D1432753

WITHDRAWN

GNOSIS

SUNY SERIES IN WESTERN ESOTERIC TRADITIONS
DAVID APPELBAUM, EDITOR

Gnosis

An Esoteric Tradition
of Mystical Visions and Unions

Dan Merkur

State University of New York Press

Published by
State University of New York Press, Albany

For information, address State University of New York
Press, State University Plaza, Albany, N.Y., 12246

Production by Diane Ganeles
Marketing by Fran Keneston

Library of Congress Cataloging-in-Publication Data

Merkur, Daniel.
    Gnosis: an esoteric tradition of mystical visions and unions /
Dan Merkur.
        p. — cm. — (SUNY series in western esoteric traditions)
    Includes bibliographical references and index.
    ISBN 0-7914-1619-4 (hard : alk. paper). — ISBN 0-7914-1620-8
(pbk. : alk. paper)
        1. Visions—History.   2. Mysticism—History.   3. Gnosticism-
–History.   4. Imagination—History.   5. Psychoanalysis and religion.
6. Jung, C. G. (Carl Gustav), 1875–1961.   I. Title.   II. Series.
BF1101.M47   1993
291.4'2—dc20   92-35390
                                                                      CIP

10 9 8 7 6 5 4 3 2 1

Incredulity is given to the world as a punishment.
        —Elias Ashmole, "Prolegomena"
        Theatrum Chemicum Britannicum (1652)

Contents

Preface

In 1913 Carl Gustav Jung developed a procedure for inducing visions that he termed "active imagination." He combined hypnagogic states with visualization techniques in order to induce waking imaginations that were autonomous, as are dreams, and not consciously directed, as are daydreams. Jung's procedure has since had a variety of successors. Related practices have also been developed in Western occultism and New Age spirituality.

The significance of active imagination for the history of religion remains to be assessed. Several intriguing speculations have been offered. Jung alleged the use of active imagination in gnosticism, alchemy, *The Spiritual Exercises* of St. Ignatius Loyola, and Friedrich Nietzsche's *Thus Spake Zarathustra*. Henry Corbin made a case for active imagination in the Islamic gnosis of medieval Isma'ilism, Avicenna's Neo-Aristotelian mysticism, and theosophical Sufism. Antoine Faivre has suggested that a blend of gnosis and active imagination has been part of Western esotericism since its systematization in the Italian Renaissance.

The present study is, to my knowledge, the first systematic history of active imagination in Western culture. As I am not a Jungian, I have reconceptualized the topic in terms of both method and perspective. My historical findings remain exploratory. I hope to have identified the major trends of the history, but at this stage in the research all results must be considered provisional. I have cited the data that I have happened to find; there must be oversights, small and large.

It is my thesis that a paired use of visionary and unitive experiences, dependent for the most part on active imagination, constituted the *gnosis*, "knowledge," at the mystical core of the gnostic trajectory in Western esotericism from late antiquity to modern times. No one has previously written a history of visionary practice in the West. Much less has anyone suggested that Western mystics, some of whom are known to have experienced both visions and unions, ever made a tradition of the dual practice. Evidence that scholars have often treated as marginal or peripheral to the general history of Western mysticism or, at best, have discussed as minor curiosities or oddities have here been presented as a discrete trajectory. My demonstration that there has been such a tradition is, in many ways, as significant as its identification as gnostic.

The gnostic uses of active imagination were transmitted, I argue, by much the same routes as Greek philosophy and science: through early Islam, where they were considerably developed before passing through medieval Judaism, which made important contributions before passing the tradition onward to the Latin West, where gnosis entered alchemy for the first time.

For reason, in Melville's phrase, of "Time, Strength, Cash, and Patience," I have deferred discussion of one of the most interesting episodes in the history of gnosis: the origin and early development of the kabbalah. The omission will be repaired as circumstances permit.

Most of this book was written from 1990 to 1992 when I was a Research Reader at the Centre for Religious Studies, of the University of Toronto, Canada. At different points over the years, this project has profited from the help of Antoine Faivre, Ithamar Gruenwald, David J. Halperin, Moshe Idel, Todd Lawson, June McDaniel, Jordan Paper, Richard Pero, Robert A. Segal, Charles and Dena Taylor, Steven M. Wasserstrom, Elliot R. Wolfson, and the members of the Alchemical Society of Canada. I extend my thanks to all. An earlier version of chapters 3 and 4 was published in *Ambix* 37 (1990), 35–45.

Part One

Jung, Active Imagination, and the
Gnostic-Alchemical Hypothesis

Chapter 1

The Study of Mystical Experiences

The modern study of mysticism was begun in the late nineteenth century when medical psychologists noted that phenomena resembling those recorded of Christian mystics were being produced by inmates of mental asylums.[1] To defend the sanity of the saints, Catholic and Anglican apologists mounted counteroffensives along two fronts. One was *literary*. The historical mystics were studied, explained, and made to serve as precedents for modern theologies of mysticism. The second front was *experiential,* but there was no living tradition within Western Christianity on which to draw. Mysticism had been in disrepute since the turn toward science and rationalism two centuries earlier. The mysticism that was available in Europe in the late nineteenth century consisted, in the main, of practices that had been imported from India in the interim. Yoga was what the apologists knew, and the aspects of Christian mysticism that they understood best were those that most closely resembled Hindu Yoga. The apologists were not content, however, to acknowledge that other historical mystics were beyond their comprehension. Yoga rapidly became a Proscrutean bed for the interpretation of Christian mystics without exception. Thomas Merton, for example, made St. Bernard of Clairvaux read like Patanjali.[2]

The debate between mysticism's detractors and apologists needlessly polarized research. It is no accident that the greatest of Western mystics were among the most insightful psychologists of their religious traditions: Augustine and Teresa, Maimonides, and ibn al-'Arabi. Success in the practice of mysticism requires competence in its psychological understanding. It was in order to perfect their experiences that the mystics kept abreast of, and often contributed originally to the front line of, psychological research in their eras and cultures.

Because most students of mysticism have neglected to acquire an equivalent competence in psychology, the historical existence of

Western mystical practices that differ significantly from Yoga went unsuspected for decades. The sophistication of William James's observations were ignored and misrepresented.[3] A generation of scholars maintained that despite superficial differences, mysticism is everywhere one and the same. Evelyn Underhill suggested that "mysticism, in its pure form, is . . . the science of union with the Absolute, and nothing else, and . . . the mystic is the person who attains this union."[4] Underhill's effort to translate a type of religiosity into a discrete psychological state was widely imitated. Prophets,[5] spirit mediums,[6] and shamans[7] were each defined by reference to a distinctive religious experience. The general paradigm was tidy, but it flew in the face of the facts.

The Diversity of Mystics' Experiences

The idea that mystics must conform with a modern definition of mysticism, or are not to be counted as mystics, is a criterion for assessing authentic and inauthentic mysticism. It privileges certain experiences over against others. Mystical union has been treated as the essence of mysticism. Visions, by contrast, have occasionally been noted, but have regularly been treated as an afterthought, an addendum, a peripheral concern.

Important as normative value-judgments may be for theologians, they express sectarian desiderata for the future. They are not impartial descriptions of the past. Historians, who define mysticism on historical principles, must instead consider the actual practices of people who have traditionally been considered mystics (pneumatics, kabbalists, sufis, yogis, and others). What the mystics of Hinduism, Buddhism, Taoism, Judaism, Christianity, and Islam traditionally or presently consider to be mystical, may not be a sufficient or complete account of mysticism. But no approach to mysticism that is less extensive can pretend to adequacy. Mysticism may entail more than what the traditionally recognized mystics have practiced, but it certainly encompasses nothing less. With saints and sinners, the orthodox, heterodox, and heretical, normative and eccentric, mainstream and marginal all counted in together, we find a tremendous diversity among mystical experiences.

Comparative perspectives are not necessary to establish this point. Consider the evidence of Western Christianity alone. In his discussion of "The Paradise or Third Heaven Seen by St. Paul,"[8] St. Augustine of Hippo introduced what subsequently became the authoritative Catholic distinction among three types of vision.

(1) The *corporeal vision* seems subjectively to be apparent to one or more of the bodily senses. The contents of the vision are seen against a background of sense perception. Corporeal visions include phenomena such as apparitions of Jesus, the Virgin Mary, and various saints.

The following report was recorded by Church authorities within days after the sighting, in Spain in 1483.

> Praying on his knees he went to the door of the chapel, and after he prayed as God ordained and started to arise he heard within the chapel the lamentations of a little girl. The witness was very disturbed and surprised by the cries and sobs, and when he started to arise and ring the pardon the doors of the chapel, which, as he said, were locked, opened miraculously.
>
> From his kneeling position the witness saw through the open doors, three or four paces within the chapel before him, a very beautiful girl between seven and eight years old, all dressed in clothes as white as the snow. She was continuously wringing her hands and with them joined she cried and asked for pity from Jesus Christ, beseeching him that it be his mercy and pity to take mercy and pity on his people. She was crying out loudly in a very sweet voice, and when the witness saw and heard her from his kneeling position, he made an effort to pull himself together, although he was very frightened, and questioned the girl with these or similar words: "O sweet child, will you tell me what is troubling you so?"
>
> The girl replied as follows: "O my son, I charge you by your soul to charge the souls of the men of the parishes. . . . "
>
> After the girl said all these words and things to the witness she disappeared, and he saw nothing more except that the doors of the chapel closed and locked themselves as miraculously as they had opened, with the witness still on his knees in the doorway. Then the witness stood up and went home.[9]

(2) The *interior vision* is apparent only to the mind. It is also termed the *imaginative vision* in reference to the medieval understanding of imagination as a faculty that is limited to the fanciful combination of elements of perceptual memory. The term signifies that the visions are understood during or following their occurrence as intrapsychic events that proceed within the soul's faculty of imagination. Interior visions do not necessarily seem imaginary in the sense of fictitious. Mystics may instead regard them as valid revelations, or as extrasensory perception.

Interior visions are dreamlike experiences that may involve images, beings, sceneries, events, and so forth. As in dreams, the mental presentations consist primarily of visual images, but auditory or other sensory representations may occur as well. The following self-report is from *The Spiritual Dialogue* of St. Catherine of Genoa:

> One day there appeared to her inner vision Jesus Christ incarnate crucified, all bloody from head to foot. It seemed that the body rained blood. From within she heard a voice say, "Do you see this blood? It has been shed for your love, to atone for your sins." With that she received a wound of love that drew her to Jesus with such trust that it washed away all that previous fright, and she took joy in the Lord.[10]

Catherine appreciated that Jesus had not appeared to her bodily senses, but only to her soul. She had no doubt, however, that she beheld an objectively existing, external, supernatural being. At the same time, it is possible and perhaps probable that she regarded the rain of blood as an imaginative symbol of the "wound of love . . . that washed away" her fright.

The Catholic tradition gave individual names to a few subcategories of the interior vision. An interior vision in which the mystic's soul flies out of the body was termed a *transport,* while visions in which the body itself was seen to fly were understood as *levitation.* Some visions straddle the categories. When the discorporeal soul is transported out of its body, it may drag the decapitated corporeal head, or the decapitated head and then the body, along with it in its wake.[11] Levitation is popularly reputed to be a physical feat, rather than the content of a vision, because interior visions may reproduce the external physical environment so very completely that mystics mistake interior visions for corporeal ones.[12]

(3) The *intellectual vision* is again apparent only to the mind. It was defined with reference to the medieval understanding of the intellect, reason, or spirit—the medieval terms were synonymous—as a faculty that accomplishes abstract conceptual thinking. It is the only faculty that has access to metaphysical beings and phenomena. Intellectual visions sometimes consist of *locutions* or distinctly verbal ideas, and otherwise of nonverbal ideas or comprehensions.[13] Classic examples include the sense of presence (the spiritual betrothal), mystical union, and the prophetic inspiration of verbal ideas.

Augustine classified visions in conformance with the best understanding of psychology available in his day. He gave the psychological categories theological importance, by arguing that the bodily senses were less reliable than the mind, and the imagination less reliable than the intellect, in the apprehension of spiritual truths. In Augustine's theology, a spiritual being—God, an angel, or a demon—was rightly perceived as an imageless idea. Whenever the spiritual being was portrayed by the imagination as a dreamlike image, or by the senses as a corporeal apparition, it was apprehended less accurately, and the possibility of doctrinal error increased.

The historian of religions Ernst Arbman established that Augustine's categories are not discrete. What begins as a corporeal vision may continue as an interior vision and end as an intellectual one:

> One morning while praying in tongues I saw the cross in a red glow—everything was red, but there were two red beams coming down from the cross to two people. One was a lady in the hospital who had fallen down one flight in an elevator shaft and was in critical condition in the hospital. . . . The other was a dear friend of mine. I was told [internally, by God] to pray for these two people and did.[14]

Because the cross was a physical sense perception, its red glow may be considered a corporeal vision. When the mystic recognized two people who were known to be elsewhere, the vision was understood to be interior. By definition, however, the concluding locutions were intellectual.

The sequence of transformations is variable. The following self-report by Angela of Foligno describes a mystical experience that began as an intellectual vision but concluded as an interior one. Mystical union took vivid pictorial form:[15]

> When I am immersed in this good and contemplate it, I no longer recollect the humanity or incarnation of Jesus Christ, nor anything, whatever it might be, which has a form. Yet I see everything and see nothing. But when I leave this good, then I see the Man-God. And He draws me mildly to Himself all the time until He says: Thou art I and I am thou. I see His eyes and His countenance full of compassion. He embraces my soul and presses it to Him with an immense force.[16]

Also violating Augustine's categories are instances of the sense of presence, traditionally classed as an intellectual vision of an unseen presence, which take palpable form as a corporeal vision.[17] Again, precisely the same image of Christ may occur to the same mystic, sometimes as a corporeal vision, and other times as an interior one.[18]

Although varieties of mystical experience that Augustine had not taken into consideration were interpreted by later Catholic writers as subdivisions within his categories, the fit was often inexact. Phenomena such as ecstatic preaching, prophesying, and glossolalia were categorized as the *spoken ecstasy*. Although it is pronounced with the bodily voice, the spoken ecstasy is considered a variety of intellectual vision because the bodily actions depend on the inspiration of verbal ideas.

The spoken ecstasy may occur alone. Alternatively, either an imaginative vision or a purely intellectual vision may occur immediately prior to, or during, the audible manifestation of the spoken ecstasy.[19] St. Catherine of Ricci provided a classic example. Every Thursday evening and Friday morning for twelve years she beheld the passion of Christ in a series of interior visions. The drama involved seventeen scenes from the Last Supper through the conclusion of the crucifixion. Within her visions, Catherine experienced herself either as Christ or alongside him. People in her physical environment saw her body assume the positions and gestures that she, as Christ, had in her interior visions. She spoke in a loud voice and misperceived people around her as fellow participants in the events of the passion. For their part, Catherine's companions respected her mystical experience sufficiently that they enacted their assigned roles.[20]

Unlike St. Catherine, who performed complete dramatic actions and spoke in a loud voice during her interior visions of Christ's passion, most passion mystics, such as St. Francoise Romaine and Mary of Moerl, were given only to limited pantomimic gestures and silence.[21] Theirs was a *mobile ecstasy*, but not a spoken one.

Closely akin to the spoken and mobile ecstasies and best considered as their literary equivalent is the experience that modern psychologists term "automatic writing." St. Teresa of Avila wrote many of her works, including poetic verse, very rapidly while in ecstatic states, by hearing intellectual visions distinctly and functioning as a copyist.[22] In other cases, the writing proceeded without the owner of the hand having an advanced notion as to what was about to be written. Sometimes the text was not comprehended even when it was complete.[23]

The spoken, mobile, and written ecstasies of Catholic mystics are all instances of what anthropologists term "spirit possession,"—

that is, positively valued experiences of involuntary bodily activity, which are attributed to the presence of spiritual beings.

Stigmata involve the involuntary rather than voluntary nervous system, but they too are related phenomena. When St. Catherine of Ricci alerted from her trance at the conclusion of her experience of the Passion, her body bore the marks of ropes, scourging, and the five stigmata:[24]

> Stigmatization . . . or more precisely the experience of having oneself personally suffered in the nailing of Jesus to the cross . . . is a well-documented, shockingly realistic ecstatic dream, experienced by the mystic from beginning to end in every detail and with all his senses in exactly the same way as an actual crucifixion and having an innate suggestive power sufficient to give rise to the marks of the wounds on hands, feet and in the side that were inflicted on the Saviour when He was crucified.[25]

The diversity of Catholic mystics' experiences is consistent with mystics' experiences elsewhere. It is absurd to contrast ecstatic religious traditions, such as shamanism, mediumship, prophetism, and mysticism, on the basis of distinctions among religious experiences. People everywhere are able to experience all possible types of religious experience. The world's ecstatic religious traditions tend to accommodate a tremendous diversity of personal experiences. Conformity is required in matters of doctrine much more than experience. Indeed, the vagueness or nonspecificity of many traditional doctrines, which has so complicated modern research, arises precisely from the need for formulations that may be applied simultaneously to diverse religious experiences.

Ecstatic religious traditions do generally favor certain experiences over against others. However, the favoritism is not the product of access to certain varieties of experience, as distinct from others. Conscious choices are made for a variety of historical factors: ideological, socio-political, economic, ecological, and so forth.

This circumstance has important consequences for historians. If the "common core" hypothesis were correct that mystical experiences are everywhere one and the same, it would no more be possible to write a history of mysticism than a history of sense perception. Histories would be restricted to beliefs and theories (philosophies, theologies, and so forth) about mysticism, but mysticism as such would be a topic for psychologists.

Because mystical experiences are various, however, it is possible to write a history of the very practice of mysticism. Just as

complex mystical doctrines must be learned in order to be transmitted, so too must techniques for the induction and direction or control of mystical experiences. Choices among techniques influence
the content of the resultant experiences and so contribute to mystics' doctrines. Refering to Buddhism, Conze remarked: "each and
every [philosophical] proposition must be considered in reference to
its spiritual intention and as a formulation of meditational experiences acquired in the course of the process of winning salvation."[26]
With appropriate adjustments to different religions' goals, the same
program of research may be applied cross-culturally. Historians
must, however, possess an expertise in the psychology of mysticism
that is at least equal to that of the mystics, if this research program
is to proceed; but there is no valid reason that it should not.

As though to rationalize their neglect of the psychology of ecstasy, many scholars have expressed doubt as to the possibility of
discussing the mystics' experiences on the basis of the textual evidence. Their studies purport to discuss mystics' doctrinal formulations; but because words have meaning only in the context of their
referents, a study of mystical doctrines in isolation of mystical experiences is necessarily uncertain. It cannot assess whether a discussion refers to experienced realities, learned opinions, or
completely mistaken speculations. It may not even be able to decide
whether a term is to be understood at face value or metaphorically.
A number of Islamicists have consequently recognized that they are
studying not mystical theologies, but mystical semantics. The
translation of the study of mysticism into a study of semiotics is,
however, of little relevance either to mystics or to their historical
study.

Again, it is emphatically not adequate to allege the presence
of mysticism on the basis of doctrines or semantics that exhibit
unitive turns of thought. Unitive thinking is a universal human
tendency. It may erupt into consciousness during a mystical experience, but it may also occur during normal waking sobriety. Classic
examples include the antireligious but extremely unitive sociologies
of Karl Marx and Emile Durkheim.

What, in my opinion, finally distinguishes mystics from other
types of religious ecstatic is their standing in society. Shamans, mediums, and prophets are public social functionaries who act on behalf their coreligionists in contacting their gods or spirits.
Coreligionists may perform similar practices for personal or private
reasons. For example, Plains Indians who were not shamans often
engaged in vision quests. Many African and Afro-American religions

engage in group spirit possessions. The Old Testament records group prophesying in Canaanite and north Israelite religion. These individuals should not be considered mystics, however, because they needed only to acquire public followings in order to become shamans, mediums, or prophets.

The social circumstance of mystics differs. Mystics have no public social authority. Neither have they the possibility of acquiring any. Most of the world's mystics belong to religions that invest authority in scriptures and their interpreters. Mystics sometimes also occur in oral religions where authority is firmly invested in ritual (for example, classical Greece, earliest Taoism). In all cases, mystics' religions deny public authority to religious experiences. This social circumstance impacts on the resultant experiences. In order to avoid conflict with their religions' authorities, mystics tend to seek experiences of exclusively private concern. Private orientations may be achieved through religious experiences of many different types. Mystical union is merely one example. In all cases, it is the inward turn, due to the impossibility of possessing public religious authority, that I think to characterize mysticism wherever it is found.

Some Unitive Experiences

Mystical experiences are religious uses of otherwise secular alternate states of consciousness—or more precisely, alternate psychic states. What makes an alternate state experience a religious one is its personal or cultural valuation. A vision of Jesus, for example, is not intrinsically religious. It is necessary to believe in Jesus for the experience to be more than a secular hallucination.

As a brief synonym for "religiously interpreted alternate state experiences," I use the word *ecstasy*. In the English language, ecstasy has been a general cover term for prophetic, mystical, and poetic experiences since the seventeenth century.[27] It is used somewhat differently in other languages. In the writings of St. Teresa, which many Catholic writers follow, ecstasy names the final step of the *scala contemplationis*.[28] In psychological terms, Teresa wrote of ecstasy where we today would speak of deep trance. Her usage should not be endorsed, however, because other Catholic authorities—for example, St. Bernard of Clairvaux—wrote of ecstasies that did not involve a *scala contemplationis*.[29] Eliade's effort to equate "ecstasy" with out-of-the-body experiences[30] is still less satisfactory; out-of-the-body experiences were traditionally termed "transports."

It is characteristic of all ecstasies that they involve at least some autonomous phenomena—what the Catholic tradition terms "contemplation" and contrasts with "meditation." Autonomous psychic materials seem subjectively to the ecstatic to be independent of control by will. The relationship between willful thinking and the autonomous materials is highly variable. Although all autonomous materials are passively received by consciousness, further passivity is not necessary to their occurrence. In the "concentrative meditation" on the *jhanas* in Mahayana Buddhism, for example, active discursive reasoning is resumed after each moment of autonomous development, until nirvana is reached.[31] Hasidic meditations that culminate in contemplations of *'ayin*, "naught," are similarly active until they climax in passivity.[32] The extent of mystical passivity has often been overestimated by mystics whose meditations are monotonous. With repeated performance, monotonous meditations become more or less automatic. Will is not required to make new decisions and mystics may quite forget that their ongoing meditations are mental activities. Passive in the face of habit, mystics may fantasize their complete passivity, which is by no means the case. Rather, the circumstance is analogous to a seated person who stands up and remains standing while conversing with another person. The continuation of standing proceeds automatically, but by no means passively.

Autonomous and autosuggested materials are mutually exclusive. Erika Fromm theorizes that " 'unbidden' imagery arises from the unconscious while 'bidden' imagery—as can be produced voluntarily by an act of attention—stems from the preconscious."[33] No philosophic prejudice should be attached to the terminology. What is unconscious is simply that which is not conscious. The term does not prejudge whether specific unconscious materials have their origin in biogenetic or constitutional endowment, experience and development, extrasensory perception (as Freud and Jung believed possible), or divine revelation.

In order to develop a crosscultural formulation that reflects the autonomy of contemplations, I define ecstasy as *any state of involuntary belief in the reality of the numinous*.[34] Like sense perception during normal waking sobriety and dream hallucinations during sleep, the autonomous contents of an ecstasy have a compelling psychic reality for at least the duration of their occurrence. The ecstatic is then convinced that the numinous is real—as real or more real than the perceptible world. In contrast with sober faith in the numinous, which requires an act of will, ecstatic belief in the reality of the numinous is involuntary. Whether or not the occurrence of ecstasy was voluntarily sought, once the experience is underway faith in the reality of the numinous is not subject to volition. Doubt can be entertained, but it cannot be sustained for the duration of the experience. Uniquely among the varieties of religious experience, ecstasies have the power not only to confirm religious faith that already exists, but also to induce conversions from unbelief to belief.

The Catholic tradition is apparently unique among the world's mysticisms in distinguishing its types of vision from its *scala contemplationis*, "ladder of contemplation." The allusion to Jacob's ladder (Gen 28:12) refers to variations in the intensity or metaphoric "depth" of trance. This treatment of the ecstatic state and its content as independent variables is not paralleled, so far as I know, in other mystical traditions. The hierarchical sequences of the kabbalah, Sufism, Hindu Yoga, and Buddhist meditation list the contents of ecstasies. The intensity of trance is either ignored or treated as a dependent variable.

Catholic accounts of the *scala contemplationis* divide trance into a number of steps (e.g., four or seven) that commence with normal waking sobriety and culminate in intense states of trance. However, current scientific thinking endorses Ronald Shor's proposal that traditional concepts of trance depth confabulate what are in fact three independent factors.[35]

Shor described the first variable as a fading of the "general reality orientation."[36] It consists of a gradual and increasing inhibition of the normal functions of consciousness, beginning with reality-testing and will, and proceeding through sense perception, memory, and fantasy, to verbal and nonverbal thinking.[37] The repression of these ego functions permits ordinarily unconscious psychic functions to manifest autonomously in their place. Because the autonomous manifestations cannot be reality-tested, they are inevitably reified. For example, daydreams are converted into hallucinations, and speculative ideas into delusional certainties. Even though the autonomous manifestations may exhibit a "trance logic,"[38] their "special reality orientation" may seem valid at least for the duration of the trance.

The intensity of role-taking—or, to coin a term, creative elaboration—describes the extent to which autonomous materials are produced and elaborated. Are the manifestations simple and brief? Or are they richly detailed and protracted in time?

The third independent variable is the intensity of "archaic involvement"—or, to use older terms, "psychic depth"[39] or absorption. To what extent is self-observation maintained? Does emotional detachment prevail? Or are the autonomous materials subject to intense emotional involvement?

The contents of the trance state form a fourth category of independent variables. Every type of thought that the mind produces during wakefulness and sleep may occur during an ecstasy, but two types of ecstatic content warrant special attention. As *narrative ecstasies,* I refer to corporeal and imaginative visions, spoken and mobile ecstasies, and all comparable phenomena crossculturally. These ecstasies, whose scope corresponds to a modern understanding of fantasy, all have narrative storylines. The narrative may be extensive scenarios; in other cases, they may be brief: a single static visual tableau, a momentary gesture, an audible sound.

A second major category of ecstatic content may be described as *unitive.* Their study is surrounded by a lively debate. In highly polemic efforts to deny that psychedelic experiences can be mystical, R. C. Zaehner proposed that differences among mystics' doctrines reflect actual differences in the phenomenologies of their experiences.[40] Ninian Smart responded with the suggestion that mystical experiences differ from their interpretations by mystics both during their occurrence and after the experiences have ended.[41] H. P. Owen added that the mystics' beliefs, practices, and expectations contribute interpretive content to the experiences themselves.[42] A consensus has since been reached that personal, cultural, and universal factors are interwoven in mystical experiences much as they are in nocturnal dreams.[43] Religious ideology makes at least some contribution to the contents of all mystical experiences.[44]

Arbman went so far as to postulate a complete correspondence of mystical faith and mystical experience. He maintained that ecstasies convert religious ideas into religious experiences, but do nothing more:

> The ecstasy . . . can from the psychological point of view only be understood as a specific religious form of suggestive absorption in the complex of beliefs which in the state preceding it has constituted the sole, exclusive, or totally dominating object of the consciousness, and from which it may thus always be shown to derive its content and predetermined, strictly closed and organized visionary dream or experience.[45]

Arbman's argument proceeded from theory. His restriction to a phenomenological psychology made it necessary to account for ecstatic experiences by reference to consciousness alone. Ecstasies had then to be products of previously held religious ideas.

Rather a different position was taken at the turn of the century by William James, who was willing to embrace the theory of the "subconscious":

> The mystical feeling of enlargement, union, and emancipation has no specific intellectual content whatever of its own. It is capable of forming matrimonial alliances with material furnished by the most diverse philosophies and theologies, provided only they can find a place in the framework for its peculiar mood.[46]

James described mystics' philosophies and theologies as "over-beliefs." They are ideas that a person brings to a religious experience, not only postexperientially in the process of its interpretation and reportage, but also preexperientially as a contribution to the experiences' contents.[47]

Narrative ecstasies may perhaps be derived, as Arbman claimed, from religious beliefs that are entertained prior to the narratives' occurrence, but the unitive element in unitive experiences cannot be explained so simply. Autosuggestions are certainly involved. Meditation on the idea of God leads to union with God. Meditation on the idea of a chair leads to union with the chair. The Yogic practice of union with anything and everything, which is used to teach the illusory character of all, takes for granted that union is possible with any topic of meditation.[48] The same data indicate the inadequacy of Arbman's theory. Deikman showed experimentally that the act of staring at a vase, so far as possible without thinking anything further, suffices in some cases to induce a unitive experience.[49] The unitive idea that discovers self and all existence in the one vase is not part of the meditation, but is added to it in the process of its conversion into a passively received contemplation. Meditations involving Tantric mantras, Sufi *dhikr*, the Greek Orthodox Jesus prayer, and so forth, are similarly able to account for only some of the contents of the subsequent contemplations. Indeed, it is unlikely that mystics would believe in their experiences if they were nothing more than the products of autosuggestions.

The unitive ideas of unitive experiences are inherent in the structure of the ecstatic apperceptions. They are not topics of thought, but modes of thinking. The unitive ideas are thought *with*, rather than *about*. Just as, in seeing a tree, one knows immediately how far and large it is; so too, in having a unitive experience of the tree, one directly experiences its unity—for example, with self and all existence. The unitive ideas are structures or lenses through which the ecstatic mind apperceives and orders whatever it may happen to think. The unitive ideas function in an automatic manner, outside consciousness, as its presuppositions.

Several varieties of unitive experience have been described as mystical union by different writers.[50] For present purposes, it will suffice to distinguish three types.

Introspective Union

The term *unio mystica,* mystical union, has most often been applied to the particular variety that Rudolf Otto described as "the Inward Way" or "Mysticism of Introspection."[51] The unitive experience is instanced in the following self-report by Mechthilde of Magdeburg:

> As He draws her to Himself, she gives herself to Him. She cannot hold back and so He takes her to Himself. Gladly would she speak but dares not. She is engulfed in the glorious Trinity in high union. He gives her a brief respite that she may long for Him. She would fain sing His praises but cannot. She would that He might send her to Hell, if only He might be loved above all measure by all creatures. She looks at Him and sayings, "Lord! Give me Thy blessing!" He looks at her and draws her to Him with a greeting the body may not know.[52]

Introspective union consists of a blissfully serene sense of timeless, boundless, and solitary uniqueness, in which self is the only existent. Introspective unions involve no experience of any actual union, uniting, or joining; neither is there a process in which subject-object distinctions disappear. There is simply and suddenly the experience that self is the unique or solitary existent, that the subject is infinite, eternal, and alone. Mystics who are theists experience introspective union as the selfhood of God. Postexperiential interpretations of the experience are much more various.

Extrovertive Union

Otto also noted a second type of unitive experience. He termed it "the Outward Way" because its "unifying Vision" apprehends the perceptible world. W. T. Stace called the outward way "extrovertive" mysticism.[53] An example may be seen in the following self-report by Angela of Foligno:

> And immediately the eyes of my soul were opened and I beheld the plenitude of God, whereby I did comprehend the whole world, both here and beyond the sea, and the abyss and all things else; and therein did I behold naught save the divine power in a manner assuredly indescribable, so that through excess of marvelling the soul cried with a loud voice, saying, "This whole world is full of God!" Wherefore did I now comprehend that the world is but a small thing; I saw, moreover, that the power of God was above all things, and that the whole world was filled with it.[54]

Extrovertive unions are the type of unitive experience that discover the one in the many. When its ideas are reified, extrovertive union may disclose that all are somehow one. In both events, the unitive element is a union that encompasses the perceptible cosmos in its full complexity.

Communion

A third type of unitive experience was identified by Abraham Joshua Heschel, who attributed classical biblical prophecy to an experience that he termed *unio sympathetica*.[55] Heschel's category was taken up by Gershom G. Scholem, who recognized its pertinence to kabbalists' experiences of communion (*devekut*).[56] The unitive ideas within the experience involve bonding with the divine in a dyadic "I-Thou" unit. There is a sense that two—not all, but two—are at one. A good example is provided by the continuation of Angela of Foligno's experience:

> Then said He unto me, "I have shown thee something of My power," the which I did so well understand that it enabled me better to understand all other things. He said also, "I have made thee to see something of My power; behold now and see Mine humility." Then was I given so deep an insight into the humility of God towards man and all other things that when my soul remembered His unspeakable power and comprehended His deep humility, it marvelled greatly and did esteem itself to be nothing at all, for in itself it beheld nothing save price.[57]

Henry Corbin suggested that interpretations of *unio mystica* as *unio sympathetica* are common in theosophical Sufism. Sufis who experience identity with God are obliged to conform their doctrinal understanding with Islam's teachings on prophecy, which involves a dialogic communion with God.[58]

In a discussion of American conversion experiences, Rodney Stark listed four types of experience. Each may occur alone or develop sequentially into the next. They all meet James's criteria for "the sense of presence,"[59] but only the last three involve the reciprocation by the presence that constitutes communion:

1) The human actor simply notes (feels, senses, etc.) the existence or presence of the divine actor.

2) Mutual presence is acknowledged, the divine actor is perceived as noting the presence of the human actor.

3) The awareness of mutual presence is replaced by an affective relationship akin to love or friendship.

4) The human actor perceives himself as a confidant of and/or a fellow participant in action with the divine actor.[60]

Johannes Lindblom noted an important difference between communion and introspective union. Communion experiences are a "personal mysticism" in which "the personality is preserved, both the personality of the divine and the personality of the religious man." The "impersonal mysticism" of introspective union is instead marked by a "complete oneness with the divine conceived of as a more or less impersonal substance."[61]

St. Teresa sometimes experienced the two phenomena as different phases of single ecstasies:

> There is the same difference between the Spiritual Betrothal [= communion] and the Spiritual Marriage [= introspective union] as there is between two betrothed persons and two who are united so that they cannot be separated anymore. . . . [In] the Betrothal. . . . the two persons are frequently separated, as is the case with union, for, although by union is meant the joining of two things into one, each of the two, as is a matter of common observation, can be separated and remain a thing by itself. . . . In the union of the Spiritual Marriage . . . the Lord appears in the centre of the soul. . . . the soul (I mean the spirit of this soul) is made one with God. . . . For He has been pleased to unite Himself with His creature in such a way that they have become like two who cannot be separate from one another. . . . the soul remains all the time in that centre with its God. We might say that union is as if the ends of two wax candles were joined so that the light they give is one.[62]

Teresa reported intellectual visions, but a transition from communion to union may also occur in a narrative ecstasy. Hadewijch, a Flemish Beguine of the thirteenth century, reported the following experience:

> The eagle, who had previously spoken to me, said: "Now see through the Countenance, and become the veritable bride of the great Bridegroom, and behold yourself in this state!" And in that very instant I saw myself received in union by the One who sat there in the abyss upon the circling disk, and there I became one with him in the certainty of unity.[63]

Psychoanalytic theory explains the differences among the three types of unitive experiences in developmental terms. Communion is explained as an intense and prolonged experience of conscience.[64] The timeless, boundless, solitary bliss of introspective union is thought to depend, however, on memories of intrauterine life before birth, when the human fetus naively imagined itself to be the whole of existence.[65] The application of the same solipsistic assumption, shortly after birth, to the perceptible world is thought to underlie extrovertive unions.[66]

Due to the complexity of human development after birth, there are "a great variety of [extrovertive] mystic experiences according to the depth of regression."[67] In some cases, for example, the ecstatic has a sense of encompassing the entire cosmos. In others, the ecstatic feels a part of a cosmic whole. Others differ yet again.[68] Assuming, as I have suggested elsewhere,[69] that the regressive materials are developmentally early forms of conscience, we must be alert to the further aspects of unitive experiences: the willful thoughts and fantasies to which conscience is momentarily responding, the role of conscience in the life of the individual, and so forth. In all cases, "regression occurs together with the retention of a sense of identity" and "is not literally a return" to the infantile state.[70] Julia Kristeva explains:

> Overcoming the notion of irremediable separation . . . reestablishes a continuous fusion with an Other that is no longer substantial and maternal but symbolic. . . . What we have here is fusion . . . transposed from the mother's body to an invisible agency. . . . This is quite a wrench from the dependency of early childhood, and it must be said that it is a compromise solution, since the benefits of the new relationship of dependency are entirely of an imaginary order, in the realm of signs.[71]

A psychoanalytic approach to unitive experience is reductive, but it is not necessarily inconsistent with a negative theology. At no point, negative theologies maintain, does any mystic have direct access to God, void, *'Ein Sof,* Ungrund, the unnameable Tao, or the like. Whatever can be experienced is necessarily not transcendent. Unitive experiences occur within the human person, and the reality that they concern is a human one. Union may access the ground of being, but it is the mystic's own personal being and not the being of all. As Martin Buber reflected:

> From my own unforgettable experience I know well that there is a state in which the bonds of the personal nature of life seem to have fallen away from us and we experience an undivided unity. But I do not know—what the soul willingly imagines and indeed is bound to imagine (mine too once did it)—that in this I had attained to a union with the primal being or the godhead. That is an exaggeration no longer permitted to the responsible understanding. Responsibly—that is, as a man holding his ground before reality—I can elicit from those experiences only that in them I reached an undifferentiable unity of myself without form or content. I may call this an original prebiographical unity and suppose that it is hidden unchanged beneath all biographical change, all development of the soul . . . existing but once, single, unique, irreducible, this creaturely one: one of the human souls and not the "soul of the All"; a defined and particular being and not "Being"; the creaturely basic unity of a creature.[72]

The psychic nature of unitive experiences is not inconsistent, however, with the proposition that they correspond to the reality of the cosmos. In the same way that Pythagoras's theorem is a mental computation that proceeds wholly within the mind, but happens, through the design of the cosmos, to correspond to the actual physical circumstances of objects that have the shapes of right triangles, so too some unitive experiences, rightly understood, may happen to correspond to the actual order of existence. It is only the collapse of this correspondence into an identity, the unfounded supposition that unitive experiences directly reveal what is necessarily the true order of being as such, that a psychoanalytic approach cannot accommodate.

I would further emphasize that my discussion of conscience as a natural faculty of the mind does not preclude the possibility of divine intervention within it, as within all else in the cosmos. Neither does my assertion that some manifestations of conscience are infantile in form, rather than mature, imply that infants have no access to divine providence.

Reification and Reality-Testing

One of the most spectacular aspects of the trance state is its effect on the sense of reality. Reality-testing is the capacity to decide whether a mental presentation represents a perceptible phenomenon or is intrapsychic alone (a memory, fantasy, concept, or the like). It is a basic function of the portion of the mind that psychoanalysis terms the ego. The sense of reality is also dependent, however, on the accumulated memory of past reality-testing. What reality has been found (or thought) to be in the past influences the reality-testing of the moment. Trance states may repress both aspects of the sense of reality, but they commence with reality-testing. Memories are inhibited only in advanced trances.

The repression of the ego's reality-testing function makes it impossible for the person in trance to determine whether mental presentations are nonrepresentational. By inhibiting reality-testing, trance serves to reify whatever may be its contents. Mental presentations are assumed to represent perceptible realities, whether they do or not. Daydreams, for example, are turned them into hallucinatory states that may seem subjectively to be extrasensory perceptions. Speculative ideas may receive apparent validation and become delusional certainties. Playacting may become a possession state.

Most religious doctrines accommodate the process of reification. The unwillingness of religions to come to agreement with physical science has generally its basis in fantasies that have been reified, sometimes by trance states, and otherwise by the weight of received tradition. Reified fantasies are scarcely less than a mystical stock-in-trade. Visions of ghosts have been endorsed by afterlife doctrines, celestial ascensions by accounts of divine abodes in heaven, and so forth.

In a few cases, the reification of fantasies by trance states is particularly noticeable because efforts have been made to struggle against it. In the Buddhist tantra of Tibet, novices are taught to meditate on topics whose very absurdity provides an object lesson of the illusory nature of the gods:

> The six syllables of the formula [*Aum mani padme hum*] are connected with the six classes of sentient beings and are related to one of the mystic colours as follows:
> *Aum* is white and connected with gods (lha).
> *Ma* is blue and connected with non-gods (lhamayin).

Ni is yellow and connected with men (mi).
Pad is green and connected with animals (tudo).
Me is red and connected with non-men (Yidag or other mi-ma-yin).
Hum is black and connected with dwellers in purgatories. . . .

One identifies the six kinds of beings with the six syllables which are pictured in their respective colours. . . . They form a kind of chain without end that circulates through the body, carried on by the breath, entering through one nostril and going out through the other.

As the concentration of mind becomes more perfect, one sees mentally the length of the chain increasing. Now when they go out with the expiration, the mystic syllables are carried far away, before being absorbed again with the next inspiration. Yet, the chain is not broken, it rather elongates like a rubber strap and always remains in touch with the man who meditates.

Gradually, also, the shape of the Tibetan letters vanishes and those who "obtain the fruit" of the practice perceive the six syllables as six realms in which arise, move, enjoy, suffer and pass away the innumerable beings, belonging to the six species.

And now it remains for the meditator to realize that the six realms (the whole Phenomenal world) are subjective: a mere creation of the mind which imagines them and into which they sink.[73]

Reification here proceeds along two lines. Tibetan tantrists are aware that their meditative states make their fantasies seem real. They deliberately cultivate absurd fantasies in order to promote belief in the fallacy of reality. They are unaware, however, of the reification present in their argument that the illusory nature of meditative experience proves the illusory nature of sense perception. The inference is not logical, but its reification during trance makes it seem certain.

Several of the medieval Bridal mystics of western Europe sought to experience allegorical visions, consistent with the texts of St. Hildegard of Bingen.[74] Their efforts met repeatedly with failure, however. The mystics were unable to sustain an allegorical point of view because their visions were invariably reified. The following example was reported by St. Gertrude of Helftha:

On one occasion, when I assisted at a Mass at which I was to communicate, I perceived that Thou wert present, by an admirable condescension, and that Thou didst use this similitude to instruct me, by appearing as if parched with thirst, and desiring that I should give Thee to drink; and while I was troubled thereat, and could not even force a tear from my eyes, I beheld Thee presenting me with a golden cup with Thine own Hand. When I took it, my heart immediately melted into a torrent of fervent tears.[75]

Here it was not the vision that was symbolic. The vision seemed an accurate perception. Jesus was really present. It was merely that Jesus inexplicably performed symbolic actions.

The Experience of Nothingness

Stace established that mystical doctrines in several religious traditions discuss an experience of the consciousness of nothing, and he undertook to defend its reality:

Suppose that, after having got rid of all sensations, one should go on to exclude from consciousness all sensuous images, and then all abstract thoughts, reasoning processes, volitions, and other particular mental contents; what would there then be left of consciousness? There would be no mental content whatever but rather a complete emptiness, vacuum, void.[76]

Stace's formulation was inadequate to the mystical phenomena that he sought to describe. There is no such thing as "pure consciousness,"[77] "zero experience,"[78] or any such comparative construct. These formulations misrepresent the nature of consciousness. Consciousness is not analogous to a radio or television that may be on, even though no program is being received. There is no homunculus, no little person within the mind, observing the play of perceptions, memories, fantasies, and ideas as though on a movie screen. Such a postulation would imply yet another homunculus, inside the first, and so on in series through an infinite regress.[79] Consciousness instead occurs when a mental presentation becomes sufficiently important to attract attention.[80] In the absence of mental contents, there is no consciousness whatever.

Although some mystics do seek states of unconsciousness, others seek an impossibility: a conscious experience of nothing. What they seem subjectively to experience may be described, from their point of view, as nothingness, as something that is nothing. Both unconsciousness and experiences of nothingness may be self-induced by means of the *via negativa* or "negative way" of meditation. The procedure involves meditations on a series of negations or denials that collectively maximize the capacity of trance to repress ego functions. For example, Buddhist *samatha* ("calming-down") meditation uses negative autosuggestions in order to achieve a series of *jhanas*.

The first stage:
Detached from sense-desires, detached (also from the other four) unwholesome states, he dwells in the attainment of the first jhana, which is accompanied by applied and discursive thinking, born of detachment, rapturous and joyful. . . .

The second stage:
From the appeasing of applied and discursive thinking, he dwells in the attainment of the second jhana, where the inward heart is serene and uniquely exalted, and which is devoid of applied and discursive thinking, born of concentration, rapturous and joyful. . . .

The third stage:
Through distaste for rapture, he dwells evenmindedly, mindful and clearly conscious; he experiences with this body that joy of which the Ariyans declare, "joyful lives he who is evenminded and mindful." It is thus that he dwells in the attainment of the third jhana.

The fourth stage:
From the forsaking of joy, from the forsaking of pain, from the going to rest of his former gladness and sadness, he dwells in the attainment of the fourth jhana, which is neither painful nor pleasurable,—in utter purity of evenmindedness and mindfulness.

The fifth stage:
By passing quite beyond all perceptions of form, by the going to rest of the perceptions of impact, by not attending to the perception of manifoldness, on thinking "Endless Space," he dwells in the attainment of the station of endless space.

The sixth stage:
By passing quite beyond the station of endless space, on thinking "endless consciousness," he dwells in the attainment of the station of unlimited consciousness.

The seventh stage:
By passing quite beyond the station of unlimited consciousness, on thinking "There is not anything," he dwells in the attainment of the station of nothing whatever.

The eighth stage:
By passing quite beyond the field of nothing whatever, he dwells in the attainment of the station of neither perception nor non-perception.[81]

Successful completion of the eighth stage results in *samapatti*, "unconsciousness," whose doctrinally correct (i.e., Buddhist, not Hindu) understanding permits nirvana.[82]

Several other mystical traditions have their own hierarchical sequence of negations. Each utilizes the trance state in a similar way. Whatever is not negated is permitted to remain conscious. The need to continue monitoring the progress of the contemplations in order to decide when to proceed from one negation to the next, prevents meditation from becoming automatic and habitual. The process of meditation remains active and alert. Self-awareness of the activity of meditation continues right up until the final meditation triggers the desired contemplation.

Nothingness—something that is nothing—is a selfcontradictory idea. Nothingness cannot exist; but it can seem subjectively to be experienced in trance when the trance state reifies the idea, preventing its illogic from being appreciated. What is actually experienced at the moment of ostensible nothingness was described by Paul Federn as the "mental ego alone."[83] Albert Deikman terms it "the observing self" and explains it as the basic function of consciousness: "The observing self is the transparent center, that which is aware. . . . [It is] prior to thought, feeling, and action, for it experiences these functions."[84]

These formulations are unacceptable, however, because they imply a homunculus. They also fail to explain why the observing self, which experiences nothingness, is experienced as the Self of an Other (atman, nirvana, *keter*, God, and so forth). In keeping with my general theory that autonomous trance phenomena are superego manifestations that compensate for the general repression of ego functions by the trance,[85] I understand the experience of nothingness as an *awareness of absence*—specifically, the superego's awareness of the ego's absence. The "observing self" is the superego's function of self-observation[86] or, more precisely, ego observation, as it manifests during an almost complete repression of the ego. The experience is analogous to having a word on the tip of one's tongue. There is conscious certainty that the desired mental content is not conscious. In experiences of nothingness, it is not a word alone, but the whole of the ego that may be inaccessible. The bare minimum of consciousness, nothingness is never ordinarily experienced as the sole content of sober consciousness. It is only when trance or shock represses all else from consciousness that the observing function alone remains.

The negative way does not always go so far as to become an experience of nothingness. Mystics arrive at whatever experiences they have not previously excluded. St. John of the Cross was willing to negate everything except an experience of fiery love.[87] For Jan van Ruysbroek it was sunlight.[88] By negating everything that can be thought, unconsciousness can be induced. An experience of nothingness occurs when meditation stops just short of unconsciousness.

Not only are there differences within single traditions of the negative way, but we must also avoid facile comparisons between traditions. Experiences of nothingness are not rendered uniform by the innate structure of the mind. When Buddhist nirvana is not "bliss-unspeakable,"[89] it may be a sort of nothingness, as is Hasidic *'ayin,*[90] but they are not the same sort. The one is achieved through an acosmist denial of existence, the other as the endproduct of a cosmological argument for the creative transcendence of God.[91] What remains is whatever has not been excluded. An acosmist void is not to be confused with a creative one. Their unconscious associations, their feeling-tone, their implications, all differ.

The experience of nothingness has been produced in heterohypnotic experiments with very deep trance states. Unity may be experienced on the way to nothingness. Just before the climactic moments of absence, there may be a passage through postnatal and intrauterine depths of regression. One may feel oneself to contain all, before one feels oneself alone to exist. Only then is nothingness reached.[92] Nothingness is a nonbiographical aspect of thought; but because it comes after moments of increasingly regressive union, it may mistakenly be regarded as *prebiographical.* The return from consciousness of absence to normal waking consciousness may reverse the sequence by progressing through the different orders of union.

Because experiences of nothingness require deeper states of trance than unitive experiences do, we may assume that a mystical tradition that seeks to experience nothingness will regularly experience unity en route to the desired depth of trance. A tradition that instead aims at unity may experience nothingness only by accident.

Ecstasy without Trance

The historical debt of the study of mysticism to the practice of Yoga has meant that the occurrence of ecstatic states that are not trances was unimagined until the 1950s and even today remains little acknowledged.

Psychedelic Drug Use

The big breakthrough was, of course, the controversial case of psychedelic experiences. To the essay that introduced "psychedelic therapy," Sherwood, Stolaroff, and Harman appended some comments, described by them as tentative, that remain among the most precise phenomenological observations of psychedelic ecstasies:

> There appears to emerge a universal central perception, apparently independent of subjects' previous philosophical or theological inclinations. . . .
>
> This central perception, apparently of all who penetrate deeply in their explorations, is that behind the apparent multiplicity of things in the world of science and common sense there is a single reality, in speaking of which it seems appropriate to use such words as infinite and eternal. All beings are seen to be united in this Being; in our usual state we are not consciously aware of this and see ourselves and the objects of the world as individual and separate entities. . . .
>
> The perception of this in the psychedelic experiences is an immediate one, somewhat like the immediate perception upon awakening in the morning that I am the same "I" that went to bed here last night. It is not inconsistent with rational examination of our more usual experiences, but it does not arise from such rational examination.
>
> This entrance into seeming awareness of the nature of reality may take various forms. . . . After such an experience, the person is never the same: in a sense he is born anew, even if it occurs just once, since never can he completely forget the knowledge of the underlying reality which he has glimpsed.[93]

The phenomena proceed at the level of "immediate perception"—or, more precisely, of apperception. During the extrovertive mystical experiences that Sherwood and others discussed, sense perception of the physical world persisted, as did its realistic understanding. Unity was discovered "behind the apparent multiplicity of things" rather than instead of finite plurality. As we all do unless there is reason to do otherwise, drugtakers take their continued reality-testing for granted.

In discussing the distinction between the quality and contents of the ecstatic fantasies, Havens made a pertinent point:

> The whole experience could be reinterpreted as a kind of dream, in which one withdraws from the real world and experiences an imagined realm. . . . Yet during the drug experience itself, the new and unfamiliar Reality is compelling, indisputable, unmistakably real! . . . One subject discovered he had not been in the realm of One Mind in the manner he had assumed. In spite of this discovery, however, he found it impossible to dismiss it all as illusory. After much weighing and consideration, he finally decided that his experience of Unity was true in a *symbolic, if not in a literal,* sense. His transcendental experience dramatized for him the fact that there is less separation, less discrete individuality among men, than his everyday consciousness assumed. Rational confirmation of this fact was attested, for him, by other interpersonal experiences and by some of the discoveries of science . . . and in the influence of culture on personality.[94]

Once the ecstatic moment has passed, drugtakers must decide whether to endorse the contents of their fantasies in a voluntary manner. Some do not. Others do. The reason that some do so is, quite simply, that reality-testing was never inhibited during the ecstasies. The fantasies that the drugtakers experienced were required to conform with reality-testing at the time of their occurrence. Consider the following self-report:

> Emotionally there is a profound feeling of oneness. . . . I was joyful to understand the concept "all things are animate." It is true for one who witnesses the supposed inanimate fibres of her dress, breathing and undulating. The proposition presenting matter as the interaction of light energy is something I feel as though I could confirm. I beheld the One and the Many emphasized in Eastern philosophy. It seemed true—the tree, my companion, and I—we were all the same thing—dying in and out. Status and classifica-

tion appeared as mere superficial differentiation, in the light of the harmony I saw among all beings.[95]

The initial "feeling of oneness" was qualified as emotional. It was not literal or actual; it was not reified. The verbal inspiration that "all things are animate" was accompanied by a visual illusion. A dress was "breathing and undulating"; but reality-testing immediately rationalized the experience as signifying the constitution of matter by pulsating light energy. The Eastern philosophy of the One and the Many then became self-evident—implicitly as an account of the uniformity of mass-energy. A second illusion occurred next. The inanimate undulations acquired the animate significance of "dying in and out." Reality-testing set in immediately, however, with an observation of the superficiality of categorization—implicitly, including both animation and death—"in the light of the harmony of all beings."

Because reality-testing during psychedelic experience reconciles the autonomous materials with the drugtaker's general understanding of the perceptible world, reality-testing after the event evaluates them no differently. Like creative experiences, psychedelic ecstasies are "reality-oriented."[96] The fantasies are consistent with the perceptible world. And like creative experiences, psychedelic ecstasies are rationally compelling, not in all respects, but in sufficiently many that their dismissal as mere illusions is impossible for many drugtakers.

The overwhelming majority of writers competent in the academic study of religion who discussed psychedelic experiences maintained that drug-induced ecstasies are genuinely religious, mystical, and highly desirable.[97] A few commentators who were well versed in one or more mystical traditions emphasized the differences between mysticism and psychedelic experiences. Sectarian prejudices as to the nature of true religion have no place, however, in scientific discussion.[98] Mysticism, as understood by these authors, variously designated one, several, or all varieties of the religious use of trance states.

Peak Experiences

In 1962, Abraham Maslow introduced the term "peak experience" in order to describe the superlative or optimal character of esthetic, creative, mystical, and other exceptionally positive, temporary experiences.[99] Maslow was concerned with peak experiences that occur spontaneously as interruptions of normal waking sobriety, without recourse to meditation, psychoactive drugs, or any other means of induction.

Peak experiences are indistinguishable from psychedelic experiences that occur at lower dosage levels. Reality-testing proceeds throughout. Consider the following self-report:

> In the loveliness of the morning, and the beauty of the hills and valleys, I soon lost my sense of sadness and regret. For nearly an hour I walked along the road. . . . On the way back, suddenly, without warning, I felt that I was in Heaven—an inward state of peace and joy and assurance indescribably intense, accompanied with a sense of being bathed in a warm glow of light, as though the external condition had brought about the internal effect—a feeling of having passed beyond the body, though the scene around me stood out more clearly and as if nearer to me than before, by reason of the illumination in the midst of which I seemed to be placed. This deep emotion lasted, though with decreasing strength, until I reached home, and for some time after, only gradually passing away.[100]

The experience of being "in Heaven" was metaphorical; it was not reified. The experiences of "being bathed in a warm glow of light" and "a feeling of having passed beyond the body" were evidently illusory. The sense of reality was, if anything, heightened. "The scene around me stood out more clearly and as if nearer to me than before."

Peak experiences differ significantly from psychedelic experiences at higher dosage levels. Masters and Houston suggested that psychedelic ecstasies are typically of longer duration, lasting from fifteen minutes to two hours, and occasionally as long as four hours. Most peak experiences last no more than a minute or so. There is consequently less opportunity for a peak experience to impress itself on consciousness and to have profound and lasting effects.[101]

Sensory Deprivation

Sensory deprivation is known to induce an alternate psychic state whose visual effects have repeatedly been compared with the psychedelic phenomena induced by mescaline. They exhibit much the same range from simple, geometric abstractions, through brief pictorial images, to extended dreamlike narratives. Since the mid-1960s, the sensory deprivation phenomena have been termed "reported visual sensations" and divided into two main classes. The first resembles daydreams and hypnagogic states, but blends imperceptibly into the second, whose images are largely spontaneous in occurrence and impossible to control by efforts of will. In both cases, the images are self-evident to the subject as imaginations.[102]

John Lilly established experimentally that profound sensory deprivation can induce unitive experiences.[103] Traditional religious uses of sensory deprivation have also been documented. In a study of Inuit shamanism and initiation,[104] I established that Inuit vision quests depend on various techniques of sensory deprivation. Visions were pursued in complete isolation while immobile and fasting in the darkness of caves or miniature snow huts. Inuit vision quests might also combine constant vigilant alertness with a boring activity: standing at a seal's blow hole, waiting to spear it; rubbing a small stone around and around the surface of a large rock; swaying back and forth atop a boulder. The resultant state was consistent with so-called highway hypnosis. In the following song, a Netsilik Inuit hunter reported visions that he had seen while hunting seal at a breathing hole in the ice:

> While I stood longing for
> While I yearned for women
> My comrades!—yes, then it was
> Their women—yes, then it was
> That they swam past me
> Out in their great sea out yonder
> By day it was
> Early in the forenoon
> That I took into the camp
> One with dark face-hair
> A comrade Inugtigjuaq
> Yes, it was I ayayaiya
> I, who have no children to come running to meet me,
> A poor dog and nothing else
> Is all I know of.—
> While one longs for
> While one yearns for women
> It was that a tiny little calf, no more,
> There, where there were cows with calf
> I found the trail of,
> In vain I was annoyed
> I, ayayaiya
> I came upon it from behind, and it was unafraid
> And I was not to give it

> The great bearded seal's skin
> The one for making into seal thong.
> I came upon it from behind, and it was unafraid
> And I did not give it
> The big white one's (bear's) skin there
> Yes, it was I, ayayaiya.[105]

The hunter was staring at the water in a blow hole when he saw seals that he understood to signify women. He saw his male comrades in similar fashion. At line 9, the vision abruptly shifted. The hunter no longer saw himself at the blow hole, but envisioned himself being greeted by people in the camp. His yearning for children and women next transformed into a caribou hunting scene. The women, earlier seen in the forms of seals, were now seen in the forms of caribou cows.[106]

Throughout his vision, the hunter knew that the seals and caribous signified people. The images were not reified. In keeping with Netsilik Inuit beliefs concerning the goddess of the sea, who controls both species,[107] the hunter saw seals and caribous; but he did not think the animals real. Neither did he think that his vision pertained to real animals. His emotions and concepts concerned Inuit women, men, and children.

In a study of ancient Jewish apocalypticism, I established that the visionaries combined darkness, solitude, fasting, and sleep deprivation with deliberate mood alteration by mourning, grieving, and weeping, in order to trigger a compensatory elation. The resultant experiences were visions that often included moments of communion.[108]

Another historical instance has been noted by Moshe Idel. The thirteenth-century kabbalist Abraham Abulafia meditated on:

> A constantly changing object: one must combine the letters and their vowel signs, "sing" and move the head in accordance with the vocalization, and even lift one's hands in the gesture of Priestly Blessing. . . . Abulafia is not interested in relaxing the consciousness by means of concentration on a "point," but in . . . the necessity to concentrate intensely on such a large number of activities that it is almost impossible at that moment to think about any other subject.[109]

Abulafia experienced both visions, which he interpreted allegorically, and communion, which he interpreted in Aristotelian fashion as union with an immanent God. Idel recognized that Abulafia's technique of letter combination, which was later popularized among east European Hasidism,[110] was inconsistent with a practice of self-hypnosis.[111] It is an instance, I suggest, of sensory deprivation.

Discursive Meditation

Buddhists have traditionally distinguished the "mindfulness" (*satipatthana*) or "insight" (*vipasyana*) meditation of Theravada Buddhism[112] from the "calming-down" (*samatha*) meditation on the *jhanas* in Mahayana Buddhism.[113] The mindfulness technique begins by maintaining "a simple nonjudgmental, noninterfering precise awareness and examination of whatever mental or physical phenomena enter awareness."[114] Once detailed "mindfulness" of the stream of consciousness is achieved, it is made the basis of interpretive "insight." The epistemological fact of the psychic character of all *experience* is translated, through philosophic skepticism, into an ontological claim of the psychic character of all *realities,* and the Buddhist doctrine of the illusion of all things is seen to be confirmed. Although the meditations are discursive and rational, they inadvertently trigger an alternate state whose manifestations include both narrative and unitive ecstasies.[115] As the autonomous materials manifest, they too are made the topics of further meditative analyses and understood to be both intrapsychic and illusory. The successful practice of insight meditation requires reality-testing to be performed almost constantly throughout the procedure.

Another use of discursive meditation has been documented in historical accounts of the *logos* (word) mysticism of Philo,[116] St. Clement of Alexandria, and Origen,[117] and the *nous* (mind or intellect) mysticism of their fellow Alexandrines, Alexander of Aphrodisias and Plotinus.[118] The mysticism of the word or intellect consisted, in my view, of communion experiences that were interpreted in the idioms of late Greek philosophy. *Logos* mysticism was transmitted in Christianity through St. Gregory Nyssa,[119] *The Celestial Hierarchy* of pseudo-Dionysius the Areopagite,[120] Syriac monasticism,[121] and St. Bernard of Clairvaux, among others. *Nous* mysticism was transmitted in late antiquity by Hermetists, Neoplatonists, and Neoaristotelians, before being revived by medieval Muslim and Jewish philosophers,[122] who bequeathed the practices to Sufism and the kabbalah.[123] Not only were the meditations discursive and rational, but the allegorical character of the mystics' occasional visions[124] is a further indication of active reality-testing.

The Concept of Reverie

The range of ecstatic phenomena that occur through psychedelic drug use provides a standard against which the available data on peak, sensory deprivation, and discursive meditation experiences can be measured. In all cases, the experiences are known subjectively to be intrapsychic. They may be interpreted variously, however, as imaginations, extrasensory perceptions, or divine revelations.

I have elsewhere proposed that psychedelic, peak, and sensory deprivation experiences should be treated together as instances of an alternate psychic state that I identify as "reverie."[125] Less intense forms of reverie are common to daydreaming, hypnagogic states, play, creative inspirations, and esthetic experiences. As reverie states intensify, the relative proportion of auto-suggested materials lessens, and autonomous materials increase.

In marked contrast with trance, which involves the increasing repression (counter-cathexis) of ego functions, reverie would seem to involve their increasing relaxation (decathexis). The process of relaxation is consistent with falling asleep and does not imply an inhibition or inability to function. Just as ego functions may become active during sleep, resulting in lucid dreaming,[126] ego functions may return to vigilance once a waking reverie has gotten underway.

The contents of ecstatic reveries are largely but not entirely consistent with the contents of trances. A full range of narrative and unitive ecstasies occur, but there are no parallels to trance phenomena that depend specifically on reification—for example, possession states and experiences of nothingness. On the other hand, a class of phenomena that are not produced in trances is common to psychedelic, peak, and sensory deprivation experiences. The best-known instance has been described in historical studies as "ecstatic death,"[127] "mystic death,"[128] and "initiatory death."[129] It consists of an acute anxiety attack that manifests as a vision of immediately impending death.[130] Grof regards ecstatic death as one of three intensely anxious varieties of psychedelic experience.[131] The others are experiences of severe depression and unending struggle. The phenomena are not unique to drug use, however. Ecstatic depression has also been documented as a spontaneous peak experience.[132] The occurrence of anxiety attacks is consistent with the continuing activity of the ego during reveries, and inconsistent with its inhibition during trances. It is only when the ego's unconscious defenses are actively resisting repressed materials that the potential manifestation of disturbing materials can precipitate panic. By contrast, when the ego's defenses are inhibited during trance, not only may repressed materials manifest unopposed, but they may do so without arousing intense anxiety.

Both Abulafia's letter combinations and Buddhist insight meditations serve to induce reverie states, but do not guide or shape the materials that manifest autonomously. Although psychedelic users are generally hypersuggestible,[133] once a unitive experience commences it runs its own course and cannot be influenced through suggestion.[134] My studies of Inuit shamanism and Jewish visionary apocalypticism indicate, however, that visions are able to conform more or less closely with traditional cultural expectations. Meditation and visualization techniques that are able to produce comparable effects were discovered—or, at least, discovered to scientific knowledge—by the analytic psychologist, Carl Gustav Jung.

Chapter 2

Jung, Silberer, and Active Imagination

A measure of mystery surrounds Jung's practice of active imagination. Jung first discussed the visualization technique in an article that he wrote in 1916 but did not publish until 1957. He first discussed the phenomenon in public in 1921, in six brief paragraphs in his *Psychological Types*. He then used the term "active fantasy" and attributed its activity to a "transcendent function." In 1929, he linked the technique to the practice of alchemy in three brief paragraphs of his "Commentary on 'The Secret of the Golden Flower,'" a Taoist alchemical text.[1] Similarly enigmatic references in passing occurred at intervals thereafter.[2] Jung was evidently using the visualization procedure in psychotherapy by the late 1920s, when a patient used the technique. From 1932 to 1934, Jung gave a private seminar about the patient's visions at the Eidgenossische Technische Hochschule in Zurich. The seminar notes were not published during Jung's life.[3]

Jung seems to have introduced the term "active imagination" during the question period following the last of his Tavistock lectures in the autumn of 1935. The lecture notes were circulated privately in mimeograph in 1936 but were not published during Jung's life.[4] From June 1939 until March 1940, Jung gave a private seminar at the Eidgenossische Technische Hochschule on the *Spiritual Exercises* of St. Ignatius Loyola, which he described as a historical forerunner of active imagination. The seminar notes were privately mimeographed.[5] Only lectures 8–11 have been published, and only posthumously.[6]

The first detailed account of active imagination was published in 1953 by Barbara Hannah.[7] Michael Fordham, a leading British Jungian, published a crucial clarification three years later.[8] Even so, it was only at the urging of James Hillman in 1957 that Jung finally published his 1916 article, "The Transcendent Function."[9]

The article was followed by an extended discussion in Jung's autobiography.[10]

Why did Jung exhibit such tremendous reticence concerning active imagination? In her 1953 article, Hannah warned of the possibility of adverse reactions. Active imagination "may be *the worst imaginable poison to people who are not reasonably adapted. . . .* It can even be dangerous if it is used by the wrong person, at the wrong time, or above all in the wrong way." [11] Hannah urged that active imagination should be used only with the assistance of an analyst or another experienced person.[12] Humbert suggested that "active imagination is indicated for persons terminating analysis, by means of which they learn to find in themselves the relationship to the unconscious originally set up through someone else as an intermediary." [13] As long as the transference remains directed at the person of the therapist, analysis is interminable. Shifting the transference to an internal object within the analysand's psyche permits independence of the therapist.

Jung's co-worker, Marie-Louise von Franz, who considered active imagination "*the* most powerful tool in Jungian psychology," believed, however, that Jung's reticence had been motivated by other concerns. She wrote that Jung "probably" declined to publish his findings "because he realized how far removed these documents were from the collective, conscious views of his time." [14] Although Jung was an eminent psychiatrist whose scientific contributions won him international fame prior to his widely publicized break with Sigmund Freud, Jung was also a visionary mystic[15] with a lifelong interest in the paranormal[16] and personal associations with occultists.[17] Where Freud tended to downplay his own belief in extrasensory perception, Jung's analytic psychology grew increasingly mystical as the years progressed. Like Freud, but much less convincingly, Jung regularly denied the subjectivity of his work and emphasized its scientific character. Jung's pursuit of scientific respectability proved vain, however, and many of his followers have openly acknowledged the mythico-religious character of his system.

In the assessment of the historian of psychology Henri Ellenberger, "Jung's analytic psychology, like Freud's psychoanalysis, is a late offshoot of Romanticism, but psychoanalysis is also the heir of positivism, scientism, and Darwinism, whereas analytic psychology rejects that heritage and returns to the unaltered sources of psychiatric Romanticism and philosophy of nature." [18] The historian of esotericism Antoine Faivre similarly recognized Jung as "the last representative" of Romantic *Naturphilosophie,* whose "scientific work renewed psychoanalysis by exploring the visionary, or imaginal, dimensions of the psyche." [19]

The First Experiments

According to Jung's autobiography, around Christmas of 1912 he had a dream that he was unable to interpret fully.[20] One association, to an alchemical text named the *Emerald Table* of Hermes Trismegistos, led to a recurring fantasy of something dead that was also still alive. Unable to explain the dream to his own satisfaction, Jung "consciously submitted" himself "to the impulses of the unconscious." [21] At first, Jung reenacted childhood games, but in October 1913 he had two visions.[22] Although he regarded his activities as a "scientific experiment," Jung experienced "violent resistance" to his efforts to immerse himself in unconscious material. He "was afraid of losing command" of himself and "becoming a prey to the fantasies." [23] On December 12, 1913, he nevertheless took "the decisive step":

> I was sitting at my desk once more, thinking over my fears. Then I let myself drop. Suddenly it was as though the ground literally gave way beneath my feet, and I plunged down into dark depths. I could not fend off a feeling of panic. But then, abruptly, at not too great a depth, I landed on my feet in a soft, sticky mass. I felt great relief, although I was apparently in complete darkness. After a while my eyes grew accustomed to the gloom, which was rather like a deep twilight. Before me was the entrance to a dark cave, in which stood a dwarf with leathery skin, as if he were mummified. I squeezed past him through the narrow entrance of the cave where, on a projecting rock, I saw a glowing red crystal. I grasped the stone, lifted it, and discovered a hollow underneath. At first I could make out nothing, but then I saw that there was running water. In it a corpse floated by, a youth with blond hair and a wound in the head. He was followed by a gigantic black scarab and then by a red, newborn sun, rising up out of the depths of the water. Dazzled by the light, I wanted to replace the stone upon the opening, but then a fluid welled out. It was blood. A thick jet of it leaped up, and I felt nauseated. It seemed to me that the blood continued to spurt for an unendurably long time. At last it ceased, and the vision came to an end.[24]

Jung's account of his first use of active imagination does not contain the claim that he invented or discovered the practice, but

only that he decided to use it. His very first attempt proved successful, and the vivid visionary experience was followed by a series of
dreams and daydreams. Six days later, Jung had a dream that pertained to this vision,[25] and in April, May, and June 1914 he had
three further dreams on the same theme.[26] Jung felt that he "was
menaced by a psychosis." He believed that "such visions and dreams
are fateful" and he felt pursued by fears. The vision and dream imagery provided content to his daydreams. "An incessant stream of
fantasies had been released." [27]

Having once been given the opportunity to manifest, unconscious materials took the occasion to permeate consciousness. The
experience taxed Jung's sanity. He was "in a constant state of ten-
sion." "One thunderstorm followed another," but he endured through
"brute strength." Engaged as he was in self-analysis, Jung persevered in his practice of active imagination, because he was determined to "find the meaning of what [he] . . . was experiencing in
these fantasies."

To cope with "these assaults of the unconscious," Jung employed "certain yoga exercises" that held his emotions in check. As
soon as he was calmed, however, he "abandoned this restraint upon
the emotions and allowed the images and inner voices to speak
afresh." "To the extent that I managed to translate the emotions
into images—that is to say, to find the images which were concealed
in the emotions—I was inwardly calmed and reassured. Had I left
those images hidden in the emotions, I might have been torn to
pieces by them."[28] Jung's visions developed a cast of recurring characters. One, whom he named Philemon, was an Egypto-Hellenistic
Gnostic who functioned as Jung's "superior insight" and "guru." [29]

The Practice of Active Imagination

Jung believed that his experiences involved "the same psychic
material which is the stuff of psychosis and is found in the
insane,"[30] but he persevered. In 1916, he twice attempted to write
up the conclusions of his experiment. One presentation, in an article entitled "The Transcendent Function," remained unpublished
until 1957. Jung added a prefatory warning in 1958:

> A . . . danger—and this may in certain circumstances be a very se-
> rious matter—is that the subliminal contents already possess
> such a high energy charge that, when afforded an outlet by active

imagination, they may overpower the conscious mind and take possession of the personality. This gives rise to a condition which—temporarily, at least—cannot easily be distinguished from schizophrenia, and may even lead to a genuine "psychotic interval." The method of active imagination, therefore, is not a plaything for children.[31]

The basic technique of active imagination is quite simple. It consists of "systematic exercises for eliminating critical attention, thus producing a vacuum in consciousness." Unconscious fantasies that are pressing for consciousness are then able to manifest.[32]

Because the basic procedure depends on the availability of unconscious fantasies that are pressing for consciousness, additional techniques must be employed when unconscious fantasies are not immediately available.[33] Jung assumed that unconscious fantasies always exist. When the suspension of critical attention is not a sufficient technique, psychic energy must be made available to the unconscious fantasies, so that they may manifest. To accomplish this end, it is necessary to devote attention to one's mood until the mood begins to generate fantasies and other associations that are consistent with it:

> The whole procedure is a kind of enrichment and clarification of the affect, whereby the affect and its contents are brought nearer to consciousness, becoming at the same time more impressive and more understandable. . . . The previously unrelated affect has become a more or less clear and articulate idea, thanks to the assistance and co-operation of the conscious mind.[34]

Once access to unconscious fantasies has been established, it becomes possible to direct them onto desired topics. The procedure is a delicate one, as it requires both the direction and the suspension of critical attention in rapid sequence:

> Critical attention must be eliminated. Visual types should concentrate on the expectation that an inner image will be produced. As a rule such a fantasy-picture will actually appear—perhaps hypnagogically—and should be carefully observed and noted down in writing. Audio-verbal types usually hear inner words, perhaps mere fragments of apparently meaningless sentences to begin with, which however should be carefully noted down too. Others at such times simply hear their "other" voice. . . .

There are others, again, who neither see nor hear anything inside themselves, but whose hands have the knack of giving expression to the contents of the unconscious.[35]

Jung explained his technique somewhat differently in the revised version of his essay "The Relations between the Ego and the
Unconscious." Here he started with the common experience of talking to oneself, which he described from his theoretic perspective as
a dialogue with the anima:

We know that practically every one has not only the peculiarity,
but also the faculty of holding a conversation with himself. Whenever we are in a predicament we ask ourselves (or whom else?),
"What shall I do?" either aloud or beneath our breath, and we (or
who else?) supply the answer. . . . The psyche not being a unity but
a contradictory multiplicity of complexes, the dissociation required
for our dialectics with the anima is not so terribly difficult. The art
of it consists only in allowing our invisible partner to make herself
heard, in putting the mechanism of expression momentarily at her
disposal, without being overcome by the distaste one naturally
feels at playing such an apparently ludicrous game with oneself, or
by doubts as to the genuineness of the voice of one's interlocutor.[36]

Jung argued that "the things one says when in the grip of an
affect sometimes seem very strange and daring." They are subject to
a "mechanism of deprecation and denial" that makes them "easily
forgotten, or wholly denied." Neurotic symptoms may then ensue:

As a result of the repressive attitude of the conscious mind, the
other side is driven into indirect and purely symptomatic manifestations, mostly of an emotional kind, and only in moments of overwhelming affectivity can fragments of the unconscious come to the
surface in the form of thoughts or images.[37]

Jung suggested that it would be "far better to make use of an
affect so as to give the other side an opportunity to speak." By way
of technique, he explained only "that one should cultivate the art of
conversing with oneself in the setting provided by an affect, as
though the affect itself were speaking." Rational criticism was to be
suspended "so long as the affect is speaking." Jung urged the exercise of criticism after the affect was exhausted. "Once it [the affect]
has presented its case, we should begin criticizing as conscien-
tiously as though a real person closely connected with us were our

interlocutor."[38] Jung's concept of criticism was limited, however. At no point did he suggest abandoning the personification of the unconscious.

The earliest public use of the term "active imagination" occurred, so far as I know, in Jung's Tavistock lectures of 1935. In this presentation, Jung claimed that imagination is ordinarily passive. An effort of will must be expended in order to direct the course of a daydream or a creative experience. Active imagination refers to occasions when imagination seizes the initiative, coming alive on its own. "Active imagination, as the term denotes, means that the images have a life of their own and that the symbolic events develop according to their own logic—that is, of course, if your conscious reason does not interfere." [39]

In his explanation of the technique, Jung emphasized its cognitive aspects:

> You begin by concentrating upon a starting point. . . . When you concentrate on a mental picture, it begins to stir, the image becomes enriched by details, it moves and develops. Each time, naturally, you mistrust it and have the idea that you have just made it up, that it is merely your own invention. But you have to overcome that doubt, because it is not true. . . . We cannot do much in the way of conscious invention; we over-estimate the power of intention and the will. And so when we concentrate on an inner picture and when we are careful not to interrupt the natural flow of events, our unconscious will produce a series of images which make a complete story.[40]

Jung also remarked that "in the later stage of analysis, the observation of images replaces the dreams. The images anticipate the dreams, and so the dream-material begins to peter out." [41]

Although Jung named "active imagination" in reference to the lucidity of the imaginations, his term has come to be identified closely with his analytic psychology. Jungian patients use active imagination in order to achieve desired sorts of relations with archetypal symbols of the unconscious. They typically encounter the shadow, anima, animus, and self in a fairly strict sequence. The books on active imagination by Marie-Louise von Franz[42] and Barbara Hannah[43] seek, in the main, to sustain Jung's interpretive system. Von Franz made two important contributions to the phenomenology of active imagination. "There is a chance that markedly synchronistic events will occur." [44] In other words, the practice

of active imagination increases the likelihood that random co-
incidences will be found personally meaningful and regarded as
providential miracles. As well, because the contents of active imagination are not necessarily moral, their postexperiential evaluation
should integrate ethical considerations.[45]

Active imagination is, I suggest, a powerful alternate state,
closely resembling the hypnagogic state between waking and sleeping. Although reflective self-consciousness, the ability to exert effort, logical thinking, and reality-testing are always suspended as
advanced hypnagogic states blend into sleep,[46] active imagination
reverses the process of relaxation by initiating conscious interaction
with the unconscious manifestations.[47] Active imagination may be
considered a *lucid hypnagogic state,* whose relation to ordinary hypnagogia compares with the relation of lucid dreams to ordinary
dreams. Lucid hypnagogia is a form of reverie. Reality-testing remains uninhibited. Whether the autonomous manifestations are interpreted as imaginations, extrasensory perceptions, or divine
revelations, they are known to be intrapsychic.

Since Jung introduced it, lucid hypnagogia has been integrated
with other systems of psychotherapy. Robert Desoille blended
Jungian and Pavlovian approaches in devising his own "Directed
Daydream" technique.[48] Desoille had his patients close their eyes
and relax. They were next to visualize a series of motifs that Desoille selected, in order that the autonomous manifestations pertain
to desired topics. The patients reported the results verbally as a
running commentary on their occurrence:

> There are a series of imaginative happenings, as a rule character-
> ized by unexpected adventure. The patient is constantly surprised
> by what he witnesses; he enjoys the pleasantly surprising views,
> wonders at meetings never foreseen, is annoyed at sudden obsta-
> cles, and is confused by unpredictable changes of mood and
> feeling.[49]

Among the various visualization exercises, Desoille's directions
"to descend to the deepest depths and to ascend to the greatest
heights" resulted in imagery of considerable interest to students of
religion:

> The barrier the neurotic meets on his way is regularly embodied in
> a person, an animal, a figure, or in any case a living being that ex-
> pressly forbids any advance—*the keeper of the threshold.* . . the na-

ture, the form of the *keeper of the threshold* was dependent on the level on which he appeared. From the bottom to the top these forms were, roughly speaking the following: goblins, dwarfs, dragons; giants and strong male figures; female figures, angels and spirits, and in the very highest region, God. In cases where a figure appeared at what might be termed a non-autochthonous level, which was no exception, still its form and substantiality nearly always agreed with the colouration and the materiality of the level on which it appeared. . . . Going upwards the image grows light, more transparent, more volatile, more euphorious, milder, more all-embracing. In harmony with this the feelings of the ascender become better, more sublime. On the highest level the light becomes inexpressibly white, colourless; all images lose their outline as they dissolve into an all-conquering light. . . .

The unbelieving patient is somewhat painfully surprised to find himself so immediately confronted with heaven and hell, God and the angels. One of my patients could not refrain from uttering again and again the apologetical correction, "but I don't believe in any heaven," and "I don't believe in angels."[50]

Jung was evidently wrong in claiming that a "vision . . . in accordance with dogmatic expectation . . . is only possible when someone has had a great deal of practice in manipulating his unconscious." [51] The unconscious production of autonomous images that conform with learned motifs may happen spontaneously. Conformity may even occur in the absence of conscious belief in the motifs. For some imagers, the apparent confirmation of received tradition by personal experience may have profound religious consequences.

Because Desoille aimed at identifying "maladaptive dynamic patterns" and introducing "possible emotional responses which are entirely new" to the patient,[52] his technique accommodated and encouraged the psychological naivety of the patient. In reporting imagined adventures with imagined beings, "more often than not, he [the patient] is not aware that he is talking about himself. Hence our work is not impeded by censorship or resistance." [53] Freud made a similar observation. In treating an adolescent boy, Freud had once had the patient experience and report hypnagogic fantasies for diagnostic purposes. Freud remarked that "long-repressed memories and derivatives from them which had remained unconscious slipped into consciousness by a roundabout path in the form of meaningless pictures." [54] Freud used ordinary hypnagogic images, but the consequences for symbolization are the same in cases of lucidity.

Unconscious ideas are able to evade censorship when they take symbolic form as images.

In contrast with Freud, who interpreted the latent meaning of symbolism for his patients, Desoille followed Jung in encouraging his patients to achieve desired relations with the imagery evoked. For example, disturbing materials were to be confronted:

> *Symbol Confrontation* is one way of dealing with those archaic, symbolic figures which emerge from the forest, cave, ocean or swamp. . . . Perhaps the most important single element . . . is persistent staring into the eyes of the frightful creature. Its purposes are to discover the message or meaning which the creature's existence conveys and to banish the creature henceforth from one's daydreams. During this confrontation the therapist actively supports the patient even by holding his hand, if necessary.
>
> By demanding an accurate description of the terrifying image, we force the patient to replace his archaic anxiety by a critical and analytic attitude which is effective for testing reality.[55]

Desoille's therapeutic technique may be compared with the play therapy of children. Both permit the patients to remain innocent of the latent meanings of symbols that their therapists teach them to manipulate. Desoille's publications drew the attention of the philosopher Gaston Bachelard, from whom I have adopted the term "reverie" in designation of the altered psychic state.[56]

Desoille's procedure was wedded to Freudian theory by Hanscarl Leuner,[57] who described his "Guided Affective Imagery" as a means to "provide the psychodynamic material needed for a genuine depth psychotherapy."[58] Like Desoille, Leuner addressed his patients' concerns through imagery whose symbolic significance the patients did not necessarily understand. However, both his selection of images and his own interpretation of their latent content were informed by Freudian theory.

Joseph Reyher's "Emergent Uncovering Psychotherapy" is a guided imagery therapy that conforms still more closely with Freudian procedures. It offers the analysand insight into the unconscious meaning of the symbolism.[59] Roberto Assagioli used guided imagery techniques as a component within the total regime of his system of psychosynthesis.[60] Further therapies have used lucid hypnagogia as well.[61]

Guided imagery techniques have also entered the world of Western occultism, where "creative visualization" has become a mainstay of New Age spirituality.[62] Consider, for example, the self-report of an occultist who learned active imagination during a Jungian analysis:

> I attempted to . . . invent . . . a staircase that would take me within to those archetypal images I was seeking. And it worked! I reached a room at the bottom of my stairway, thought of the *High Priestess,* and she was *there,* a *living* presence in that inner world, different from the picture on the tarot card, but without a doubt the *High Priestess* as a reality within me. And the experience seemed to be happening *there,* in some other dimension or reality, totally unconnected with the *here* of the normally experienced outer world.[63]

A later attempt to visualize the devil precipitated an acute anxiety attack:

> I was inside the room where I came into contact with the archetypal forms when an image of *Old Pan* or *Devil* appeared, unsummoned and unwanted. It was a classic Christian devil with an emanation of "evil" . . . . I tried to end the experience by opening my eyes, but I discovered that I was unable to move or perform this simple feat. I was paralyzed. I began to panic. I seemed to be frozen in the chair. The *Old Pan* entity became even more menacing than before, placing himself in my inner world between me and the stairway to the outer world and safety. The panic finally subsided (although not the fear), and I further tried to maneuver to the stairway around the figure, but to no avail. This entity of the inner world blocked my every move. . . .
>
> Finally, I was able to calm myself and concentrate on my outer body sufficiently to try to move a finger on my right hand. Using all my will and ignoring the *Old Pan* figure entirely, I managed this feat, and it broke the state in which I had been locked.[64]

In order to avoid further experiences of panic, the subject sought the aid of a guide:

> I found my inner stairway and cautiously descended. I reached the bottom. The room was deserted. Standing close to the stairs, I called out for a guide to appear. At first nothing happened, but then a feeling of love and warmth touched me from my left. Slowly I moved away from the staircase through an opening that I now noticed on the left. I passed through the opening, and, to the right of it, I saw an old, old man standing. He was dressed in striped

robes of muted colors, had white whiskers, was of medium height
and wore a turban. Kindness and gentleness radiated from him. I
asked if he were a "guide." He responded that he was *my* Inner
Guide and that his name was "Aman." I told him of my terrifying
experience with the *Old Pan* energy, and he explained that it was
my fear that had made the experience so potentially dangerous. I
asked him if he could truly guide and teach me in this strange,
beautiful, but frightening, inner world and if he could protect me
from such experiences as I had had with *Old Pan*. He stated simply that he *had* always tried to guide and protect me and always
would if I requested and allowed him to do so.[65]

Importantly, it was the autonomy of the imagined beings that
led their imager to believe in their reality:

It was during this initial . . . phase that I experienced the difference between *ego* and *non-ego* elements in my own psyche. My
imagination took on a life of its own. Conflicting archetypal forms
would not be pushed into agreement or easy reconciliations. Where
I had supposed, "I'm making most of this up," I soon found experiences full of surprises. It became dramatically clear to me that
these were *living* entities I was dealing with, and that my ego
could not get them to cooperate or come together just because I
thought they should or asked them to. They seemed to be separate,
sometimes alien, entities totally unlike any familiar aspect of myself. They had their own likes and dislikes, interests and aversions,
moods and temperaments. Their behaviors, as I observed and in-
teracted with them, were often completely unpredictable. Occasionally they were hostile to me. Sometimes they totally ignored
my presence, and only with the greatest effort could I attract their
attention and get them to communicate with me. To get behavior
change or cooperation from them, *I* usually had to agree to make
changes in my outer world, modify my behavior or agree on new
actions. They were most explicit about the changes they required
from me or from my life in exchange for their cooperation or
assistance.[66]

To express the paradoxical status of active imaginations that
are known to be intrapsychic and are nevertheless experienced as
real, Corbin coined the term "imaginal":

The forms and figures of the *mundus imaginalis* do not subsist in
the same manner as the empirical realities of the physical
world . . . [but] these forms and figures could not subsist in the

purely intelligible world [either] . . . they had indeed extension and dimension, an "immaterial" materiality compared to the sensible world, but . . . a corporality and spaciality of their own.[67]

We need not follow Corbin in ascribing "subtle bodies" to the imaginal in order to use his term in reference to beliefs such as his own.

Gnosticism and the Occult

Jung's article, "The Transcendent Function," was one of two attempts in 1916 to write up his findings on active imagination. The second took form as a Gnostic apocryphon that he entitled "The Seven Sermons to the Dead by Basilides of Alexandria." [68] Originally printed privately as a gift for friends, it was first made available to the public in 1961 as an appendix to Jung's autobiography.[69]

Jung's interest in Gnosticism had begun at least as early as 1902, when his doctoral dissertation, "On the Psychology of So-called Occult Phenomena," described the views of a séance medium as Gnostic. In a Victorian condemnation of Gnosticism as a Christian heresy, Charles William King had asserted that medieval Gnosticism had been practiced by the Knights Templar and later made its way into Western occultism.[70] The speculation that Gnosticism was an antecedent of occultism was subsequently adopted and popularized by Helena Petrovna Blavatsky, who founded the Theosophical Society in 1875.[71] Jung's doctoral dissertation gave academic standing to the historical hypothesis. Later, between 1918 and 1926, Jung "seriously studied the Gnostic writers, for they too had been confronted with the primal world of the unconscious and had dealt with its contents, with images that were obviously contaminated with the world of instinct." [72] Robert A. Segal has shown that most of the affinities that Jung perceived between Gnosticism and analytic psychology were doctrinal. Ideas that the Gnostics had expressed in metaphysical terms corresponded to similar observations that Jung had formulated in psychological terms.[73] However, Jung also contended that some Gnostic "symbolism may well have been based, originally, on some visionary experience, such as happens not uncommonly today during psychological treatment." [74]

Was Jung indebted to unacknowledged sources in Western occultism for his introduction to active imagination?[75] Although Robert Desoille's Directed Daydream therapy was indebted to Jung and Pavlov, Desoille had first learned of lucid hypnagogia from an occult work that had been published *the year before Jung* first associated active imagination with the occult.[76] The occult procedures were employed in the late nineteenth century by the Hermetic Order of the Golden Dawn, an English occult society whose teachings have since come to dominate Western occultism. The Golden Dawn taught two techniques of visualization, which were known as "path-working." In active path-working, occultists visualized imagery whose complete details they had planned in advance. In passive path-working, however, visualization techniques determined the initial selection of imagery, but the images were later permitted to unfold or develop on their own.[77] Both active and passive path-working might be performed in either trance or lucid hypnagogic states.

Silberer's Contribution

In searching for a historical link between Gnosticism and "the modern psychology of the unconscious," Jung settled on alchemy:[78]

> The experiences of the alchemists were, in a sense, my experiences, and their world was my world. This was, of course, a momentous discovery: I had stumbled upon the historical counterpart of my psychology of the unconscious. The possibility of a comparison with alchemy, and the uninterrupted intellectual chain back to Gnosticism, gave substance to my psychology.[79]

Jung was not the first depth psychologist to take a serious interest in alchemy. The psychoanalyst Herbert Silberer published a book on alchemy in 1914.[80] Despite Jung's break with Freud the year previously, Jung and Silberer had corresponded about the book's ideas. At the time, Jung was uninterested in Silberer's account of alchemy but appreciative of his concept of "the anagogic or constructive point of view." [81] Given the extent of Jung's later fascination with alchemy, this apparent denial of Silberer's influence is astonishing—until the remark is unpacked.

In 1913, when Jung and Freud met for the last time, Jung delivered a paper entitled "A Contribution to the Study of Psychological Types." In it, Jung advanced the concepts of extroversion and introversion. Silberer's book on alchemy built on Jung's concept of psychological types. Silberer maintained that symbols that originally occur in dreams "only incidentally to signify some idea content, wish content, etc., return and become a persistent or typical form." [82] In the process of their repetition, the symbols undergo changes in meaning. They become less particular and more "representative of a whole group of similar experiences, a spiritual capital, so to speak, till finally we can regard it simply as the representative of a spiritual current (love, hate, tendency to frivolity, to cruelty, to anxiety, etc.)" [83] In their development, typical symbols retain the unconscious instinctual significance that gave them origin. Through sublimation, however, they also acquire a second order of significance that Silberer termed "anagogic." [84] The two levels of meaning are not in conflict. It is simply that symbols that were originally used egotistically later acquire ethical value.[85] For example, the infantile desire to kill the father acquires the anagogic significance of killing the old Adam. The desire for the mother—to be passive while she attends to one's needs—is sublimated into introversion. The desire for incest develops into love toward an ideal. Infantile autoerotism is sublimated as ecstasy; and so forth.[86] Having established the general theoretic principle with reference to sublimations of the Oedipus complex, Silberer analyzed alchemical symbols in close detail.

The question of precedence is intricate. In a passage prior to the section of his book that referred to typical symbols as "types," Silberer used the term "imago," which Jung had introduced during his Freudian period. As an example of an imago, Silberer remarked that "the earth is the mother"[87]—the earth has the symbolic meaning and unconscious importance of the mother imago. In all, it would seem that Jung advanced the concepts of both the imago and the type, but that Silberer recognized their harmony and synthesized them. Building on Freud's concept of sublimation, Silberer further innovated the concept of the development of a type from egotistic to anagogic significance. Jung's later concept of the "archetype" retained Silberer's concern with anagogic meanings, while jettisoning the Freudian heritage of developmental, sexual, and egotistic concerns. The seminal importance of Silberer's work for Jung's theory system may explain why, by 1928, Jung had quite forgotten what Silberer had written about alchemy, as distinct from anagogic types.

On the other hand, there is reason to believe that Jung failed to accord Silberer the credit that he was due. In 1909, Silberer had published an article outlining a use of hypnagogic imagery as a means to confirm Freud's theory of symbol formation.[88] He claimed independent discovery of phenomena that he had since found mentioned in existing literature:

> The conditions for the phenomenon . . . were two: (a) drowsiness, (b) an effort to think. The former is a passive condition not subject to will, the latter an active one manipulatable by the will. It is the struggle of these two antagonistic elements that elicits the experience which I call the "autosymbolic" phenomenon.
>
> It can be described as an hallucinatory experience which puts forth "automatically," as it were, an adequate symbol for what is thought (or felt) at a given instance. . . .
>
> The "autosymbolic" phenomenon comes about only in a transitional state between sleep and waking, that is, in the hypnagogic state, the twilight between sleep and waking.[89]

In hypnagogic states, Silberer found that his thoughts underwent involuntary or automatic conversion into visual images that allegorized the verbal ideas. The unconscious was involved in the production of the images, but not in the development of the ideas that they allegorized.

Silberer's book on alchemy presented a variant of the technique that he had adapted to address the anagogic level of symbolic function:

> In a drowsy state I reflect upon the nature of the judgments that are transsubjectively (= for all men) valid. All at once the thread of the abstract thought is broken and autosymbolically in the place of it is presented the following hypnagogic hallucination:
>
> Symbol. An enormous circle, or transparent sphere, floats in the air and men are putting their heads into this circle.
>
> Interpretation. In this symbol everything that I was thinking of is expressed. The validity of the transsubjective concerns all men without exception; the circle goes through all the heads. This validity must have its cause in something common to all. The heads all belong to the same apparently homogeneous sphere. Not all judgments are transsubjective; with their bodies and limbs men are outside of and under the sphere and stand on the earth as separate individuals.[90]

Jung did not develop active imagination in a vacuum. However much he may have had independent sources and however much he may have altered or adapted Silberer's techniques, he was following Silberer's lead. Jung's innovation was nevertheless substantial. Where Silberer had explored the unconscious symbolization of conscious ideas, Jung sought the manifestations of symbols and ideas that had never before been conscious.

Jung and Alchemy

Jung's interest in alchemy was renewed in 1928 when Richard Wilhelm made him a gift of a Chinese alchemical work, *The Secret of the Golden Flower.*[91] Also in 1928, Jung had a patient whose dreams included alchemical symbolism that she interpreted for Jung.[92] In his collaboration with Wilhelm in 1929, Jung asserted that Taoist alchemists had used "the art of letting things happen, action through inaction," as he then described active imagination.[93] Jung took up systematic study of Western alchemical literature the next year. He was soon astonished to discover in alchemy a historical precedent for his own system of psychology.[94] Jung contended that alchemists had traditionally used techniques that closely resembled active imagination,[95] and he argued that Gnosticism, which included a practice of visions, had anciently been a primary source of alchemical thought and symbolism.[96] Was Jung correct? Were there parallels with Jung's system of analytic psychology? If so, were the parallels coincidental? Did Jung rediscover psychological findings that had been known to the Gnostics and Western alchemists? Or was Jung indebted to occult sources for his ideas?

The possibility of a direct debt can be neither established nor discounted. While studying medicine at the University of Basel late in 1895, Jung immersed himself in occult literature. "I read virtually the whole of the literature available to me at the time."[97] Beginning in 1898, he attended spiritualist séances on Saturday evenings for two years.[98]

At least as early as his association with Freud, Jung had the opportunity personally to meet deeply learned occultists. Rudolf Steiner, one of the most knowledgeable occultists of the time, tutored a Viennese family that Joseph Breuer frequently visited. Friedrich Eckstein, who introduced Steiner to Theosophy, was a lifelong friend of Sigmund Freud.[99] Sandor Ferenczi, one of Freud's closest disciples, developed an interest in parapsychology. In 1910, he began to visit psychics, and he even dragged Freud along on one occasion. By 1912, he was trying to convince both Freud and Ernest

Jones that he was a mind reader. Wilhelm Fliess, who had been Freud's intimate friend in the 1890s, found the main reception of his theories among occultists; scientists considered him a mystic.[100] It is most improbable, to say the least, that anyone with Jung's interests would have failed to avail himself of at least some of the social opportunities that Freud's circle provided. Of course, if Jung did know occultists and was given access by them to esoteric matters, he may well have respected the confidences by concealing his sources.

On the other hand, a debt to occultism need not have been direct. If we allow that Jung improvised active imagination on the basis of Silberer's scientific publications, the question might instead be phrased in terms of Silberer's sources. Jung acknowledged that the mystical dimension of his system was indebted to Silberer's discussion of alchemy.[101] Was Jung's debt to Silberer more than he stated or perhaps even consciously knew? Silberer, who claimed that Freemasonry was heir to the secret practices of the alchemists,[102] wrote occasionally in the cryptic style of an initiated mason.[103] He asserted, for example, that the philosopher's stone of the alchemists had the same meaning as the cornerstone of Freemasonry, but he declined to say anything more.[104] Silberer was also familiar with literature on the psychic techniques of occultists.[105] Indeed, he was sufficiently knowledgeable about the phenomena to remark that occult initiations sometimes go awry until they verge on psychosis.[106] Was it an accident that Jung's experiences of 1912 to 1917 resembled such an initiation? Did Jung receive from Silberer just enough traditional esoteric lore, dressed up in modern psychoanalytic garb, to undertake the equivalent of a self-initiation?

These questions cannot be answered directly, but the problem can be approached from another direction. What was the history of lucid hypnagogia before Silberer and Jung? Did alchemy transmit Gnostic teachings as Jung claimed?

Chapter 3

Theories of Spiritual Alchemy

In 1845, Baron Karl von Reichenbach, a German industrialist and research chemist, published his pioneering studies of what has since come to be termed parapsychology. Reichenbach claimed that all physical bodies have invisible force fields that are visible to "sensitives" in Mesmeric trances. When examined as they occur in crystals, these force fields are bipolar. They feel cool and appear blue at one pole, but are lukewarm and yellow-red at the other. Reichenbach identified the force with Mesmer's animal magnetism but named it Odic after the Scandinavian god Odin.[1]

Although Reichenbach presented himself as a scientist, several motifs that I have cited may be alchemical. Since the Romans identified Odin with Mercury, an Odic force is Hermetic by definition. Reichenbach's discussion of crystal is similarly notable. In the Gold-und Rosenkreuz, a development of the alchemical tradition of Paracelsus and Boehme in late eighteenth-century German, the insignia of the ninth and highest degree, *Majus,* consisted of a "gleaming and fiery" Urim and Thummim, with a Schemhamphorash.[2] It is at least probable that the German alchemists named their engraved brooches in allusion to their use in crystal-gazing or scrying. The biblical Urim and Thummim, or high priest's breastplate, had been used in divination (Ex 28:15–30); and the English import of the Gold- und Rosenkreuz system by the Hermetic Order of the Golden Dawn[3] associated Rosicrucianism with crystal-gazing.[4] Crystal also alluded to salt, which, in Paracelsian alchemy, designated the quintessence.

Complementing Reichenbach's early efforts, Mary Anne South, later Mary Anne Atwood, addressed the historical dimension of the problem. Western alchemists never themselves claimed that transmutation was spiritual rather than metallic or physical. However, the literary works were designed to be incomprehensible to the uninitiated, and they have done their task well. The writings abound in allegories, ciphers, uses of common words in secret technical manners, allusions, intimations, and outright misdirections.[5] What the texts were intended to conceal remains a matter of highly variable interpretation.

The thesis that alchemical literature concerned a secret practice of mysticism was first put forward in *A Suggestive Inquiry into the Hermetic Mystery*. The book was published anonymously in London in 1850, but its author withdrew it from circulation six weeks later for fear that it had revealed too much. The book claimed that both the Eleusinian mysteries and alchemy secretly concerned the quintessence or ether, the substance of which souls are composed. Texts that manifestly discuss the transmutation of base metal into gold were to be interpreted as secret allegories of the soul's perfection through Mesmerism.[6] Jung, who considered the book "a thoroughly medieval production garnished with would-be theosophical explanations as a sop to the syncretism of the new age,"[7] asserted that "no secrets are betrayed" by it. The book was written in a traditional alchemical style, and few of its readers seem ever to have understood it. *A Suggestive Inquiry* was not reissued until 1918, when the name of its author, Mary Anne Atwood, was first attached to it.

With Reichenbach's failure to win the approval of scientists, Atwood's book had found appeal chiefly among occultists. It was endorsed by Eliphas Levi in 1855[8] and embraced in the 1880s by English occult circles. Atwood herself enjoyed a personal following among members of the Theosophical Society, to whom the esoteric exegesis of her book was apparently transmitted. The only writers on alchemy, who have come to my attention, who wrote of the same esoterica as Atwood, were Arthur Edward Waite, whose *Azoth* was published by the Theosophical Society's press in 1893;[9] Rudolf Steiner, who headed the Theosophical Society in Austria until he founded Anthroposophy; and Carl G. Jung.

Most modern writers on spiritual alchemy have interpreted the initial blackening and final golden perfection of the alchemical opus as symbols, respectively, of ecstatic death[10] and introspective union.[11] Opinions differ regarding the middle of the opus. Atwood's account of "the experimental method" claimed to follow "the Paracelsian Alchemists and some others."[12] The possible existence of other alchemical traditions should not be discounted.

The Paracelsian Tradition

Atwood began her exposition by emphasizing that "Intellect . . . possesses an universal knowledge of every thing, and is in the highest sense powerful." Intellect had, however, no elemental substratum. It "is not mingled with any thing; but is alone itself by itself. . . . For it is the most attenuated and pure of all things."[13] Paracelsus had spoken similarly of spirit, and Atwood sometimes used his idiom. She wrote, for example, of "the purified spirit or intelligence, that is Isis."[14]

Immediately after introducing her discussion of intellect, Atwood turned to the topic of "putrefaction:"[15]

> Darkness, made visible by the appearing light, shrinks more and more condensing; and falsehood, as it were, trembling for her kingdom, puts on every sinister guise, to combat and eclipse the living truth, as, increasing in power and armed with bright effulgence, it arises, threatening to dissipate the total fabric, and dissolve its very foundation.[16]

This passage explains ecstatic death as a by-product of the experience of Intellect. Because ecstatic death occurs in reverie states, but not in trances, we may infer that the associated experience of an omniscient Intellect was similarly attained during a reverie. In view of the two thousand year history of the mysticism of the *nous* or Intellect, the experience may confidently be identified as communion.

As though to veil the mystery that she had so briefly and allusively exposed, Atwood continued with several pages of mythological allusions that made mention of death and dying. When she next returned explicitly to the opus, she made her meaning somewhat more clear: "Enter in even to the *Cross,* then seek gold and you will not be deceived. You must seek in another world for the pure child . . . ; in this world . . . enter in even to the cross . . . ; there you have Sol and Luna together; bring them through an anguish into death."[17]

An anguished experience of death formed part of the alchemical opus. Following the ecstatic death, gold, "the pure child," was to be sought "in another world." Although the otherworldly operation involved both Sol and Luna, gold was the metal of the sun. Because Atwood elsewhere identified Sol explicitly as the soul,[18] the operation involving gold may be interpreted as a vision of the disembodied soul. "The Quintessence and hidden thing of our Stone is nothing else than our viscous celestial and glorious soul, drawn by our magistery out of its mine, which engenders itself and brings itself forth."[19] The mine where the soul was quarried was presumably the body; the soul's self-creation implied its divinity. Atwood maintained that the soul "is changed into the likeness of an immortal god."[20] But since she also maintained, with Neoplatonism and the kabbalah, that God "is unknown, or known as nothing,"[21] the soul's divinizing transformation presumably pertained to its life after death.

Mystical union with God played no part in Atwood's account of the opus. Her God was wholly transcendent. The alchemical opus involved mystical union, but the union was limited to what was manifest: "the most beautiful and Universal Mystery of Nature."[22] Atwood maintained that the ether, which might be seen in Mesmeric trances,[23] was inherently hylic or chaotic. "*A Nature primarily vital which is also formless, indestructible and immortal...*is made *manifest* and imparted through arcane and blessed visions."[24] The hylic condition of ether became evident, I suggest, upon the dissolution of the Many into the One at the climax of introspective union.

Not only did Atwood interpret mystical union as a reversion to hylic ether, and not to God, but she maintained that intellect or spirit imparted form to the ether. "Whatever soul possesses greater or lesser, over all these Intellect has dominion":[25]

> No sooner, it is said, does the Divine Light pierce to the bosom of the *matter*, but the pattern of the whole universe appears in those Subject Waters, as an image in a glass, conceived and divided forth in all the vastness of ideal distinction and effulgence upon that glorious metaphysical height where the Archetype shadows the intellectual spheres.[26]

To summarize, in Atwood's presentation, the alchemical opus was an initiation that consisted of four ecstatic experiences: (1) ecstatic death; (2) communion with the Intellect of nature; (3) a flight of the disembodied ethereal soul; and (4) an introspective union, which was understood to reduce matter and ether to a hylic condition. Her mystical doctrine sought to reconcile the ecstasies through an alchemical marriage of Luna and Sol: a conjunction of the Intellect that imparts nature to matter, with the hylic substance of ether.

Arthur Edward Waite (1857–1942) was a Londoner who wrote mystical poetry, novels, and highly learned historical studies of Christian mysticism and the esoteric mystical dimension of alchemy, Rosicrucianism, Freemasonry, Arthurian romance, the kabbalah, magic, and the tarot. He also published English editions or translations of medieval and Renaissance alchemical texts. A frequent visitor of the Theosophical Society in the early 1880s, he joined the Hermetic Order of the Golden Dawn in 1891, Freemasonry in 1901, and the Societas Rosicruciana in Anglia in 1902. In 1903, when the Golden Dawn split into two groups, Waite led the Independent and Rectified Rite, which he reorganized as a mystical rather than a magical society. In 1915, he founded the Fellowship of the Rosy Cross, whose esoteric doctrines were exclusively mystical, Christian, and Rosicrucian. Under his direction, the higher grades of the Fellowship of the Rosy Cross became the Ordo Sanctissimus Roseae et Aureae Crucis in 1922.[27]

Waite's claim that the various major branches of Western occultism each formed part of a "secret tradition" should not be understood as a claim that they shared the same esoterica.[28] Although he was self-taught, Waite was a judicious empirical historian. He believed that all Western esoterica led ultimately to Christ, but his studies explicated a variety of different esoterica. For example, Waite wrote a work of spiritual alchemy[29] that was considerably indebted to Atwood's book,[30] but he also insisted that the secrets of historical alchemists had been chemical rather than mystical.[31] He attributed the origin of spiritual alchemy to "Henry Khunrath and the anonymous author of the treatise concerning Mary of Alexandria, with a few Rosicrucian philosophers" in the late sixteenth or early seventeenth century.[32]

Because occultists each adapt the traditions they receive in order to accommodate their own abilities, experiences, and beliefs, Waite organized his presentation of spiritual alchemy into "seven distinct stages of the Soul's ascent towards God."[33] Atwood's four ecstasies became the second through fifth in Waite's version of the opus.

Waite began with a state of aspiration, or first sublimation, which "is the transfiguring and subliming of sense." The experience transforms sense perception. "The essence of the sublimation of the senses is in their elevation into the region of religion."[34] Waite referred to the transvaluation of the sensible world in an experience of extrovertive union.

The state of mental aspiration, or second sublimation, carries the same process further, into "the mind's transfiguring." It was an experience of "enlightenment and . . . clarifying." "In its highest development there is the consciousness already of that contact between the individual and the Universal Mind which is a foretaste of mystical union."[35] As did St. Teresa of Avila, Waite regarded communion as an anticipation of introspective union. For Waite, however, a crucial feature of "the quintessential rapture of pure intelligence . . . the illumination of Nature" was the identification of the unifying principle as the universal mind, nature, pure intelligence, ideal being, and so forth.[36]

As the third of his seven stages, Waite counted "the Obscure Night."[37] "It is the Black State of the Matter of the Alchemists. It is the portentous darkness of initiation, the passage of the Soul through Hades, the Kingdom of Pluto, and the mystical death of Tartarus."[38]

Waite's fourth stage was "the Absorption of Quietism." Its "complete immobilation of self and unreserved surrender into the hands of God . . . is not to be confounded with insensibility."[39] It was not to be confused, then, with the inhibition of sense perception and mobility during trance states. It also involved "the evolution of the inner light and the education of the withdrawn glory."[40] Waite was being secretive, but he was also writing of a generality. The fourth stage was, I suggest, any order of trance in whose course "the inner light" or "withdrawn glory" was seen in a vision. The euphemisms pertained to the ether.

The fifth stage was "the state of Union."[41] This "second psychal state" entails "a common comprehension in the psychic potencies of the unseen."[42] For the purposes of the alchemical opus, it was crucial that this vision of introspective union accomplished a "union of mind and Soul."[43] The concept of nature as pure intelligence, developed in the second stage of the work, was to be brought to union with the concept of the ether and soul. Under these conditions, the mystical reduction of all to one—the production of mercury, or the philosopher's stone—implied that the ether was subject to the intelligent ordering processes of nature.

Atwood's account of the opus ended at this point, but Waite added a Christianizing sequel. His sixth stage was "the Ecstatic Absorption, or the Soul's transport above and outside itself."[44] Waite wrote of "transport" in its technical sense as an ecstatic vision of the soul's disembodied transport by God. "It is . . . the passage of the mind or soul into the other world, as took place with Enoch, Elias, and others."[45] The sixth stage developed directly into the seventh:

> It is a state of sanctification, beatitude, and ineffable torrents of delight flowing over the whole being. . . . Love, which is a potency of the Soul, or of that *Anima* which vivifies our bodies, has passed into the Spirit of the Soul, into its superior, divine, and universal form, and this process, when completed, comprises the seventh

and final stage of pneumatic development, which is that of Entrancement.[46]

In the entrancement, "man, unified with his Spirit, is united in the Spirit with God."[47] It was a second experience of introspective union, but it had a novel significance. In the union of the fifth stage, an alchemist came to comprehend the macrocosm as a union of universal intelligence with matter and ether. In the final entrancement, however, alchemical initiation passed beyond the macrocosm to a union with the third person of the Christian trinity.

Rudolf Steiner (1861–1925) was a white magician and, by his own lights, a Christian. He was also one of the most knowledgeable and creative occultists of his time. He earned a PhD at Rostock for his work on Goethe and spent six years at the Goethe archive in Weimar while editing Goethe's scientific writings for the then-projected standard edition. During his academic years, Steiner was a Theosophist. Around 1906, Steiner was installed for a time as the head of a lodge of the Ordens Tempel des Ostens. In addition to a blend of Hindu tantra and Sufism, the Ordens Tempel practiced Grail mysticism and Rosicrucianism, which was then still an explicitly alchemical tradition. In 1913, Steiner led a schism within continental Theosophy and founded the Anthroposophical Society.[48]

Steiner followed the Romantic practice, descended from Schelling,[49] that made overt discussion of metaphysics rather than ecstasies[50] and simplified by referring to a dualism.[51] Rather than the four stages of the opus, this tradition referred to its two basic ingredients, sulfur and mercury, which were also known as the king and queen, Sol and Luna, fire and ice, Apollo and Dionysius, and so forth. In the following passage, Steiner used a traditional Freemasonic and Rosicrucian symbolism that had been suggested by the biblical verse, "I am a rose of Sharon,/ A lily of the valleys" (Song of Songs 2:1):

> If one went back . . . [to] Flor and Blancheflor, one could see that in them lived the rose and the lily. . . . One could see in the rose, in Flor or Flos, the symbol for the human soul who has taken into itself the personality-impulse, the ego-impulse, allowing the spiritual to work out of the individuality, who has brought into the red blood the ego-impulse. In the lily, however, was seen the symbol of the soul who can only remain spiritual because the ego remains without, comes only to the boundary of the soul's existence. Thus rose and lily are polar opposites. The rose has taken the

consciousness of itself wholly into itself; in the lily it has remained outside. But there has once been a union between the soul who is within, and the soul who, outside, enlivens the world as World-Spirit. Flor and Blancheflor express the finding of the World-Soul, the World-Ego, by the human soul, the human ego.[52]

The passage becomes comprehensible when the metaphysical conceptions are understood to have their esoteric basis in ecstatic experiences. The rose, we are told, symbolizes the human soul that has absorbed a spiritual "ego-impulse," which latter manifests within the soul's individuality. The rose is also the spiritual ego-impulse, which "has taken the consciousness of itself wholly into itself," obliterating the individuality of the human soul in the process. The rose thus symbolizes both the many and the one or, to put the same matter in experiential terms, the metaphysical essence of introspective union.

The lily symbolizes a different conception. Here the ego remains outside the human soul, coming "only to the boundary of the soul's existence." Steiner's phrasing presupposes a communion between an "I" and a "Thou." For Steiner, however, the experience was not theistic but anthroposophic. Elsewhere, in an extended description of what he termed "Initiation," Steiner portrayed communion as proceeding, successively, with the Spirits of one's youth and old age.[53]

The final union of the individual human soul, or "soul who is within," with the soul of the "World-Spirit" combined the ideas of introspective union and communion. The synthesis was doctrinal, but perhaps also occurred in a further experience of union. In either event, the reconciliation of opposites may be treated as a tacit instance of the alchemical marriage.

In his Anthroposophical period, Steiner sometimes discussed his metaphysical dualism by referring to Lucifer and Ahriman.

> What we can trace as supersensible in the external world, we call for certain reasons spiritual; what is more active inwardly within the human being, we assign to the soul. Ahriman is a more spiritual being, Lucifer is more soul nature. Ahriman can be called the lord of all that takes place in external nature, Lucifer penetrates with his impulses into the inner nature of man.[54]

Lucifer had to do with the soul, the "inner nature of man." Ahriman, by contrast, manifested in the supersensible spirituality of the external world—that is, in extrovertive union.

Ahriman was linked with the intellect, which, in the presentations of Atwood and Waite, involved experiences of communion. "Ahriman has more to do with our thinking, Lucifer with the feelings, with the life of the emotions, passions, impulses and desires."[55] Ahriman had also a further role as "the Lord of Death, far and wide the ruler of all the powers that have to bring about in the physical world what this world has to have, the annihilation and death of its entities."[56]

These attributions imply a view of ecstatic death, extrovertive union, and perhaps also communion as aspects of a single metaphysical principle. Ahriman was presumably associated with reverie states, since ecstatic death occurs in reveries, but not in trances.

Lucifer, by contrast, was the soul of the macrocosm, the one soul that tragically fell to become the many: "Lucifer stands before the clairvoyant vision, preserving in his life and soul the divine spiritual glories of world creation. . . . To perceive the macrocosmic resemblance of Lucifer to the microcosmic nature of the human soul . . . is to perceive the profound tragedy of this figure of Lucifer."[57]

Not only could Lucifer be seen in "clairvoyant vision," but he was also implicated in introspective union: "The human soul . . . has a moment where it is a mere 'has-been' and confronts nothingness; it is a single point in the universe, experiencing itself only as a point. But then this point becomes a spectator and begins to observe something else."[58]

After the human soul experiences nothingness during an ecstatic trance, it experiences itself as a single point, which seems the only point, but the point is next recognized as a point in the macrocosm.

Not only did the material realm of Ahriman differ from the etheric realm of Lucifer, where elemental beings lived; but beyond the etheric plane, there was a spiritual or astral plane:

> A person lives in his physical body in the physical world around him. When he comes away from it and has experiences outside the physical body, he is having those experiences in his etheric body with the elemental world around him; and when he comes out of that world as well, he is experiencing the spiritual realm in his astral body.[59]

Steiner's schema of three realms—material, etheric, and astral or spiritual—corresponded to St. Augustine's classification of visions as corporeal, imaginative, and intellectual. Spirits are nevertheless active in the material world of the senses, for example, in experiences of extrovertive union. "The sense world is the world of self-contained forms, for here the Spirits of Form rule."[60]

Spirits were also responsible for imparting forms to the ether. Magic depended on the ability to control the forms that ether assumed during visionary experiences:

> The elemental world is the world of mobility, of metamorphosis, of transformation. . . . What is it that makes the human being capable of transformation? It is his living in imagination, in mental images, the ability to make his ideas and thoughts so mobile . . . he can dip down into other beings and happenings.[61]

Because magic could not act directly on the ether but was obliged to enlist the aid of form-imparting spirits, Steiner's magic always proceeded through the intermediacy of Christ.

In keeping with St. Augustine's scheme, Steiner located experiences of communion on the astral plane of the spirit. However, in keeping with Steiner's Anthroposophical doctrine, communion proceeded not with God, but with an astral double:

> With this experience—feeling oneself in the astral body—there will be a meeting in the spiritual world, the meeting with the other self, the second self. . . . Whatever we have brought with us in the way of thought content unfolds a spirit conversation in cosmic language with a living thought-being of that realm. . . . We experience this other self . . . in such a way that we feel almost as though . . . we confront what we might call our past, brought into the spirit world in the form of memory and transformed into something spiritual by being brought there. And this past of ours begins a conversation in the region where living thought-beings converse.[62]

Steiner recognized that the presence encountered in communion experiences is at least partly a psychological projection of one's own personality. It was not God but Man (anthropos) that Steiner claimed to encounter:

> Our true ego is actually our constant companion within us . . . oneself, the other self, the true ego. . . . And this other self, this true ego, decks itself out in our weaknesses, in everything we should really forsake but don't wish to forsake. . . . The Guardian of the

Threshold . . . arrays himself in everything that arouses in us not only anxiety and distress but also disgust and loathing. . . . Our fear of separating from him makes us shudder, or it makes us blush, overcome with shame, to have to look at what we are.[63]

Steiner explained experiences of extrovertive union by reference to the astral body. With its separation from "the true ego" that was projected in "the other self," the astral body ceased to be limited to the ego or self and become coextensive with the world:

When this astral body detaches itself from the true ego . . . it is not like a snake slipping off its skin but rather a loosening on every side, a growing larger and larger until the astral body becomes one with the whole cosmic sphere. In doing this, it becomes ever thinner, while being absorbed by the whole surrounding world. . . . This experience is very similar to the one created voluntarily by a human being seeking the discovery of his true ego in the spiritual world.[64]

Steiner's Anthroposophical metaphysics was used to explain five ecstatic experiences. Ecstatic death and extrovertive union were considered spiritual events that proceeded on the material plane. Etheric visions, including transports of the soul, were associated with introspective union on the etheric plane. Communion was located at a purely spiritual level.

Unlike Waite and Steiner, Jung followed Atwood's sequence quite closely. Although he interpreted the opus from his own perspective in analytic psychology, his philosophical commitment to phenomenologism[65] permitted him to eschew theology while refusing to question the validity of the apparently parapsychological character of religious experiences. To account for the apparent phenomena, Jung went so far as to refer to "projections" that belonged not to personal psychology, but to a collective unconscious. Importantly, the collective unconscious was not restricted to people's nervous systems, but instead belonged to the cosmos.

I think one should . . . not attribute to our personal psyche everything that appears as a psychic content. After all, we would not do this with a bird that happened to fly through our field of vision. It may well be a prejudice to restrict the psyche to being "inside the body." . . . There may be a psychic "outside-the-body," a region so utterly different from "my" psychic space that one has to get outside oneself or make use of some auxiliary technique in order to get there. . . . The alchemical consummation of the royal marriage in the *cucurbita* could be understood as a synthetic process in the psyche "outside" the ego.

As I have said, the fact that one can get into this territory somehow or other does not mean that it belongs to me personally. . . . The primitive mind senses the psyche outside the ego as an alien country, inhabited by the spirits of the dead. On a rather higher level it takes on the character of a shadowy semi-reality, and on the level of the ancient cultures the shadows of that land beyond have turned into ideas. . . .

This region, if still seen as a spectral "land beyond," appears to be a whole world in itself, a macrocosm. If, on the other hand, it is felt as "psychic" and "inside," it seems like a microcosm.[66]

In Jung's view, psychic experiences were invariably restricted to symbols of the archetypes. The symbols became conscious; the archetypes, which together formed the collective unconscious, did not. Single archetypes might issue in a variety of symbols, not only in the same historical era, but also with the passage of history. The collective unconscious, or objective psyche "outside-the-body," had historically been appreciated by means of symbols, among other manners, as spirits of the dead, Otherworlds, and Platonic ideas. Jung's remarks on the psychology of alchemy must be understood in the context of his belief that the archetypes of the collective unconscious were psychic phenomena simultaneously of the macrocosm and the microcosm. Although Jung shunned the word, he was fully as metaphysical as were Atwood, Waite, and Steiner.

Jung acknowledged that some alchemists had engaged in chemical activities, but he maintained that "a parallel psychic process" had been the more important activity.[67] The psychic process took the form of mystical visions: "While working on his chemical experiments the operator had certain psychic experiences which appeared to him as the particular behaviour of the chemical process."[68] "During the practical work certain events of an hallucinatory or visionary nature were perceived, which cannot be anything but projections of unconscious contents."[69] In Jung's view, the visions were induced while alchemists watched the alchemical processes in their apparatus. Once the visions commenced, the hallucinatory materials obliterated the field of sense perception. The alchemists no longer saw the chemical processes. The symbols that they presented in their writings were products exclusively of their visionary states.

For Jung, there was finally no difference between the alchemical opus and his system of analytic psychology. He described both "the analytic process" and the alchemical opus in terms of the successive manifestation of four archetypes: the shadow, the anima, the animus, and the self.[70]

Jung described the alchemical blackening as an experience of the shadow: "The *nigredo* not only brought decay, suffering, death, and the torments of hell visibly before the eyes of the alchemist, it also cast the shadow of its melancholy over his own solitary soul."[71] By the shadow, Jung most frequently referred to negative aspects of the personality that a person ordinarily fails to acknowledge. "The shadow is a moral problem that challenges the whole ego-personality. . . . To become conscious of it involves recognizing the dark aspects of the personality as present and real."[72] Ending self-deception and hypocrisy may resolve the personal shadow, but an objective or archetypal shadow then remains. "With a little self-criticism one can see through the shadow—so far as its nature is personal. But when it appears as an archetype . . . it is a rare and shattering experience . . . to gaze into the face of absolute evil."[73]

Jung's concept of the shadow provided an explanation, among other matters, for experiences of ecstatic death. Death experiences had an archetypal dimension: "Death means the total extinction of consciousness and the complete stagnation of psychic life, so far as this is capable of consciousness. So catastrophic a consummation . . . must surely correspond to an important archetype."[74]

The second phase of the alchemical opus in Jung's presentation was the manifestation of the anima. "The anima . . . represents the collective unconscious. . . . The unconscious appears in projected and symbolized form, as there is no other way by which it might be perceived."[75] As a symbol for the unconscious, the anima may be an idea, but "whenever she appears, in dreams, visions, and fantasies, she takes on personified form, thus demonstrating that the factor she embodies possesses all the outstanding characteristics of a feminine being."[76] Because the unconscious is responsible for the projections of its archetypes, the anima symbolizes the "projection-making factor. . . . Maya, who creates illusion by her dancing."[77] In the alchemical opus, the anima manifests as Luna, who represents the physical.[78] Luna has also a second aspect, however, that appears at the *albedo* or whitening, when the anima manifests as the salt or white woman. She is then "the soul or spark of the *anima mundi*." She is Eve, but transformed now from "the body into light," from eros into wisdom.[79] "Apart from its lunar wetness and its terrestrial nature, the most outstanding properties of salt are bitterness and wisdom."[80]

Wisdom, the intellectual principle, was identified by Jung as the salt or philosopher's stone; but he referred only in passing to the experience that salt symbolized. "The human soul imprisoned in the body as the *anima mundi* is in matter ... undergoes the same transformations by death and purification, and finally by glorification, as the lapis."[81] The salt, which is a stone or lapis, is achieved through "glorification." The glorification of Wisdom may be identified as an experience of communion.

The third stage in Jung's opus pertains to the animus. Here Jung located the alchemical motifs of the sun, gold, the king, and masculinity.[82] Although "the apotheosis of the king, the renewed rising of the sun" represents "the daylight of the psyche, consciousness," it is not consciousness as experienced from a subjective ego perspective. "The king represents ego-consciousness, the subject of all subjects, as an object."[83] What Atwood, Waite, and Steiner had presented as ecstatic experiences of the disembodied soul, Jung described as "an observation of the ego-complex from another standpoint somewhere in the same psyche. ... The critical portrayal of the ego-complex in dreams and in abnormal psychic states."[84] Jung limited himself to a phenomenological perspective on visions of the disembodied soul that avoided the question whether the visionary's psyche was in the body, or outside it.

The fourth and final stage of Jung's opus was the alchemical marriage. It was a union of the anima and animus. "There is in the *coniunctio* a union of two figures, one representing the daytime principle—that is, lucid consciousness, the other a nocturnal light, the unconscious."[85] The alchemical marriage was experienced as a mystical union,[86] a manifestation of the archetype that Jung termed the self. "The self, or ... personal atman. ... I have defined the self as the totality of the conscious and unconscious psyche."[87] "The self ... is a God-image, or at least cannot be distinguished from one."[88]

Jung's psychological account of the opus referred to the same four stages as Atwood had.[89] He explicated a great many more symbols than Atwood had discussed, but his interpretations concerned the psychology of the same esoteric subtexts.

Jung's claim that "alchemy is ... the forerunner of our modern psychology of the unconscious"[90] depended on his belief that "the alchemists had a dim presentiment" of the "state of *participation mystique,* or unconscious identity ... between them and the chemical substance."[91] In speaking of metals, they had believed that they were speaking simultaneously of the soul. They were unaware that their notions of correspondence between the metals and their own souls were psychological projections; they never imagined that in speaking of metals, they were actually speaking of their psyches alone.[92] Still, because the alchemists had based their symbols, concepts, and theories on psychological data, Jung felt justified in deriving his psychological categories from the religious categories of the alchemists:

> It is the medical investigators of nature who, equipped with new means of knowledge, have rescued these tangled problems from projection by making them the proper subject of psychology. This could never have happened before, for the simple reason that there was no psychology of the unconscious. But the medical investigator, thanks to his knowledge of archetypal processes, is in the fortunate position of being able to recognize in the abstruse and grotesque-looking symbolisms of alchemy the nearest relatives of . . . the healing processes at work in the psychogenic neuroses.[93]

For Jung, it was not a question of fitting psychological categories to alchemical texts. He did not proceed, as Silberer, to detect the presence of the Oedipus complex,[94] or as Fabricius, to note the pertinence of Kleinian object-relations theory.[95] Jung did not apply clinical theories to alchemical data. He expressed Atwood's theories of alchemy in psychological terms and called them scientific.

Jung believed that the manifestations of the unconscious through active manifestations had an innate tendency to promote personality transformations:

> Continual conscious realization of unconscious fantasies, together with active participation in the fantastic events, has . . . the effect firstly of extending the conscious horizon by the inclusion of numerous unconscious contents; secondly of gradually diminishing the dominant influence of the unconscious; and thirdly of bringing about a change of personality.[96]

Assuming that the process of transformation was determined not by historical cultural factors, but exclusively by psychical ones, the alchemists would have observed the same processes as scientific psychologists, and it would be reasonable to adopt alchemical categories and call them psychological. Jung naively failed to realize that no personality transformation occurs in isolation of historical cultural factors.

Jung's psychology of alchemical symbolism was indifferent to the psychic states in which the symbols manifest. For Jung, it was immaterial whether the shadow, anima, animus, and self manifested in waking fantasies, nocturnal dreams, active imagination, or any other context. Eliade commented:

> The uninitiated person who has alchemical dreams and comes close to a psychic integration, also goes through the ordeal of an "initiation": however, the result of this initiation is not the same as that of a ritual or mystic initiation, although, functionally, they are akin. . . . Imagination, dream, hallucination—all disclose a similar alchemical symbol—and by this very fact place the patient in *an alchemical situation*—and achieve an amelioration which, at the psychic level, corresponds to the results of the alchemical operation.[97]

In contrast with Jung's psychologizing of the opus, the ecstatic experiences discussed by Atwood, Waite, and Steiner involved a combination of reverie and trance states. Reveries must be postulated for ecstatic death, which does not occur in trances; and reveries may consequently be inferred for the associated experiences of communion and extrovertive union. Trance states must be presupposed, however, for the reification of ether in both the transports of the soul and the final introspective unions.

A Rival Tradition?

The theory of spiritual alchemy that was known to Atwood, Waite, Steiner, and Jung was not widely shared. Eliade offered a significantly different interpretation. He suggested that Greek alchemy had been influenced not only by classical Greek philosophy, but also by the Hellenistic mystery cults. Alchemy was, in effect, a mystery in which matter had the role of the god: "It is the mystical drama of the God—his passion, death and resurrection—which is projected on to matter in order to transmute it. . . . The alchemist treats his Matter as the God was treated in the mysteries."[98]

Eliade's link to mysticism was necessarily speculative. We know that "initiation into the Mysteries consisted of participation in the passion, death and resurrection of a God," but we are ignorant of the manner of participation. Eliade was willing, however, to "conjecture that the sufferings, death and resurrection of the god, already known to the neophyte as a myth or as authentic history, were communicated to him during initiations, in an 'experimental' manner."[99] Eliade noted the initiatory visions in which shamans suffer, die, and resurrect.[100] He concluded:

> At the operational level, "death" corresponds usually to . . . the reduction of substances to the *materia prima,* to the *massa confusa,* the fluid, shapeless mass corresponding—on the cosmological plane—to chaos. Death represents regression to the amorphous, the reintegration of chaos. . . . The alchemical regression to the fluid state of matter corresponds, in the cosmologies, to the primordial chaotic state, and in the initiation rituals, to the "death" of the initiate.[101]

In *The Visions* of Zosimos, the alchemist reported visions with similar motifs, but the deaths and resurrections were not his own. Rather, he "projected on to Matter the initiatory function of suffering."[102]

Even with its qualifications, Eliade's contention remains speculative. No differently than alchemy, Christianity adopted language and symbolism from the Hellenistic mysteries; but it would be absurd to suggest that *imitatio Christi* has invariably consisted of a visionary experience of crucifixion and resurrection.

Eliade described the final phase of the opus as an introspective union. He argued that "the *opus alchymicum* had profound analogies with the mystic life,"[103] but he stopped short of asserting that analogy implied identity.

> The phase which follows the *nigredo,* that is, the "work in white", the *leukosis,* the *albedo,* probably corresponds, on the spiritual plane, to a resurrection expressed by the assumption of certain states of consciousness inaccessible to the uninitiated. . . . The two subsequent phases, the *cinitritas* and the *rubedo*...further develop and fortify this new initiatic consciousness.[104]

> The *coniunctio* and the ensuing death is sometimes expressed in terms of *hieros gamos:* the two principles—the Sun and Moon, King and Queen, unite in the mercury bath and die (this is the *nigredo*): their "soul" abandons them to return later and give birth to the *filius philosophorum,* the androgynous being (Rebis) which promises the imminent attainment of the Philosopher's Stone.[105]

Ecstatic death, flight of the ethereal soul, and their conjunction in introspective union. How is it possible to proceed from these three ecstasies to the general theory that the material and ethereal planes are in parallel?

What is missing from the interior logic of Eliade's interpretation is the role of spirit or intellect imparting the coherence, structure, and order of nature to ether and matter alike. The tripartite opus of Eliade's description takes for granted the orderliness of the ether and does not justify the doctrine through experiences of communion.

Consistent with the opus of Eliade's description is the view widely held among modern occultists that the astral plane is ethereal, for which reason magic is thaumaturgical rather than theurgical. Magic depends on manipulations of the ether directly, without the intermediation of spirit.

Henry Corbin attributed the thaumaturgical alchemy to medieval Sufis;[106] but his well-known tendency to extemporize should be taken into account. His theory, like that of Eliade, shows sufficient similarity, for example, to the occult views of René Guenon[107] and R. A. Schwaller de Lubicz[108] that I prefer to treat it as evidence of its own time and place. Corbin's explication of Sufi alchemy was informed, I suggest, by the common understanding of alchemy in Parisian occultism in the 1930s and 1940s:[109]

> One and the same spiritual Energy of light is just as much the constituent of the essence of what is qualified as material as it is of the essence of what is qualified as spiritual. . . . "Spirits are being-light in the fluid state . . . whereas bodies are being-light in the solidified state. . . . The difference between the two is like the difference between water and snow. Now, the final result of the alchemical Operation is exactly this *coincidentia oppositorum:* once a body has been treated and perfected by this Operation, it is in the state of "solid (or 'congealed,' 'frozen,' . . .) liquid."[110]

> This transsubstantiation was accomplished in the world of Imaginative Presence, not of material, sensible data. . . . One does not look for the Angel on the plane of material evidence; transsubstantiation is not a phenomenon of material laboratory chemistry.[111]

The same line of thought, the same notion of correspondence between the ethereal and material planes of existence, is a commonplace of modern Western occultism. Its immediate source would appear to have been the Hermetic Order of the Golden Dawn, an English occult society whose teachings have since come to dominate

Western esotericism. Some Golden Dawn members understood spiritual alchemy as the conjuring of spirits.[112] Others regarded alchemical mysticism as a metallic symbolism for cabalistic magic.[113] Although these occult traditions come to the same thing, it is clear that they were not originally alchemical. In the Italian Renaissance, spirit conjuring was known to be a cabalistic practice newly imported from Judaism,[114] where its antecedents can be traced for over a millennium.[115] Cabalism was syncretized with alchemy in the early sixteenth century by Paracelsus. The association of alchemy with spirit conjuring originated no later than the Elizabethan period when Dr. John Dee and Edward Kelly happened to engage in both practices.[116]

In this context, it is easy to perceive the correspondences that led H. P. Blavatsky, who founded the Theosophical Society, to trace modern occultism to ancient Gnosticism. Experiences of reverie were limited to ecstatic deaths. Neither extrovertive union nor communion was experienced. Alchemical doctrines surrounding matter were unrelievedly negative. Only ethereal phenomena, which were accessed in trance states, were seen as potentially benign. This matter-renouncing or anticosmic approach to alchemy was readily forced onto the surviving literary evidence of Gnosticism, by misunderstandings it references to spirit as references to ether.

The Medieval Origin of Alchemical Ether

The history of research on spiritual alchemy originated with Atwood's theory of a Paracelsian tradition, whose opus consisted of a secret initiation into an ecstatic mysticism of nature. Nature was understood to consist of spiritual ideas that impart lawful order to both ether and matter. Another theory, which may be traced back to the Golden Dawn, dispensed with the role of spirit. Forms were held to be inherent in the ether. Because ethereal forms were believed to determine the forms of material phenomena, manipulations of the ether during ecstatic visions were understood to have magical consequences in the material world.

Both theories presupposed the existence of an ethereal plane. Their terminus a quo may consequently be fixed in the Late Middle Ages. From its Hellenistic origins, Western alchemy had depended on the four physical elements: earth, water, air, and fire. Aristotle's theory of a fifth element did not enter alchemical tradition until the medieval Latin period. Aristotle's *Metaphysics* was translated from

Greek to Latin circa 1210.[117] Alchemists were not at first concerned
with its theory that the substance of starlight was a fifth element,
ether. For example, the *Summa* of the Latin Geber, a highly influential pseudonymous work that appeared toward the close of the
thirteenth century,[118] mentions the fifth essence only in passing:
"In Animals, and other Living Things . . . there is (according to the
Opinion of Many) a Soul, which is from the Occult Recesses of Nature, as from a Quintessence, or from the first Mover."[119]

Neither the living soul nor its substance were pertinent to the
concerns of alchemists who worked with the inanimate and often
exclusively with the inorganic. Alchemists adhered to the theory of
four elements and generally mentioned the fifth essence only as
metaphor. Because it descended from the heavens—that is, from
the top of the alchemical apparatus—"fifth essence" served as a secret name for the newly discovered distillate, alcohol.

Alchemists began to treat the notion of a fifth element as a serious postulate only in the middle of the fourteenth century. John of
Rupescissa's *Consideration of the Fifth Essence* may have been the
first text to introduce the doctrine that there is a fifth essence to
each thing; he referred to alcohol.[120] Also influential was a commentary by Ortolanus on the *Emerald Tablet of Hermes*. In his preface, Ortolanus discussed the fifth essence as a term for *aqua
ardens,* "burning water" or alcohol,[121] but his text of the *Emerald
Tablet* permitted a significantly different inference. A crucial line in
the Arabic version cited by Jabir ibn Hayyan reads: "That which is
above is from that which is below, and that which is below is from
that which is above."[122] The text means that vapors above derive
from solids below, but presently condense to fall below once more.

The same sense is conveyed in one of the three Latin render-
ings: "These things below with those above and those with these
join forces again." The other Latin versions have different implications. The formulation "Whatever is below is similar to that which
is above"[123] is likely derivative of the more famous rendition of Ortolanus, *Quod est superius est sicut quod inferius, et quod inferius
est sicut quod est superius,*[124] "That which is above is as that which
is below, and that which is below is as that which is above." Ortolanus's commentary interpreted the text in the traditional manner
as a reference to solids and vapor—he wrote "earth" and "spirit."[125]
However, his phrasing has since supported other interpretations
that postulate a supernal plane or dimension of existence that is in
parallel with the physical universe.

An unmistakably metaphysical theory of ether was advanced late in the fourteenth century by Thomas of Bologna, who contrasted the conventional search for the fifth essence in "the potency of combustibles,"—that is, in alcoholic spirits—with his own investigation of "the force of things indissolubly joined." In his conception, the fifth essence was responsible for imparting form to minerals.[126] Rupescissa's account of the fifth essence was plagiarized in late fourteenth- or early fifteenth-century writings falsely attributed to Ramon Lull.[127] A generation later, Marsilio Ficino identified spirit, the substance on which his magic depended, with the fifth essence.[128]

Let me underscore this last point. The Renaissance practice of occult syncretism, whose beginning D. P. Walker and Frances A. Yates traced to Ficino in the mid-fifteenth century,[129] built on a prior innovation in alchemy. The newly rediscovered Hermetism of the *Corpus Hermeticum* was prized by Renaissance Platonists precisely because it was associated with the traditional Hermetism of alchemy. When alchemists postulated a fifth essence as the substance of souls and the Platonic world of forms, they inaugurated a search for its theoretic understanding and practical technology. The search led to magic and mysticism: pseudo-Lullism and the Renaissance developments of Hermetism, Pythagorism, Orphism, Cabala, Druidism, pseudo-Egyptianism, and the like.

Historians of chemistry, seeking to date the origin of spiritual alchemy, have followed different paths to the era immediately following. John Read named Paracelsus, in the early sixteenth century, as the originator of a form of alchemy that had both chemical and spiritual ingredients.[130] Citing the example of Jacob Boehme, F. Sherwood Taylor maintained that "alchemical terminology was used in purely mystical writings as early as the sixteenth century."[131]

Chapter 4

The Alchemical Production of Gold

Students of alchemy are wrong to assume that a practice of spiritual alchemy goes back to the origin of Western alchemy in Hellenistic Egypt. No one has ever established that alchemical mysticism existed in antiquity, and it is not adequate to assume that "alchemical symbolism . . . can be taken to refer either to man or to a mineral substance."[1] The methodological premise has not been earned. Where an alchemical document pertains to metallic alchemy, we have no *necessary* evidence that it pertains to anything more. The student of alchemical literature is engaged in a hermeneutic akin to psychoanalysis: the interpretation of symbolic materials in terms of an expected subtext. In many alchemical texts, the expected subtext happens to be the chemistry of gold-making.

In the nineteenth century, historians of chemistry incorrectly assumed that because the artificial manufacture of gold is not chemically possible, alchemists must without exception have been liars, frauds, and swindlers. The hypothesis precluded serious investigation of the alchemists' belief systems.

Hopkins's Color Theory

Only in 1925 did Arthur John Hopkins suggest that alchemists had been sincere in their efforts. He argued that Western alchemy had originated as an extension of the dyeing of textiles, in a deliberate attempt to color inexpensive metals for the costume jewelry trade. In Hellenistic Egypt, precious metals were routinely given superficial surface colors by means of bronzes. Gold, for example, was bronzed purple, and silver black. The Leyden papyrus X,[2] which is dated to the third century, explains how to produce similar bronzes in base metals. Hopkins urged that these procedures, which

77

are plainly stated in a metallurgical text, should be used to interpret the cryptic references to changes in color in alchemical texts.

Alchemists continued to make cryptic references to the same color changes through the seventeenth century. In the context of classical Greek physics, changing the color of a metal constituted its transmutation.[3]

Taylor's Theory of a Copper-Lead Alloy

F. Sherwood Taylor built on Hopkins's "color theory," but he argued that alchemists' references to changes in color pertained to the productions of alloys, rather than superficial bronzes. Taylor also emphasized that alchemical gold was believed to be genuine. Natural variations in the quality of different gold ores combined with limited refining and assaying techniques to produce a considerable variation in the quality of natural gold. Alchemical gold was often indistinguishable. Taylor found that the Hellenistic texts contain four techniques for producing gold-resembling alloys, but only one combined metallurgy with religious imagery, philosophy, and an esoteric literary style. Equally uniquely, its procedure involved distillation, a process that alchemists apparently invented but kept secret. Stills were first used for nonalchemical purposes in the West some seven centuries after their earliest description in alchemical texts. In Taylor's view, the alchemical tradition commenced no later than the third century in the person of Maria the Jewess, whom Zosimos of Panopolis (c. 300 C.E.) credited with the introduction of the still.[4]

Among later alchemists, those who adopted empirical and/or innovative attitudes to chemical experimentation—for example, the Islamic schools of Jabir ibn Hayyan and al-Razi, and the later Paracelsians of Europe—have attracted most of the attention of historians of chemistry. We remain comparatively ignorant of Muslim alchemy in Egypt and the Mediterranean basin, where gold-making, antiquarian Hellenism, and pseudepigraphy were prominent.[5] Possibly because they are repetitive, monotonous, and boring, the gold-making recipes in European alchemical literature have not been systematically explicated either. Under the circumstances, historians of chemistry have rarely given more than cursory attention to the relation of spiritual alchemy and the chemistry of gold-making.

Taylor was an important exception. He described alchemical spirituality as an expression of "wonderful analogies . . . between

the great world with its seasons, and growth and death and generation, and the process of the alchemical work. It is . . . a sort of re-
joicing in the wonderful phenomena of chemical change."[6]

A related understanding informed H. J. Sheppard's definition of
alchemical mysticism as "ideas of a supra-rational nature concerning the origin, nature and destiny of the soul."[7] His views come to
close agreement with Taylor's position once we allow that alchemists routinely interpreted correspondences among events in the
cosmos, the chemical apparatus, and the soul.

It must be emphasized, however, that historians of science have
consistently employed the term "mysticism" in reference to any un-
scientific or religious point of view. The term is used very differently
by occultists and historians of religion, and confusion regarding the
term has repeatedly concealed disagreements of substance. Religious evaluations of chemical events, as demonstrated by Taylor
and Sheppard, are instances of religious philosophy but not of
mysticism.

Taylor's reconstruction of the process[8] is, I suggest, very nearly
correct. The basic equipment was a reflux apparatus, termed a *kerotakis*. It consisted of a closed chamber with a shelf (or hook) in its
middle. On the shelf were placed the metals to be treated: copper,
lead, perhaps also minute quantities of gold and silver. Other ingredients were placed on the bottom of the chamber. Sulphur is frequently mentioned, but Taylor cautioned that we do not know what
was actually intended by the term.[9] When the base of the *kerotakis*
was heated, the ingredients inside the bottom of the chamber
turned to smoke and vapor, which singed the outer surfaces of the
metals on the shelf, accomplishing *melanosis,* "blackening." A small
vent hole permitted heated air to escape near the top of the apparatus, but the vapors condensed on a condensing cover. The condensate fell to the bottom of the *kerotakis,* vaporized anew, and
attacked the metals once again. *Leucosis,* "whitening," referred to
the corrosive action of the vapors on the metals. The process was
allowed to continue until the solids on the shelf were thoroughly
discolored and permeated with corrosion. The heat was then increased and the metals gently roasted. The annealing, which
yielded a soft heavy yellow alloy, was termed *xanthosis,* "yellowing."

An alternate means of whitening, also mentioned by Taylor,[10]
involved use of a still, termed an *alembic*. In this distillation procedure, once the gases had singed the outer surfaces of the metals
and risen to the top of the apparatus, they were led out through a
pipe and cooled. Taylor assumed that distillation precipitated an

efflorescence of salts. The salts were returned to the fluid in the chamber, yielding an acid of greater intensity than before. The acid was then applied to the solid metals on the shelf.

Taylor was unable to explain the significance of *iosis,* which may mean either "imparting the color of a violet (*ion*)" or "removal of rust or tarnish (*ios*)."[11] Hopkins argued that *iosis* originally pertained to the dyeing of textiles the color of royal purple. The term was secondarily applied to the violet bronzing of gold. Among other proof texts, Hopkins convincingly cited a passage in which Maria the Jewess described the violet bronzing of alchemical gold.[12] However, *The Visions* of Zosimos (and many later texts) associated reddening (an alternate of empurpling) with the distillation of the salt.[13]

I conclude that some alchemists sought to produce gold that had a purple bronze, while others sought gold that had its natural yellow color. In the latter event, *iosis* was necessarily a metaphor. A change of color was no longer of reference. The term instead referred to a change in potency from common to royal: the production of the salts necessary to transform a weak acid into a strong one.

Fulcanelli's Preparation of the Great Work

Taylor's reconstruction of alchemical gold-making was anticipated by Fulcanelli, the only twentieth-century alchemist who is reputed to have successfully completed the opus. Fulcanelli was a pseudonym, almost certainly of Jean-Julien Champagne (c. 1885–1932), a Parisian painter, draftsman, and occultist.[14] The first French publication of *Le Mystère des Cathédrales*[15] established Fulcanelli's reputation in 1926 as the most accomplished alchemist of modern times.[16] Fulcanelli wrote in alchemists' traditional literary style, but his esoteric subtext offers a slightly better recipe for the opus than Taylor knew.

By way of preface to a reading of Fulcanelli's subtext, I would note his discussion of an "iron-bound chest" that was portrayed in Renaissance art.[17] Fulcanelli immediately went on to denounce Renaissance artists for their ignorance of the medieval esoterica of his own interest.[18] Iron was implicitly not one of the metals that Fulcanelli employed. Neither was the Renaissance innovation of spiritual alchemy consistent with the medieval alchemy that he proposed to discuss.

Fulcanelli elsewhere mentioned lead,[19] common copper,[20] physical sulphur that was nonetheless termed mercury,[21] metallic sulphur,[22] and finally realgar, or natural sulphur of arsenic.[23] He also mentioned arsenic, but only by way of misdirection:

> What, then, is this RER? . . . Let us suppose that the matter represented by RE is *realgar,* or natural sulphur of arsenic. R, half RE, could then be the *sulphur* of the realgar or its *arsenic,* which are similar or different according to whether you consider the sulphur and the arsenic separately or combined in the realgar. In this way the RER will be obtained by *augmenting* the realgar with sulphur, which is considered as forming half the realgar, or with arsenic, which is seen as the other half in the same red sulphide.[24]

Fulcanelli's recipe called for realgar plus an equal measure of either sulphur or arsenic. But which? His next sentence told the story: "Here is some more advice: seek *first* the RER" (emphasis added).[25] The first alternative, sulphur, was to be employed.

Fulcanelli's recipe of lead, copper, sulphur, and realgar corresponds closely to Taylor's reconstruction of the Greco-Egyptian recipe, which lists "sulphur, sometimes mixed with arsenic sulphides" together with "the several metals to be treated: copper, lead, perhaps gold and silver also."[26] Fulcanelli explicitly stated, however, that "it was apparently necessary to exclude . . . common gold."[27] Since gold and silver would not have been active ingredients in any event, the only chemically significant discrepancy was Taylor's reference to cadmia, an ore containing both arsenic and zinc.[28] Fulcanelli mentioned arsenic but rejected its use.

Fulcanelli's recipe apparently required precisely four minerals. Symbolic considerations were presumably at work. In discussing alchemical color symbolism, Fulcanelli stated that "there are several elemental colors—the color blue belongs particularly to earth, green to water, yellow to air and red to fire."[29] For the colors of the opus to have been elemental, the four elements must have been represented by four minerals. Earth was represented by lead, which was symbolized—for reasons I have been unable to trace—by the color blue. Copper represented water, because oxidized copper is green, the color symbolic of water. Because purified sulphur is yellow, the mineral represented "the Air [which] becomes more yellow, the nearer it approaches the Sun."[30] Finally, realgar represented fire because both are red in color. Within the Neo-Aristotelian philosophy of late Arabic and Latin alchemy, Fulcanelli's recipe had elegance. Earth, water, air, and fire were represented in the mineral realm—and in the opus—by lead, copper, sulphur, and realgar.

The alchemical microcosm was made still more complete, so I suggest, by the actual presence of the four elements within the opus. Lead, copper, sulphur, and realgar are minerals and, as such, kinds of earth. Fire heated the alchemical processes. Air was contained within the vessel.

Fulcanelli's use of water was more esoteric. Most of his references to water are almost certainly special uses of the common word. Water usually signified the liquid state; for example, both *"water which does not wet the hands"*[31] and "secret fire enclosed in water"[32] described a corrosive, liquid acid. However, Fulcanelli twice referred unmistakeably to ordinary water. Using a Gothic cathedral as a symbol for his apparatus, he termed its crypt a "low, damp, cold place." Later he asserted that "the esoteric tradition of the *Fountain of Life* or the *Fountain of Youth* may be found in material form in the *sacred Wells* associated with most gothic churches in the Middle Ages."[33] The second reference was the more explicit; it associated the esoteric liquid with material—that is, ordinary— water. However, the first reference was more conclusive. Paradoxical references to water that is dry or fiery pertain to acids, but description as both damp and cold is proper to elemental water alone. Moreover, Fulcanelli's account of the opus described a series of chemical reactions that would have been impossible unless a quantity of water were added to the four minerals.

In addition to the color symbolism of the four minerals, Fulcanelli mentioned that the *"colours of the Work,* which are described in all the classical works" are three in number.[34] "The three colours succeed one another in an invariable order, going from *black,* through *white,* to *red."*[35] However, Fulcanelli tells us of no events prior to "the crow, symbol of the *colour black*...or the first appearance of decomposition."[36] Because Fulcanelli did not explain how the initial blackening is achieved, I improvise on the basis of Taylor's reconstruction. Sulphur and realgar are placed near the bottom of the vessel. Water is placed separately nearby. Lead and copper—the "matter" of the work—are placed above on a shelf that is nearer the bottom than the top of the apparatus. It is difficult to be certain of the proportions. Fulcanelli recommended seven parts of the agents to one of the matter; he also cited other alchemists who variously recommended six, seven, nine, and ten.[37] However, he did not indicate whether these proportions pertain to the sulphur and realgar, or also include the water. In all events, once the ingredients are placed in the vessel, the external fire below the vessel is lit. The sulphur and realgar presently burn and rise as fumes, blackening the outer surface of the lead and copper.

Use of water must be postulated—or, as Taylor instead concluded, alchemists' references to sulphur cannot possibly refer to the metal that we know by the name. Burning sulphur yields sulphur dioxide (SO_2) and a small yield of sulphur trioxide (SO_3). The latter reacts readily and violently with water to form sulphuric acid (H_2SO_4), a chemical reagent that is also used in cleaning the surfaces of metals and as a bleaching agent. Sulphur dioxide both dissolves in water and forms sulphurous acid (H_2SO_3), an unstable compound that breaks up into sulphur dioxide and water. However, when sulphurous acid is heated to about 500° C, the sulphur dioxide unites with atmospheric oxygen to form sulphur trioxide, which water converts to sulphuric acid. Both sulphurous and sulphuric acid are dibasic and form both normal and acid salts.[38] If we assume that the alchemical opus burned sulphur and allowed the fumes to cool and fall into water, we may understand that the resultant sulphuric acid was used to cleanse an alloy of copper and lead, making it resemble gold. Water (H_2O) would then have been the *prima materia* of the opus—the secret ingredient whose identity alchemists never revealed.

Of the second stage, the whitening process that puzzled Taylor,[39] Fulcanelli presented two accounts:

> Few alchemists will admit the possibility of two ways, one short and easy, called the *dry way*, the other, longer and less rewarding, called the *moist way*. This may be due to the fact that many authors deal exclusively with the longer process, either because they do not know of the other, or because they prefer to remain silent about it, rather than to teach its principles. . . . Chemically speaking, there is no objection to a method, employing the moist way, being replaced by another, which makes use of dry reactions, in order to arrive at the same result.[40]

Taylor came very close to an explanation of the dry way with his speculation that "if, as is probable, the black product was dried before smelting, it might be whitened as a result of the efflorescence of salts derived from the 'divine water'."[41] Fulcanelli's account differed in only a single important detail: "An old saying tells us that *all dry colouring is useless in its dryness*. It is, therefore, expedient to dissolve this earth or this salt again in the same water which gave it birth, or—which amounts to the same thing—*in its own blood*. In this way it may *become volatile again*."[42]

In the dry way, once the fumes combine with water to produce acids, the acids are vaporized, drawn out the top of the vessel, and distilled into a salt. Fulcanelli styled the salt variously: the philosophic stone, philosopher's salt, celestial salt, philosopher's mercury, mercurial salt, and Babylonian dragon.[43] To this list I would add several symbolic references to the salt's "whiteness": white powder, white man, and various white metals (mercury, silver, iron, antimony, etc.). After its distillation, the salt is dissolved in a quantity of liquid acid. Fulcanelli mentioned a proportion of two parts fluid to one part salt.[44] The resultant acid is then applied to the lead and copper.

The wet way depends on the same chemical reactions, but does not involve the distillation and resolution of the salt as an intermediate phase in the process. Fulcanelli described the process as follows:

> Now, *the wheel* is the alchemical hieroglyph of the time necessary for the coction of the philosophical matter, and consequently of the coction itself. The sustained, constant, and equal fire, which the artist maintains night and day in the course of this operation, is for this reason called the *fire of the wheel*. Moreover, in addition to the heat necessary for the liquefaction of the philosophers' stone, a second agent is needed as well, called the *secret* or *philosophic fire*. It is this latter fire, sustained by ordinary heat, which *makes the wheel turn* and produces the various phenomena which the artist observes *in his vessel*.[45]

Fulcanelli's emphasis on the phrase "in his vessel" leads me to infer that the vaporization of the sulphurous and sulphuric acids proceeds within a hermetically sealed vessel that traps the vapors, permits them to condense on its upper surface, and allows them to drip from the condensing cover onto the blackened lead and copper below. Condensate that falls not onto the metals on a shelf but to the bottom of the vessel, vaporizes yet again, renewing the process. The "wheel" refers to the cyclical process of vaporization and condensation. The condensed vapors are termed the "fire of the wheel" and "the secret or philosophic fire" because they are corrosive. Fulcanelli further named them: living water, solvent, the elixir, the universal medicine, the fountain, virgin's milk, spirit, chaos, philosophers' mercury, secret fire, burning water, fiery water, watery fire, primitive and celestial water.[46]

Fulcanelli's account of the final stage of the opus requires amplification by Taylor's reconstruction. Among other symbols, Fulcanelli emphasized the green and red lions: "As for the *Red Lion,* according to the Philosophers it is nothing more than the same matter, or the *Green Lion,* brought by certain processes to this special quality which characterizes hermetic gold or the *Red Lion.*"[47]

A variety of references to the color green, including green vitriol, the philosopher's emerald, the herb of Saturn, the vegetable stone, allude to the idea of a "*green and sour* fruit, compared with the *red, ripe* fruit."[48] The difference is a question of maturity. The chemical composition is the same in both events.

Once the acid has thoroughly permeated the lead and copper, what remains to be done is, in Taylor's words, "the gentle roasting and smelting"[49] that reveals the yellow of the heavy brass alloy that alchemists regarded as gold.

Fulcanelli also mentioned that the color coding of the stages of the process could be expanded from three to four if an additional process were added to the end of the opus: "White succeeds black, yellow succeeds white and red succeeds yellow. And every matter reaching the fourth colour . . . is the *tincture* of things of its kind."[50] Here yellow signified the third stage, which was otherwise symbolized as red; while red described a tincture that was added to the alchemical gold.

The metallic opus was a self-contained microcosm that literally contained the four elements. The element earth was represented, moreover, by four minerals that are types of the elements in the mineral realm. Another recipe might have produced a heavy brass that successfully passed for gold in prescientific times; but only a microcosm could have had the religio-philosophic significance of the opus. Four minerals, plus water, heated by fire, in an apparatus containing air, underwent change into acidic vapors and blackened matter, only to recombine in a process termed "whitening" and eventually turn yellow. In the wet way, the vessel was even hermetically sealed. The alchemical opus was a proof, in what the medievals termed natural theology, of the perfectibility of matter.

The Visions of Zosimos

Let us confront these theories of the alchemical opus with some early examples of Hellenistic alchemy. Zosimos of Panopolis lived in Alexandria in the late third or early fourth century.[51] Taylor stated

that *The Visions* "stand quite apart from his other writings, and indeed from all other Greek Alchemy, which contains nothing else of
his elaborately allegorical character."[52] Jung insisted that the text
was not allegorical but visionary.[53] I shall argue that it was both.
The Visions is an apocalypse in genre.[54] The text narrates revelations to a visionary by cosmic mind, regarding the resurrection of
the dead.

To begin, let us collect information that Zosimos dispersed at
intervals throughout his text.[55] He mentioned copper by name
seven times, lead five times, silver once, and gold once. The moon
was mentioned once and the sun twice, possibly alluding to silver
and gold, respectively. Reference was once made to *theion hudor,*
which may mean either "divine water" or "sulphurous water."

The Visions refer to three colors: white six times, yellow once,
and red twice. The color black, which signified the first stage of the
opus, is not mentioned in *The Visions.* Zosimos expressed the esoterica in other manners. The text, which is divided by subheadings
into three lessons, begins: "The composition of waters, the movement, growth, removal, and restitution of corporeal nature, the separation of the spirit from the body, and the fixation of the spirit on
the body."[54]

As so often with ancient texts, the opening epitomizes the
whole. The four stages of the chemical process were outlined in as
many phrases:

1) "The composition of waters" is the initial phase, the production of the "sulphurous water."
2) Since "corporeal nature" signifies a solid state, its "removal
   and restitution" refer to the transformation of a solid into
   either a fluid or a vapor, and vice versa. The vaporization
   and condensation of the acid were meant.
3) "The separation of the spirit from the body" refers to the
   separation of a gas from a solid—that is, of the acid from
   the metals being treated.
4) "The fixation of the spirit on the body" refers to the action of
   the acid, to corrode and so be absorbed by the metals being
   treated.

The balance of the opening section has nothing to do with chemistry:

> . . . are not due to foreign natures, but to one single nature react-
> ing on itself, a single species, such as the hard bodies of metals and
> the moist juices of plants.

And in this system, single and of many colours, is comprised a research, multiple and varied, subordinated to lunar influences and to the measure of time, which rule the end and the increase according to which the nature transforms itself.[57]

Zosimos invoked the classic Aristotelian argument concerning alchemical transmutation. Within Aristotelian philosophy, transmutation was considered possible within a single species, but not among the species of a genus. Indeed, the possibility and impossibility of transmutation were the defining characteristics of species. In this passage, Zosimos took for granted that "the hard bodies of metals" and "the moist juices of plants" are each a species. However, the "one single nature reacting on itself" to which he compares metals and plant juices encompasses all four elements: earth, air, fire, and water. He refers, in short, to "one single Nature," the cosmos.

Zosimos asserted that his research was sublunar and temporal in order to emphasize its pertinence to "the end and the increase." Since *The Visions* later refers explicitly to resurrection, I interpret "the end and the increase" as a reference to death and resurrection. For Zosimos, the possibility of alchemical transmutation was a proof in nature of the possibility of bodily resurrection.

The beginning of the second paragraph is most astonishing. "Saying these things I went to sleep and I saw. . . . "[58] The preceding sentences were evidently recited prior to Zosimos's experience of a vision. Since the discursive recital of cosmology is known to be able to induce mystical experiences,[59] Zosimos's recital may be interpreted as a deliberate effort to induce a visionary state. The contents of the ensuing vision were almost wholly chemical:

. . . and I saw a sacrificing priest standing before me at the top of an altar in the form of a bowl. This altar had 15 steps leading up to it. Then the priest stood up and I heard a voice from above saying to me, "I have accomplished the descent of the 15 steps of darkness and the ascent of the steps of light and it is he who sacrifices, that renews me, casting away the coarseness of the body; and being consecrated priest by necessity, I become a spirit." And having heard the voice of him who stood on the bowl-shaped altar, I questioned him, wishing to find out who he was. He answered me in a weak voice, saying "I am Ion, the priest of the sanctuary, and I have survived intolerable violence. For one came headlong in the morning, dismembering me with a sword, and tearing me asunder according to the rigour of harmony. And flaying my head with the sword which he held fast, he mingled my bones with my flesh and burned them in the fire of the treatment, until I learnt by the transformation of the body to become a spirit."

And while yet he spoke these words to me, and I forced him to speak of it, his eyes became as blood and he vomited up all his flesh. And I saw him as a mutilated little image of a man, tearing himself with his own teeth and falling away.[60]

Jung noted the debts of these images to the self-sacrifice of Christ, the dismemberment of Dionysius, and the flaying of Marsyas and perhaps Mani.[61] The motifs were used, however, to convey an alchemical allegory. The image of the speaking man, whose eyes become blood and who vomits up his flesh, signifies a solid turning to fluid. At first there are pockets of fluid visible in the solid, but later only patches of solidity remain in a mass of fluid. Mutilation and tearing suggest the actions of an acid.

The dialogue has much the same significance. The priest stands by an altar above fifteen steps. We later learn of an altar above only seven steps. The higher altar may be understood to represent the top of the apparatus; the lower altar would be a shelf or hook in its middle. The priest identifies himself as a spirit—that is, a gas—who has cast off "the coarseness of the body,"—solidity. His "weak voice" alludes to the initial weakness of the acid. His name is Ion, "purple," the royal and final color of the opus. But the violence that he suffered occurred "in the morning,"—that is, early in the experiment. Since alchemists understood chemical change as the death of one form and the birth of another, the "sword" that attacked Ion may be understood to signify the death-dealing heat of fire. The separation of his head from his bones and flesh refers to the emission of gas from metallic ores; the latter, as slag, were abandoned to the fire.

The priest's claims to "have accomplished the descent of the 15 steps of darkness and the ascent of the steps of light" refers to the transition from the blackening to the whitening. After the sulphur has been burned, the oxides that rise as black smoke cool and fall as powder into the water at the bottom of the apparatus, where the powder reacts to form an acid.

The clause, "and I forced him to speak of it," indicates that Zosimos was in control of his visionary experience. His claim is consistent with his vision's fidelity in allegorizing the chemical process in his *kerotakis*. Zosimos's visions bear comparison with several other ancient apocalypses—Daniel, 1 Enoch, 4 Ezra, the Apocalypse of St. John, and so forth—that narrate visions that allegorized past or future history.[62] The autosuggestive allegorization of chemistry was presumably accomplished in a similar manner. The occurrence of Zosimos's visions upon going to sleep suggests his use of a hypnagogic state. The autosuggestive and allegorical character of the visions is consistent, however, not with Jung's practice of active imagination, but with Silberer's production of autosymbolic phenomena. The images did not have the imaginal character of active imaginations; they were self-evidently allegorical. The chemical ideas that the visions allegorized were presumably entertained consciously immediately before their experience in the forms of imagery.

If Zosimos's visions were autosymbolic imagery in hypnagogic states, their production would have commenced as discursive meditations on chemical events. "The alchemist *projects* on patiently worked substances his own unconscious, which accompanies and parallels sensory knowledge."[63] The images were not merely daydreams, however. Jung argued that alchemists' visions *replaced* sense perception of the chemical apparatus. Although the passages that Jung cited in support of his hypothesis sometimes refer to shapes that were discerned in the swirling vapors at the top of the apparatus,[64] and otherwise to discoloration of metals by corrosive acid vapors,[65] we may assume that Zosimos's meditations took form as autosymbolic images only after he closed his eyes and entered a hypnagogic state.

The next sentences in *The Visions* function, as so often in apocalypses, to provide explanatory commentary on the vision: "And being afraid I awoke and thought 'Is this not the situation of the waters?' I believed that I had understood it well."[66]

The first vision, so we are told, concerns the acidic waters. Zosimos apparently expected the initiated reader to need no further key to the cipher.

The further materials, waking in fear, thinking about the vision's meaning, becoming satisfied with its interpretation, and returning to sleep, should not be passed by too quickly. Zosimos was telling us that his visions were allegorical. He did not treat his vision as evidence of any transcendence of nature. He did not journey in sleep to an earthly temple. He did not meet a mythic redeemer. All that he experienced were hypnagogic images that allegorized "the situation of the waters."

Lesson 1 continues with an account of a second vision:

> . . . and I fell asleep anew. And I saw the same altar in the form of a bowl and at the top the water bubbling, and many people in it endlessly. And there was no one outside the altar whom I could

ask. I then went up towards the altar to view the spectacle. And I saw a little man, a barber, whitened by years, who said to me "What are you looking at?" I answered him that I marvelled at the boiling of the water and the men, burnt yet living. And he answered me saying "It is the place of the exercise called preserving (embalming). For those men who wish to obtain virtue come hither and become spirits, fleeing from the body." Therefore I said to him "Are you a spirit?" And he answered and said "A spirit and a guardian of spirits." And while he told us these things, and while the boiling increased and the people wailed, I saw a man of copper having in his hand a writing tablet of lead. And he spoke aloud, looking at the tablet, "I counsel those under punishment to calm themselves, and each to take in his hand a leaden writing tablet and to write with their own hands. I counsel them to keep their faces upwards and their mouths open until your (*sic*) grapes be grown." The act followed the word and the master of the house said to me, "You have seen. You have stretched your neck on high and you have seen what is done." And I said that I saw, and I said to myself, "This man of copper you have seen is the sacrificing priest and the sacrifice, and he that vomited out his own flesh. And authority over this water and the men under punishment was given to him."

And having had this vision I awoke again and I said to myself "What is the occasion of this vision? Is not this the white and yellow water, boiling, divine (sulphurous)?" And I found that I understood it well.[67]

Zosimos's interpretation of his second vision refers to the acid; but the people in the water, who implicitly have bodies, signify the solids that the acidic vapors are attacking. "The boiling of the water" refers to the repeated vaporization of the condensing acid. "The men, burnt yet living" allude to the metals being attacked by the vapors. Because base metals are perfected by this process, it is also termed "the exercise called preserving." The barber, who talks to Zosimos, is described as "whitened by years." The motif identifies this process as the whitening. The motif of the barber is consistent with the notion of preserving or embalming. Like embalmers, ancient barbers were concerned with cosmetics and beautification.[68] But unlike embalmers, they worked with the living, not the dead. The notion of "men who wish to obtain virtue" pertains to the same chemical process. Although vapors arrive at the top of the *kerotakis* by becoming "spirits, fleeing from the body," they commence as men—that is, as solids. Those "under punishment" who were "to keep their faces upwards and their mouths open" are the metals. Their depicture as people undergoing the torments of Hades[69] alludes, through the location of Hades in the cosmos, to the position of the metals on a shelf in the lower part of the alchemical apparatus. The grapes allude by their color, purple, to the royal character of the condensate that drops onto the metals from above. The motif of Zosimos stretching his neck on high agrees with the motif of beheading in the first vision. The body or solid remains on the shelf. The head or ascending gas climbs on high.

The religious concerns of the second vision are few but notable. Jung suggested that the bowl-shaped altar alludes to the krater of Poimandres, which was filled with *nous*.[70] Zosimos may have alluded to the doctrine found in Book 4 of the *Corpus Hermeticum*, entitled *The Krater*, to the effect that people may have mind, but nonhuman creatures do not. Human mind is one with the mind who is the cosmos.[71] The symbolization of metals by people would then signify the presence of universal mind in metals, as in people.

Another religious concern of the text is expressed in the sentence, "For those men who wish to obtain virtue come hither and become spirits, fleeing from the body." What virtue entails is not stated. Zosimos employed the symbols as references to gaseous and solid states; but because he disagreed with the religious doctrine of body-soul dualism, he identified the "spirit and . . . guardian of spirits" as "a man of copper" who was holding "a writing tablet of lead." The equation of spirit with base metals conveys a religious monism.

Monism is central not only to Zosimos's doctrine, but also to his further uses of symbolism. The chemical process entails two groups of ingredients—the solids on the shelf or hook, and the circulating vapor-condensate—but neither can be described in terms of their ingredients. The solids have absorbed some of the vapor, and the remaining vapor includes traces of the solids. The proportions differ, but the chemical composition of both the solids and the vapor-condensate has become the same. Reference to the chemical composition now results in paradoxical or self-contradictory symbolism. For example, the "barber, whitened by years," is both the sacrificing priest and the sacrifice: the vapors that attack the metals, and the metals being attacked. Chemically, both have the same composition.

The text asserts that the barber was given authority over the vapors and metals, but it does not explain who gave the authority. Since the barber symbolizes mind, the cosmos, we may interpolate the doctrine in *The Krater* and understand the unnamed source of authority as an allusion to God, the Father, creator of mind.[72]

However, instead of developing the allusion to God, Zosimos alerts from his second vision. He does not experience fear this time. Once again, he finds that he has rightly understood his vision's meaning.

Following his second vision, Zosimos expounded at length on its significance. Like the opening of *The Visions,* the passage seems to have been a recital:

> And I said that it was fair to speak and fair to listen, and fair to give and fair to receive, and fair to be poor and fair to be rich. For how does the nature learn to give and to receive? The copper man gives and the watery stone receives; the metal gives and the plant receives; the stars give and the flowers receive; the sky gives and the earth receives; the thunderclaps give the fire that darts from them. For all things are interwoven and separate afresh, and all things are mingled and all things combine, all things are mixed and all unmixed, all things are moistened and all things dried and all things flower and blossom in the altar shaped like a bowl. For each, it is by method, by measure and weight of the 4 elements, that the interlacing and dissociation of all is accomplished. No bond can be made without method. It is a natural method, breathing in and breathing out, keeping the arrangements of the method, increasing or decreasing them. When all things, in a word, come to harmony by division and union, without the methods being neglected in any way, the nature is transformed. For the nature being turned upon itself is transformed; and it is the nature and the bond of the virtue of the whole world.[73]

The third sentence of the recital commences a series of chemical allusions. The copper man who gives symbolizes the metals at the start of the process. The watery stone that receives symbolizes the vapors, which acquire some copper even as they attack the metals. The metal that gives would be copper, while the plant that receives would be the rising vapors. With the next images, the sequence of parallels reverses. The stars are in the heaven—that is, at the top of the apparatus. The flowers that receive are the colors produced in the metals by the acid. The sky that gives is the condensing vapor at the top of the apparatus. The receptive earth is the metals. The thunderclaps are the condensing vapors; their fire is their acidic potency.

At the start, Zosimos's recital pertains only to the chemical process, but it contains a passage that develops a universal relevance. Zosimos mentions the four elements and generalizes about "breathing in and breathing out." He refers here to the Hermetic doctrine concerning the participation of all individual souls in the one atmospheric mind.[74] The nature, its method, the bond of the virtue of the whole world, and so forth, is the universal mind.

Following Zosimos's recital, Lesson 1 ends with instructions to the reader:

> And that I may not write many things to you, my friend, build a temple of one stone, like ceruse in appearance, like alabaster, like marble of Proconnesus, having neither beginning nor end in its construction. Let it have within it a spring of pure water glittering like the sun. Notice on which side is the entry of the temple and, taking your sword in your hand, so seek for the entry. For narrow is the place at which the temple opens. A serpent lies before the entry guarding the temple; seize him and sacrifice him. Skin him and, taking his flesh and bones, separate his parts; then reuniting the members with the bones at the entry of the temple, make of them a stepping stone, mount thereon, and enter. You will find there what you seek. For the priest, the man of copper, whom you see seated in the spring and gathering his colour, do not regard him as a man of copper; for he has changed the colour of his nature and become a man of silver. If you wish, after a little time you will have him as a man of gold.[75]

Since ceruse is white lead,[76] the temple's appearance like ceruse is once again an allusion to the base metals of the opus. The spring of water glittering like the sun is the vapors. As previously, the sword symbolizes heat. The sword is able to discover the narrow entry of the temple because a place of entry is also a place of exit that escaping vapor will find once heat is applied to the *kerotakis*. The serpent guarding the temple is, I suggest, a pipe that leads from the *kerotakis* to a still. Although the text seems to suggest that the serpent is to be seized and sacrificed, I suggest that Zosimos engaged here in literary misdirection or sleight of hand. The pronoun "him" refers not to the serpent but to something unnamed. Anyone able to identify the serpent as a pipe leading to a still would know that it was the gas, rather than the pipe, that was to be drawn out of the *kerotakis*. The vapors were to be separated into their parts, of which at least some were flesh and bones—that is, solids. The reunion of the members signifies the resolution of the salts into a portion of the fluid acid. This acid of increased potency is the "stepping stone" with which to enter the temple—that is, the *kerotakis*. There the acid produces what is sought: through the application of the acid to the metals within the *kerotakis*, "the priest, the man of copper," becomes "a man of silver"—that is, undergoes the whitening. He will presently undergo the yellowing, becoming "a man of gold."

Lessons 2 and 3 of *The Visions* are considerably shorter. Their subtexts provide further details on the later aspects of the opus. For present purposes, it will suffice to discuss the opening of Lesson 3:

> And again I saw the same divine and sacred bowl-shaped altar, and I saw a priest clothed in white celebrating those fearful mysteries, and I said "Who is this?" And answering, he said to me "This is the priest of the Sanctuary. He wishes to put blood into the bodies, to make clear the eyes, and to raise up the dead."[77]

In this, the fifth of Zosimos's visions, the subtext again concerns the shelf and the vapors whitening the metals. We now learn the religious significance of the chemical process. By liquefying the metals that have been attacked by the vapors, the opus was able "to raise up the dead." Zosimos regarded the opus as a proof of the physical possibility of bodily resurrection: the capacity of biochemical science to resuscitate the dead.

Isis the Prophetess to Her Son Horus

Although a considerable number of alchemical sayings were transmitted in the name of Hermes,[78] other sayings were attributed to other gods. It was probably due to the personal influence of Zosimos that alchemy came to be described as the "hermetic" philosophy. Zosimos was the only Hellenistic alchemist known to us who was a Hermetist—that is, a practitioner of the religious mysticism that is attested in the *Corpus Hermeticum*. Other early alchemists had other points of view. Consider, for example, the pseudonymous *Isis the Prophetess to Her Son Horus*. The bulk of the text consists of metallurgical recipes that are ignorant of distillation. The archaic recipes are prefaced, however, by a narrative whose orientation is alchemical:

> Isis the prophetess to her son Horus: "You decided, my son, to set out and go to battle with the infidel Typhon, for the throne of your father. Myself, I went to Hermonthis, a town (where one practices) the sacred art of Egypt. I stayed there some time. In the course of events and the necessary revolution of the spheres, one of the angels who reside in the first firmament saw me from above and

wanted to unite with me. He advanced, intending to arrive at his goal, but I refused to yield, wanting to learn from him the preparation of gold and silver. When I questioned him, he told me that he was not permitted to explain in this regard, in view of the high importance of these mysteries, but that the following day, a greater angel, the angel Amnael would come and would be able to provide me with the answer to the question.

He told me that he [Amnael] would carry a sign on his head and would display a small vase that was not covered with pitch, [but] full of transparent water. He would be able to reveal the truth.

Next day, before the sun was neared its course, the angel Amnael appeared, greater than the first. Taken by the same desire with my regard, he descended towards me. He did not stay immobile, but hastened to where I held myself. And I, I did not stop asking him the question.

And when he delayed (to answer me), I did not yield a bit. But I resisted his desire until he let me see the sign which he had on his head and transmitted to me without reserve and with sincerity the mysteries that I sought.

At last, he showed me the sign and began the revelation of the mysteries. Offering oaths, he expressed himself this way: "I adjure you by heaven, earth, light, and darkness. I adjure you by fire, water, air, and earth. I adjure you by the height of the heaven, by the depth of the earth and of Tartaros. I adjure you by Hermes, by Anubis, by the roaring of Kerberos, by the serpent who guards the temple. I adjure you by the Ferry and by the Boatman of the Acheron. I adjure you by the Three Fates, by the Furies, and by the Sword."

After all these oaths, he demanded that I communicate nothing to anyone whatever except my beloved and legitimate son, so that you might be he and he you. So then, observe in passing, ask the farmer Acharantos and learn from him what is sown and what is harvested, and you will learn from him that the man who sows wheat also harvests wheat, and the man who sows barley also harvests barley. . . .

The adepts having participated in the divine power, and having recourse to divine assistance, clarified by virtue of the question (of Isis): they must make preparations with certain metallic minerals, without using other substances. . . . Now the mystery has been revealed.[79]

The revelation of an alchemical secret by a spirit is a leitmotif of Greco-Egyptian alchemy. The significance of the motif was preserved in a historical notice of Maria the Jewess by the Muslim alchemist ibn Umail:

> MARIYA also said: "The 'Water' which I have mentioned is an Angel and descends from the sky, and the earth accepts it on account of its (the earth's) moistness. . . .
>
> (As for her statement regarding the Angel) "She meant by this the 'Divine Water,' which is the 'Soul.' She named it 'Angel' because it is spiritual, and because that 'Water' has risen from the earth to the sky of the *Birba* (i.e., from the bottom to the top of the Alembic).
>
> "And as for her statement (The Water) descends from the sky,' she meant by this its return to their Earth."[80]

One source of *Isis the Prophetess* was a Jewish midrash. Expanding on the biblical account of an antedeluvial period when fallen angels mated with the daughters of men (Gen 6:1–4), the midrash accounted for the origin of alchemy through revelation by an angel named Amnael.[81] As the midrash was reworked in *Isis the Prophetess*, the Egyptian goddess has been euhemerized and identified as the woman whom Amnael approached. The alchemical cipher also depends on the well-known Hellenistic identification of Isis with the earth.[82] Isis symbolizes the copper-lead metals. The approach of the first angel, whom she is able to refuse, corresponds to the initial attack of smoky vapors, the blackening. Amnael, the angel whose advances she welcomes at a price, symbolizes the corrosive vapors that attack the metals, accomplishing the whitening. The vase that Amnael exhibits presumably signifies a still. The vessel has not been coated with pitch, in the sense that it has not been involved in the blackening; yet it is filled with transparent waters, meaning vapors. The sign on Amnael's head, whose display coincides with Isis's surrender to his lust, alludes to the discoloration of the vapors upon their corrosive contact with the metals.

The passing reference to a sword, in the last of Amnael's oaths, signified the death-dealing agency of heat. The text does not otherwise allegorize the increase of heat necessary to transform the corroded metals into a gold-resembling alloy. Instead of a description of Isis and Amnael in the heat of union becoming Horus, the text identifies Amnael with Horus but otherwise refers chastely to a secret communication involving Isis. The secret, we are also told, is that what one sows is what one harvests. In other words, with the attack of the vapors on the metals, the chemical ingredients of alchemical gold are all present.

So far is *Isis the Prophetess to Her Son Horus* from spiritual alchemy that it is distinguished by an iconoclastic irreverence for religion. Much in the text is meant to be absurd. The great mother goddess of Egypt is merely a mortal prophetess, and she is seduced by a Jewish angel. Mercenary in her morality, she is a willing party to her seduction, providing only that she is told the alchemical secret of silver and gold. For his part, the Jewish angel takes no Jewish oaths. He swears by the four elements and otherwise by a variety of Egyptian and Greek numina. Finally, Isis no sooner swears an oath of secrecy than she breaks it by writing the text that we are reading.

These calculated insults to Greco-Egyptian religion are all present in the manifest level of the text. The subtext adds the further sacrileges that Isis and Amnael are names for mineral substances. Heaven and Tartaros name the top and the bottom of the alchemical apparatus. The serpent who guards the temple is the pipe leading from the apparatus to the distillation equipment. These uses of religious language are reductive. They interpret the divine and angelic as mere terminology for the physical and material.

Physika kai Mystika

An attitude consistent with *Isis the Prophetess* may be found in *Physika kai Mystika,* which is sometimes regarded as the oldest alchemical writing extant. The text is a collection of metallurgical recipes, comparable to the Stockholm and Leyden X papyri, that was subsequently revised and expanded from an alchemical perspective. The ostensible author, the classical philosopher Democritus of Abdera, was identified in antiquity as Bolos of Mendes. A reference to Democritus in the metallurgical Stockholm papyrus[83] obliges us to associate Bolos with the first literary stratum in *Physika kai Mystika:* the metallurgical recipes of the first century C.E.[84] rather than their alchemical revision.

A number of Greco-Egyptian magical recipes were also attributed to Democritus. One is entitled "Pythagoras's request for a dream oracle and Demokritos's dream divination."[85] The

recommended procedure compares closely with the practice described in the alchemical preface of *Physika kai Mystika*. The anonymous alchemist who revised Bolos's text presumably drew on the
reputation of Democritus in the magical papyri in developing the
account of Democritus's use of spirit-conjuring to acquire the alchemical secrets of an Egyptian priest. That the tale is alchemical,
rather than metallurgical, is evident from its assertion, "They [the
uninitiated] think we are proclaiming a Logos which is a myth
[*muthikos*], not a mystery [*mustikos*], and they make no examination of the Forms."[86] The following tale of the origin of alchemy is
not a mythical narrative, but a riddle, allegory or cipher that con-
ceals a secret subtext:

> Recollecting these ideas of our ordained master and knowing the
> diversity of matter we endeavoured to bring the natures into har-
> mony. But as our master died before we were initiated and at a
> time when we had not attained the complete knowledge of matter,
> we were told that we must evoke him from Hades. And as I set out
> to do this, I called upon him directly in these words. "Grant me
> gifts, in return for that which I have accomplished for you," and
> having thus spoken, I kept silence. And as I called upon him many
> times, asking now how I should harmonise the natures, he told me
> that it was difficult to speak without the permission of the dae-
> mon. And he only said "The books are in the temple." Returning to
> the temple I set myself to search if by chance I might gain posses-
> sion of the books: for when he was alive he had said nothing of
> them. For he died leaving no testament, having, as some say, taken
> poison to separate his soul from his body; or better, as his son says,
> having taken poison in error. Before his death, he had intended to
> show the books to his son alone when he had passed his first
> prime. None of us knew anything about these books. As after a
> search we found nothing, we were most anxious to know how the
> substances and natures were made one and combined. As we had
> completed the combination of matter, and it was time for a cere-
> mony in the temple, we made a common feast. Then as we were in
> the temple one of the columns suddenly opened but we saw noth-
> ing within. For neither he nor anyone had said the books of his fa-
> ther were hidden there. Advancing, he led us to the column;
> leaning forward we saw with astonishment that nothing had es-
> caped us except the precious formula which we found there:
>
> "The Nature rejoices in the nature and the nature conquers
> the nature and the nature masters the nature."
>
> We were much surprised that he had summed up all his writ-
> ings in so few words.[87]

On the face of it, this passage concerns the conjuring of a ghost, but the subtext is chemical. Consider the tale. A dream succeeds in raising a dead father who says no more than that the books are in the temple. Is this a historical notice on the Egyptian priestly origin of the metallurgical recipes? Possibly. But it is certainly a use of the *imago templi* to designate the alchemical apparatus.

The reference to poisoning involves a wordplay. The word *ios*, "purple, rust," can also mean "poison." The son's claim that his father poisoned himself accidentally signifies that he chanced to discover the technique of empurpling.

The same notion is conveyed by further images. A search yields no evidence of books: no one teaches how to accomplish the empurpling. But a column suddenly opens and a formula is revealed. Here the allegory depends on understanding a column of ascending gas in place of a column of stone. The secret, I suggest, was the significance of the fumes produced by burning sulphur.

Much the same intimation may be read in a letter by Zosimos of Panopolis to his sister Theobesia:

> In the same way your priest Nilus moved me to laughter, burning his lead-copper alloy in a baker's oven, as if he was baking bread, burning it with cobathia for a whole day. Blinded in his bodily eyes he did not realize his method was bad, but he blew up the fire and after cooling and taking out his product, showed you cinders. Being asked where the whitening was, he was at a loss and said that it had penetrated into the interior. Then he put in copper and coloured the cinder, for meeting nothing solid it passed out and disappeared into the interior, the same being true for the whitening of magnesia. Hearing this from his opponents, Paphnutia was much laughed at, and you will be laughed at, too, if you do the same. Greet Nilus, the cobathia-burner.[88]

Zosimos did not assert that Nilus was employing the wrong ingredients, but only that "his method was bad." To scorn the fumes, to allow them to escape, is to be unable to produce the divine water, sulphuric acid.

The alchemical formula, "The Nature rejoices in the nature and the nature conquers the nature and the nature masters the nature," emphasizes the idea of the unity of nature through its allusions to the interactions of the solid metals and the vapors. The metals rejoice in the vapors, because the acidic vapors conquer the metals, after which the corroded metals master themselves.

Physika kai Mystika employs the image of spirit-conjuring as a cipher for the production of gas. The choice of imagery was apparently dictated by the existing reputation of Democritus as a magician, but the alchemical significance of the imagery was metallic. Of the alchemist's religiosity, we may infer a willingness to satirize the practice of necromancy,[89] but it is difficult to say more.

Isis the Prophetess and *Physika kai Mystika* may conceivably have been the works of atheists. It is equally possible, however, that the authors were devoutly religious. A willingness to satirize Egyptian, Greek, and Jewish mythologies would not necessarily have been inconsistent, for example, with Maria the Jewess's interpretation of scientific creativity as divine revelation. Zosimos quoted her as having said: "Here is what God said: Know that according to experience, in burning copper (first), the sulphur produces no effect. But if instead you burn sulphur (first), then not only does it render the copper without stain, but it also makes it approach gold."[90] Although Jewish and Christian mystics generally sought creative inspirations for the purpose of scriptural exegesis, alchemists may certainly have desired revelations concerning both the sacred art and its literature.

Alchemical Philosophy

The founders of Greek alchemy, Maria the Jewess and Zosimos of Panopolis, were almost certainly mystics, but two early instances do not constitute a tradition. There are no claims to revelation in the writings of other Hellenistic alchemists. Neither is mysticism to be found in the works of Arabic alchemy that I have been able to consult.[91] Mysticism is not demonstrable in Western alchemy prior to the Late Middle Ages. It is only a religio-philosophical evaluation of chemical change that has been a constant of Western alchemy since its Hellenistic origins.

Hopkins argued persuasively that the Hellenistic alchemists were heirs to Greek science, most notably that of Aristotle.[92] However, the thoroughgoing Aristotelian interpretation of alchemy that contributed to the rise of science was an Arabic innovation that found its way to the West in such texts as the Latin *Morienius* and the *Turba Philosophorum*.[93] Greek alchemy was instead indebted to a blend of late antique philosophies.

Sheppard attempted to prove that "the main source from which alchemical mysticism derived was Gnosticism,"[94] but his several efforts to substantiate Jung's hypothesis[95] remained inconclusive. Zosimos was assuredly a Hermetic, but the Gnostic character of Hermetism, which was taken for granted in Jung's day, may not be assumed. Some Hermetic writings show the influence of Valentinian Gnosticism, but most, including the writings of Zosimos, do not. Hermetism was primarily an intellectualist mysticism—a mysticism of the *nous* or mind—that was consistent with related trends in Middle Platonism, Neo-Aristotelianism, and early Christianity. Again, the motifs of creation out of an egg and the tail-eating serpent, and Stoic ideas of transformation and redemption, were shared by Greco-Egyptian alchemy not only with Gnosticism, but with a variety of other Hellenistic movements.

The alchemical "vision of Nous entangled in the embrace of Physis"[96] that Jung, Sheppard, and others have mistaken for Gnosticism is better regarded, I suggest, as a Stoic contribution to both alchemy and Gnosticism. The Stoics were responsible for developing the doctrine of the sympathy of all things.[97] They were also responsible for the theory of species that alchemists took for granted in formulating their ideas about transmutation.

The Stoics held that plants and animals reproduced their species because the semen of each species contained its *spermatikos logos* or "seminal formula." For example, a *logos* is responsible for causing matter to take form as a lion. The semen of lions contains a *spermatikos logos* that transmits their *logos* to the wombs of lionesses, as is necessary for the reproduction of the species. The Stoic term *logos* conveyed a variety of meanings. The Stoics, like the Middle Platonists who followed them, held God to be the *logos*. F. H. Sandbach suggested that the Stoics used *logos* (pl. *logoi*) to mean: (1) language, speech, expression; (2) formula, explanation; (3) purpose; (4) reason, rationale, correct reason, plan; and (5) dynamic process, tending toward consummation.[98] The term evidently had a technical sense that is not conveyed by its literal translation. At bottom, a *logos* is a concept or idea inherent in a thing, that makes the thing what it is. God is the *logos* of the world; but lesser *logoi*, which are all portions of God, are responsible for particular things. The thing may be an individual, or an entire type, class, or species.

A *logos* is invariably a processual structure. It is both the structure of the thing and its dynamic activity or process. The *logos* consequently encompasses a thing's cause, reason, motive, purpose, rationality, function, and goal. In all cases, a *logos* exists in matter, causing a specific amount of matter to assume the form that it does. The Stoics recognized an immanent God and rejected the idea of divine transcendence. In their view, God had no discrete existence as *logos* apart from matter. God was composed of *pneuma*, "breath" or "spirit," a particular blend of air and fire. Since God was the soul of the world, the human soul (*psyche*) was thought to be composed of the same mixture. Matter was essentially *hylé*, substance in an indeterminate or chaotic condition. Particular *logoi* caused *hylé* to take form as the four elements—earth, water, air, and fire—of which all else is composed.[99]

In a second sense of the term, or perhaps a second context of its activity, a *logos* might be expressed in language as a word, or visually as an image. In cases of what we may term its representation, it is then the same *logos*, but it is present in a substance—for example, sound or light, thought or imagination—whose species is determined by other *logoi*. For example, seeing or thinking of a lion does not cause a person to become a lion, because the human soul continues to be determined by its own *logos*. To explain the phenomenon, the Stoics contrasted two physical concepts. As "blending," they conceived of two substances that occupy the same space but retain their individual identities and qualities. In "fusion," the original qualities are lost and the two substances combine to form a third.[100]

The Stoic theory of the *spermatikos logos* was adapted by Hellenistic alchemists to the circumstances of metals.[101] The alchemical theory of transmutation depends on it. Metals that changed their form were held to have changed their very species. Copper and lead that had been made to appear to be gold were indeed gold. The copper and lead were said to have died. The gold was said to have been born. Sulphuric acid, which was understood to produce the transmutation, was considered the pneumatic source of the new form.

This doctrine is explicated at the beginning of the *Poimandres*, the first book in the *Corpus Hermeticum* collection. The doctrine occurs in a passage where the microcosm of the alchemical opus is presented—without identification or explanation—as the type or model of cosmogenesis:

> And I beheld a boundless view; all was changed into light, a mild and joyous light; and I marvelled when I saw it. And in a little while, there had come to be in one part a downward-tending darkness, terrible and grim. . . . And thereafter I saw the darkness changing into a water substance, which was unspeakably tossed about, and gave forth smoke as from fire; and I heard it making an

indescribable sound of lamentation; for there was sent forth from it an inarticulate cry. But from the Light there came forth a holy Word, which took its stand upon the watery substance; and methought this Word was the voice of the Light.[102]

The narrative describes the initial brightness of the burning of sulphur, its production of dark smoke, the precipitation of the sulphur oxides into the water, and the violent and noisy formation of sulphuric acid. The Word that "took its stand upon the watery substance"—that is, was responsible for the final emergence of the acid—was a structuring principle that had logically already to have been present in the initial light.

When added to the blackened mass—that is, the corpse—of copper and lead, sulphuric acid functioned like a seed which, taking root in soil, grew by converting the soil into plant flesh. In alchemical gold-making, the soil consisted of blackened copper and lead. To ensure the success of the transmutation, a small quantity of natural gold was sometimes added to the alchemical recipe. It too functioned as a *spermatikos logos,* the seed whose species would transmute the whole of the metals present. The transmutation proceeded in two stages. The whitening, or addition of sulphuric acid to the blackened copper and lead, accomplished a blending that was equivalent to the planting of the seed of gold. The yellowing, by annealing the metals, accomplished the growth of gold through fusion.

The alchemical use of Stoic philosophy was ancient and rudimentary science, not yet fully separated from religion, speculating wildly in premature attempts to understand the structural concepts that underlie the table of the atomic elements and structural chemistry. It was not mysticism, but a religio-scientific philosophy. Neither was it the only religio-scientific philosophy that influenced alchemy; Platonism and Aristotelianism each had notable impact in later eras. Stoicism left a permanent mark, however, on alchemical symbolism.

Alan de Lille

The *Anticlaudianus* of Alan de Lille, a major document of the Platonic revival of the twelfth century, was perhaps the first literary (as distinct from alchemical) discussion of alchemical gold-making in the Latin West. Alan allegorized the three stages of the alchemical opus—the blackening, whitening, and yellowing—as three mirrors. The composition of the first was not specified, but may be assumed to have been an ordinary medieval mirror of bronze with a large (30%) proportion of tin. The second and third mirrors were made of silver and gold, respectively. The interpretation given to the alchemical opus was expressed in Platonic language, but the concepts perpetuated the Stoic perspective that had given rise to Western alchemy a millennium earlier.

Alan began his allegory with an account of the blackening:

> Reason devotes her close attention to the use of one of the mirrors. In this mirror she sees the system of causes; she examines the primordial elements of things. She sees the marriage of matter and form; she sees the kisses which the union shares; she sees what this temporary union toasts as it weds matter to form.[103]

The "system of causes" and "primordial elements of things" refer to the ingredients of the alchemical opus. Once the opus was begun, the sulphur and arsenides of sulphur would burn and the fumes would briefly attack the lead and copper. This brief contact was "the marriage of matter and form," "kisses," a "temporary union." In this symbolism, the solids were designated as matter, and the fumes as form—the Platonic equivalent of Stoic *logoi*.

In order to convey the idea that these fumes were not to be allowed to escape, but were instead to be used throughout the course of the opus, Alan next outlined the diverse functions of the "form": "She sees which form gives matter existence, which completes that existence; which sets a thing on the road to existence, which brings it to the end of the road, which produces it, which changes it, which preserves it in a being."[104] The "end of the road" of existence referred to the loss of a species' form. The loss was conceptualized as the reduction of a discrete phenomenon to the chaotic or formless condition of primordial matter.

Alan's account of the silver mirror allegorized the whitening phase of the alchemical opus and continued its Stoic-Platonic interpretation. The fumes were described as "pure form" returning to "her place of origin." The image alluded to the soul's ascension to God after death, but allegorized the descent of the powdery oxides into the water, there to form acids:

> Here she sees matter divorced from form return to primordial chaos and pure form seek again her own source, regain her youth in her proper state and no longer have to bemoan her disgust with

degenerate matter. She sees how form joyfully finds rest in her own being and no longer suffers, like one ship-wrecked, the changing tides of matter but how, like a wanderer, she returns to her place of origin, escapes the destruction of matter and avoids sharing its death.[105]

The subsequent action of the acid on the blackened solids, which accomplished their whitening, was described in two aspects. Throughout this operation, the acid retained the integrity of its chemical composition. "The youth of form, not ravished by aged matter, keeps form forever a fair maid."[106] As well, through their condensation, the acidic vapors at the top of the apparatus fell onto and united with the solids below: "With unruffled countenance and profound mind, she perceives how the composite is simple; the heavenly, mortal; the different, identical; the heavy, light; the moving, stationary; the dark, bright; the dear, cheap; the jocose, tearsome; the eternal, temporal; the revolving, fixed."[107]

The condensate that missed the solids and fell to the very bottom of the apparatus would vaporize, condense, and fall anew, accomplishing the "moving" or "revolving" that Alan mentioned.

Once the acid had thoroughly saturated and discolored the solids, the alchemical opus required an increase of heat to anneal the metals. The alloy that this yellowing produced was a soft heavy brass that considerably resembled gold:

The excellence of gold, more refined than any known gold, and scarcely deigning to recognise its own genus and species, lends it reflection to a mirror, the third one, which cannot counterfeit the shadow of things but shows every thing with more definiteness and reflects the whole with greater clarity. Here she sees the fount of things, the genus of the universe, the idea, exemplar, species, cause, first beginning and ultimate end of the world.[108]

For Alan de Lille, alchemical gold was a "reflection" of the "first beginning and ultimate end of the world," a testament to nature, but so also to God. The direct evidence consisted of the reflection, nature; but the image that the mirror reflected was the image of God.

Not only did Alan regard alchemy as a proof of the validity of the idea of nature, but he envisioned an analysis of nature. His method was qualitative and teleological. He sought the divine purposes and ideas that were manifest in nature:

She measures each and every thing by definite boundaries. She sees by what plan, by what causes, why, how, when, this unstable, generated, unsteady, changing universe got its shape, being, condition, species, life and origin from the ungenerated, stable and fixed; how the heavenly idea begets the earthly form, transforms chaos into the species we know and sends abroad the forms which it destines for earth; how the child degenerates from the father, lays aside her father's face and forgets the mien of her parent of old. Here it was possible to see how the image of the idea is reflected in the universe and the idea's pure splendour is sensed in its copy; how the river, winding its way from the fount of forms, loses its native sparkle through corruption by matter; what fate determines; what comes to pass by chance; what the power of free-will, keeping its place between the two, can do. Reason devotes herself entirely to these mirrors. For the present she gives freer rein to her eyes, racks her brain, gives her soul free-play that she may draw from within the mirrors something approved by Reason that would be well worth bringing to ears so important.[109]

This passage in *Anticlaudianus* took for granted the distinction between ideas and forms that Bernard of Chartres had introduced at the beginning of the twelfth century. Forms were the reflection in nature of the ideas in the mind of God.[110] Alan described sulphuric acid as form because its addition was responsible for introducing the form of gold—better, the form of what was mistakenly understood as gold—to the blackened mass of copper and lead. Form was analogous to soul, but form had no existence apart from matter. As a vapor, form might be said to have a subtle body; but it invariably remained a body that was composed of the four elements. The concept of form was a distant forerunner of the modern concept of "structure" in structural chemistry. It was a bridge not to mysticism but to physical science.

To conclude. Jung based his account of the alchemical opus on symbols that allegorized the chemistry of gold-making, of which Jung was unaware. Jung followed Atwood closely in mistaking the symbols as evidence of visionary and unitive experience. Historians of alchemy date the origin of alchemical mysticism to the Renaissance; its presupposition of Aristotle's theory of ether was not even available until the Late Middle Ages.

The possibility of direct continuity from the ancient Gnostics to the alchemists may be eliminated. Jung confused two radically different approaches to the relation of spirit and matter.[111] For Gnosticism, matter was evil and spirit or soul were trapped within it. For alchemists, as for Stoics, matter was good and God's presence within it imparted its structures, forms, and processes. Hellenistic alchemy was proto-scientific in character, and its Muslim and Latin successors preserved the optimistic physicalism of late Greek physics during centuries whose popular cultures were dominated by Christian, Gnostic, Neoplatonic, and Muslim doctrines of the body's irredeemable imperfection and the soul's salvation alone.

A modified version of Jung's theory that alchemists had visions that they projected onto matter may nevertheless be sustained. We may not assume that all alchemists were visionaries. We are instead obliged to demonstrate the particular individuals who were. Those, such as Zosimos, who were visionaries, used hypnagogic states in autosuggestive manners in order to produce allegorical visions. They did not use lucid hypnagogic states in order to produce imaginal visions. If lucid hypnagogic states and Gnostic doctrines were used by alchemists, as Jung claimed—and it will be my case to demonstrate that they were—they must have entered the alchemical tradition at a later date and by a more complicated route than Jung imagined.

Part Two

A History of Gnosis

Chapter 5

Defining Gnosis

The Greek word *gnosis* means "knowledge." Since late antiquity, a variety of Western religions have referred to gnosis in a technical sense. In most cases, the significance of the term was partly or wholly esoteric. The knowledge to which the term referred was a secret whose disclosure was reserved to initiates. Modern scholars are in considerable disagreement regarding the precise meaning or meanings of the term.

At an international colloquium held at Messina, Italy, in 1966, scholars agreed to define gnosis as "knowledge of the divine mysteries reserved for an elite." This broad definition conformed with the studies of Hans Jonas[1] and the Bultmann school of New Testament theology. However, Gnosticism was defined more narrowly, in keeping with traditional Christian heresiology, by reference to "Second-Century sects" that believed in "a divine spark in man, deriving from the divine realm, fallen into this world of fate, birth and death, and needing to be awakened by the divine counterpart of the self."[2] Most scholars have added the further qualification that Gnosticism possessed a world-rejecting dualism that contrasted the virtue of spirit and the evil of materiality.[3]

This scholarly agendum perpetuates a Judeo-Christian bias. For the fathers of the Christian church, what was most striking about Gnosticism was its rejection of the God of Israel. In the Gnostics' view, because spirit was good and matter was evil, the creator of the material world had to be evil, and all the God-loving heroes of the Old Testament had to be villains. Under these circumstances, it was not a man from Nazareth but, for some Gnostics, the serpent in Eden who had appeared on earth as Christ the savior.[4] As may be expected, the church fathers saw Gnosticism as a deliberately anti-Christian heresy, a diabolic inversion or mockery of Christianity, and they emphasized the aspects of Gnosticism that most alarmed or appalled them.

Jewish scholars, such as Jonas, arrived at a similar bias for different reasons. The Gnostic description of the God of Israel as a demonic being has been understood by Jews as an intellectual or doctrinal anti-Semitism. The growing body of evidence that Gnosticism originated, perhaps only in part, among non-Christians who were deeply versed in Jewish midrash and halakhah[5] compounds the monstrosity by revealing the Gnostic villification of Judaism's God as a species of Jewish self-hatred.

Not only is the Messina terminology based on Judeao-Christian prejudices, but it adds to the confusion of the issues. Were we to fall in with the Messina terminology, we would find that some Gnostics were not dualists but monists,[6] as were a majority of the Hermetists.[7] Monistic Gnostics were not favorable to the world. Like Neoplatonists, they were acosmists. They rejected the world because they held matter to be an illusion. Hermetists instead agreed with Aristotelians and Stoics in espousing a monism that affirmed the reality and virtue of the physical world. Why should scholars lump dualists together with two very different sorts of monists, while setting all three apart from Christians?[8] Plainly, it is a heresiological agendum, a desire to protect the purity of some normative conception of Christianity, that informs the scholarly consensus.

The construction cannot be defended on the basis of ancient usage. Christians anciently used *gnosis* to mean "knowledge by personal acquaintance." The term was used freely by Paul, for the most part in reference to the knowledge that people have of God.[9] Paul discussed gnosis in parallel with prophecy. "Our knowledge is imperfect and our prophecy is imperfect" (1 Cor 13:9). Prophecy was verbal; gnosis could be visual. "God . . . has shone in our hearts to give the light of the knowledge of the glory of God in the face of Christ" (2 Cor 4:6). Although John did not use the noun, he wrote frequently of knowing (*gignoskein*) God or Christ, and the Fourth Gospel portrays John as a perfect gnostic—although without using the term.[10] The New Testament writings were the common source of the prominence that both Christian mystics and Gnostics gave the word *gnosis*.[11]

The term *gnostikos*, "knower," was not used by the ancient practitioners of the religion currently termed Gnostic.[12] Most called themselves Christians. They were called *gnostikoi* by their opponents or rivals within the Christian communities.[13] Most uses of the term were probably contemputous of a standard of spirituality that was ostensibly inferior to faith.

The people in late antiquity who referred to themselves as *gnostikoi* were Platonists and Pythagoreans. St. Clement of Alexandria and Origen described themselves as *gnostikoi* in a blend of the New Testament and Platonic senses.[14] An analogous blend of Quranic and Neoplatonic tendencies may be seen in Sufism. The term *maʿrifa*, "gnosis," earliest occurred in the sayings of early Sufi ascetics. Dhu 'l-Nun the Egyptian (d. 245/860) gave the term wide currency as a reference to unitive mysticism.[15] *ʿArif*, "gnostic," and *maʿrifa*, "gnosis," later gained generic significance in reference to Sufi mystics and their experiences.

The Messina terminology is all the more inadequate, however, because it has led to the neglect of an older body of scholarship that used the terms differently. Gershom G. Scholem protested this development:

> The discussion as to what exactly is to be understood by "gnosis" has gained in prominence in scholarly literature and at conferences during the last decades. There is a tendency to exclude phenomena that until 1930 were designated gnostic by everyone. To me it does not seem to matter greatly whether phenomena previously called gnostic are now designed as "esoteric," and I for one cannot see the use or value of the newly introduced distinctions.[16]

Is this a case of a rose by any other name? Not quite. Because they are addressing different topics, students of gnosis and Gnosticism, in the Messina senses of the terms, have no reason to read studies that used the terms in their older senses. The term "esoteric" is so very general, however, that its investment with a narrow technical sense has not proved successful. It is not going too far to say that for want of an effective name, the very topic of the older studies has come to be forgotten.

Jung, who attributed both visions[17] and unitive experiences[18] to the Gnostics, suggested that "gnosis is undoubtedly a psychological knowledge whose contents derive from the unconscious."[19] Scholem defined gnosis in terms of "a mystical esotericism for the elect based on illumination and the acquisition of a higher knowledge of things heavenly and divine."[20] But the materials he examined regularly involved celestial or otherworldly journeys:

> One of the chief preoccupations of the second and third century gnostics . . . [was] the ascent of the soul from the earth, through the spheres of the hostile planet-angels and rulers of the cosmos,

and its return to its divine home in the "fullness" of God's light, a
return which, to the gnostic's mind, signified Redemption. Some
scholars consider this to be the central idea of Gnosticism.[21]

In the present context, it is not important whether gnosis was
essentially or only occasionally a vision of ascension. What matters
is that a definition of Gnosticism in terms of a matter-rejecting dualism results in a different history than a definition in terms of visionary practices.

If we follow the trail of dualism, we perpetuate the skewed perspective of Christian heresiology. We are not then interested in
Gnosticism on its own terms, but only insofar as it aroused the hos-
tility of ecclesiastic authorities. We do not permit the historical evidence to define Gnosticism for us; we use a heresy's definition as a
criterion for admitting and excluding the relevance of historical
data. We have then the familiar history that Hellenistic Gnosticism
began to be suppressed by Roman Catholic Christianity in the
fourth century; that its eastern offshoot, Manicheism, was suppressed by early Islam; and that only a few small sects survived
thereafter. We may argue historical continuity[22] or, as Couliano
contended,[23] independent developments of several different sorts of
dualism in a number of medieval sects that were distributed from
Armenia and Asia Minor up the Danube to Lombardy and southern
France. In the east, dualism remained a going concern until the
Turkish conquest of Bosnia in 1463. In the west, the Cathars or Albigensians of Provence were exterminated by a series of crusades
between 1208 and 1238, and Catharism was abandoned in Italy by
the middle of the next century. With the exception of the Mandaeans of Iraq, who have survived to the present day,[24] Gnosticism has
been extinct for centuries.

If we instead trace the aspects of Gnosticism that were most
important not to Christian heresy-hunters but to the history of religion in the West, we may ignore the rejection of matter as an occasional extravagance. Most gnostics have been content to adhere to
Christian, Jewish, or Muslim views of matter and the body. The element of Gnosticism that succeeded in finding a place within the
three Western monotheisms was not its anticosmic dualism but a
distinctive type of visionary experience. The visions were not regarded as ("extrasensory") perceptions of objectively existing external realities. They did not disclose the real appearances of heavenly
beings and locations in manners consistent, for example, with the
celestial journeys of Jewish and Christian apocalyptists. Gnostics

recognized their visions as subjective mental experiences whose contents varied from moment to moment and individual to individual. There are, however, many different understandings of subjectivity. Gnostics did not treat their visions as allegories; they did not interpret the envisioned images as metaphoric presentations of abstract ideas, as was the major trend in early Christian and Talmudic mysticism, Hermetism, and the Aristotelian tradition within the three Western monotheisms. Between the two extremes of mythological objectivity and allegorizing subjectivity, gnostics devised a middle path.

The gnostics' approach to visionary experiences was motivated, I suggest, by their additional practice of unitive experiences. Because gnostics attempted to reconcile the two classes of experience, their doctrines were invariably paradoxical. They knew that their visions were subjective experiences, but from a unitive perspective they were obliged to regard the perceptible world equivalently. Whatever reality they accorded the world, they had to accord also to their visions.

The desire to reconcile visionary and unitive experiences is natural and human. It may arise independently, in any culture at any time. However, the doctrinal option to reconcile the two classes of experience by affirming the manifest contents of both is not widely attested on the planet. Within the history of religion in the West, the gnostic approach to visionary and unitive experiences was integrated with a variety of distinctive doctrines whose recurrence across time and space cannot reasonably be ascribed to chance reinvention. Gnostic visions included but were not limited to heavenly ascensions. Ecstatic deaths were frequent. The visions were known to be intrapsychic but were accorded a special reality of their own. Their contents were related to the spiritual status of the visionary: one saw what one merited. The associated unitive experiences were understood in terms of a conjunction of the gnostic with a divine hypostasis that was distinguished from a wholly transcendent extracosmic godhead. The hypostasis was simultaneously divisible into a plurality of hypostases, whose discussion constituted a theosophical analysis of both the cosmos and the divine.

The gnostic inventory should not be defined too rigidly, however, for it was not fixed and immutable, as scientific and metaphysical categories may be. Gnosis was and is a historical phenomenon that has undergone change over the centuries. A detailed definition for the gnosis of the second century will not fit the gnosis of the eighteenth, but the process of change can be traced. Gnosticism appears to have made its way from late antiquity to modern times, in a manner and by a route that compares with the transmissions of both Aristotelianism and the practice of science.

Such, at least, is the history whose evidence I have assembled. To avoid confusion, I refer to Gnostics and Gnosticism with a capital *G* when intending the Messina definition, but to gnosis, gnostics, and gnosticism, all with a lowercase *g*, when referring to the history of gnosis as an esoteric practice of visionary and unitive mysticism.

Chapter 6

The Gnostic Journey to the Ogdoad

It is conventional to speak of the "Copernican revolution" and to discuss the intellectual consequences of the humbling discovery that we are not at the center of the cosmos. More recently, the fallout from Einsteinian physics has included cultural relativity, moral ambiguity, and deconstruction. It has not been appreciated, however, that zodiacal astronomy resolved a scientific paradigm crisis in late antiquity that had comparably profound significance for the intellectual cultures of the Hellenistic world. Few movements were affected more deeply than Gnosticism.

Monumental architecture that is oriented to the sun, the moon, or a star does not go out of alignment. The great temple of Amen-Ra and the temple of Ra-Hor-Ahkty, both at Karnak, are in ruins but still faithfully point to the mid-winter solstice sunrise.[1] Other monuments lose accuracy with the passage of time. The great pyramid of Khufu (Cheops), for example, no longer points at the pole star. Its shaft remains aligned to Alpha Draconis, the star that was the pole star at the time of the pyramid's construction.[2] Pole stars change. Due to a slow wobble in the earth's rotation, a line that extended the earth's axis, as the cosmic pole was anciently thought to do, would describe a circle among the northern stars over a period of about 25,800 years.

The inaccuracy of monuments motivated the astronomical observations that gave rise to the zodiacal paradigm. By 700 B.C.E., Babylonian astronomers had recognized that the sun, moon, and planets always remain within a belt of stars, known as the zodiacal belt, whose center is the ecliptic, an imaginary line drawn in a circle at a 23° angle to the earth's axis. In a Babylonian text from 419 B.C.E., the division of the zodiacal belt into constellations had been replaced by its mathematical division into houses (mansions or signs) of 30° of arc each. By 410 B.C.E., Babylonians had developed birth or natal horoscopes that charted the positions of the seven

117

planets (sun, moon, and five visible planets) against the twelve zodiacal houses.[3]

Greek innovations in mathematics made possible a further aspect of zodiacal astrology. Beginning with Meton and Euctemon in 420 B.C.E., Greek astronomers made exact observations of the equinoxes and solstices that enabled Hipparchus to note the regularity of change that he conceptualized as precession.[4] Hipparchus's achievement, around 128 B.C.E.,[5] made possible the recognition that the constellations in the zodiacal belt themselves undergo precession. They do not remain forever each within its own zodiacal house. Rather, they pass through the entire zodiacal belt over a period of 25,800 years.

Two systems of zodiacal astrology were consequently possible. The Babylonian system, which had been ignorant of precession, made use of the actual positions of the zodiacal constellations. Termed a fixed or sidereal zodiac, it was used in the Hellenistic world until the period of Augustus. The younger, Greco-Babylonian system was founded by Hipparchus. It made use of the mathematical constructs of the houses, through which the planets and constellations pass. Termed the tropical or moving zodiac, it was popularized in a simplified form in the *Almagest* and *Tetrabiblos* of Claudius Ptolemy (c. 120–150 C.E.), works of astronomy and astrology, respectively.[6]

Another crucial contribution to zodiacal astrology was the Stoic doctrine of the sympathy of all things.[7] Unlike Aristotle, who maintained that different laws prevailed in the celestial and sublunar worlds, the Stoics insisted on the unity of the heavens and earth. In its Alexandrine development, Stoicism validated belief in an intricate system of correspondences among the celestial bodies, the parts of the human body, and the parts of the soul. The popularity of Stoicism among Rome's ruling class was responsible for the initial popularization of zodiacal astrology in the first century B.C.E.. Astrology spread throughout the Greek-speaking cities of Hellenistic Egypt and the Near East during the next two centuries. The famous Egyptian "zodiacs" of Dendera and Esna, the horoscope of Athribis, and the coffin of Heter all date to the first and second centuries C.E.[8]

David Ulansey has argued that the idea of a divine power that controlled the wobble of the cosmic pole was a central premise of the mysteries of Mithras.[9] Zodiacal astronomy had a different doctrinal consequence, I suggest, in Hellenistic Egypt. The new scientific paradigm made it impossible to maintain the ancient Egyptian belief that the sun combats stellar demons in its nightly passage through the celestial netherworld. The regions of the sky through which the sun passed were now understood to be limited to the twelve zodiacal houses. The traditional Egyptian doctrine of salvation could be reconciled with the new astrology, but only at the expense of relocating the netherworld. If the sun combated stellar demons, the demons could be no stars other than those of the twelve houses. The sun remained savior, not because it passed by night through the region below the celestial equator, but because it passed each year through the zodiacal belt.

As the new soteriology was worked out, the older concept of solar salvation through a vertical motion upward, toward the top of the sky, was retained. The zodiacal belt was divided horizontally into seven heavens, corresponding to the assumed distance of the seven planets from the earth. The Babylonians and Egyptians each developed a different sequence for the seven heavens. The order called "Chaldean," which was actually Greek in origin, came into standard use in the second century B.C.E.. It depended on mathematical calculations of the planets' periods of rotation around the ecliptic and consequently their assumed distances from the earth.[10]

It is this idea of a salvific journey through seven divisions of heaven that we meet in Gnosticism.[11] The seven divisions corresponded to, but were not identical with, the seven planets. Seven archons governed the seven planets and dominated the days of the week. They may also have been held responsible for the seven days of biblical creation.[12] In contrast with the view that the astrology was a secondary and superficial addition to an already dualistic Gnostic mythology, I suggest that the integration of astrology and cosmology was thoroughgoing. The seven archons and the salvific ascension to the Ogdoad were inherently astrological conceptions. Indeed, it is entirely possible—if indemonstrable—that Gnostic anticosmic dualism itself had origin as a speculative interpretation of the new astronomy.

Irenaeus of Lyons, writing in the second century C.E., attested to the astrological learning of the Basilidean Gnostics: "They distribute the positions of the 365 heavens as the mathematicians do; they accept their theorems, it is true, but have applied them to their own specific doctrine."[13] Basilides, a Christian Gnostic, had been active in Egypt in the first half of the second century.

Astrological references in the Coptic texts discovered at Nag Hammadi are several, but aimed at nontechnical readers. A notable example occurs in a text of the Christian Gnostic school that

Valentinus founded in Egypt in the middle of the second century. In *The (First) Apocalypse of James,* dialogue between James and Jesus introduced the innovation of the twelve zodiacal houses: "James said, 'Rabbi, are there then twelve hebdomads and not seven as there are in the scriptures?' The Lord said, 'James, he who spoke concerning this scripture had a limited understanding'. "[14]

The text went on to subdivide the twelve into "seventy-two heavens, which were their subordinates,"[15] in reference to the division of the twelve zodiacal houses into 72 pentans, or units of 5° of arc of the sky. Each of the houses was also counted as a hebdomad, or unit of seven, because they could also be divided horizontally into the seven (planetary) heavens.

Another Valentinian text, *The Testimony of Truth,* named the "Ogdoad, which is the eighth [heaven], and . . . [place] of salvation."[16] The Ogdoad was, I suggest, the region of the fixed stars above the twelve houses of the zodiacal belt. Its attainment conferred immortality in *The Paraphrase of Shem,*[17] a work of Christian Gnosticism. In the Sethian Gnosticism of *Zostrianos,* attainment of the Ogdoad produces immortality by accomplishing a transformation into an angel.[18] In the Sethian *Gospel of the Egyptians,* the Father, the Mother, and the Son formed a trinity of powers in the Ogdoad, while twelve angels governed twelve aeons. In the same passage, a sentence that has only been partially preserved speaks of "the number of seven," presumably in reference to the heavenly powers below the Ogdoad.[19]

Gnosticism was unique in developing an extraordinary implication of the zodiacal world picture. The border between heaven and the netherworld was no longer identified with the celestial equator. Half of the zodiacal belt lies above the celestial equator, stretching northward to the celestial tropic of Cancer. Gnostic texts drew an appropriate conclusion. In *The Apocryphon of John,* a Christian Gnostic text, the archon creates twelve authorities or kings: "And he placed seven kings—each corresponding to the firmaments of heaven—over the seven heavens, and five over the depth of the abyss."[20] Here the twelve houses of the zodiac were divided, presumably by the celestial equator, so that seven were ruled by the same powers that ruled the seven planets, while five powers presided over houses in the netherworld. The diurnal rotation of the zodiac meant, however, that each zodiacal house was demonic during some hours each day. The Sethian *Gospel of the Egyptians* generalized appropriately. The twelve angels who governed the twelve aeons were "the ones who preside over Hades."[21]

In Gnosticism, the demonic powers of the netherworld ascended daily into the sky with the seven planets, and the earth was
subject to netherworldly powers.[22] The Gnostics believed that astrology worked, but they did not seek to know their horoscopes.
Quite the reverse! They sought salvation from astral determinism,
because they regarded fate as demonic.[23]

Ignorance and Knowledge

For the Gnostics, the astrological division of the cosmos into the
realm of astral determinism and the transcendent Ogdoad implied
that matter and the body were evil, while spirit and the mind were
good. Underlying these much-remarked antitheses[24] was another
pair of opposites: ignorance and *gnosis,* "knowledge." The knowledge
under question pertained to the unknowable, transcendent God.[25]
Gnostic teachings tended to emphasize that ignorance promotes an
arrogance that results in wrongdoing toward others. The ignorance
was variously caused. Gnostic systems regularly postulated a series
of gradations in the hierarchy of being. In some Gnostic systems, an
unknown, infinite, indescribable God, who is pure spirit, light, and
thought, gave rise to a thought, about himself, and so created the
first of all beings. Different formulations identified the first hypostasis variously as the son of god, the son of man (Jesus, Seth,
and the like), the feminine (Sophia, Achamoth, Barbelo, etc.), or an
androgynous being. Since all further creation proceeded by emanation from it, the first hypostasis was equivalent to being as such. It
was the all, the cosmos. When the first hypostasis was considered
androgynal, the hierarchy of being might continue with several
equally androgynal hypostases before the sexes were separated.

In some Gnostic systems, the first hypostasis was regarded as
a mirror image or replica of the transcendent godhead. The godhead
was not known directly, but its nature was inferred from its hypostasis. The godhead was sometimes considered the first or primal
person (anthropos) and the prototype of both the first hypostasis
and humanity.[26] Whether it was the unknown God or the first hypostasis that was identified as the anthropos, the anthropos was often explicitly androgynal.[27] When the godhead was considered
androgynal, it might even be treated as two gods, rather than one.

In most Gnostic systems, the first hypostasis engendered the
second, which was termed the totality or pleroma, and considered
equivalent to the Ogdoad. Ignorance came into being soon after, but

here the details varied considerably. In the *Tripartite Tractate,* God and the pleroma created the *logos,* but then drew away from him, leaving him in ignorance.[28] In many cases, however, Sophia attempted to create on her own, without the aid of the masculine principle(s) above her; her progeny were consequently ignorant of the higher beings.[29] The attribution of the origins of both matter and evil to a feminine entity combined the biblical notion of Eve's responsibility for the fall from paradise with the conception of Wisdom as a "master workman" (Prov 8:30) that contributed to God's work of creation.

Hans Jonas, whose interpretation dominated research for over a generation, regarded myth as the central premise of Gnosticism. The myth of the cosmogonic fall was balanced by the mythic descent of a heavenly redeemer who taught of an equally mythic salvation that was attained through the soul's ascent to heaven after death. Unlike the anthropos, who was considered perfect, immobile, and absolutely or relatively transcendent,[30] the redeemer entered into the physical cosmos in order to bring gnosis to human beings. The gnosis consisted of the perfection of the anthropos that the redeemer replicated, both in himself and in Gnostics to whom he made the anthropos known. The *Three Steles of Seth* addresses the anthropos: "We bless thee, once we have been saved, as the perfect individuals, perfect on account of thee, those who [became] perfect with thee who is complete, who completes, the one perfect through all these, who is similar everywhere."[31]

Some presentations of the anthropos myth, for example, by the Naasene sect,[32] Valentinus,[33] and the *Three Steles of Seth,*[34] named the anthropos Adam (Adamas, Geradamas). The redeemer might then be termed the "son of man" and identified as Seth, the son or "seed" of Adam. The motif of "seed" reflects the Stoic concept of *spermatikos logos,* the "seminal idea" responsible for replicating a parent's form in its offspring.

In Jonas's construction, which was unconsciously modeled on early Christianity, Gnosticism contrasted with Christianity chiefly in its rejection of matter, its nihilistic mood, and its claim that salvation was attained not by faith (*pistis*) but by knowledge (*gnosis*). Because gnosis often concerned secret mythic lore, its so-called knowledge frequently amounted to no more than faith in myth.[35]

An alternative perspective was presented initially by the Buddhologist Edward Conze, who remarked on the striking parallels of Buddhism and Gnosticism.[36] In this scholarly construction, Gnosticism is seen as a philosophy or hermeneutic, comparable to Buddhism and Neoplatonism, for the understanding of life in the world:

> Valentinus intends readers to understand Gnostic and biblical narratives not so much as stories but as representations of modes of being—of the ever present possibilities of spiritual blindness or insight, nonexistence or existence. . . . Rather than taking place sequentially in time, "actions" seem to occur within one another, as physical states of being dissolve into one another in metaphysical space, within the all inclusive field of the Father.[37]

Jung's claims regarding the Gnostics' uses of active imagination may be treated as a third, significantly different interpretation. In Jonas's construction, salvation was not possible for Gnostics until after death, and their experience of mortal life in the physical and intrinsically evil world was bleak and nihilistic. The hermeneutic approach permits the Gnostics to be seen as abstemious, ascetic personalities who were perhaps able to achieve a limited happiness through a smug sense of superiority that they nourished through self-comparisons with the ignorant or uninitiated. Jung claimed, however, that the Gnostics accessed the unconscious through active imagination and interpreted their experiences in a psycho-theological manner. As a result, they would have undergone personality transformations that would have made them some of the best adjusted, happiest, and most wholesome personalities of their age.

In my own view, Jung overestimated the capacity of religious ecstasy to induce personality transformations. Pagels rightly emphasizes the Gnostics' positive regard for creativity,[38] but even the best of modern psychotherapists, using all the techniques presently available, cannot produce the success rate imagined by Jung. I am also not prepared to endorse Jung's claim that the psycho-theological character of Gnostic doctrines would necessarily have facilitated transformation significantly more efficiently than many other mystical theologies. We have at present neither the evidence nor a cogent theory to support meaningful comparisons. Even with these qualifications, however, Jung's view of the Gnostics as a community of innovative mystics differs significantly from their interpretation as dour ascetics, much less as nihilists.

Certainly the debate whether a myth of otherworldly salvation or a philosophic theology was central to Gnosticism belabors unduly literal readings of myth. It has not been sufficiently recognized that because myths tell of the numinous powers that are held to be responsible for the providential miracles, misfortunes, and religious experiences of everyday life, myths are inherently and inalienably metaphoric.[39] Whether individual Gnostic formulations were cosmogonic myths or philosophical doctrines, they invariably discussed metaphysical phenomena that were believed to determine real experiences in the world. Gnostic myths never concerned cosomogony alone.

The Gnostic concept of ignorance is a case in point. It is the way of the world for people to be nonreligious, secular, and materialistic. The ignorance of religiosity that is the natural condition of humanity[40] is the cause of evil. In the absence of humility before God, people seek "to command one another, overcoming one another [in] their vain ambition." The "lust for power" causes people to be "fighters ... warriors ... troublemakers ... apostates ... disobedient beings."[41] A Gnostic, that is, a person who knows God, instead acts in "harmony and mutual love."[42] A Gnostic avoids sin and neither wrongs others nor causes them to suffer. These observations from human conduct cannot be made to explain all evil, however, and the Gnostics consequently maintained that evil was also caused by the wrongdoing of the powers, termed archons, who determine astrological fate. As wrongdoers, the archons had to be sinners who were ignorant of God; and since they were deficient in spirituality, they had to be material in composition.

The Gnostics' identified the leader of the archons as a demiurge. The concept of a demiurge, or world-creating deity who differed from the ultimate God, originated with Plato and was widespread in Hellenistic culture.[43] In Gnosticism, however, the demiurge was an ignorant and sinful wrongdoer, who imparted his or her failings to the creation. In some Gnostic systems, the creator of the world repented of his or her ignorance at some time after the act of creation.[44]

A more complicated scheme is found in *On the Origin of the World,* which was influenced by Jewish merkabah mysticism,[45] possibly in the early fourth century. Here the demiurge Yaldabaoth created seven evil heavens: "Seven appeared in chaos, androgynous. ... They are the [seven] forces of the seven heavens [of chaos]." Repenting in response to a revelation by Pistis, Sophia, the feminine portion of the sixth power, leagued with Sabaoth, the masculine portion of the second power, to overthrow Yaldabaoth, their father and creator, who had the seventh heaven as his place of rule.

The "great war in the seven heavens" ended with the repentant Sabaoth ruling "over everyone so that he might dwell above the twelve gods of chaos." Sabaoth made his abode "in the eighth heaven," the Ogdoad, where he made himself "a mansion . . . huge, magnificent, seven times as great as all those that exist in the seven heavens."[46]

The spiritual beings of the Ogdoad constituted the *pleroma*, "fullness" or "totality," in two different senses. As the source of the lower regions of the cosmos, they contained the lower regions within themselves. Unlike the lower regions, however, they were filled with a full measure of spirit, knew the truth of their origin, rendered glory to the transcendent godhead, and did not occupy themselves with sin. A Gnostic might seek to acquire a similar fullness by acquiring *gnosis*. Gnostic dualism pertained less to the theory of evil than to the practical problem of "awakening,"[47] as the Gnostics termed conversion.

Like Christians, Gnostics learned of salvation through the teachings of their savior, but came actually to be saved through a personal experience of revelation.[48] A Gnostic's salvation from fate by ascending into heaven remained an imitation of the descending and ascending redeemer,[49] who was often but not always identified with Jesus. In Sethian Gnosticism,[50] for example, the redeemer was identified as Seth, the Son of Adam (Man).[51] Other Gnostic redeemers included Adam, Eve, Enoch, Melchizedek, the angel Baruch, the angel Eleleth, Sophia (wisdom), Spirit, Understanding (*nous*), Insight (*epinoia*), the power of thought (*ennoia*), the Word (*logos*), and the Illuminator or Light-Bearer (*phoster*).[52]

Ugo Bianchi emphasized the docetic character of Gnostic christology.[53] Most Gnostics rejected the doctrine of the incarnation because they considered the body evil. Gnostic saviors generally resemble the spiritualized views of Melchizedek that we find in the Dead Sea scrolls, the New Testament, and Gnosticism, of Moses in Samaritanism[54] and of the patriarch Jacob Israel in both Gnosticism[55] and some Jewish texts of the period.[56] In keeping with the Gnostics' negative evaluation of materiality, Gnostic saviors were purely spiritual beings who descended from heaven to earth in order to save humanity from further enslavement by the powers of ignorance. Gnostic docetism (from *dokesis*, "appearance") varied from pure spirituality to spirituality that assumed the appearance of materiality. Some texts went so far toward Christian incarnationism as to allow that the spiritual Christ entered the flesh of the man Jesus at his baptism. Gnostics did not concede, however, that Christ incarnated as Jesus from his conception onward.[57]

Between Mystery and Mysticism

Jonas's construction of Gnosticism as a religion based in myth precluded the assignment of a role to mysticism, because he regarded myth and mysticism as mutually exclusive phenomena:

> The doctrine of the soul's ascent through the spheres . . . is one of the most constant common features in otherwise widely divergent gnostic systems. . . . In a later stage of "gnostic" development (though no longer passing under the name of Gnosticism) the external topology of the ascent through the spheres . . . reappears "internalized" in the shape of a psychological technique of inner transformations by which the self, while still in the body, might attain the absolute as an immanent, if temporary, condition. An ascending scale of mental states replaces the stations of the mythical itinerary; the dynamics of progressive spiritual self-transformation replaces the spatial thrust through the heavenly spheres. . . . With this transposition of a mythological scheme into . . . self-performable experience whose culmination has the form of *ecstasis* or mystical union, gnostic myth passes into mysticism.[58]

Jonas suggested that the myth of the soul's ascension was applied to "stages of an intra-psychic process" through the myth's "psychologization."[59] He implicated allegory in the transition,[60] which, he felt, imposed "a certain temporal order" on "mystical philosophy and gnostic myth."[61] Myth might be allegorized and psychologized as mysticism, but mysticism could not be parent to Gnostic myth. Under the circumstances, Jonas made bold to remark: "Is there evidence of ecstasy as the culmination of experience? It would surely be in keeping with the whole gnostic attitude if there were. But my own impression is on the whole negative."[62]

Most scholars continue to share Jonas's assumption of the mutual exclusion of myth and mysticism. Rudolph maintains, for example, that the ascension to heaven was "first realized by the gnostic at the time of his death."[63] What Jung assumed and Corbin termed "imaginal" was a third alternative that was intermediate between myth and allegory. Once heavenly ascensions were Platonized in late antiquity, the itineraries constituted a sequential experience of different metaphysical ideas. Ascensions could be understood as internal and transformative within human beings, even though the ideas remained external and objectively given, due to their existence in the divine mind (*logos, nous,* and the like).

Scholarly reluctance to view Gnostic ascensions as visionary experiences dovetails with the purposes of Christian apologetics. It is generally recognized that various schools of Hellenistic Gnosticism were organized socially in the manner of the mysteries.[64] Their more advanced teachings were maintained as secrets that were reserved to an inner circle within their membership.[65] Gnostics explicitly boasted that their teachings were mysteries. For example, the second-century *Gospel of Thomas* states: "Jesus said, 'It is to those [who are worthy of my] mysteries that I tell my mysteries'. "[66] Gnostics even kept statues in a fashion consistent with the mysteries.[67] Scholars are prepared to allow that Gnosticism appropriated the terminology of the mysteries, as did Christianity and Greek philosophy; but they deny any closer connections.[68]

This flight in the face of the evidence is heir to the church fathers' treatment of Gnosticism as a heresy that was commensurate with Christianity. If Gnosticism was a mystery, so might Christianity have been—and as Jonathan Z. Smith has shown, Christian apologetics have consistently prejudiced the scholarly consensus against any such acknowledgment.[69]

In seeking an impartial account of Gnosticism, it would be an error, however, to interpolate the model of a Hellenistic mystery without allowing for the influence of Judaism. Walter Burkert recently argued that neither the classical Greek mysteries nor their Hellenistic successors were religions. In his view, "Mysteries were initiation rituals of a voluntary, personal, and secret character that aimed at a change of mind through experience of the sacred."[70] So understood, mysteries were optional additions to the conventional religions of their cultures. They bear comparison not with complete religions but with religious practices of limited scope, such as pilgrimages or religious vows and their fulfillments. In the mysteries, the optional religious practices consisted, Burkert argues, of secret initiations. The initiations consisted partly of lore and partly of ritual observances. Invariably, a mystery initiation also involved one or more religious experiences.[71] In the mysteries of Dionysus, and perhaps some few others, ecstasies were also practiced at certain festivals, but the ecstatic practices of most mysteries were initiatory alone.

Burkert's reevaluation of the social organization and religious function of the mysteries has important consequences for the interpretation of Gnosticism. In tribal societies, initiation is a rite of entrance into the tribe, in whose course various experiential and doctrinal secrets are communicated.[72] With the disintegration of

tribalism in the imperial cities of late antiquity, initiations ceased
to have political functions. Ritual acts remained integral to mystery
initiations as long as membership in the group of initiates retained
importance, but the raison d'être of the mysteries came increasingly to be their secret experiences and doctrines.

The transition was accelerated by the encounter with Judaism.
Jewish prophets and apocalyptists—including Jesus and his disciples—were members of a national religion whose rite of entrance
was public and nonecstatic. Differing institutional allegiances divided Jews into sects, but none were distinguished, so far as we
know, by initiations. Where we have evidence of initiatory practices,[73] we are dealing with subgroups that ecstatics formed within
sects. The "sons of the prophets" were only part of the cultic per-
sonnel at the Bethel sanctuary, as were the prophets of the Jerusalem temple. The ecstatic practices of Jewish prophets and
visionaries were not one-time initiations, but permanent ways of
life. Their successors, the mystics of Judaism and Christianity, perpetuated similar modes of social organization. They belonged to
their parent religions, kept the common practices, and had little use
for special—much less secret—rites. The mystics instead invested
the religious activities of their coreligionists with ecstatic dimensions. Ascesis, prayer, and scriptural study, for example, were made
mystical by being performed during ecstatic states. Mysticism was
developed into a way of religious life.

Gnosticism may usefully be regarded as a mystery that was in
process of developing into a mysticism. The social group that most
Gnostics acknowledged was Christianity. It was only their opponents who set them apart with the derogatory label *gnostikoi.* Yet
some of their texts, such as the Coptic *Gospel of Thomas,* were sufficiently Christian to divide modern scholarly opinion regarding
their orientations. The status of rituals varied among Gnostics. In
at least some cases, ritual terminology was metaphorized as a
means to discuss religious experiences. On the other hand, initiations remained esoteric, were not integrated with the practices of
noninitiates, and seem to have been ends in themselves, rather
than introductions to a mystical way of life.

Where Gnosticism broke company with Christianity was not in
the matter of ecstasy—for the heavens opened for the apostles, and
Paul even ascended into heaven (2 Cor 12:2–4)—but in the value
that was placed on the experience. Wilson remarked "that from Irenaeus to Harnack the traditional view of Gnosticism saw in it the
contamination of Christianity not through the mystery religions

but through Greek philosophy."[74] Christianity's problem with Gnosticism was not that it was a mystery, but that its mystery was heretical.

Gnostic Visions

Elaine Pagels noted that Gnostics recognized three sources of religious authority. They acknowledged "secret lines of apostolic succession, which relate visions and revelations given to the apostles, but shared only with the initiates." They followed "inspired teachers like Valentinus, whom they revered as visionaries." And they finally accorded authority to their own "spiritual experience and inspiration."[75] Irenaeus complained that "every one of them generates something new everyday, according to his ability . . . they ascribe whatever they recognize themselves as experiencing to the divine Logos!"[76]

Puech suggested that Gnostic narratives portray visions that have several typical features. "The scene is laid on a mountain, after the Resurrection; the Saviour appears in supernatural, luminous form; those present . . . are struck with astonishment and terror; then begins immediately a dialogue in the course of which the risen and glorified Christ imparts to His hearers the most sublime revelations."[77] Pagels noted, however, that these conventions are more often absent than present. "What is essential is the claim . . . to have access to continuing revelation through visions."[78]

Corbin drew attention to the "docetic" character of the visions in two Christian apocrypha that "were particularly esteemed and meditated upon in Gnostic and Manichean circles."[79] In Acts of Peter 20–21, Peter explained both the incarnation and the transfiguration as divine manifestations whose extents were adjusted to the capacities of their human observers:

> The Lord in his mercy was moved to show himself . . . in the form of a man. . . . For each of us saw (him) as he was able, as he had power to see. . . . Our Lord wished me to see his majesty on the holy mountain; but when I with the sons of Zebedee saw the brilliance of his light, I fell as one dead, and closed my eyes and heard his voice, such as I cannot describe, and thought that I had been blinded by his radiance. And recovering my breath a little. . . . And he gave me his hand and lifted me up. And when I stood up I saw him in such a form as I was able to take in.

Aged widows, who were blind and disbelieving, happened to be present, and Peter told them: "See with your mind what you do not see with your eyes; and (though) your ears be closed, yet let them open in your mind within you." After everyone prayed, "the room in which they were shone as if with lightning, such as shines in the clouds. Yet it was not such light as (is seen) by day, (but) ineffable, invisible, such as no man can describe, a light that shone on us so (brightly) that we were senseless with bewilderment." This light entered into the blind widows: And they said, "We saw an old man, who had such a presence as we cannot describe to you"; but others (said), "We saw a growing lad"; and others said, "We saw a boy who gently touched our eyes, and so our eyes were opened."

Peter remarked, "God is greater than our thoughts, as we have learnt from these aged widows, how they have seen the Lord in a variety of forms."[80]

In Acts of John 88–89, John and James were returning home after being away at sea all day, when they first saw Jesus standing on the shore. Jesus appeared differently to each:

> He came to me and to my brother James, saying, 'I need you; come with me!' And my brother said this to me, 'John, what does he want, this child on the shore who called us?' And I said, 'Which child?' And he answered me, 'The one who is beckoning to us.' And I said 'This is because of the long watch we have kept at sea. You are not seeing straight, brother James. Do you not see the man standing there who is handsome, fair and cheerful-looking?' But he said to me, 'I do not see that man, my brother. But let us go, and we will see what this means.
>
> And when we had brought the boat to land, we saw how he also helped us to beach the boat. And as we left the place, wishing to follow him, he appeared to me again as rather bald-<headed> but with a thick flowing beard, but to James as a young man whose beard was just beginning.[81]

Later in Acts of John 97–102, John could not bear to watch the crucifixion and fled into a cave on the Mount of Olives. At the sixth hour of the day, when Jesus was being crucified and darkness came over the earth, Jesus appeared to John in the cave:

> And my Lord stood in the middle of the cave and gave light to it and said, 'John, for the people below in Jerusalem I am being crucified and pierced with lances and reeds and given vinegar and gall to drink. But to you I am speaking. . . .

He showed me a Cross of Light firmly fixed, and around the Cross a great crowd, which had no single form; and in it (the Cross) was one form and the same likeness. And I saw the Lord himself above the Cross, having no shape but only a kind of voice; yet not that voice which we knew, but one that was sweet and gentle and truly (the voice) of God, which said to me, '.... This Cross of Light is sometimes called Logos by me for your sakes, sometimes mind, sometimes Jesus, sometimes Christ, sometimes a door, sometimes a way, sometimes bread, sometimes seed, sometimes resurrection, sometimes Son, sometimes Father, sometimes Spirit, sometimes life, sometimes truth, sometimes faith, sometimes grace; and so (it is called) for men's sake. . . .

But this is not that wooden Cross which you shall see when you go down from here; nor am I the (man) who is on the Cross, (I) whom now you do not see but only hear (my) voice. I was taken to be what I am not, I who am not what for many others I was. . . .

What I am is known to me alone, and no one else. . . . You hear that I suffered, yet I suffered not; and that I suffered not, yet I did suffer; and that I was pierced, yet I was not wounded; that I was hanged, yet I was not hanged; that blood flowed from me, yet it did not flow; and, in a word, that what they say of me, I did not endure, but what they do not say, those things I did suffer.[82]

In the Acts of Peter and the Acts of John, Christ was described as having a form that varied according to the capacity of whomever beheld him. It was as a purely spiritual being that Christ performed all the actions described in the Gospels. There was no hypostatic union, no God-man, no word made flesh. There was instead a word that had the ability to appear to have taken the form of flesh. At the very moment when the word appeared as flesh, it was also not flesh. It was scourged, yet it was not scourged. It was crucified, yet it was not crucified. It bled, yet did not bleed.

Corbin suggested that the conception of Christ in these apocryphal texts may loosely be termed "docetic." The conception was consistent not only with the early Christian heresy known as Docetism, but also with the conceptions of Christ in the Quran, the Imam in Shiite gnosis, and the Buddha in Mahayana Buddhism.[83] Corbin also noted the influence of this conception on Origen. In discussing the transfiguration in his *Commentary on Matthew,* Origen asserted that Christ appeared not two ways but three. Not only was he seen in his common way and as transfigured, but "he appeared to each one according as each man was worthy."[84]

The mystery of the cross of light in the Acts of John was its provision of the power of salvation to visionary practice:

The multitude around the Cross that is <not> of one form is the inferior nature. And those whom you saw in the Cross, even if they have not (yet) one form—not every member of him who has come down has yet been gathered together. But when human nature is taken up, and the race that comes to me and obeys my voice, then he who now hears me shall be united with this (race) and shall no longer be what he now is, but (shall be) above them as I am now. For so long as you do not call yourself mine, I am not what I am; but if you hear me, you also as hearer shall be as I am, and I shall be what I was, when you (are) as I am with myself.[85]

The cross of light was surrounded by a multitude of people, who had different forms in reflection of the different forms in which they saw Christ. The cross contained further people who shared a single form, which was the form of Christ as he was with himself. In other words, a vision of Christ that revealed the true form of Christ accomplished salvation by transforming the visionary into the form of Christ. Every vision of lesser accuracy accomplished a lesser salvation.

Corbin emphasized the psychological character of these visions. The visionary experiences were recognized as such. They were not regarded as perceptions of objectively existing external realities. The visions did not disclose the real appearances of otherworldly beings and locations in a manner consistent with the celestial journeys of Jewish and Christian apocalyptists. Gnostics did not see Jesus as he was to himself, but only as he chose momentarily to appear to the Gnostics. Their understanding of the heavens was consistent. Visions were subjective experiences whose form varied from moment to moment and individual to individual. On the other hand, the visions were not allegorical; they were not consistent with Christian mysticism, Talmudic tradition,[86] Hermetism, or Neo-Aristotelianism. In these texts, because the visions were caused by Christ, whatever they portrayed was Christ—and yet was also not Christ. It was Christ "as toward men," but it was not Christ as he was "with himself."

Like most ancient documents, Gnostic texts seldom report visions in the name of historical individuals. By far the majority of visionary narratives ascribe the visions to characters of myth or auspicious legend. Since the contexts of the alleged visions are plainly fictitious, most scholars have inferred that the visions are fictions as well. The portraits of visions in Acts of Peter, Acts of John, and equivalent texts are assumed to be unreliable; and their doctrinal implications are considered accidental.

In my own view, the equation of pseudepigraphy with fraud is both anachronistic and ethnocentric. It presupposes that theological integrity cannot exist in the absence of uncompromising truthfulness, as though myth, allegory, and parable had no honorable place in the history of religion. Pseudepigraphic visionary narratives are not reliable historical reports of actual visions, but they were never intended to be. They are mystical theologies couched in the form of narratives. Like the oral folkore genre that Lauri Honko termed the belief-legend,[87] pseudepigraphic texts ascribe visions to fictional characters not for purposes of imposture, but as exemplars of the living practice of visionary experience.

Several Gnostic texts that were discovered at Nag Hammadi describe visions that are consistent with those narrated in the apocryphal Acts of Peter and Acts of John. Jesus appeared to John in a succession of different forms in *The Apocryphon of John,* a text whose main teachings date before 185 C.E.:[88]

[Behold I] saw in the light [a youth who stood] by me. While I looked [at him he became] like an old man. And he [changed his] likeness (again) becoming like a servant. There was [not a plurality before me, but there was a likeness] with multiple forms in the light, and the [likenesses] appeared through each other, [and] the [likeness] had three forms.

He said to me, "John, John, why do you doubt, or why [are you] afraid? You are not unfamiliar with this image, are you?—that is, do not [be] timid!—I am the one who is [with you (pl.)] always. I [am the Father], I am the Mother, I am the Son. I am the undefiled and incorruptible one."[89]

Because Jesus' self-description as the Father, the Mother, and the Son refers to the trinity of Sethian Gnosticism, his visual forms as a youth, an old man, and a servant may not be correlated with the three persons of the Christian trinity. They attest instead to the versatility of visionary imagery in Gnostic conception.

Visionary experiences of variable imagery were given a mythological explanation in *The Second Treatise of the Great Seth,* a text with affinities to both the apocryphal Acts of John and the Gnostic school of Basilides. In order to evade the evil archons during his descent through the heavens to the earth, Seth assumed a variety of appearances: "As I came downward no one saw me. For I was altering my shapes, changing from form to form. And therefore, when I was at their gates I assumed their likeness."[90] As in the cross of light, each appearance of the son of man was appropriate to whomever envisioned him.

In *The Gospel of Philip,* a Valentinian work that dates perhaps to the second half of the third century,[91] Jesus appeared differently to each person who beheld him, because he appeared in a manner that was comprehensible to each:

> Jesus took them all by stealth, for he did not appear as he was, but in the manner in which [they would] be able to see him. He appeared to [them all. He appeared] to the great as great. He [appeared] to the small as small. He [appeared to the] angels as an angel, and to men as a man. Because of this his word hid itself from everyone. Some indeed saw him, thinking that they were seeing themselves, but when he appeared to his disciples in glory on the mount he was not small. He became great, but he made the disciples great, that they might be able to see him in his greatness.[92]

The variability of visionary imagery was not doctrinal alone. It was not an interpretation that was imposed on visionary experiences whose contents were themselves uniform. Rather, the doctrine arose from the very nature of the Gnostics' visionary experiences. Consider, for example, the visions attributed to the apostles James and Peter, immediately that the risen Christ leaves them at the end of *The Apocryphon of James:*

> Having said these words, he departed. But we bent (our) knee(s), I and Peter, and gave thanks and sent our heart(s) upwards to heaven. We heard with our ears, and saw with our eyes, the noise of wars and a trumpet blare and a great turmoil.
>
> And when we had passed beyond that place, we sent our mind(s) farther upwards and saw with our eyes and heard with our ears hymns and angelic benedictions and angelic rejoicing. And heavenly majesties were singing praise, and we too rejoiced.
>
> After this again, we wished to send our spirit upward to the Majesty, and after ascending we were not permitted to see or hear anything, for the other disciples called us and asked us, "What did you (pl.) hear from the Master? And what has he said to you? And where did he go?"
>
> But we answered them. . . . [93]

Although the pseudepigraphic narrative is fictional, its portrait of visionary experiences may be treated as a reflection of actual practice. Visionary techniques were apparently employed deliberately: "we . . . sent our heart(s) upwards to heaven. . . . We sent our mind(s) farther upwards. . . . We wished to send our spirit upward." The resultant experiences were said to have manifested to the bodily senses of Peter and James: "we heard with our ears, and saw with our eyes." The experiences were both aural and visual. It is possible that the visionaries did not resolve the logical paradox that their hearts, minds, or spirit ascended while ears and eyes continued to function. Paul too testified that he did not know whether he ascended in the body or out of it (2 Corinthians 12:2–4). A similar paradox was remarked in the *Gospel of Thomas:* "The kingdom is inside of you, and it is outside of you."[94] It is clear, however, that the visionaries knew their visions to be visions, even at the time of their occurrence. The visions did not involve deep trance states, in which anesthetized visionaries were oblivious to their bodies and physical surroundings. The arrival of other people, asking questions, was able to interrupt the visionary experiences.

A passage in *The Paraphrase of Shem* suggests the equivalence of divine light and thought: "I marveled when I received the power of the Light and his whole thought."[95] The equivalence of light and language, here as also in John 1:1, 4, likely reflected the psychological fact that single meditation techniques lead some people to experience visual images but others to experience verbal inspirations. In Gnosticism, where variations in religious experience were attributed not to the source but to the receiver of the revelations, visible light was equivalent to the audible word or verbal thought.

In common with several Jewish apocalypses,[96] Matthew 23, and much Christian monasticism, *The Apocryphon of John* portrayed solitude and grieving as means by which a visionary experience was induced: "[When] I, [John] heard these things [I turned] away from the temple [to a desert place]. And I grieved [greatly in my heart]. . . . Straightway, [while I was contemplating these things,] behold, the [heavens opened].[97] The topics of John's meditations were the descent and ascent of the savior—rational topics, consistent with a use of active imagination, but inconsistent with the monotony appropriate to the induction of trance states.

The Gnostics' texts were otherwise silent concerning their methods for inducing ecstasies. They tell us a good deal, as we shall shortly see, concerning the regulation and guidance of ecstasies that were already underway. To these ends, the Gnostics employed visualizations and meditations of types consistent with lucid hypnagogic states. It is uncertain, however, that they induced their ecstasies through hypnagogia alone. They may well have done so. They may instead have used lucid hypnagogia as an adjunct to other practices, such as sensory deprivation and psychedelic drug use, that induce compatible or related reverie states. There is no evidence of the latter, but because the Gnostics were secretive about their ecstatic practices, the possibility cannot be excluded.

With this caution, let us move on to the Gnostics' management of their experiences. The Nag Hammadi texts are consistent in presenting the idea that what beheld a vision, and might journey through the heavens to the Ogdoad, was not the soul but the mind.[98] Because the unknown God was both spirit and mind,[99] the human mind was generally considered spiritual. However, *The Gospel of Mary*, which dates to the second century,[100] contrasted the human mind with the spirit: "I said to him, 'Lord, now does he who sees the vision see it <through> the soul <or> through the spirit?' The Savior answered and said, 'He does not see through the soul nor through the spirit, but the mind which [is] between the two—that is [what] sees the vision'. "[101] The contrast pertained to the different functions that the human mind and the divine spirit had during visionary experiences and did not imply a lack of consubstantiality.

The soul differed. The Gnostics did not greatly value it. *The Gospel of Thomas* states: "Jesus said, 'Woe to the flesh that depends on the soul; woe to the soul that depends on the flesh'. "[102] The Gnostics allowed that the soul had a spiritual origin, but it later became contaminated and material through its contact with the body. "When the spiritual soul was cast into the body, it became a brother to lust and hatred and envy, and a material soul."[103] The soul was able to re-orient itself through repentance. The process was described in rather lurid language in *The Exegesis on the Soul*. The text probably derives from Alexandria at the beginning of the third century:[104]

> As long as the soul keeps running about everywhere copulating with whomever she meets and defiling herself, she exists suffering her just deserts. But when she perceives the straits she is in and weeps before the father and repents, then the father will have mercy on her and he will make her womb turn from the external domain and will turn it again inward, so that the soul will regain her proper character. For it is not so with a woman. For the womb of the body is inside the body like the other internal organs, but the womb of the soul is around the outside like the male genitalia, which are external.[105]

The soul's promiscuity and prostitution consisted of idolatry; the tract quotes Jeremiah, Hosea, and Ezekiel in some detail to this effect. The metaphor of the womb's location may be explained in similar fashion. Idolatry consists of a devotion to the external things of the material world. Devotion to God instead requires the soul's attention to the internal spirituality of the mind. The reorientation of the soul's womb consequently implies a practice of asceticism.

Although some Gnostics were libertines, most Gnostics, including those whose texts were preserved at the Nag Hammadi, instead made a practice of asceticism or abstinence.[106] The spiritual function of the practice was explained in a passage in *Zostrianos:*

> After I parted from the somatic darkness in me and the psychic chaos in mind and the feminine desire . . . in the darkness, I did not use it again. After I found the infinite part of my matter, then I reproved the dead creation within me and the divine Cosmocrater of the perceptible (world).[107]

Ascesis was not pursued in its own right as a sacrificial devotion. Ascetic behavior was a means to acquire the mental discipline necessary to a successful practice of ecstasy. Once Gnostics learned to distinguish among conscious experiences of the body, soul (*psyche*), and mind, they attempted to avoid body and soul while remaining with their portions of the infinite.

Occasional passages that might be taken to describe disembodied journeys while anesthetized in deep trance are better interpreted in other terms. Consider the following account of a celestial journey in *The Paraphrase of Shem:* "My thought which was in my body snatched me away. . . . It took me up to the top of the world. . . . I saw no earthly likeness, but there was light. And my thought separated from the body of darkness as though in sleep."[108]

The narrative states explicitly that the ascension was accomplished by the mind "which was in my body." It was only as the vision progressed that Shem is described as having lost awareness of his body. The phenomenon may be interpreted, I suggest, as a hypnagogic state that became increasingly advanced, resulting in inattention to bodily sensation.

In Gnosticism, the ascension to heaven was equivalent to a spiritual resurrection. *The Treatise on the Resurrection* states: "The Savior . . . transformed [himself] into an imperishable Aeon and raised himself up, having swallowed the visible by the invisible, and he gave us the way of our immortality. . . . We are drawn to heaven by him, like beams by the sun, not being restrained by anything. This is the spiritual resurrection."[109]

In *The Exegesis on the Soul,* the ascension and the resurrection both designated the soul's recovery of her original spiritual character: "Now it is fitting that the soul regenerate herself and become again as she formerly was. The soul then moves of her own accord. . . . This is the resurrection that is from the dead. This is the ransom from captivity. This is the upward journey of ascent to heaven. This is the way of ascent to the father."[110]

The resurrection was accomplished in this life, as a precondition for life after death: "Those who say they will die first and then rise are in error. If they do not first receive the resurrection while they live, when they die they will receive nothing."[111]

It was possible, indeed, it was the Gnostic objective to achieve immortality while yet in this life. "Whoever, then, is able . . . to confess the God of truth and agree in everything concerning him, he is immortal, dwelling in the midst of mortal men."[112]

The resurrection might consist of a "disclosure" or "revelation" of the dead, as, for example, in the disciples' vision of Elijah and Moses during Christ's transfiguration on the mount (Matthew 17:1–9): "What, then, is the resurrection? It is always the disclosure of those who have risen. For if you remember reading in the Gospel that Elijah appeared and Moses with him, do not think the resurrection is an illusion. It is no illusion, but it is truth!"[113]

A second sense of the term is indicated, however, by the many passages that refer to the deaths of Gnostics. *The Gospel of Philip* states that "Jesus came to crucify the world."[114] *The Apocryphon of James* had Jesus advise his disciples to seek death, in order to examine it: "Become seekers for death, like the dead who seek for life; for that which they seek is revealed to them. And what is there to trouble them? As for you, when you examine death, it will teach you election. Verily I say unto you, none of those who fear death will be saved; for the kingdom <of God> belongs to those who put themselves to death.[115]

A later passage provided the appropriate analysis. "It is the spirit that raises the soul, but the body that kills it; that is, it is it (the soul) which kills itself."[116] The soul was to experience death, while the spirit was to accomplish its resurrection.

The significance of the soul's experience of death was indicated in a striking passage in *The Gospel of Truth* that scholars have termed the "nightmare parable." The text dates possibly from the second half of the second century:[117]

> They were ignorant of the Father, he being the one whom they did not see. Since it was terror and disturbance and instability and doubt and division, there were many illusions at work by means of these, and (there were) empty fictions, as if they were sunk in sleep and found themselves in disturbing dreams. Either (there is) a place to which they are fleeing, or without strength they come (from) having chased after others, or they are involved in striking blows, or they are receiving blows themselves, or they have fallen from high places, or they take off into the air though they do not even have wings. Again, sometimes (it is as) if people were murdering them, though there is no one even pursuing them, or they themselves are killing their neighbors, for they have been stained with their blood. When those who are going through all these things wake up, they see nothing, they who were in the midst of all these disturbances, for they are nothing. Such is the way of those who have cast ignorance aside from them like sleep, not esteeming it as anything, nor do they esteem its works as solid things either, but they leave them behind like a dream in the night. The knowledge of the Father they value as the dawn. This is the way each one has acted, as though asleep at the time when he was ignorant. And this is the way he has <come to knowledge>, as if he had awakened.[118]

Sleep and awakening were used by the Gnostics as metaphors for life without and with gnostic understanding.[119] Scholars have assumed that the "nightmare parable" referred to the general human condition,[120] but something else was surely intended by the reference to taking "off into the air though they do not even have wings." The remark did not pertain to the content of a dream, but to an experience of ignorance that was analogous to a disturbing dream. This ignorance was not a simple absence of knowledge. It had positive content as "terror and disturbance and instability and doubt and division," which generated "illusions" and "empty fictions" that resembled dreams. The experiences evidently had visual content. The text remarks that "when those who are going through all these things wake up, they see nothing," as though they had been seeing something previously. The statement "sometimes (it is as) if people were murdering them" suggests that ecstatic death was among the disturbing visionary experiences.

The Gospel of Philip asserts that the ascension, which was equivalent to the resurrection, was a precondition of the Gnostic's experience of death: "Those who say that the lord died first and (then) rose up are in error, for he rose up first and (then) died. If one does not first attain the resurrection he will not die."[121]

The Gnostics of the nightmare parable did not spurn physical reality. Rather, it was a class of visions that they "cast . . . aside from them like sleep, not esteeming it as anything, nor do they esteem its works as solid things either, but they leave them behind like a dream in the night." The Gnostics apparently regarded anxiety-laden visions as products of the body's influence on the soul. The visionary phenomena were to be dismissed as material rather than valued as spiritual. Anxious visions were typical or normative for novices. "This is the way each one . . . has <come to knowledge>, as if he had awakened." The variety of anxiety-laden visions are consistent with modern evidence regarding anxiety attacks during reverie states.[122]

Gnostics coped with the experiences in a distinctive manner. In contrast, for example, with shamans who seek repeatedly to experience and to withstand visions of their deaths,[123] Gnostics sought entirely to avoid ecstatic death experiences.[124] *The Gospel of Thomas* explained that avoidance required an ascension to the unknown God. "Blessed is he who will take his place in the beginning; he . . . will not experience death."[125] Ascension to the Father was equivalent to an achievement of repose within oneself. "He said to them, 'You too, look for a place for yourselves within repose, lest you become a corpse and be eaten'. "[126] A poorly preserved passage in *The Dialogue of the Savior* seems to offer similar advice:

> When the time of dissolution arrives, the first power of darkness will come upon you. Do not be afraid and say, "Behold! The time has come!". . . . Truly, fear is the [power . . .] . . . . So if you are going to be [afraid] of what is about to come upon [you], it will engulf you. . . . look at [the . . .] in it, since you have mastered every word on earth. It [. . . take] you up to the . . . [. . . place] where there is no rule [. . . tyrant]. . . . [. . . you] will see those who [. . .] . . . and also . . . [. . . tell] you . . . [. . .] . . . the reasoning power [. . .] reasoning power . . . [. . . place] of truth.[127]

Fear was to be avoided, because it was fear that would "engulf you." It was instead appropriate to ascend above the rule of the tyrant, where reasoning power could be exerted.

Elaine Pagels noted that Zostrianos "tells how one spiritual master attained enlightenment, implicitly setting out a program for others to follow."[128] Its consecutive narrative of an initiatory sequence is sufficiently idiosyncratic that the account was likely drawn closely from life. After Zostrianos "found the infinite part" of his matter, he reproved "the dead creation . . . and the divine Cosmocrater of the perceptible (world) by preaching powerfully about the All." Zostrianos's intellectual conversion enabled him to gain control over his bodily appetites and conscious thought. The two exercises of self-discipline led him to recognize that he possessed a "sinless soul." He then grew "strong in a holy spirit." A vision then occurred, apparently spontaneously. "It [came] upon me alone as I was setting myself straight, [and] I saw the perfect child."[129] The child was the divine mind in visible form.

Zostrianos "pondered these things to understand them" and eventually decided to risk an experience of ecstatic death. "As I was deeply troubled and gloomy because of the discouragement which encompassed me, I dared to act and to deliver myself to the wild beasts of the desert for a violent death." The text does not say how Zostrianos proceeded to induce his experience. It tells us only that it was highly positive:

> There stood before me the angel of the knowledge of eternal light. He said to me, "Zostrianos. . . . "

> When he had said this [to me], I very quickly and very gladly went up with him to a great light-cloud. I cast my body upon the earth to be guarded by glories. I was rescued from the whole world and the thirteen aeons in it and their angelic beings. They did not see us, but their archon was disturbed at [our] passage, for the light-cloud. . . . Its beauty is ineffable. With strength it provides light [guiding] pure spirits as a spirit-savior and an intellectual word, [not] like those in the world . . . with changeable matter and an upsetting word.

> Then I knew that the power in me was set over the darkness because it contained the whole light. I was baptized there, and I received the image of the glories there. I became like one of them. I left the airy-[earth] and passed by the copies of the aeons, after washing there seven times [in] living [water], once for each [of the] aeons. I did not cease until [I saw] all the waters. I ascended to the Exile which really exists. I was baptized and [. . .] world. I ascended to the Repentance which really exists [and was] baptized there four times. I passed by the sixth aeon. I ascended to the [. . .] I stood there after having seen light from the truth which really exists, from its self-begotten root, and great angels and glories, [. . .] number.[130]

Later in the text, Zostrianos outlined five of his seven baptisms in close detail. Following the first, he stated, "I was purified"; following the second, "I became an angel of the male race"; following the third, "I became a holy angel"; following the fourth, "I became a perfect angel";[131] and following the fifth, "I became divine."[132]

The motif of baptism is notable. The rite of baptism had the esoteric significance of an initiation into the mystery of gnosis.[133] *The Gospel of Philip* stated, however, that the rite had to be performed in a manner that was attended by a spiritual experience: "If one go down into the water and come up without having received anything and says, 'I am a Christian,' he has borrowed the name at interest. But if he receive the holy spirit, he has the name as a gift. . . . This is the way [it happens to one] when he experiences a mystery."[134]

In *The Exegesis of the Soul,* the relocation of the soul's womb—that is, its reorientation from the body to the spirit—was termed a baptism. "When the womb of the soul, by the will of the father, turns itself inward, it is baptized and is immediately cleansed of the external pollution which was pressed upon it."[135] The seven baptisms of Zostrianos during his ascension formed a series of spiritual purifications. They collectively accomplished the visionary's transformation. Zostrianos outlined the process in two brief sentences. "I received the image of the glories there. I became like one of them." These ideas need to be unpacked.

A passage in *The Gospel of Philip* presented a coherent theory of variation in visionary experience. It drew on alchemical ideas that the Valentinian Gnostics adopted in the late second century.[136] The concept of alchemical transmutation, which alchemy had developed on the basis of Stoic philosophy, was here adapted to the explanation of visionary experiences. In the following passage the archaic term "dyer" described God as an alchemist and located his activity in the context of baptism in water:

> God is a dyer. As the good dyes, which are called "true," dissolve with the things dyed in them, so it is with those whom God has dyed. Since his dyes are immortal, they become immortal by means of his colors. Now God dips what he dips in water.
>
> It is not possible for anyone to see anything of the things that actually exist unless he becomes like them. This is not the way with man in the world: he sees the sun without being a sun; and he sees the heaven and the earth and all other things, but he is not these things. This is quite in keeping with the truth. But you (sg.) saw something of that place, and you became those things. You saw

the spirit, you became spirit. You saw Christ, you became Christ. You saw [the father, you] shall become father. So [in this place] you see everything and [do] not [see] yourself, but [in that place] you do see yourself—and what you see you shall [become].[137]

Gnosis accomplished salvation because gnosis consisted of the revelation of a *spermatikos logos* that caused the soul's transformation.[138] No longer are we speaking of the Stoic concept of a *logos,* such as a lion, that could be thought or imagined without transforming a human soul into a leonine one. Gnosis concerned *logoi* that produced transmutations of the soul. *The Gospel of Thomas* consequently equated transformation into Jesus with both Jesus becoming the gnostic and the moment of gnostic revelation: "Jesus said, 'He who will drink from my mouth will become like me. I myself shall become he, and the things that are hidden will be revealed to him'. "[139] *The Concept of Our Great Power* expressed the doctrine through Jesus' assertion that visions of his form were salvific: "everyone in whom my form will appear will be saved."[140]

The negative consequences of the doctrine were expressed in a saying in *The Gospel of Thomas:* "Jesus said, 'Blessed is the lion which becomes man when consumed by man; and cursed is the man whom the lion consumes, and the lion becomes man'. "[141]

The motif of the lion alluded to Ariel, "lion of God," which was an alternate name of the lion-headed demiurge Yaldabaoth.[142] The saying meant that the demiurge was blessed when he was transformed through a Gnostic's transformation, but a person was cursed when transformed and dominated by the demiurge. The path of ascension was a path of transformation through images; the path of descent was the entrapment of spirit in matter.

The Gnostic concept of the symmetry of visionaries and their visions was a necessary consequence of the construction of the world by means of images. Because they can be seen and envisioned, images are implicitly material: "Truth did not come into the world naked, but it came in types and images. The world will not receive truth in any other way. There is a rebirth and an image of rebirth. It is certainly necessary to be born again through the image. Which one? Resurrection. The image must rise again through the image."[143]

A similar distinction was made in *The Tripartite Tractate,* a work of the Valentinian school that dates to the first half of the third century.[144] "All the spiritual places are in spiritual power. They are separate from the beings of the thought, since the power is established in an image, which is that which separates the Pleroma from the Logos."[145] Spiritual places, spiritual power, and the Pleroma were to be contrasted with the beings of the thought, which entailed power in images. Images were the province of the *logos,* as the demiurge was designated in this document.

Another passage in *The Tripartite Tractate* identified the word, together with all that it supported, as thoughts belonging to the Father. Originally, they had no knowledge of themselves. Later, they were brought into existence—that is, the cosmos came into being— "as mental substance":

> They were forever in thought, for the Father was like a thought and a place for them. . . . While they were in the Father's thought, that is, in the hidden depth, the depth knew them, but they were unable to know the depth in which they were; nor was it possible for them to know themselves, nor for them to know anything else. That is, they were with the Father; they did not exist for themselves. . . . Like the word he begot them, subsisting spermatically. . . . The one who first thought of them, the Father—not only so that they might exist for him, but also that they might exist for themselves as well, that they might then exist in [his] thought as mental substance and that they might exist for themselves too,— sowed a thought like a [spermatic] seed.[146]

The distinction between truth and its images may be interpolated here. What has being, what exists, is an image. Its hidden or unknown depth is known only to the unknown God. The passage also implies that visions are expressions of ideas that are thought by the Father—even as the whole universe is nothing other than the "mental substance" of the Father.

As the Gnostics understood visionary experiences, visionaries and their visions were isomorphic. What a visionary beheld reflected the extent of the visionary's spirituality. Spiritual development was necessary before visions of advanced content could be seen. At the same time, it was impossible to advance in spirituality without a transformative vision to lead one onward. Gnosis had salvific transformative power, but gnosis became available only through revelation. The *Treatise on Resurrection* expressed this doctrine by reference to resurrection:

> But the resurrection. . . . It is the revelation of what is, and the transformation of things, and a transition into newness. For imperishability [descends] upon the perishable; the light flows

down upon the darkness, swallowing it up; and the Pleroma fills up the deficiency. These are the symbols and images of the resurrection.[147]

In *The Gospel of Philip,* transformation through revelation was the precondition of a successful ascent to the Ogdoad: "Not only will they be unable to detain the perfect man, but they will not be able to see him, for if they see him they will detain him. There is no other way for a person to acquire this quality except by putting on the perfect light [and] he too becoming perfect light."[148]

Successful ascensions to the Ogdoad were also possible, however, by magical means. The consistency of Gnostic doctrine was preserved by myths that narrated the revelatory origin of the magic. In *The Apocalypse of Paul,* a text that may date as early as the second century,[149] there were not eight heavens but ten. Instead of archons barring the way in every heaven, there were sinners being punished in the fourth and fifth heavens; and only the demiurge, in the seventh heaven, proved an obstacle. He was countered by means of a sign:

> The old man replied to me, saying, "How will you be able to get away from me? Look and see the principalities and authorities." [The] Spirit spoke, saying, "Give him [the] sign that you have, and [he will] open for you." And then I gave [him] the sign. He turned his face downwards to his creation and to those who are his own authorities.
>
> And then the <seventh> heaven opened and we went up to [the] Ogdoad.[150]

In *The Gospel of the Egyptians,* Mother Barbelo made a similar use of five seals: "[She . . . the five] seals which [the Father brought] forth from his bosom, and she passed [through] all the aeons."[151] The motif was more fully developed in *Trimorphic Protennoia,* which is dated to the first quarter or half of the second century:[152]

> And [he received] the Five Seals from [the Light] of the Mother, Protennoia, and it was [granted] him [to] partake of [the mystery] of knowledge, and [he became a light] in light. . . . These are the glories that are higher than every glory, that is, [the Five] Seals complete by virtue of Intellect. He who possesses the Five Seals of these particular names has stripped off <the> garments of ignorance and put on a shining Light. And nothing will appear to him

that belongs to the Powers of the Archons. Within those of this sort darkness will dissolve and [ignorance] will die. . . . And I proclaimed to them the ineffable [Five Seals in order that I might] abide in them and they also might abide in me.[153]

When they were pronounced aloud, the names on the seals had transformative powers to end ignorance, to permit passage beyond the archons, and to induce ecstatic death in the ignorant.

Religious transformations may consist of a cognitive shift in religious belief. Alternatively, they may involve integrations of belief and desire, so that the prospect of transgressing religious scruples ceases to be tempting. They may accomplish the reparative work of psychotherapy. They may also foster a growth of the personality toward whatever may be its standard of integrity and excellence. Gnostics may have been concerned with the full range of transformations. Their visionary experiences encouraged the manifestation of unconscious materials, and for doctrinal reasons they were eager for transformative insights.

Some Gnostic visions had the versatility of Jung's active imagination. Others were more consistent with the use of standardized motifs in guided imagery therapies. As in the modern psychotherapies, the work of transformation would have proceeded both consciously and through the latent or unconscious meanings of the images that the visionaries beheld. The effectiveness of stereotypical or standardized insights would have depended on their content and appropriateness, whether expressed discursively or only in symbolic manners. The signs and seals may have encouraged transformations, but it is more likely that the texts refer to ritual objects[154] whose magical efficacy depended on the Gnostics' belief in them. As sources of security and calm, magical objects may have helped Gnostic visionaries to avoid anxiety during their experiences.

Gnostic Unions

Several authors have remarked on the Gnostic practice of mystical union. Menard described it as a "technique of reaching the Divine through the Intellect or the *Nous*."[155] The experiences were of the type that scholars have termed "communion," "personal mysticism," and *unio sympathetica*. It proceeded by means of an interior dialogue. *The Gospel of Truth* discussed the experience as follows:

One who has knowledge is the one whose name the Father has uttered. For he whose name has not been spoken is ignorant. Indeed, how is one to hear if his name has not been called? . . . Therefore, if one has knowledge, he is from above. If he is called, he hears, he answers, and he turns to him who is calling him, and ascends to him. And he knows in what manner he is called. Having knowledge, he does the will of the one who called him, he wishes to be pleasing to him, he receives rest. Each one's name comes to him. He who is to have knowledge in this manner knows where he comes from and where he is going.[156]

The dialogue, which was a form of knowledge or gnosis, began as a divine call but developed into a conversation, an obedience, and an awareness that origin and destiny coincide in rest.

Although single ecstasies included both interior dialogues and the receiving of rest, the two phenomena should not be confused. *The Gospel of Mary* portrayed the achievement of rest as the culmination of an ascension past the seven heavens until release had been obtained even from heavenly types. The motifs imply a transition beyond the envisionable into the purely intelligible:

The fourth power . . . took seven forms. . . . These are the seven [powers] of wrath. They ask the soul, "Whence do you come, slayer of men, or where are you going, conqueror of space?" The soul answered and said, "What binds me has been slain, and what surrounds me has been overcome, and my desire has been ended, and ignorance has died. In a [world] I was released from a world, [and] in a type from a heavenly type, and (from) the fetter of oblivion which is transient. From this time on will I attain to the rest of the time, of the season, of the aeon, in silence."[157]

The motifs of standing and rest, which may be traced to Jewish apocalypticism, pertained to the supreme mystical experience in the Middle Platonism of Philo and Albinus and the Neoplatonism of Plotinus, Proclus, Gregory of Nyssa, and Augustine of Hippo. Different varieties of ecstatic experience were considered supreme by different Platonists,[158] and the Gnostic conception differed yet again. *Allogenes,* dating early in the fourth century,[159] connected the motifs of silence and rest with the unknowability of the One. The narrative began with an account of an ascension to a place of light, where the Gnostic was taught by the divine mind Barbelo. Some of the instructions concerned the universals—that is, the categories of intelligible thought. But others explained the meditations by which Allogenes was to encounter the unknown God:

When <I> was taken by the eternal Light out of the garment that was upon me, and taken up to a holy place whose likeness can not be revealed in the world, then by means of a great blessedness I saw all those about whom I had heard. And I praised all of them and [stood] upon my knowledge and [I inclined to] the knowledge [of] the Universals, the Aeon of Barbelo.

And I saw [holy] powers by means of the [Luminaries] of the virginal male Barbelo [telling me that] I would be able to test what happens in the world: "O Allogenes, behold your blessedness how it silently abides, by which you know your proper self and, seeking yourself, withdraw to the Vitality that you will see moving. And although it is impossible for you to stand, fear nothing; but if you wish to stand, withdraw to the Existence, and you will find it standing and at rest after the likeness of the One who is truly at rest and embraces all these silently and inactively."[160]

Barbelo began by advising Allogenes to recognize the silence of the unknown God and then to revert to himself—that is, to return his mind to his soul or life principle. Because the soul would be moving or unstable, there was risk of a negative development of the visionary experience, but Allogenes was not to fear. If he wished to stand, he was to turn his thoughts to the topic of Existence—that is, the virginal male Barbelo—who would be found to be stable, having derived his stability from the unknown God. The idiomatic expression "to be upright" or "to stand" was frequent in Gnosticism[161] and may here warrant a literal interpretation. An ecstatic who was able to stand upright was not then undergoing an anxiety attack. It goes without saying that standing upright while experiencing celestial ascent would have required a visionary state that permitted ongoing attention to the body: lucid hypnagogia, but not deep trance.

Barbelo's speech continued with advice concerning the revelations that Existence mediated from the unknown God:

And when you receive a revelation of him by means of a primary revelation of the Unknown One—the One whom if you should know him, be ignorant of him—and you become afraid in that place, withdraw to the rear because of the activities. And when you become perfect in that place, still yourself. And in accordance with the pattern that indwells you, know likewise [that] it is this way in [all such (matters)] after this (very) pattern. And [do not] further dissipate, [so that] you may be able to stand, and do not desire to [be active] lest you fall [in any way] from the inactivity in [you] of the Unknown One. Do not [know] him, for it is impossible; but if by means of an enlightened thought you should know him, be ignorant of him.[162]

Revelations were revealed by the unknown One through the mediation of Existence. Fear might arise, however, if the distinction between God and his hypostasis were unclear. It then became necessary to retreat from the experience of revelations in order to regain equanimity. Calm would occur once ignorance of God was reasserted—presumably because a feeling of humility would pervade the mind. In this manner, it would be possible to stand. What was to be avoided was the presumption that a revelation or enlightened thought might convey knowledge of the unknown One. It was knowledge *from* the unknown One, but it was knowledge *of* his hypostasis, Barbelo or Existence.

The Gnostic experience of communion with a transcendent God through the mediation of a manifest hypostasis had its parallels in pagan and Christian Neoplatonism. Plotinus understood experiences of union with the *nous* to indicate the transcendence of the Good.[163] Gregory of Nyssa regarded experiential union with Christ the word as the exclusive means of knowing the transcendent Father.[164]

The text of *Allogenes* went on to describe the Gnostic putting these techniques into practice and appreciating the many attributes that do *not* pertain to the superiority of the unknowable God.[165] Similar instructions were given in *Eugnostos,* a Sethian text that outlined a further doctrinal distinction: "Now if anyone wants to believe the words set down (here), let him go from what is hidden to the end of what is visible, and this Thought will instruct him how faith in those things that are not visible was found in what is visible. This is a knowledge principle."[166]

One began with "what is hidden," the human mind within the human soul, and proceeded to the Ogdoad, at "the end of what is visible." Divine "Thought" would then provide revelations concerning the presence of the invisible in the visible—that is, the hypostatic manifestation of the unknown God in the world.

The Sophia of Jesus Christ reworked the same passage from a Christian Gnostic perspective. There were no substantive changes in the ecstatic technique. "The perfect Savior said: 'Come (pl.) from invisible things to the end of those that are visible, and the very emanation of Thought will reveal to you how faith in those things that are not visible was found in those that are visible, those that belong to the Unbegotten Father'. "[167] The unknowing of the unknown God was accomplished while engaging in communion with Him. The unknown God did not become manifest, but the occurrence of an "emanation of thought" implied its invisible source, the unbegotten Father. The thoughts themselves were hypostases.

The Gnostics were led by their mysticism to appreciate all things as hypostatic manifestations of the unknown God. In *The Tripartite Tractate,* for example, the Father is described, among other manners, as:

> the power of those to whom he gives power,
> the assembly [of] those whom he assembles to him,
> the revelation of the things which are sought after,
> the eye of those who see,
> the breath of those who breathe,
> the life of those who live,
> the unity of those who are mixed with the Totalities.

> All of them exist in the single one. . . . And in this unique way they are equally the single one and the Totalities. . . . He is wholly himself to the uttermost. [He] is each and every one of the Totalities forever at the same time. He is what all of them are.[168]

Because all exists in and of God, all things are hypostases of the unknown God. A saying in *The Gospel of Thomas* proceeds to similar effect:

> Jesus saw infants being suckled. He said to his disciples, "These infants being suckled are like those who enter the kingdom."

> They said to him, "Shall we then, as children, enter the kingdom?"

> Jesus said to them, "When you make the two one, and when you make the inside like the outside and the outside like the inside, and the above like the below, and when you make the male and the female one and the same, so that the male not be male nor the female female; and when you fashion eyes in place of an eye, and a hand in place of a hand, and a foot in place of a foot, and a likeness in place of a likeness; then will you enter [the kingdom]."[169]

The language here was uniformly reductive of two into one, but the items whose unions were described were selected with care. The union of the inside and the outside, and vice versa, pertained to the paradoxical location of Gnostic visions. The union of the above and the below pertained to the unknown God and his hypostasis, the cosmos. The male and the female were another way of describing the same. The four exchanges—an eye in place of an eye, hand for hand, foot for foot, and likeness for likeness—expressed the concept of theosophy. A Gnostic's eyes were the eyes of God; a Gnostic's hand, the hand of God. Only in such a manner might the unknown God be known.

A saying in *The Gospel of Thomas* stated: "When you come to know yourselves, then you will become known, and you will realize that it is you who are the sons of the living father."[170] Another saying explained that Jesus, who was the first hypostasis, was the means of access to the unknown God. "Jesus said, 'I shall give you what no eye has seen and what no ear has heard and what no hand has touched and what has never occurred to the human mind'."[171]

The Western tradition of theosophy, which encompasses branches of both kabbalah and Sufism, as well as the art of Ramon Lull and the philosophies of Jacob Boehme and Schelling, discuss hypostases as a basis for inferences regarding their transcendent source. Apart from their cosmologies, the Nag Hammadi texts do not preserve detailed theosophical systems, but the seminal idea of a theosophical mode of cosmological analysis was already present in Hellenistic Gnosticism.

Among its various presentations, the Gnostic doctrine of theosophy was articulated as a philosophy of language. *The Tripartite Tractate* identified hypostases as names:

> Each one of the aeons is a name, <that is>, each of the properties and powers of the Father, since he exists in many names, which are intermingled and harmonious with one another. It is possible to speak of him because of the wealth of speech, just as the Father is a single name, because he is a unity, yet is innumerable in his properties and names.[172]

The hypostatic character of names was metaphoric. It was not possible to perform magic by manipulating names. The text entitled *Marsanes* explicitly rejected an idealistic view of language in favor of a representational one: "[Form] by [form], <they constitute> the nomenclature of the [gods] and the angels, [not] because they are mixed with each other according to every form, but only (because) they have a good function. It did not happen that <their> will was revealed."[173]

The theosophical implication of unitive experience was remarked in a saying of *The Gospel of Thomas*. It amended the notion that the Father was within all people, by asserting that the fullness was within them all. The fullness (*pleroma*) designated the second hypostasis, the many names of the aeons that together comprised the one name of God:

He said, "Go into your (sg.) chamber and shut the door behind you,
and pray to your father who is in secret" (Mt 6:6), the one who is
within them all. But that which is within them all is the fullness.
Beyond it there is nothing else within it. This is that of which they
say, "That which is above them."[174]

Gnostics distinguished visionary and unitive experiences as
two separate phases in their pursuit of gnosis. They attached the
motif of spiritual baptism to their visionary experiences of resurrection and ascension; but they associated their unitive experiences
with the motif of the bridal chamber. In *Authoritative Teaching,* the
sequence of the ecstasies is explicit. It was after the soul had
achieved her rising—that is, her resurrection or ascension—that
she went on to discover her rest in the bridal chamber:

But the rational soul who (also) wearied herself in seeking—she
learned about God. She labored with inquiring, enduring distress
in the body, wearing out her feet after the evangelists, learning
about the Inscrutable One. She found her rising. She came to rest
in him who is at rest. She reclined in the bride-chamber. She ate of
the banquet for which she had hungered. She partook of the immortal food. She found what she had sought after. She received
rest from her labors, while the light that shines forth upon her
does not sink.[175]

Although I am sympathetic to ethnopharmacological arguments regarding religious uses of psychoactive drugs, the Gnostic
rejection of the world of matter leads me to doubt that "the immortal food," the manna or bread of the angels, was an esoteric allusion
to a psychedelic, such as ergot. The soul's food consisted, I suggest,
of images and ideas that transformed her. The experience of rest, of
not presuming to know the unknowable God, was such a transformation. It made possible her experience of theosophical light.

The motif of the bridal chamber was metaphoric, but likely also
pertained to a Gnostic sacrament whose precise ritual details are
not fully understood.[176] *The Gospel of Philip* described the bridal
chamber as the restoration and identified it with the production of
the name or first hypostasis of God: "The bridal chamber and the
image must enter through the image into the truth: this is the restoration. Not only must those who produce the name of the father
and the son and the holy spirit do so, but <those who> have produced them for you."[177]

According to Irenaeus, the rite of the bridal chamber was said by some Valentinians to be "a 'spiritual marriage,' after the image of the conjunctions (syzygies)."[178] The *Apocatastasis,* "restoration," was an eschatological concept in Valentinian Gnosticism that referred to the reversal of the cosmogonic fall. The "unchangeable voice" and "thought of the invisible," through whose fall the world came into being, achieved her restoration through a provision of *gnosis* by her consort, the Christ.[179] The restoration of the individual soul in the bridal chamber was modeled on the restoration of Sophia[180] and presumably contributed to the world's end.

The association of unitive experience and the restoration of the female hypostasis whose fall gave origin to the world may also be found in *Zostrianos,* which is a non-Christian text:

> Apophantes and Aphropais, the Virgin-Light, came before me and brought me into Protophanes, (the) great male perfect Mind. I saw all of them as they exist in one. I joined with them all (and) blessed the Kalyptos aeon, the virgin Barbelo, and the Invisible Spirit. I became all-perfect and received power. I was written in glory and sealed. I received there a perfect crown.[181]

Chapter 7

The Recital of the Chariot

Ma'aseh Merkabah, the "story," "narrative," or "recital of the chariot," was a phrase used in Mishnah *Hagigah* 2:1 in reference to the Glory of God enthroned on the cherubim in the first chapter of Ezekiel. The phrase entered the Mishnah from synagogue sermons on the text of Ezekiel, but it was later applied to visions of the chariot throne by Jewish gnostics. Visions of the merkabah were a dominant form of Jewish esotericism from the second or third century[1] until the thirteenth century rise of the kabbalah.

Gershom G. Scholem referred to the visionary practice as both "merkabah mysticism" and "throne mysticism."[2] Several of the surviving texts that discuss merkabah mysticism use the term *hekhalot* in their title. The texts, which may have been compiled in the early Muslim period on the basis of oral traditions or literary units that were sometimes as much as half a millennium older, are consequently known as the *hekhalot* literature. The term has generally been translated as "palace" or "temple," but it is more coherent when understood in its original sense. In the Hebrew Bible, the term *hekhal* designated the vestibule or antechamber in front of the Holy of Holies within the Jerusalem temple.[3] Similarly, in merkabah mysticism, the seven *hekhalot* are sometimes fascinating locations in their own rights, but they remain preludes to the climactic unitive experiences.

The *hekhalot* texts attribute their teachings about heavenly ascensions to several rabbis of the second century. These rabbis, and not the authors of the texts, are said to have accomplished ascensions. However, the fictional format of the texts does not invalidate a critical assessment of the authors' knowledge of mystical techniques.[4] Just as it is valid to discern the authors' implicit knowledge of personality theory in the construction of many modern novels, so too we may fairly use the *hekhalot* literature as evidence of their authors' knowledge of mystical practice.

In recent years, several scholars have challenged Scholem's assessment of merkabah mysticism as "Jewish gnosis" or "Jewish Gnosticism." David Flusser's argument was nominalistic. Gnosticism had been defined by the fathers of the Christian church as "the rebellion against the God of Israel." By definition, then, Judaism and Gnosticism were mutually exclusive.[5] Flusser failed to consider, however, that this definition originated with ancient Christians and did not reflect the views of either Gnostics or merkabah mystics. It is true that the merkabah mystics were not world-renouncing dualists; but neither were some of the Gnostic authors of the Nag Hammadi library. In Scholem's view, merkabah mystics were dualists, but not of a world-renouncing or anticosmic type. They worshiped God as king and regarded the demiurge as a hypostatic "appearance of God on the 'throne of Glory'."[6]

Ithamar Gruenwald's objections to Scholem were more sophisticated. Gruenwald acknowledged the striking resemblances of Gnosticism and merkabah mysticism, and suggested that both religious traditions were historically derived from Jewish apocalypticism.[7] However, he contrasted the two movements sharply. Gnosticism was both antinomian (i.e., opposed to Jewish law) and anticosmic. It found salvation in secret knowledge that was revealed to an elite and concerned a heavenly ascension that occurred only after death. Merkabah mysticism, by contrast, was nomian, cosmic, and concerned with heavenly ascensions that were envisioned during mortal life and did not have the power of salvation.[8]

Gruenwald's arguments collapse, however, with my demonstrations in the last chapter that Gnostic ascensions were visionary experiences, and in the present one, that merkabah mysticism was indeed a path of salvation. The differences between the two traditions of gnosis—anticosmism among them—should not be permitted to conceal their generic resemblance. As I shall show, both Hellenistic Gnosticism and merkabah mysticism were esoteric initiatory adjuncts to parent religions. Both used lucid hypnagogic states. Both sought visions and unions, in a sequence that was considered transformative. Both regarded the contents of visions neither at face value nor allegorically, but as subjective realities appropriate to a visionary's stage of spiritual progress. Both attributed metaphysical power to language. Both offered salvation. Both ascribed the origin of their doctrines to a heavenly teacher. Both distinguished a transcendent God from his visible manifestations.

Another objection to Scholem's presentation of merkabah mysticism has been the claim by David J. Halperin and Peter Schäfer that the *hekhalot* literature is more magical than mystical.[9] These criticisms wrongly assume that the practices of magic and visions are mutually exclusive. Scholem, by contrast, always maintained that merkabah mysticism shared with both Hellenistic Gnosticism and the Greek magical papyri "a magical and theurgic aspect to the technique of ascent."[10] Halperin and Schäfer rightly emphasize that the *hekhalot* literature also discusses a type of magic that did not pertain to ascension. The adjurations invoked an angel, known as *sar torah*, the "archon" or "prince of the Law," to help in the exegetical study of the Bible. However, the *sar torah* magic was a visionary practice consistent with heavenly ascensions. The *hekhalot* literature derive from more than one school of Jewish mystics.[11] At least in *Hekhalot Rabbati*, "Greater Hekhalot," the *sar torah* materials were a secondary addition to a text that was originally concerned with ascension alone.[12]

Following the lead of Hai Gaon in the tenth century, most modern scholars have associated rabbinical discussions of the "recital of the chariot" with the contents of the *hekhalot* literature. It has been assumed that the secrets to which the rabbis alluded were committed to writing as the *hekhalot* texts. The *hekhalot* treatises have been pronounced rabbinical on the assumption that they explain enigmatic statements by various rabbis. Halperin has argued, however, that the terminology that the rabbis developed in exegetical and homiletic contexts, was given new meaning in the *hekhalot* texts. Moreover, the studies of rabbinic mysticism by Chernus and Halperin mainly bear witness to an allegorizing tradition, inconsistent with gnosis, but consistent with the interpretation of dreams by the biblical Joseph.[13] Much work remains to be done on rabbinic mysticism. For the present, however, it seems best to base my account of merkabah mysticism, so far as possible, on the *hekhalot* literature alone.

Techniques for Inducing Ecstasies

The Gnostic *Apocryphon of John* portrayed solitude and grieving as techniques to induce visions. Moshe Idel noted that the technique, which had been adopted from Jewish apocalypticism, was also employed by merkabah mystics. The technique was discussed in *Midrash Hallel,* a late midrash that elaborated on *’Avot de-Rabbi Nathan:*

> Who turned the rock into a pool of water, the flint into a fountain of water. We have taught that R. ’Akiva and ben ’Azzai were as

arid as this rock, but because they were anguished for the sake of the study of Torah, God opened for them an opening to [understand] the Torah. . . . And matters that were closed to the world were interpreted by R. 'Akiva, as it is said: "He binds the floods that they trickle not; and the thing that is hidden, he brings forth to light [Job 28:11]." This demonstrates that R. 'Akiva's eye had seen the *Merkavah,* in the same manner that Ezekiel the prophet had seen it.[14]

The midrash quoted a biblical passage that had used the Hebrew word *bekhi,* "weeping," in a context that required a metaphoric reading as "trickle." In the midrash, however, Job 28:11 was applied to R. 'Akiva, so that *bekhi* had to be taken in its literal sense, as weeping. The text described the induction of a vision of the merkabah.[15]

Weeping was also mentioned as an induction technique in *'Aggadat R. Ishmael,* an eschatological treatise.

R. Ishmael said: I devoted myself to the pursuit of wisdom and the calculation of the holidays and moments and of the [eschatological] dates and times and periods [of times], and I turned my face to the Supreme Holy One through prayer and supplications, fasting and weeping. And I said: "God, Lord of Zevaot, Lord of Israel, until when shall we be neglected."[16]

Although this passage portrayed R. Ishmael seeking to learn the era of the messianic redemption, the treatise as a whole was related to the *hekhalot* literature.

A close variant of the induction technique was portrayed in *The Vision of Ezekiel.* A midrash based on synagogue sermons that commented on Ezekiel's vision, it has often and incorrectly been counted among the *hekhalot* texts,[17] but it does contain several passages that were conversant with a living practice of merkabah mysticism. According to the text, Ezekiel's induced his experience by speaking in complaint and protest at the injustice of God.[18] The technique, which occurs in Job and several apocalypses, may be considered a variant of speaking lamentation while grieving or weeping. "No sooner did Ezekiel speak thus than the Holy One, blessed be He, opened seven compartments down below."[19]

Curiously, it was by gazing into seven netherworlds that Ezekiel beheld the seven heavens:

As Ezekiel gazed, the Holy One, blessed be He, opened to him the seven heavens and he saw the Power. A parable was told. To what can this be compared? To a man who visited his barber. After the barber had cut his hair he gave him a mirror in which to look. As he was looking into the mirror the king passed by and he saw the king and his armies passing by the door (reflected in the mirror). The barber said to him: Look behind you and you will see the king. The man replied: I have already seen. Thus Ezekiel stood beside the river Chebar gazing into the water and the seven heavens were opened to him so that he saw the Glory of the Holy One, blessed be He, the *hayyot*, the ministering angels, the angelic hosts, the seraphim, those of sparkling wings, all attached to the *merkavah*. They passed by in heaven while Ezekiel saw them (reflected) in the water. Hence the verse says: "by the river Chebar."[20]

This concept of seeing the heavens in the netherworlds is not paralleled in any *hekhalot* text.[21] Halperin noted, however, that Hellenistic Gnosticism regarded the material cosmos as a reflection of the pleroma in the primordial waters of Genesis 1:2.[22] So understood, the motif of the mirror in *The Visions of Ezekiel* may have intended a practice of theosophy: a drawing of inferences concerning God on the basis of observations of the creation.

Techniques for inducing visions were also mentioned in other *hekhalot* texts. *Maʿaseh Merkabah,* "Recital of the Chariot," referred to an unspecified practice of meditation. "R. Akiba said: Who is able to meditate on the seven palaces /and to catch sight/ of the heaven of heavens and to see the chambers of the chambers and to say I saw the chambers of YW?"[23] *Hekhalot Rabbati,* "Greater Palaces," explained that the techniques were so very effective that "all the *haverim* [i.e., the initiated] liken this to a man who has a ladder in the middle of his house, who ascends and descends on it and there is no creature who stops him."[24] *Hekhalot Rabbati* also provided detailed instructions. A string of meaningless names was to be recited one hundred twelve times:

When anyone would want to "go down to the Chariot" he would call upon Surya, the Angel of the Presence, and make him swear [to protect him] one hundred and twelve times in the name of Tootruseah-YHVH who is called Tootruseah Tzortak Totarkhiel Tofgar Ashrooleah Zevoodiel and Zeharariel Tandiel Shoked Hoozeah Dahivoorin and Adiriron-YHVH, Lord of Israel.

He may not do it more than one hundred and twelve times, or less, for he who adds or subtracts has his blood on his own head. Rather one's mouth brings forth the names and one's fingers count one hundred and twelve times. He then immediately goes down and [successfully] masters the Merkabah.[25]

The monotony of the technique may be expected to have induced trance states. This expectation is strongly supported by another passage in *Hekhalot Rabbati:*

> Rabbi Ishmael said: The members of the *Havura,* then, said to me: Son of the Proud Ones, you are as much a master of the light of Torah as R. Nehunya ben Hakkanah. See if you can bring him back from the visions which he has glimpsed. . . .
>
> Immediately I took a piece of very fine woolen cloth and gave it to R. Akiba, and R. Akiba gave it to a servant of ours saying: Go and lay this cloth beside a woman who immersed herself and yet had not become pure, and let her immerse herself [a second time]. For if that woman will come and will declare the circumstances of her menstrual flow before the company, there will be one who forbids [her to her husband] and the majority will permit. Say to that woman: Touch this cloth with the end of the middle finger of your hand, and do not press the end of your finger upon it, but rather as a man who takes a hair which had fallen therein from his eyeball, pushing it very gently.
>
> They went and did so, and laid the cloth before R. Ishmael. He inserted into it a bough of myrtle, full of oil, that had been soaked in pure balsam, and they placed it upon the knees of R. Nehunya ben Hakkanah. Immediately they dismissed him from before the Throne of Glory where he had been sitting and beholding:
>
> A wondrous proudness and a strange powerfulness,
> A proudness of exaltation and a powerfulness of radiance,
> Which are stirred up before the Throne of Glory,
> Three times each day, in the height,
> From the time the world was created and until now, for praise.[26]

This narrative portrayed R. Nehunya ben Hakkanah deep in trance and apparently oblivious to his environment. His fellow initiates did not wish or dare to arouse him from his trance through direct physical contact, so R. Ishmael resorted to the mildest of conceivable interventions. He produced a heterosuggestion, concerning the least possible ritual impurity,[27] and it sufficed to change the contents of R. Nehunya's vision. Once Nehunya had been dismissed from the seventh heaven, he returned to his fellow initiates.

Two paragraphs in *Ma'aseh Merkabah* indicate, however, that at least some visions of the merkabah mystics were experienced with open eyes while in the body:

R. Ishmael said:

> As soon as I heard from R. Nehunya ben Hakana my teacher this announcement (literally hearing) . . . I got up and asked him all the names of the princes of wisdom and from the question that I asked I saw a light in my heart like the days of heaven (or broad daylight).

R. Ishmael said:

> As soon as I stood up and saw my face shining from my wisdom <and> I began to detail off each and every angel in each and every palace. . . . [28]

R. Ishmael beheld a light in his own heart and on his own face. His experience of bodily sense perception was apparently uninterrupted by his visionary state.

These distinctions between two types of visual experience are consistent, I suggest, with the inconsistencies in a passage in *Hekhalot Rabbati* where R. Nahunya explained the difference between two categories of merkabah mystics:

> Now, the guards of the sixth palace make a practice of killing those who "go and do not go down to the Merkabah without permission." They hover over them, strike them, and burn them. . . . The mentality [of those who are killed] is that they are not afraid nor do they question: "Why are we being burned?"[29]

> Then we asked him: Who are those who are among those who descend to the Merkabah and [who are] those who are not? He said to us, *Those [who "go and do not go down to the Merkabah"] are the men whom those who do go down take with them, whom they then establish above and in front of them, and to whom they say, "Look carefully, see, hear, and write all that I say and all that we hear in the presence of the Throne of Glory.* These men, if they are not worthy of the task, are those who are attacked by the guards of the sixth palace. Be cautious, therefore, to choose men who are fit and tested *haverim.*" [italics added][30]

Those who both did and did not go down to the merkabah succeeded to induce visionary states that permitted the occurrence of ecstatic death experiences. The experiences were notable, however, for the absence of fear and logical reflection. The visions were consistent with the phenomenology of hypnagogic states. Mavromatis mentions "a lack, or considerable decrease of affect" and a loss of "reflective self-consciousness together with the ability to exert effort and think logically."[31] In lucid hypnagogic states, by contrast, the visionary materials coincide with a reawakened ego. Affect is intense, and logical reflection constant. The term "those who do and do not go down to the Merkabah" refers, I suggest, to visionaries who achieved hypnagogia without also achieving lucidity. They were unable to achieve the climactic form of lucidity: the experience of divine communion.

The materials that I have italicized may be treated as an interpolation by a later hand, by someone who did not understand the original meaning of the passage. For this author, those who went without going were not visionaries who were only partly successful. They were not visionaries at all. They were members of the audiences at séances that were held by those in trance.

The Water Test

Let us restrict attention, for the moment, to those who went down to the merkabah. They had to confront the ordeal that Gruenwald has described as the "water test." The Talmud, Hagigah 14b, related the following story: "Four entered 'Paradise': Ben Azai, Ben Zoma, Aher and Rabbi Akiba. Rabbi Akiba spoke to them: 'When you come to the place of the shining marble plates, then do not say: Water, water! For it is written: He that telleth lies shall not tarry in my sight'."[32]

Scholem asserted that "this famous passage . . . clearly enough refers to a *real* danger in the process of ascending to 'Paradise,'"[33] but his explanation was limited to a demonstration that the merkabah mystics so understood the narrative:

> But if one was unworthy to see the King in his beauty, the angels at the gates disturbed his senses and confused him. And when they said to him: "Come in," he entered, and instantly they pressed him and threw him into the fiery lava stream. And at the gate of the sixth palace it seemed as though hundreds of thousands and millions of waves of water stormed against him, and yet there was not a drop of water, only the ethereal glitter of the marble plates with which the palace was tessellated. But he was standing in front of the angels and when he asked: "What is the meaning of these waters," they began to stone him and said: "Wretch, do you not see it with your own eyes? Are you perhaps a descendant of those who

kissed the Golden Calf, and are you unworthy to see the King in his beauty?" . . . And he does not go until they strike his head with iron bars and wound him. And this shall be a sign for all times that no one shall err at the gate of the sixth palace and see the ethereal glitter of the plates and ask about them and take them for water, that he may not endanger himself.[34]

Because the term *pardes,* literally "orchard" but metaphorically "paradise," was shared by the Talmud, Hagigah 14b, with the account of St. Paul's ascension to the third heaven in 2 Corinthians 12:2–4, a considerable scholarly literature has been devoted to the "water test" of merkabah mysticism. None of the literature explains what was at issue for the merkabah mystics. Scholem recognized that once a mystic had failed the test and his vision had gone awry, it might result in an experience of "ecstatic death"[35]—that is, an anxiety attack during visionary experience[36]—but the significance of the test, with its distinction between marble and water, remains to be explained.

A partial interpretation of the images may be inferred from the *hekhalot* passages. The visions were evidently of such an order that a hermeneutic problem arose. It was possible to interpret the apparent content of the vision as the marble floor of the sixth heavenly palace, and such an interpretation made it possible for a visionary to walk across the floor. It was also possible for a visionary to doubt the reality of the marble, and skepticism about the visual experience would precipitate a series of patent illusions: a lava stream, a tidal wave of water, a vicious beating with iron bars, all of which he survived. This circumstance was consistent, I suggest, with the "pseudo-hallucinatory" character of lucid hypnagogic states, whose hallucinations are known as such during their experience. It was not consistent with self-hypnosis, whose "special reality orientation" reifies whatever happens to be its content.[37]

The *hekhalot* texts referred to a disturbance of the senses and intellectual confusion not because the envisioned images were incoherent, but out of opposition to their theological significance. Merkabah mystics desired to enter a marble palace in the sky. They did not want to know their visions to be fictions of their own improvisation. This circumstance resembles the position of Carl Jung, who expressed his "doubt whether we can assume that a dream is something other than it appears to be" and chose to "take the dream for what it is." Jung was well aware of Freud's "courageous attempt to elucidate the intricacies of dream psychology," but he stoutly rejected Freud's explanation of "the dream as a mere facade behind which something has been carefully hidden."[38] A comparable difference of opinion seems to have prevailed in antiquity.

Halperin considered "the purest, and therefore presumably the oldest, version of the 'water' test" to be a variant reading from *Hekhalot Rabbati:*[39]

> Because the guardians of the gate of the sixth palace [*hekhal*] throw and hurl upon him thousands and thousands of waves of water. Yet there is not a single drop there. If he should say, "What is the nature of these waters?," they run after him and stone him. "Fool!" they say to him. "Perhaps you are descended from those who kissed the calf and you are not worthy to see the king and his throne?" If this is true, a heavenly voice goes forth from 'Arabot Raqia': "Well you have spoken! He is descended from those who kissed the calf, and is not worthy to see the king and his throne." He does not move from there before they throw upon him thousands and thousands of iron axes [?].[40]

This version of the water test was precisely to the contrary of its majority significance in *hekhalot* literature. These images were self-evidently illusory. It was because the visionary found himself withstanding thousands of waves of water that he began to question the water's true nature. His questioning was prohibited by angels, who alluded to rabbinic midrashim that attributed the idolatry of the golden calf to a mistaken understanding of the merkabah. The midrashim asserted that the Israelites beheld an ox at the Red Sea, understood it as an aspect of the god of their deliverance, and worshiped it.[41] The analogy implied that the illusory nature of the waters was not to be investigated, and the angelic accusation was promptly confirmed by a heavenly voice. The very existence of a voice transcendent of the angels proved the error of deifying or hypostatizing the envisioned forms of the merkabah and the waters. An anxiety attack then followed.

Halperin noted that the water motif may be traced back, among other sources, to the "sea of glass" in Revelation 4:6.[42] But he overlooked the oldest instance of the water test, which occurs in Matthew 14:

> And in the fourth watch of the night he came to them, walking on the sea. But when the disciples saw him walking on the sea, they were terrified, saying, "It is a ghost!" And they cried out for fear. But immediately he spoke to them, saying, "Take heart, it is I; have no fear."

And Peter answered him, "Lord, if it is you, bid me come to you on the water." He said, "Come." So Peter got out of the boat and walked on the water and came to Jesus; but when he saw the wind, he was afraid, and beginning to sink he cried out, "Lord, save me." Jesus immediately reached out his hand and caught him, saying to him, "O man of little faith, why did you doubt?" (Mt 14:25–31)

Here as in the earliest *hekhalot* instance, the danger lay in reifying the water. It was only when Peter treated the envisioned substance as though it really were water that it ceased to support his weight. The later and majority *hekhalot* usage retained both the motif of water and the concept of a test, but reworked their narrative contexts until the danger lay in failing to reify the water.

The two varieties of water test each represented an attitude toward visionary experience. One interpreted the imagery allegorically, the other accepted it as a subjective reality. The two approaches may be traced prior to the rise of gnosticism in the apocalypticism of ancient Judaism and early Christianity. Both Jewish and Christian apocalypses may be divided into two basic categories: apocalypses whose protagonists journeyed into a netherworld or heaven; and apocalypses whose visions were to be interpreted in allegorical manners. Of necessity, apocalyptic journeys conformed with a mythological cosmology, but the allegorical apocalypses were instead able to make use of any imagery that came their way.[43] The three apocalypses that were canonized in the Bible all belonged to the allegorical school: Daniel, in the Old Testament; 2 Esdras (4 Ezra), in the Apocrypha (which form part of Roman Catholic bibles), and Revelation, in the New Testament. Allegorizing interpretations of visionary experiences became normative in both rabbinical Judaism and Christianity. Conversely, the mythological visionaries, the Jungians of late antiquity, seem to have been shunted aside. Excluded from the central political structures of the rabbinacy and the church, they became, in the Christian case, a heresy and a schism, and in the Jewish case, a marginalized and eccentric minority practice.

Managing Ecstatic Death

Merkabah mysticism produced a considerable number of prayers or hymns that found their way into rabbinic prayer books as early as the second and third centuries.[44] Several passages in

Ma'aseh Merkabah explained that the hymns functioned in gnostic contexts as means to regulate visionary experiences: "A person who wishes to make use of this great mystery, let him recite the angels who stand behind the holy beasts . . . and let him pray a prayer that they will not [destroy him] because they are more wrathful than all the hosts of the heights."[45]

The visionary's destruction by the angels of the sixth palace could be forestalled by means of an appropriate prayer. Reciting a prayer served to control the anxiety that would otherwise have led to an experience of ecstatic death. "He was praying that prayer which will rescue you from the judgment of Gehenom."[46] Because the prayers made experiences of visions possible, they functioned as petitions even when their words spoke praise. "Pray a prayer with all your power and the presence is friendly to him and gives him permission to catch sight and he is not damaged."[47]

The detailed management of visionary states by means of prayers was also portrayed in another passage of *Ma'aseh Merkabah:* "He said to R. Ishmael: How is it possible to catch sight of them and see what RWZNYM Adonai God of Israel does?" R. Akiba said to me: "I prayed a prayer of mercy and by this means I was delivered."[48]

The text of the prayer consists of nearly sixty lines of praise. The opening lines suffice to convey the poem's character:

> Blessed are you Adonai God great in might.
> Who is like you in heaven and on earth?
> Holy in heaven and holy on earth.
> He is a holy king, he is a blessed king.
> He is a king distinguished over the entire chariot.
> You stretched out the heavens, you established your throne.
> And the great name is adorned on the throne of your glory.
> You laid out the earth,
> You established in it a throne as a footstool for your feet.
> Your glory fills the world.
> Your name is great and mighty in all might.
> And there is no limit of your understanding.[49]

Immediately following his completion of this prayer, R. Akiba saw a vision: "R. Akiba said: As soon as I prayed this prayer I saw 640 thousand myriads of angels <of service> of glory who stand opposite the throne of glory and I saw the knot of the tefillin of GRWYY Adonai God of Israel and I gave praise in all my limbs."[50]

In *Hekhalot Rabbati,* the techniques for managing adverse visionary experiences were explained in a discussion of the terrors at the entrance to the seventh palace. The *hayyot* or beasts of the merkabah gazed at the visionary with their five hundred twelve eyes, and the mystic suffered an anxiety attack:

> The greatest [terror] of them all is the five hundred and twelve eyes of the four Holy Hayot opposite the gate of the seventh palace. [There are also] faces of human shape—and each "face" has sixteen faces—on each Hayah opposite the gate of the seventh palace.

> As soon as that man [i.e., the initiate] entreats to descend to the Merkabah, Anaphiel the prince opens the doors of the seventh palace and that man enters and stands on the threshold of the gate of the seventh palace and the Holy Hayot lift him up. Five hundred and twelve eyes, and each and every eye of the eyes of the Holy Hayot is hollow like the holes in a sieve woven of branches. These eyes appear like lightning, and they dart to and fro. In addition, there are the eyes of the Cherubim of Might and the Wheels of the Shekhina, which are similar to torches of light and the flames of burning coals.

> This man then trembles, shakes, moves to and fro, panics, is terrified, faints, and collapses backwards. Anaphiel, the prince, and sixty-three watchmen of the seven gates of the palace support him, and they all help him and say: "Do not fear, son of the beloved seed. Enter and see the King in His magnificence. You will not be slaughtered and you will not be burnt."

> Illustrious King, glorious King, masterful King, blessed King, chosen King, luminescent King, distinguished King, heroic King, sublime King, omniscient King, remarkable King, disciplining King, splendiferous King, majestic King, affluent King, eternal King, aristocratic King, infinite King, memorable King, worthy King, radiating King, living King, merciful King, pious King, valuable King, chaste King, righteous King, esteemed King, redeeming King, astounding King, adorned King, worshipped King, sympathetic King, commanding King, fervent King, comprehending King, possessing King, prosperous King, gilded King, faithful King, resplendent King, secretive King, wise King, modest King, benevolent King, patient King, embellished King, rescuing King, virtuous King, joyous King, radiant King, sanctified King, esoteric King, commended King, revered King, compassionate King, moderate King, attentive King, tranquil King, serene King, ornamented King, perfect King, supportive King, Blessed be He.

> They give him strength. Immediately, they blow a trumpet from "above the vault which is over the heads of the Hayot" [Ezekiel 1:25]. And the Holy Hayot cover their faces and the Cherubim and the Wheels turn their faces away and he stands erect, turns, and poses himself before the Throne of Glory.[51]

In order to cope with his terror at the eyes of the living creatures,[52] the visionary recited a string of phrases, each composed of a different adjective followed by the word "King." The words functioned to reduce his anxiety, restoring his trust in God. His vision promptly reflected his equanimity. Having ceased to frighten him, the angelic beings covered their faces or turned their heads away.

Although the phrases repeated the word "king," they were not hypnotic and would not have served to induce a trance. They were only partly mind-numbing or monotonous; they also required a considerable alertness in order to remember the many different adjectives in order to recite them. The combination of rhythmic inattention with highly thoughtful or alert attention is consistent with the phenomenology of lucid hypnagogia.

Vision and Union

The Gnostic doctrine that the contents of visions vary with the perfection of the visionaries had its parallel in *Maʿaseh Merkabah:*

> R. Akiba said to me:
> Were uprightness and righteousness in your heart
> then you would know how many measures are in heaven.
> He said to me:
> When I was in the first palace I was righteous,
> in the second palace I was pure,
> in the third palace I was upright,
> in the fourth palace I was perfect,
> in the fifth palace I arrived holy
> before the king of king of kings, blessed is his name.
> In the sixth palace I said the sanctification
> before the one who spoke and created and commanded all
>   living beings.
> so that the angel would not slaughter me.
> In the seventh palace I stood in all my power.
> I trembled in every limb and I said:
> You are the living and established God
> You created heaven and earth.
> Apart from you there is no rock.[53]

Scholem remarked that "this tendency to set the stages of ascent in parallel with the degrees of perfection obviously raises the question whether we are not faced here with a mystical reinterpretation of the Merkabah itself."[54] The motifs of the merkabah were not allegorized, however. They were considered imaginal. Like Platonic ideas, they were both internal and external, both subjectively achieved and objectively merited.

It is, I think, strongly probable that merkabah mystics were familiar with extrovertive unitive experiences: ecstasies in which sense perception of the physical world coincides with the idea of its unification by an intellectual consciousness. In *3 Enoch,* Enoch described his transformation into the angel Metatron as follows:

> The Holy One, blessed be he, laid his hand on me and blessed me with 1,365,000 blessings. I was enlarged and increased in size till I matched the world in length and breadth. . . . There was no sort of splendor, brilliance, brightness, or beauty in the luminaries of the world that he failed to fix in me.[55]

Enoch became coextensive with the cosmos—both the world or earth, and the celestial regions.

In extrovertive union, ecstatics have a sense of the spatial immanence of an intellectual consciousness in the perceptible world. Where we find doctrines that emphasize the cosmic extent of a spiritual consciousness—for example, in Proverbs 8:27–31, Middle Platonism, Neo-Aristotelianism, Hermetism, Mandaeism,[56] and rabbinical midrash on primal Adam[57]—we may reasonably suspect, even when we cannot prove, a contribution by extrovertive unitive experiences.

Having become Metatron, the "Prince of the Divine Presence," Enoch had access to universal knowledge:

> The Holy One, blessed be he, revealed to me from that time onward all the mysteries of wisdom, all the depths of the perfect Torah and all the thoughts of men's hearts. All the mysteries of the world and all the orders of nature stand revealed before me as they stand revealed before the Creator. . . . There is nothing in heaven above or deep within the earth concealed from me.[58]

The name "Metatron" likely derived from the Greek *metathronos,* which like the more common *synthronos* designated a co-ruler.[59] The name indicated that its possessor was to be distinguished from God.

These tales of Enoch may be understood both as legends of the past and as mythic precedents for the living present.[60] The narratives explained that the biblical figure Enoch anciently became the angel Metatron, whom a merkabah mystic might still meet in the seventh palace. The texts also signified that it was possible for a mortal human being such as Enoch, *or any other merkabah mystic,*[61] to be transformed into a macrocosmic being and to acquire universal knowledge.

The merkabah mystic's transformation into an angel was also expressed differently. In the so-called Ozhayah text, after the merkabah mystic arrives in the seventh antechamber, he is seated on a throne: "Look at the youth who comes forth from behind the throne to greet you; Zehubadiah is his name. He will take your hand and seat you in his lap. It is not only because you come with his permission; he seats others as well on a seat . . . that is fixed before the [throne of] glory."[62]

Elliot Wolfson noted that "youth" is a frequent epithet of Metatron. He concluded that "the act of sitting and the consequent vision of things divine indicates that at this moment the mystic has attained the rank of an angelic being and can thus see things which were hitherto invisible from the mortal perspective." Because angels ordinarily stand and do not sit on the throne of glory, "sitting on a throne . . . proximates divinization."[63] Sitting on Zehubadiah's lap may be treated as a metaphor that signified *unio sympathetica.* Single ecstatic reveries readily shift from moments of extrovertive union to moments of communion, and both may involve a sense of empathy (*unio sympathetica*) rather than identity with the divine. The empathy may be achieved, however, through union with a hypostasis (for example, the Shechinah, Metatron).

The hypostatization of the gnostic is also implied by the *hekhalot* literature's term for a merkabah mystic. *Yored la-merkabah,* literally "he who descends into the chariot," is to be understood idiomatically, in keeping with talmudic usage, as "he who enters the chariot." Since the chariot is the throne of glory, entrance into it implies an enthronment.[64]

Rachel Elior remarked that a "key innovation" of the *hekhalot* literature "pertains to the concept of *revelation,* which is no longer the divinely initiated communication of the absolute will of the Deity . . . but . . . the humanly initiated achievement of a vision of God and the celestial realms."[65] The introduction of a practice of extrovertive mysticism may have motivated the doctrinal innovation. Once the demiurgic hypostasis and the human became equivalent, revelation amounted to self-knowledge.

The enormous size of Metatron was mentioned in both *3 Enoch* and *Hekhalot Rabbati.*[66] A similar enormousness is the central topic of another text, *Shiʿur Qomah,* "Measure of the Body." *Shiʿur Qomah* may have had an independent existence prior to its inclusion within the text of *Merkabah Rabbah.*[67] Our present interest is with its significance as a component of merkabah mysticism.

Shiʿur Qomah speaks of *yoser beraiʾshit,* "the Creator" (literally, "the shaper of the beginning"), as a technical term for the demiurge, but does not identify him as Metatron.[68] Joseph Dan drew attention to the extraordinary character of the figures that the text provided. For example, "thirteen thousand times ten thousand, plus eight hundred parasangs is the height of his neck" and "the black in his right eye is eleven thousand and five hundred parasangs." *Shiʿur Qomah* did not assume a standard Persian parasang of slightly over three miles, but explicitly defined the unit of measure as ninety thousand times the width of the earth. The divine body was consequently unimaginable. Before the introduction of Arabic numerals and the zero, the figures were literally incalculable. Dan inferred that "the purpose [of the figures] is to prove that the divine 'body' is beyond all knowledge, transcending comprehension." He offered a similar interpretation of "the many hundreds of groups of letters which are in this work described as 'names' " of the parts of the divine body. Dan suggested that "probably, the names, like the numbers, were not given in order to impart definite knowledge but rather to convey the incomprehensibility of the realm of the divine."[69]

According to a passage in *Shiʿur Qomah,* the goal of merkabah mysticism was not simply an encounter with spiritual beings. Like Hellenistic Gnosticism, Jewish gnosis culminated in the mystic's salvation: "R. Ishmael said: When I said this thing before R. Aqiba, he said to me, Whosoever knows this measurement of his Creator and the glory of the Holy One, blessed be He, is secure in this world and [in] the world to come; he [lives] long in this world, and he [lives] long and well in the world to come."[70]

It is possible, of course, to interpret the verb "knows" as a reference to book learning. Perusal of the lore contained in *Shiʿur Qomah* would then have been the precondition of salvation. I suggest, however, that knowledge of the measurement of the demiurge was not considered possible through the mere agency of a text. The measurement was incalculable. It could only be known, I suggest, through a mystical union with the demiurgic world-angel.

Scholem raised the question: "Was there not a temptation to regard man himself as the representative of divinity, his soul as the throne of glory, etc.?"[71] I have not found evidence to such an effect.

I have also been unable to sustain a systematic interpretation of the various parts of the merkabah—that is, the human figure, the beasts, the wheels, and so forth—in terms of the parts of the human soul. The *hekhalot* texts do not seem to contain a doctrine of correspondence between the microcosm and the macrocosm. The reason for this circumstance is apt to have been the *extrovertive* character of their unitive mysticism. A merkabah mystic might enlarge to become one with the world-angel Metatron; but there seems never to have been a moment of introspective union, when the world collapsed into the mystic's soul.[72]

The mysticism of the *hekhalot* texts is coherent as a system of visionary and unitive practice, but it is defective as a system of myth. The texts exhibit comparatively little interest in the first five or six antechambers. Their narratives are instead preoccupied with the danger of panic that might occur, according to different traditions, in either the sixth or the seventh antechamber. The texts address the "water-test" that might induce panic, the hymns and hymnic recitations that might manage an anxiety attack, and the successful visionary's crowning—better, enthroning—achievement of extrovertive union. This scenario utilized only a portion of the older mythology of the Jewish apocalypses. There were no grand tours of the netherworlds and the heavens. There was instead a preoccupation with the throne of glory.

In a series of studies, Geo Widengren cited data on the heavenly ascension from ancient Mesopotamia, biblical Israel, Samaritanism, Gnosticism, Mandaeism, and Islam. For theoretic reasons, he interpreted all the data in a uniform manner that pertained to the ritual installations of divine or sacred kings.[73] The Mesopotamian and Israelite data amassed by Widengren sometimes pertained to the initiations of kings, but much more frequently attested to the experiences of priests and prophets. In late antiquity, heavenly ascensions sometimes retained an initiatory significance, but like religions in general, they usually acquired a pertinence to salvation. Whether ascensions took place in this life or at the beginning of the next, ascension was the precondition of an immortal existence among the imperishable angels. In rare cases, however, we do see the persisting influence of the ancient initiatory pattern. The chief instances in Jewish apocalypticism were both found among the Dead Sea scrolls. Celestial ascent accomplished the installation of a high priest in *The Testament of Levi* 2–4, and Enoch was given a mission as a prophet or seer in *1 Enoch* 72–82. In this context, merkabah mysticism's selected use of ascension mythology may perhaps indicate a debt to the Qumran community.[74] It may also or alternatively have been related to the royal ideology that surrounded the Palestinian patriarchate, prior to its extinction in 425 C.E.[75]

If most merkabah mystics proceeded as directly as possible to the throne of glory, the route that they took was determined by criteria that were psychological rather than mythological. Merkabah mystics sought much the same transformation that was discussed in the famous lines of the twenty-third Psalm:

> Even though I walk through the valley of the shadow of death,
>   I shall fear no evil;
> for thou art with me . . .
> and I shall dwell in the house of the Lord
>   forever. (Psalm 23:4, 6)

Alnaes and Grof have discussed in the context of psychedelic experiences,[76] and I have demonstrated regarding shamans' uses of sensory deprivation,[77] that experiences of ecstatic death ordinarily change character with repetition. As the individual adjusts to the prospect of dying, the idea of dying immediately—the first conscious element of the experience—ceases to arouse an anxiety attack and comes instead to be greeted with equanimity. In some cases, the equanimity turns positively joyous, and unitive experiences may ensue.

The Jewish gnosis of the *hekhalot* literature consisted of precisely this transformation, which was at once of the personality and its visionary experiences. *Hekhalot Zutarti* had R. Akiba explain to his students that a transformative process, which was indicated by a sequence of attitudes, resulted in salvation: "He said to them: 'My sons, be careful about the Name . . . For whoever uses it in terror, in fright, in purity, in holiness and in meekness—his seed will multiply, and he will be successful in all his ways and his days will be long'."[78]

The Angelic Character of Language

More emphatically than Gnosticism, merkabah mysticism attributed creative power to language. In *3 Enoch,* God provided the transformed Enoch with a crown, on which was written:

The letters by which heaven and earth were created;
the letters by which seas and rivers were created;
the letters by which mountains and hills were created;
the letters by which stars and constellations, lightning and wind, thunder and thunderclaps, snow and hail, hurricane and tempest were created;
the letters by which all the necessities of the world and all the orders of creation were created.[79]

These were no ordinary letters. "Each letter flashed time after time like lightnings, time after time like torches, time after time like flames, time after time like the rising of the sun, moon, and stars."[80]

The creative power of language was expressed in *Ma'aseh Merkabah* through the motif that God created the world by speaking:

You spoke and the world existed.
By the breath of your lips you established the firmament
and your great name is pure and elevated
over all the ones above and over all the ones below.
Privilege of the earth is your name.
And privilege of the heavens is your name.
And angels stand in your name and Just Ones feel confident in your name.[81]

Indeed, the text went so far as to assert that God is himself no other than his name. "He is his name and his name is him."[82] This doctrine may be considered a reification or concretization of the common Jewish reference to God by means of the circumlocution *hashem*, "the Name," or in Aramaic, *memra*, "the Word." *Ma'aseh Merkabah* took the doctrine a step further, however, for it described God's name as His means of creation:

Blessed are you Adonai, one God.
Creator of his world in his [one] name.
Fashioner of all by one word.[83]

If we assume that this doctrine is not to be understood in a manner that conflicts with the creation story in Genesis 1, but is instead to be treated as a commentary on it, it is necessary to infer that the one name of God contains within it all the names of all the things of creation.[84] And since God is no other than his name, God is equivalent to his creation. God is the one and the many together.

The doctrine becomes slightly less strange once we remember that it pertains to the creator—that is, to the demiurge beheld on the heavenly throne—as distinct from the God who manifests through the world-angel. The doctrine was a Jewish version of the *logos* and *nous* theologies that were common to Stoicism, middle and Neoplatonism, Christianity, Neo-Aristotelianism, and Hermetism. The world-angel was most essentially the intelligence that gives order and shape to the cosmos. It was the intellectual principle of coherence or reason by whom and through whom and in whom God made the world manifest. The world-angel is the name, in the singular absolute—the name in principle, or naming as such. The world-angel was the very principle of naming, created and creating by means of naming.

Slippage between the demiurgic world-angel and the God who manifested through him was consistent with the general status of angels. Scholem remarked:

> Fragments of *heikhalot* literature mention names like Adiriron, Zoharariel, Zavodiel, Ta'zash, Akhtriel. . . . The formula "the Lord, God of Israel" is very often added to the particular name, but many of the chief angels also have this added to their name . . . so it cannot be deduced from this whether the phrase refers to the name of an angel or to the name of God. Sometimes the same name serves to designate both God and an angel.[85]

The *hekhalot* texts do not permit conclusive statement, but I doubt that angels were conceived as objectively existing beings who went about their own affairs whether or not they were observed by visionaries. Rather, I suspect that merkabah mysticism perpetuated the concept that had been expressed in the Hebrew Bible under the term *temunah*, "likeness" (Numbers 12:8 and parallels). The concept may be compared with the Homeric *eidolon*, which pertained to the image or representation of a god that occurred in a dream or vision. The visual image was a perception not of the god, but of a symbolic image that the god conveyed to the visionary.[86] In similar fashion, Zechariah (3:1–10) envisioned an angel of Yahweh who spoke the words of Yahweh on Yahweh's behalf. So understood, a Hebrew angel was a theophanic figure or character within a vision or dream, whose existence was limited to the duration of its visual experience. An angel was a vehicle or agency of divine revelation. It was a manifestation of God's power and will, but it did not exist outside the spirit, soul, or mind that beheld it. As a hypostatic manifestation of God, an angel might be named by reference to God; but there was no need to trouble about distinguishing God from his angels. Angels had no existence outside revelations.

Philip S. Alexander argued that merkabah mysticism differed from Hellenistic Gnosticism, among other manners, in having no myth of a redeemer figure.[87] The observation is an overstatement, but it points toward an important distinction. The so-called re- deemer figures of Gnosticism were teachers of gnosis. They did not save gnostics. They taught the means by which gnostics might save themselves. The *hekhalot* literature contained a related but differ- ent conception. No heavenly being descended to earth to teach the gnosis of salvation. Enoch in *3 Enoch* was at most a trace remainder of such a concept. However, once the rabbinic protagonists arrived on high, they encountered angels, some of whom functioned as teachers of gnosis. In most cases, these angels were equivalent to the angelic guides and interpreters of Jewish apocalypticism. How- ever, at least Metatron in *Hekhalot Zutarti*[88] and *3 Enoch* had a double role (consistent with Hermes Trismegistus in Hermetism) as both an angelic teacher of gnosis and the demiurgic world-angel with whom salvific union was sought. Moreover, the *hekhalot* phi- losophy of language implied that all angels were in some sense man- ifestations not only of God, but also of God's primary manifestation, the demiurge. This doctrine was rendered explicit in *Hekhalot Rab- bati,* where ʿAnafiʾel, a gatekeeper of the seventh palace, was named by reference to the demiurge: "He resembles the demiurge. As it is pointed out about the demiurge: 'His glory covers the firma- ment) (*Habakkuk* iii,3), so it is also with ʿAnafiʾel, the minister, who is a servant that is called after the name of his master."[89]

The linguistic nature of the world-angel—that is, of God's man- ifestation within creation—did not place God's creative power at human disposal. The theology went far, however, toward explaining the power that language exhibited in determining and shaping the contents of visionary experiences. The theology validated the induc- tion and management of visionary experiences not only by prayer, but also by deliberate linguistic commands. It also furnished a par- tial theory by which to explain the workings of magic.

Magic

The magical practices of the merkabah mystics were primarily verbal. They consisted almost entirely of "incantations (or hymns), the sayings of names, charms and magical seals."[90] Gruenwald re- marked that "where autohypnotic and autosuggestive experiences were cultivated, one could expect to find the suitable soil for the theurgical and magical seeds to grow."[91] Within these general limits, *hekhalot* magic may be divided loosely into three classes of phenomena. The first consisted of names that generally had no etymological or linguistic coherence, but nevertheless functioned as words of power during visionary experiences. In the following passage from *Ma'aseh Merkabah,* for example, the names of two angels had magical function as passwords:

> When I ascended to the first palace, a prayer ... I prayed and I saw from the palace ... of the first firmament up to the palace of the seventh firmament and as soon as I ascended to the seventh palace I recited (the names of) two angels and I gazed at above the Seraphim and these are them STR HGLYWN. And as soon as I recited their names they came and grabbed me and they said to me: Human, do not be afraid. He is the holy king, for he is holy over the throne, high and exalted, and he is chosen forever and distinguished over the chariot.[92]

The magical names designated either angels or aspects of the godhead and were described as seals that were to be shown as passports to the angelic gatekeepers of the seven palaces. Seals with equivalent functions were also mentioned in various Hellenistic Gnostic texts,[93] and ritual objects may indeed have been used during ascension experiences. In trance states much more efficiently than in lucid hypnagogia, the rote association of names or ritual objects with expected narrative scenarios would have functioned to produce the desired visionary experiences.

Most of the magic in the *hekhalot* literature was not employed in the context of ascensions. Instructions for invoking the *sar torah,* "prince of the torah," depended on the names of angels and were comparatively simple acts of conjuring. Little or no ritual was involved, and the purpose of the magic was angelic aid in committing the exegeses of scripture to memory. It is significant, however, that the experiences were equivalent to visions. In *Merkabah Rabbah,* R. Ishmael said of his *sar torah* practice: "everyday it seemed to me as if I was standing before the Throne of the Glory."

Efforts to invoke the *sar torah* were also able to induce verbal revelations:

> R. Ishmael said: I was 13 years old and my heart was moved every day I was worn down in a fast. As soon as R. Nehunya ben Hakana revealed the Prince of the Torah, SWYR' Prince of the Countenance

revealed (himself), he said to me: Prince of the Torah YWPY'L is his name and everyone who seeks is revealed to me.[94]

R. Ishmael said: I sat 12 days fasting when I saw that I could not (?) I made use of the [name] of the 42 letters and PYWYQRT <and> the angel of the Countenance came down in displeasure. He said to me: Emptyhead! I will not give over until you will sit for forty days. Immediately I was frightened and I recited the three letters and he went up.[95]

Scholem suggested that the *sar torah* materials were a late replacement of merkabah mysticism, deriving from an era when visionary ascensions had been augmented or largely replaced by practices of magic.[96] The notion of augmentation warrants emphasis. The visionary ascensions and extrovertive unions constituted an initiation. The addition of further practices, which might be performed after initiation had been completed, was a historical development beyond the model of a mystery, toward the model of a mysticism.

There are no grounds for the assumption that the *sar torah* magic replaced visionary ascensions over the course of the centuries. Halperin noted an ascension that had the acquisition of a *sar torah* as its goal, and he concluded that the *hekhalot* texts originated not "in any esoteric clique, but among the Jewish masses," "far removed from the rabbinic intelligentsia," as a quick and easy means to achieve mastery of the Torah.[97] Although the passages do not permit conclusive demonstration of the procedures involved, the mnemic function of *sar torah* experiences was presumably produced by posthypnotic suggestions during trance states.

A third type of magic is represented by *Sefer Ha-Razim,* the "Book of the Mysteries."[98] Its collection of magical recipes is not ordinarily counted among the *hekhalot* literature nor regarded as a text of merkabah mysticism. Unlike the *hekhalot* literature, *Sefer ha-Razim's* blend of ritual and conjuring resembles the Greek and Demotic magical papyri.[99] The two traditions of Jewish magic had, however, a generic resemblance. Like merkabah mysticism, *Sefer ha-Rasim* was heir to the world of Jewish apocalypticism. Where the *hekhalot* literature located angels in seven antechambers within God's palace, *Sefer ha-Razim* organized its magical recipes in a sequence that proceeds from the angels of the first to the seventh heaven. Several of the recipes also took for granted at least some sort of visionary experience.

The magic of the Greek and Demotic magical papyri depended extensively on dreams,[100] on visions that were most likely of self-hypnotic character,[101] on visions that were induced, most probably through hetero-hypnosis, in young boys who were ritually pure,[102] and only very rarely on hypnapompic states.[103] *Sefer Ha-Razim* was generally less informative concerning presuppositions, but it several times described brief visions that were consistent with a practice of self-hypnosis. Consider the following passages:

> When you finish repeating the adjuration twenty-one times, look up and you will see (something) like a coal of fire descending into the blood and wine.[104]

> If you wish to question a ghost; stand facing a tomb and repeat the names of the angels of the fifth encampment. . . .
>
> He should appear immediately. But if he does not, repeat the adjuration a second time (and) up to three times. When he appears set the flask before him and after this speak your words.[105]

> If you wish to speak with the spirits, go out to "the place of the killed" and call out there in a singsong, whimpering way. . . .
>
> If you see opposite you a column of smoke, speak your words and send (her) for whatever purpose you wish.[106]

> You will see that a pillar of fire will appear to you with a cloud on it like the image of a man. Question him and he will tell you whatever you ask.[107]

> On the seventh day stand facing (the sun) when he rises and burn incense of spices weighing three shekels before him, and invoke seven times the name of the angels that lead him during the day. Then if you are not answered after these seven times, go and invoke. . . .
>
> At the completion of your adjuration, you will see him in his bridal chamber and you can ask him (to foretell questions) of death or life, good or evil.[108]

> If you wish to see the sun during the night. . . .
>
> When you finish speaking, you will hear a peal of thunder from the north and you will see something like lightning come forth and light up the earth before you. And after you see him, you

will assuredly bow down to the ground and fall upon your face to the earth and pray. . . .

Then stand up and you will see (the sun) in the north proceeding to the east. After this, put your hands behind you, and bow your head low, and ask whatever you desire.[109]

When you finish speaking the adjuration, you will see something like fog and smoke before you.[110]

These magical recipes described very brief visions that occurred as responses or answers to the magicians' performances of magical ritual and invocation. The visionary experiences were regarded as signs confirming that the magical procedures were functioning properly. The visionary episodes were not points of departure for further visions that concerned other events, beings, or sceneries. The full contents of the magicians' visions were determined by the expectations inculcated by the recipes in *Sefer Ha-Razim*. The visions did not depend on unconscious manifestations. They were autosuggestive in character and could most easily have been produced through a use of self-hypnotic trances.

Chapter 8

Muhammad and his Mi'raj

Islamic tradition dates the call of Muhammad to the month of Ramadan in the year 610 C.E., when Muhammad was about forty years of age. The Muslim calendar begins in 622 with the *Hijra,* "flight" or "migration," when Muhammad and his followers emigrated from Mecca to Medina. Muhammad first led Islam into war at the battle of Badr in 624, when he gained a victory against the superior forces of the Quraysh of Mecca. Islam suffered a serious defeat at Uhud in 625, but by 628 the Muslim position had sufficiently improved that the Meccans accorded Muhammad a treaty. In 630, the Muslims occupied Mecca almost without opposition and converted the entire population. Muhammad died in 632.

The Quran, the holy book of Islam, is a collection of prophecies that were revealed to Muhammad over the twenty-year period of his public activities. If, as scholars believe, the term Quran derives from the Syriac *qeryana,* which named the scripture readings of the Christian church,[1] Muhammad would have used the Quranic prophecies as texts for public devotion from the beginning of his career. The individual prophecies were preserved orally until their collection, according to Muslim tradition, after Muhammad's death. Critical scholars instead favor the view that Muhammad himself organized much or all of the collection at a late point in his career.

The further historical evidence of Muhammad is considerably less reliable. The extant biographical traditions and sayings of Muhammad were earliest recorded one and three centuries, respectively, after his death.

Modern scholarship on Muhammad has reflected the changing political relations of Euro-American and Muslim cultures. A period of imperial chauvinism, now known as Orientalism, has been followed in many quarters by a period of inordinate solicitude for Muslim sensibilities. Because Muslims view the Quran as a perfect and faultless incarnation on earth of the preexistent word of God, it is not surprising that a great deal of obscurity surrounds the actual, historical, and only too human circumstances of Muhammad's experience of prophecy.

The Revelation of the Quran

The Quran uses three terms for revelation. *Nazzala* and *anzala* both mean "to send down" and invoke the notion that revelations were sent down from heaven.[2] The third term was the verb *awha,* "reveal," together with its cognate noun *wahy,* "revelation." Richard Bell noted that *wahy* often refers to a practical line of conduct, such as Noah's instruction to build the ark (11.36/8f;23.27), or Moses' instruction to strike the sea and the rock with his staff (7.160; 16.123/4). When the term refers to a doctrine,—for example, "Your god is one God" (18.110; 21.108; 41.5), the "formulations . . . are always quite short, the sort of phrase . . . which might flash into a person's mind after consideration of a question, as the decision and summing up of the matter."[3] Where the term pertains to lengthy narratives, Bell contended, it does not necessarily pertain to their verbal communication, but perhaps only to their idea.

A problem is presented, however, by the Muslim tradition that *wahy* consisted of Gabriel's mediation to Muhammad of the actual words recorded in the Quran. Although the Quran exhibits the rhymed prose of a master of Arabic style, its ideas frequently lapse into momentary incoherence. Because the collation of the various prophecies into the extant book introduced many abrupt disjunctures, modern scholars generally attribute the cryptic, allusive, or enigmatic element of the texts, so far as is reasonable, to the accidents of collation.

The problem of the prophecies' style remains. The Quran indulges in mystification in order to impress its audience,[4] and some of its allusions have of course become obscure through the passage of time. There are also many points, however, at which the Quran lapses into incoherence. The Quran admits that not even Muhammad understood it all. The third sura states:

> Some of its verses are precise in meaning—they are the foundation of the Book—and others ambiguous. Those whose hearts are infected with disbelief follow the ambiguous part, so as to create dissension by seeking to explain it. But no one knows its meaning except God. (sura 3:7)

Bell attempted to explain the incoherent elements of the Quran by supposing that Muhammad's inspirations were routinely non-verbal and difficult to express in words. He further supposed that Muhammad experienced brief inspirations but elaborated them into the extant verses of the Quran on his own initiative. He acknowledged, however, that one Quranic verse cannot be reconciled with his theory. Distinctly verbal communications are indicated by the verse, "God does not speak to man except by *wahy*" (sura 42.50).[5]

In my own view, Muslim tradition may have the right of the matter.[6] The Quran may indeed record prophecies as Muhammad received them, to the best of his ability to report and collate them. It does not contain Muhammad's understanding or commentary on his prophecies. We have only the texts themselves. Incoherence that is not to be attributed to accidents of the verses' collection are consequently to be traced to Muhammad's prophetic experiences.

A good example of the conflictual character of Muhammad's prophecies may be seen in the sura al-Anfal, "The Spoils," which "came down" immediately following the victory at Badr. Although the text was written as a monologue, the text divides easily into a dialogue between two voices that engage in a quarrel. One voice expresses the desires of Muhammad's self-seeking will or ego, the other reflects his conscience:

[Will:] They ask you about the spoils. Say: "The spoils belong to God and the Apostle. Therefore have fear of God and end your disputes. Obey God and His apostle, if you are true believers."

[Conscience:] The true believers are those whose hearts are filled with awe at the mention of God, and whose faith grows stronger as they listen to His revelations. They are those who put their trust in their Lord, pray steadfastly, and bestow in alms from that which We have given them. Such are the true believers. They will be exalted and forgiven by their Lord, and a generous provision shall be made for them.

[Will:] Your Lord bade you leave your home to fight for justice, but some of the faithful were reluctant.

[Conscience:] They argued with you about the truth that had been revealed, as though they were being led to certain death while they looked on.

[Will:] God promised you victory over one of the two bands, [Conscience:] but it was your wish to take possession of the one that was unarmed. [Will:] He sought to fulfil His promise and to rout the unbelievers, so that Truth should triumph and falsehood be discomfited, though the wrongdoers wished otherwise.

When you prayed to your Lord for help, He answered: "I am sending to your aid a thousand angels in their ranks."

[Conscience:] By this good news God sought to reassure your hearts, for victory comes only from God; God is mighty and wise.

[Will:] You were overcome by sleep, a token of His protection. [Conscience:] He sent down water from the sky to cleanse you and to purify you of Satan's filth, to strengthen your hearts and to steady your footsteps.

[Will:] God revealed His will to the angels, saying: "I shall cast terror into the hearts of the infidels. Strike off their heads, strike off the very tips of their fingers!"

That was because they defied God and His apostle. He that defies God and His apostle shall be sternly punished by God. We said to them: "Taste this. The scourge of the Fire awaits the unbelievers." (sura 8.1–14)[7]

In communion experiences, such as those of the Hebrew prophet Jeremiah,[8] the Jewish apocalyptists of late antiquity,[9] Hellenistic Gnostics' bridal chamber, and much modern American Pentacostalism, the distinction between the two internal voices is evident to the ecstatics. They do not confuse the two voices, and they attribute the passively experienced voice, which for purposes of neutrality I have termed conscience, either to God or to an angelic or hypostatic mediator.

Muhammad experienced the same sort of coherent verbal inspirations, but he was unable to recognize his own willful responses to conscience as his own inventions. The products of his will, no differently than his conscience, seemed to him to be revelations. This circumstance is consistent with a hypothesis that Muhammad's efforts to achieve lucid hypnagogia were complicated by a coinciding state of trance. The autonomous activity of conscience—the voice of revelation—is ordinarily unconscious, prior to its moments of manifest inspiration. But due to Muhammad's trance, the willful thinking that constituted his lucidity similarly proceeded unconsciously. When his unconscious thinking became conscious, it was experienced passively as a spontaneous manifestation. In this manner, Muhammad's own willful thinking was able to counterfeit the revelatory or inspirative character of conscience, and Muhammad naively treated both as the words of God.

Bell suggested that sura 73.1-8 discussed the composition of the Quran:[10]

> You that are wrapped up in your mantle, keep vigil all night, save for a few hours; half the night, or even less: or a little more— and with measured tone recite the Koran, for We are about to address to you words of surpassing gravity. It is in the watches of the night that impressions are strongest and words most eloquent; in the day-time you are hard-pressed with the affairs of this world.

During his nocturnal vigils, Muhammad apparently recited existing verses of the Quran in order to direct his thoughts to the topic and phenomena of revelation. In keeping with the process of autosuggestion during trance states, the recital served to induce the onset of further prophetic experiences. New words, expressing new ideas, would enter his thoughts, sometimes augmenting existing passages, sometimes guiding the editing or collation of the book, but primarily innovating new passages entirely.

Another passage has traditionally been understood to refer to Muhammad's experience of receiving the Quran: "You need not move your tongue too fast to learn this revelation. We Ourself shall see to its collection and recital. When We read it, follow its words attentively; We shall Ourself explain its meaning." (sura 75.16–19)

Sura 75.16 forbids the effort to anticipate the end of a verse, the end of an inspired thought, from the revelation of its beginning. Tor Andrae explained that Muhammad was forbidden "any trace of intention, and any vestige of personal initiative," because these have "a negative influence upon the free and spontaneous flow of inspiration."[11] Muhammad's need to minimize his production of autosuggestions is a further indication of his use of trance.

Muhammad's habitual recourse to trance states may also be corroborated from several biographical traditions. One had Muhammad respond to the questions of Jewish rabbis: "Tell us about your sleep." "Do you not know that a sleep which you allege I do not have is when the eye sleeps but the heart is awake?" "Agreed." "Thus is my sleep. My eye sleeps but my heart is awake."[12] Sense perception is repressed in deep states of trance. In lucid hypnagogic states, by contrast, sense perception is never more than forgotten and so may be restored immediately that the "heart" desires it.

Several traditions suggest that Muhammad's trances were symptoms of pathology. Andrae summarized the evidence:

'Ayesha, Mohammed's favourite wife, relates: "Once I witnessed how the revelation came to Allah's Apostle on a very cold day. When it was completed his brow dripped with perspiration." According to another tradition Abdallah Ibn 'Umar asked the Prophet: "Do you know when the revelation comes to you?" He replied: "I hear loud noises, and then it seems as if I am struck by a blow. I never receive a revelation without the consciousness that my soul is being taken away from me." Ibn Sa'd gives this saying of the Prophet: "The revelation comes to me in two ways. Sometimes Gabriel visits me and tells it to me as though one man were speaking to another, but then what he speaks is lost to me. But sometimes it comes to me as with the noise of a bell, so that my heart is confused. But what is revealed to me in this way never leaves me."[13]

Medieval Byzantine writers concluded that Muhammad was an epileptic, and several modern scholars have agreed.[14] The diagnosis cannot be allowed, however. Trance phenomena may occur in epilepsy either in the prodromal phrase, prior to the onset of unconsciousness during which convulsions may occur, or else after the recovery from unconsciousness. Although the contents of the trances include hallucinations, delusions, and so forth, they are dreamlike in their quixotic associations.[15] If the traditions are to be trusted, Muhammad instead experienced trances during his collapses, but neither before nor after them. Further, much of his literary productivity during trance was strikingly artful and coherent. His trances bear evidence of internal conflicts and occasional incoherence, but not the utter chaos of epileptic thought.

Competent medical authorities and scholars acquainted with the medical data have concluded that Muhammad suffered hysteroepilepsy, a form of neurosis whose spells or fits superficially resemble epileptic attacks.[16] His pathology was not organic but psychological.

The only existing psychoanalytic assessment of Muhammad's personality draws attention to the repeated losses of loved ones in early childhood. His father Abdullah died before he was born. For the first months of his life, he was suckled by a slave of his uncle Lahab. His second wet-nurse, Hamila, then took him away to her own tribe, the Bani Sad. Until he was weaned two years later, he had no further contact with his mother Amina. When his mother next saw him, she so approved of his healthy upbringing that she sent him back to spend another two years with Hamila among the Bani Sad. Muhammad began to suffer seizures shortly afterward, at age four, but his mother had him continue among the Bani Sad for a further year. At age six, he accompanied his mother to visit her relatives and the tomb of his father in Medina. She died on the return journey to Mecca. Muhammad was then raised by a grandfather, Abd-ul-Muttalib, who died when the boy was eight.

Tradition maintains that Muhammad was treated well by both Abd-ul-Muttalib and his uncle, Abu Talib, who raised him to manhood. Certainly his strength of character suggests that he was dearly loved as a child. Many contradictions in his adult behavior are nevertheless coherent in perspective of his many childhood tragedies. Because children experience early loss as abandonment, Muhammad's desire for the father he never had would have coincided with intense anger at having been abandoned by him. The emotional conflict will explain the lifelong paradox of Muhammad's submissive idealization and violent resentment of authority. He warred against the Meccan polytheism of his ancestors, only to reinstate its Kaaba stone as the center of his own religion. He claimed the Hebrew prophets as his precedents, yet promoted murderous policies toward Jews. He conceived of a merciful but transcendent God, who was inflexibly cruel in the manifest punishment of sinners.

Emotional conflicts may also be noted in Muhammad's sexual activities, which were marked by both a desire for mother-figures and their extreme avoidance. Muhammad was celibate until the age of twenty-five when he married Khadijah, an affluent woman fifteen years his senior. He was faithful to her until her death a quarter century later, but he subsequently took twelve wives. He began by marrying another elderly widow, Sauda, but he also became betrothed to 'Ayesha, who was then a six-year-old child. Muhammad consummated the marriage when 'Ayesha was nine. He also required an adopted son to divorce his wife, so that he might marry her himself. Interestingly, he abolished the Arabian custom of permitting sons to inherit their father's wives.[17]

One biographical tradition of Muhammad's call is consistent with this assessment of his personality:

> When it was the night on which God honoured him with his mission and showed mercy on His servants thereby, Gabriel brought him the command of God. "He came to me," said the apostle of God, "while I was asleep, with a coverlet of brocade whereon was some writing, and said, 'Read!' " I said, "What shall I read?" He pressed me with it so tightly that I thought it was death; then he let me go

and said, "Read!" I said, "What shall I read?" He pressed me with
it again so that I thought it was death; then he let me go and said
"Read!" I said, "What shall I read?" He pressed me with it the third
time so that I thought it was death and said "Read!" I said, "What
then shall I read?"—and this I said only to deliver myself from
him, lest he should do the same to me again. He said:

> "Read in the name of thy Lord who created,
> Who created man of blood coagulated.
> Read! Thy Lord is the most beneficent,
> Who taught by the pen,
> Taught that which they knew not unto men."

So I read it, and he departed from me. And I awoke from my sleep,
and it was as though the words were written on my heart.[18]

The dream that the legend portrays was a nightmare. Not to be
confused with a merely disturbing or anxious dream, a nightmare
combines extremely intense anxiety with a sensation of pressure on
the chest and both a feeling and fear of suffocation. Jones explained
nightmares as products of inner conflicts over unresolved incestu-
ous wishes for the mother.[19] Conflicts of such an order are precisely
what motivated Muhammad to marry mother-figures and then to
reverse himself by marrying daughter-figures.

If the legend of Muhammad's nightmare had a basis in history,
the event may have come to be regarded as Muhammad's prophetic
call through the mistaken identification of his fear of suffocation as
an initiatory experience of ecstatic death. There is no evidence,
however, that Muhammad began his career through an initiation.

The enormity of Muhammad's claim to prophethood can be explained most satisfactorily by the assumption that he was ignorant
of less extravagant alternatives. Both the Quran (51.39,52; 69.42)
and early Islamic traditions[20] attest that pagan Meccans in Muhammad's day knew of diviners, sorcerers, poets, the possessed, and
the insane. The traditions do not refer, however, to the mystical experiences of the *pneumatics,* or "spiritual ones," of the Syriac
church.[21] Was Muhammad unaware that the pneumatics were able
to commune with God, that revelatory experiences, equivalent to
his own, were commonplace and not rare among the followers of Origen and St. Gregory of Nyssa? Since Muhammad was not ascetic
and did not introduce fasting until his Medinan period, when he
was imitating Jewish practice, his legendary call while secluded in
a cave on a mountain named Hira, near Mecca, may be regarded as

unhistorical.[22] Unlike his legend, his historical activities were not modeled on the practices of Syriac hermits who undertook solitary devotions in caves.[23]

According to tradition, when the Meccans initially did not know what to make of Muhammad, they sought the advice of Jewish rabbis in Medina, who categorized him a prophet.[24] The claim that Jews acknowledged his prophethood may be doubted; the subordinate claim that Jews supplied the very concept of prophethood is possible. Muhammad most frequently claimed to be a *rasul*, "messenger," a term that he applied to the Hebrew prophets.[25] The main thrust of his discussions of biblical prophets was the creation of a conceptual framework that would make him comprehensible to his Arab audiences.

Muhammad's doctrine of prophethood was borrowed, however, from Manicheism. Mani (216–276), a Mesopotamian, had been raised among the Elkasites, a Jewish Christian baptismal sect that had affinities with merkabah mysticism.[26] At twelve and again at twenty-four, he had visions in whose consequence he undertook to transform Gnosticism into a religion of explicitly universal appeal. Although he reduced esotericism to a minimum,[27] Mani claimed that he confirmed and completed a tradition of "apostles of light" that had included Seth, Noah, Enosh, Enoch, Shem, Abraham, Buddha, Aurentes, Zoroaster, Jesus, and Paul.[28] Apparently from the very beginning of his career, Muhammad transferred to himself the same doctrine of the culmination of the history of the prophets.[29]

Had Muhammad known that religious experiences of types similar to his own were common in the Syriac church, would he have presumed that he was a prophet rather than a pneumatic? At a minimum, would he have failed to justify his claim of prophethood by contrasting it with mysticism? Neither the Quran nor the early biographical traditions trouble about these questions. They presumably occurred neither to Muhammad nor to his audiences.

A further indication that Muhammad was self-taught is the fact that he did not teach his practice of ecstasy to anyone else. No legend so much as claims that he initiated anyone. Much less did he follow the Hebrew prophets in raising up generations of prophets after himself. The omission is striking.

Perhaps Muhammad did not teach his practice of prophesying because he could not. If hysteria disposed Muhammad to lapse into trance states, there would have been nothing for him to teach. To Muhammad's mind, all that he did was to pray. His neurosis would have done the rest. His nocturnal recitals of the Quran apparently served as cues that induced the onset of trance states. The recitals and prayers also autosuggested the religious character of his trances.

Muhammad's hysteroepilepsy was a precondition of his historical achievement, but no more than its partial explanation.[30] He plainly taught himself how to use his trance states as religious ecstasies. Once he had induced a trance, he directed it to take form as an experience of communion, and the unanticipated inspirations of his conscience were enabled to manifest. The result was a blend of neurosis, piety, and genius.

From God to Gabriel

Bell noted an important change in Muhammad's understanding of visionary experience in his Medinan period. The Quran mentions only two occasions on which Muhammad unequivocally saw visions.

> By the declining star, your compatriot is not in error, nor is he deceived!
>
> He does not speak out of his own fancy. This is an inspired revelation. He is taught by one who is powerful and mighty.
>
> He stood on the uppermost horizon; then, drawing near, he came down within two bows' length or even closer, and revealed to his servant that which he revealed.
>
> His own heart did not deny his vision. How can you, then, question what he sees?
>
> He beheld him once again at the sidra tree, beyond which no one may pass. (Near it is the Garden of Repose.)
>
> When that tree was covered with what covered it, his eyes did not wander, nor did they turn aside: for he saw some of his Lord's greatest signs. (sura 53.1–18)

Bell remarked that "strictly read, these verses imply that the visions were of God, since the word 'abd, 'slave' or 'servant,' describes a man's relation to God and not to an angel; this interpretation is allowed by some Muslim commentators."[31]

Bell noted, however, that a later sura reinterpreted the vision and made it to pertain to an angel:

I swear by the turning planets, and by the stars that rise and set; by the night, when it descends, and the first breath of morning: this is the word of a gracious and mighty messenger, held in honour by the Lord of the Throne, obeyed in heaven, faithful to his trust.

No, your compatriot is not mad. He saw him on the clear horizon. He does not grudge the secrets of the unseen; nor is this the utterance of an accursed devil. (sura 81.15–25)

Muhammad came finally to maintain that all revelations are mediated: "It is not vouchsafed to any mortal that God should speak to him except by revelation [wahy], or from behind a veil, or through a messenger sent and authorized by Him to make known His will" (sura 42.51).[32]

The account of Muhammad's visions in sura 53 was followed, almost certainly through a later editorial juxtaposition, by a passage that Muhammad is known to have revised, precisely in order to eliminate false prophecies. The verses presently read:

Have you thought on Al-Lat and Al-'Uzza and on Manat, the third other? Are you to have the sons, and He the daughters? This is indeed an unfair distinction!

They are but names which you and your fathers have invented: God has vested no authority in them. The unbelievers follow vain conjectures and the whims of their own souls, although the guidance of their Lord has long since come to them. (sura 53.19–23)

According to tradition, the satanic verses originally occupied a position following the first question. They began: "These are the exalted Gharaniq whose intercession is approved." In an attempt to gain the support of the pagan Meccans early in his career, Muhammad had acknowledged the intercessory function of the three "daughters of God," as the Meccans called them.[33] Muhammad later reversed himself on this doctrine. Legend relates:

Then Gabriel came to the apostle and said, "What have you done, Muhammad? You have read to these people something I did not bring you from God and you have said what He did not say to you." The apostle was bitterly grieved and was greatly in fear of God. So God sent down (a revelation), for He was merciful to him, comforting and making light of the affair and telling him that every

prophet and apostle before him desired as he desired and wanted
what he wanted and Satan interjected something into his desires
as he had on his tongue. So God annulled what Satan had
suggested.[34]

The present verses, which denounce the female deities as mere
names, were then revealed in replacement of the satanic verses; and
the theology explaining the incident was discussed in another sura:
"Never have We sent a single prophet or apostle before you with
whose wishes Satan did not tamper. But God abrogates the interjections of Satan and confirms His own revelations. God is all-
knowing and wise. He makes Satan's interjections a temptation for
those whose hearts are diseased or hardened." (sura 22:51–53)

It is significant, I suggest, that the collation of prophecies in the
Quran juxtaposed the two visions, originally of God but later reinterpreted as of Gabriel (53.1–18), with the revised text of the satanic
verses (53.19f). The two passages presumably had separate origin.
They were united, however, in their need for reinterpretation.

Muhammad's Allegorical Visions

Muhammad's hermeneutic shift may perhaps be linked with
several biographical legends that describe visions from his Medinan
period. The legend that is set earliest concerns Muhammad's prophecy of victory at the battle of Badr, when the Muslims of Medina engaged both an army and a caravan of the Quraysh of Mecca. At the
battlefield, while Muhammad waited for the fighting to begin, he
evidently sought divine assurance regarding its outcome:

Then the apostle . . . returned to the hut and entered it, and none
was with him there but Abu Bakr. The apostle was beseeching his
Lord for the help which He had promised to him, and among his
words were these: "O God, if this band perish today Thou wilt be
worshipped no more." But Abu Bakr said, "O prophet of God, your
constant entreaty will annoy thy Lord, for surely God will fulfil His
promise to thee." While the apostle was in the hut he slept a light
sleep; then he awoke and said, "Be of good cheer, O Abu Bakr. God's
help is coming to you. Here is Gabriel holding the rein of a horse
and leading it. The dust is upon his front teeth."[35]

The Quran alludes to this prophecy in the verse, "Though God
promised that one of two columns (would fall to you), you desired
the one that was not armed" (sura 8.7). The legend of the vision was
consistent. It portrayed the capture of a horse that had fled at

speed. The image implied a defeat of Quraysh warriors on horse, as distinct from the capture of the caravans' camels. The legend's claim that Muhammad interpreted the vision as a prophecy of unqualified victory may be considered an exaggeration. It is inconsistent with sura 8.7, and it overinterprets the vision described in the legend.

What was Muhammad's state of consciousness during this vision? Early Arabic discussions of consciousness were very rudimentary and limited to only two categories: waking and sleeping. When this narrative asserts that Muhammad was asleep, all that it necessarily means is that he experienced his vision in his mind as when asleep, rather than through his eyes as when awake.[36] The text should not be understood to assert that natural sleep was necessarily his precise state of consciousness. Was Muhammad in a trance? Or a hypnagogic state?

A hypnagogic state was definitely portrayed in another tradition about the battle of Badr that ascribed a similarly allegorical vision to one of Muhammad's followers:

> Quraysh advanced and when they reached al-Juhfa Juhaym b. al-Salt b. Makhrama b. al-Muttalib saw a vision. He said, "Between waking and sleeping I saw a man advancing on a horse with a camel, and then he halted and said: 'Slain are 'Utba and Shayba and Abu'l-Hakam and Umayya' (and he went on to enumerate the men who were killed at Badr, all nobles of Quraysh). Then I saw him stab his camel in the chest and send it loose into the camp, and every single tent was bespattered with blood." When the story reached Abu Jahl he said, "Here's another prophet from B. al-Muttalib! He'll know tomorrow if we meet them who is going to be killed!"[37]

The state "between waking and sleeping" is hypnagogic, by definition.

Brief visions that were interpreted allegorically were also reported of Muhammad in connection with the battle of Uhud,[38] the siege of al-Ta'if,[39] and one later occasion in his life.[40] Muhammad was likely indebted to the Bible for the idea of allegorizing interpretation. He devoted a sura in the Quran to the tale of Joseph. The narrative provides a detailed account of Joseph's practice of dream interpretation (12.4–7, 36–37, 43–49) and emphasizes that the act of interpretation was divinely revealed (12.6, 37, 43–45).

It is unlikely that Muhammad himself read the Bible or even had it read to him.[41] The Quran improvises freely in its presentations of biblical tales. It is ignorant of writing prophets other than

Jonah, and it contains elementary errors. Haman is identified as the vizier of the pharaoh (28.6,8,38; 29.39; 40.24,36), and Mary mother of Jesus is called the sister of Aaron and daughter of Imran (19.20; 66.12). Muhammad presumably owed his knowledge of the Bible to verbal communications. A Christian source is improbable, however, because Muhammad was unaware of such basic Christian teachings as the fall of man and the world's redemption through Jesus' crucifixion and resurrection. Of the Gospels, Muhammad knew of the infancy narratives, but nothing of the adult Jesus.[42]

A debt to Judaism is proved by the Quran's frequent accuracy in presenting narrative details that originated in rabbinic midrash.[43] An Islamic tradition records that Muhammad had Zaid b. Thabit learn to read "Hebrew," so that he might read some Jewish texts for him. A Judeo-Arabic dialect, written with Hebrew characters, may have been in use among Arabian Jews.[44] Muhammad may have learned of Joseph's allegorizing hermeneutic from these or similar sources.

The Quran explicitly addressed the theological problem of Muhammad's debt to a non-Muslim:

> We know they say: "A mortal taught him." But the man to whom they allude speaks a foreign tongue, while this is eloquent Arabic speech. (16.103)

> The unbelievers say: "This is but a forgery of his own invention, in which others have helped him." Unjust is what they say and false.

> And they say: "Fables of the ancients he has written: they are dictated to him morning and evening."

> Say: "It is revealed by Him who knows the secrets of the heavens and the earth. He is forgiving and merciful." (25.4–6)

Muhammad acknowledged his dependence on a teacher whose source was not in Arabic. He nevertheless regarded the inspiration of his own versions of biblical stories as their divine revelation. He cited their presentation in fluent Arabic, rather than awkward translation, as proof of his claim.[45]

Muhammad's Encounter with Gnosis

The angel that mediated revelations to Muhammad was identified in the Quran as Gabriel (2.91), but the name was not introduced until the Medinan period.[46] Muhammad presumably learned of the name from the story of Gabriel's annunciation to Mary of her conception of Jesus. However, Gabriel's double function as a visible representative of God and the invisible spirit of verbal inspirations in Muhammad's experience of prophecy bears comparison with Talmudic ideas of the archangel Michael, the "prince of the world." Importantly, Michael's functions were attributed by the merkabah mystics to the angel Metatron, who was sometimes described more abstractly as the *Geburah*, a hypostatic "power" or "dynamis." The cognate name *Gabriel* means the "power of God."[47]

That Muhammad had personal contact with merkabah mysticism during his stay in Medina was established by David J. Halperin. A number of hadiths identify *al-Dajjal*, the Muslim counterpart of the Antichrist, with Ibn Sayyad or Ibn Sa'id, a Jewish boy who lived in Medina when Muhammad was resident there. He is said later to have converted to Islam and to have died at the battle of al-Harrah in 683.[48] Because tradition is unlikely to have euhemerized al-Dajjal, the association of the eschatological figure with an ostensibly historical person implies that the extant legends of Ibn Sayyad had a basis in historical fact.

The surviving legends are notable. One has Muhammad and Ibn Sayyad each demand that the other recognize him as a prophet. Muhammad does not make retort. A group of legends have the common form of a question by Muhammad, followed by Ibn Sayyad's answer and Muhammad's decision in response. In one case, the question pertains to the Dust of Paradise, which Ibn Sayyad identifies correctly. Another tale permits us to identify the conception of paradise:

> The Apostle of God said to Ibn Sa'id, "What do you see?"
> He said, "I see a throne upon the sea (*bahr;* var., *ma'*, water), around it *al-hayyat* (var., *hayyat*)."
> The Apostle of God said, "He sees (*yara;* var., *dhaka*, that is) the Throne of the Devil (*'arsh iblis*)."[49]

Halperin suggested that the word *hayyat* "is to be explained as an Arabicized form of the Hebrew *hayyot*, 'living creatures', " who carry or surround the divine throne in the biblical book of Ezekiel and the merkabah mysticism that contemplated its images. The angelic figures were ordinarily termed "throne-bearers" (*hamalat al-'arsh*) in Islamic legends; they were termed *hayyat* only here.[50]

Another legend of Ibn Sayyad portrays Muhammad in an embarrassing fashion, which argues for its authenticity:

The Apostle of God and Ubayy b. Ka'b set out for the palm-grove (*nakhl*) in which was Ibn Sayyad, until they entered (*dakhala*) the palm-grove. The Apostle of God began to hide among the trunks of the palm-trees, deceiving (*yakhtilu*) ibn Sayyad, that he might hear something from Ibn Sayyad before he [Ibn Sayyad] could see him. Ibn Sayyad was lying on his pallet (*firashihi*), in a cloak (*qat-ifah*) of his, in which (*fiha;* = "coming from which"?) was a low, in-articulate sound (*zamzamah*). His mother saw the Apostle of God as he was hiding among the trunks of the palm-trees, and said, "O Saf!—that was his name—this is Muhammad." Then he was roused. The Apostle of God said, "If only she had left him, he would have clarified (*bayyana*)!"[51]

Halperin understands the tale as an account of Ibn Sayyad in an alternate state, wrapped in a cloak as was characteristic of Muhammad, Arabic diviners, and merkabah mystics. Ibn Sayyad's re-course to a palm grove, which must have been habitual since Muhammad expected to find him there, may be associated with a Jewish mantic practice that Talmudic and Gaonic sources termed "conversation of palm-trees."[52]

The Ibn Sayyad traditions have an important implication. During his stay in Medina, Muhammad had sufficient entree within the Jewish community to learn the identity of a young practitioner of merkabah mysticism. A date must be assigned no later than 626, when Muhammad expelled the Jews from Medina. But because positive contacts with Jews must have commenced prior to Muhammad's initial migration to Medina, Muhammad may have encountered merkabah mysticism as early as 623 or 624.

Muhammad's acquaintance with merkabah mysticism may also underlie sura 6.35, where Muhammad was told that he could satisfy his opponents "if thou couldst find a way down into the earth or a ladder into the sky to bring them a portent." The image of a ladder was presumably biblical. The Quran twice used the term *sullam* in reference to the ladder of ascension (6.35; 52.38). The Bible uses the cognate Hebrew term, *sullam,* in designation of the ladder to heaven that Jacob saw in a dream (Gen 28:12). In sura 70, the Quran instead used the term *ma'arij,* meaning "stairways," in de-scribing Allah as *Dhu 'l-ma'arij,* "the Lord of the Stairways," to whom "the angels and the Spirit mount up in a day whereof the measure is fifty thousand years." In later Arabic usage, the cognate term *mi'raj,* "ladder," gained the meaning of *'uruj,* "ascension."[53]

The motif of the ladder bears comparison with a passage in *Hekhalot Rabbati,* where "Rabbi Ishmael said: All the *haverim* [i.e., the initiated] liken this to a man who has a ladder in the middle of his house, who ascends, and descends on it and there is no creature who stops him."[54]

We do not know the quality or content of Muhammad's encounter with merkabah mysticism. The possibility that he was initiated into the esoteric gnosis rests on an enigmatic and much debated Quranic verse: "Glory be to Him who made His servant go by night from the Sacred Temple to the farther Temple whose surroundings We have blessed, that We might show him some of Our signs." (17.1)

God's "servant" was presumably Muhammad; and "the Sacred Temple" is a formulation used in the Quran in reference exclusively to the sanctuary of Mecca (2.139ff; 5.3; 8.34; 9.7ff; 22.25; 48.25ff).[55] Other Quranic references to the "surroundings We have blessed" pertain to the Holy Land (7.133; 21.71, 81; 34.17); but the identification here may be questioned because the shift of pronouns from "Him" to "We" may indicate that the phrase was added to the original text.[56] Traditional Muslim exegeses of this verse identify the sacred temple with the Kaaba of Mecca and the far-off temple with the Jerusalem temple of the Jews. Legends of Muhammad's *isra,* or night journey to Jerusalem, narrate an itinerary consistent with the exegeses. Early biographical traditions differ, however, in their claims that the *isra* was immediately followed by the *mi'raj,* or ascension to heaven. Ibn Ishaq presented the two events as a single continuous journey; but Ibn Sa'd, who wrote seventy years after Ibn Ishaq, dated them twelve and eighteen months, respectively, prior to the emigration to Medina.[57] Modern scholars have cited sura 17.1 as evidence that the earliest form of the tradition spoke of the *isra* but not the *mi'raj.*

There is a problem with the assumption. No temple stood on Mount Zion in the era of Muhammad. Solomon's temple had been destroyed by the Babylonians in 586 B.C.E., and the Second Temple had been razed by the Romans in 70 C.E.. It is possible that Muhammad was unaware of these facts and composed a Quranic verse that refers to a nonexistent temple in Jerusalem.

Alternatively, because the Quranic verse refers to a distant temple without specifying its location, it might be taken to refer to the temple that was available for Muhammad to see: the heavenly temple that Jewish apocalyptists and the New Testament had located in New Jerusalem, which continued to be visited by Jewish merkabah mystics. Exegetical speculations would then have misunderstood the verse and interpolated a preliminary journey by night from Mecca to the earthly temple mount in Jerusalem, prior to

Muhammad's ascension.[58] The Quran would instead refer to an ascension by night from Mecca to God's temple in heaven. Interestingly, this itinerary was given in a version of the legend preserved by al-Bakhari.[59]

Because the residents of the seven heavens first learn that Muhammad is a prophet in the course of his *mi'raj*, scholars regard the legend of his ascension as a legend about the beginning of his career.[60] It may more precisely be described as initiatory. Halperin has demonstrated that the oldest extant legends of Muhammad's *mi'raj* had already been significantly influenced by merkabah mysticism within a century of Muhammad's death. R. Ishmael, whom the *hekhalot* traditions portray as a visionary who undertook the ascension, appears in legends of the *mi'raj* as the angel Isma'il. The shift in roles is consistent both with Enoch's transformation into the angel Metatron in *3 Enoch* and with the regard for Muhammad as a primordial being of light in Shiite Islam[61] and Sufism.[62]

On the evidence, it is safest to conclude that Muhammad had a limited encounter with merkabah mysticism that later served as a precedent for the developments of Islamic gnosis among his followers. It is not impossible, however, that Muhammad's encounter with Jewish gnosis was more thoroughgoing than we are presently able to prove.

Chapter 9

Islamic Gnosis and the World of Imagination

Gnosis presumably entered Islam through the conversion of gnostics, but greater precision is impossible. Several schools of gnosis are represented in the Nag Hammadi texts. Others are known to us through the church fathers. The *hekhalot* literature attests to at least two Jewish schools; and further Gnostic traditions were represented by the Mandaeans, Elkasites, Bardesanites, and Manicheans of Syria and Mesopotamia. Other schools, whose names, practices, or doctrines are no longer remembered, presumably existed as well. The many parallels of Islamic gnosis and Mandaeism, for example, may owe directly to Mandaeism, but they may instead owe to one or more closely similar traditions of which no record survives.

Already in the second century, a Valentinian Gnostic named Marcos had developed a cosmology that was based on the Greek letters and their numerical values. According to St. Irenaeus of Lyons, Marcos maintained that: "When first the inconceivable and nonmaterial Father . . . willed to make utterable that of him which was ineffable and to give form to that which was invisible, he opened his mouth and sent forth a word which was similar to himself. This stood by and showed him who and what he was: a form, appearing from the invisible."[1]

The first hypostasis was the Greek word *arche,* "beginning." It was simultaneously audible and visible; and because it consisted of four letters or elements, it was called the tetrad. The addition of further words, of four, ten, and twelve letters each, resulted in a "whole name" of thirty elements or letters.

> The whole name was the Truth. Marcos saw her in a vision. Behold her head on high: Alpha and Omega; her neck: Beta and Psi; her shoulders and hands: Gamma and Chi; her breast: Delta and Phi; her diaphragm: Episilon and Upsilon; her back: Zeta and Tau; her

stomach: Eta and Sigma; her thighs: Theta and Rho; her knees: Iota and Pi; her shins: Kappa and Omicron; her ankles: Lambda and Xi; her feet: Mu and Nu. This is the body of Truth. . . . This is the form of the element, this the character of the letter. And this element he calls "Man" and says it is the source of all speech, the beginning of every sound, the expression of all that is unspeakable.[2]

The letters each had autonomous metaphysical functions. "Each element has . . . its own form, its own pronunciation, appearance, and images."[3] The elements were each separate; their future unification would accomplish the eschatological "restitution of all things." In the meantime, the letters or sounds "are those which have given form to the immaterial and unbegotten aeon, and these in fact are the forms which the Lord has called angels who continually behold the face of the Father" (Mt 18:10).[4]

The thirty letters were able to generate the full complexity of the cosmos because they were each composite. "Each one of the letters contains in itself other letters by means of which the name of the letter is expressed, and again other letters are in turn indicated by means of other letters, and the others by others still, so that the number of the letters extends to infinity."[5] The further development of Marcos's cosmology, in which the truth became mother to the demiurge, proceeded on numerological principles. It was no longer the letters and their meanings as words, but their numerical values and arithmetical computations that brought the many features of the cosmos into being.[6]

Gnostics had entertained the idea of an anthropos, an archetypal human being, from early times. However, the anticosmic dualism of the Gnostics generally made it impossible for them to equate the anthropos, whose perfection Gnostics sought to replicate, with anything having to do with the physical cosmos. Gnostic adaptations of the Platonic idea of a world-soul pertained, in the main, either to a plurality of evil powers that create the physical cosmos or, in the singular, to a fallen being—for example, Sophia, who is entrapped within matter. Mandaeism represents an exception to the general Gnostic pattern.

Mandaeism, the only Gnostic sect that has continued as a living tradition down to the present day, likely originated as a Jewish baptismal sect in or near Judea, prior to a migration to Iraq possibly as early as the first or second century C.E. The Mandaeans speak an east Aramaic dialect with a twenty-four character alphabet, and they had developed a blend of Gnostic and Zoroastrian dualisms[7] by the late third century, when some of their psalms can be dated through their adaptation by Manicheans.[8]

Like Marcos the Gnostic, Mandaeism regards the letters of the alphabet as the elements that compose both the cosmos and the many limbs and organs of human beings. Like Marcos, Mandaeism regards the cosmos as an anthropomorphic being.[9] On the other hand, Mandaeism differs from Marcosian Gnosis in equating the cosmos with the Gnostic anthropos. The Mandaeans name the macroanthropos Adam Kasia or Adam Qadmaia, and they regard him as the prototype of Adam Pagria, the first man.[10]

It was inevitable that the Stoic concept of the correspondence of the macrocosm and the microcosm, which proceeded through their common composition of the four elements, should have been syncretized with the Gnostic concept of the anthropos, whose transcendent perfection was the prototype and salvation of humanity. The logical inconsistency of the two doctrines—the one immanent and physicalist, the other transcendent and anticosmist—was no impediment to religious sensibilities that functioned more by images and symbols than by cogent reasoning.

The equation of the macrocosm and the anthropos generated an anthropomorphic conception of the cosmos that compromised the anticosmic dualism that Gnosticism had favored. For the world to be not an imperfect replica of a divine prototype, but the perfect prototype itself, meant that the world had to be valued positively. Anticosmism could be perpetuated as a negative valuation of matter; but the hypostases that were present in the material world, creating it and imparting forms to it, had to be valued positively, as Gnosticism had not previously done. This crucial limitation of Gnostic dualism, which celebrated the creation and revalorized demonic archons as holy angels, goes far toward explaining why Mandaeism, or a closely similar development, was the school within Gnosticism that Muslims found attractive.

The Ghulat

Steve Wasserstrom suggests that gnostic adaptations to Islam were so extensive in the eighth century that "these assertive reorganizing movements constitute a virtual failed takeover of Islam."[11] The Shia, which was originally a political faction devoted to the dynastic claims of ʿAli and his descendants,[12] attracted the support of a variety of religious sects, whose political agenda were similarly revolutionary. Several that the Shia termed *ghulat,* "extremists," were gnostic. As may be expected, the political ambitions of the Shia coincided with a positive valuation of the physical world. Where gnostic dualism persisted in Shiism, it was qualified severely.

Al-Mughira ibn Sa'id, who led a Shiite rebellion against the Umayyad governor of Iraq and died in 736, was as much a self-styled prophet in the Mesopotamian tradition of Elkesai and Mani, as he was a Muslim. His native tongue was apparently Aramaic, and his doctrines suggest that he came from a baptist community "closely resembling if not identical with the Mandeans,"[13] with its blend of Zoroastrian light imagery and alphabetological gnosis. He maintained that God was a man of light whose limbs had the forms of the letters of the Arabic alphabet. When God set about creating the world, he began by speaking the "Greatest Name." This name flew up to his head and there became a crown of light. Al-Mughira's cosmological teachings contrasted light and darkness as good and evil.[14] As some *ghulat* had done since the mid-seventh century,[15] he may have deified 'Ali. He is said to have claimed that he ascended to heaven, where God anointed his head and told him, "Go, my son, to earth, and tell its inhabitants that 'Ali is my right hand and my eye."[16]

The Shiite leader Abu Mansur al-'Igli (d. c. 738–744), whose followers, the Mansuriyya, were the first sect of Shiites to be organized as terrorists, claimed that prophecy had continued since Muhammad, and that he himself was a prophet. He based his claim to authority on an ascension to heaven:[17]

> He maintained, when he claimed the Imamate for himself, that he was lifted up to heaven and had seen the object of his worship, and he had patted him on the head with his hand and said to him: "O my son, descend and convey a message from me, whereupon he had sent him down to the earth." (He further believed that) he was the Fragment, fallen from heaven.[18]

The reference to "the Fragment" presupposed a gnostic myth of the fall of spirit into the world of matter.

Another early account of heavenly ascension in Islam again concerned a Shiite leader, the weaver Bazigh: "And Bazigh claimed that he had ascended to heaven and that God had touched him and spat into his mouth, and that wisdom had grown in his breast like the truffle in earth, and that he had seen 'Ali sitting at the right hand of God."[19]

The Sunni heresiographers who recorded these early *ghulat* traditions described anthropomorphic conceptions of God. Louis Massignon maintained, however, that "for all the Ghulats, God, absolutely ineffable, is unrecognizable in Himself. It is the question only of a deification by participation."[20] The need clearly to distinguish God from any hypostatic manifestation may have encouraged the development of alternative formulations.

The Mi'raj Tradition

Details derived from merkabah mysticism contributed to the legend of Muhammad's *mi'raj* by the early eighth century, and the legend[21] was used to provide authority and precedent for Islamic gnosis. For example, the famous *hadith-i kisa,* "tradition of the garment," relates that Muhammad summoned his daughter Fatima, her husband Ali, and their sons Hasan and Husayn, and gave them a cloak that covered them. The bestowal of his mantle implied the succession from him. Another Shiite tradition, also well-known, explains the nature of the cloak:

> It has been accounted of the Prophet—upon him and his family be peace—that he said: "When I was taken on the nocturnal ascension to heaven and I entered paradise, I saw in the middle of it a palace made of red rubies. Gabriel opened the door for me and I entered it. I saw in it a house made of white pearls. I entered the house and saw in the middle of it a box made of light and locked with a lock made of light. I said, "O Gabriel, what is this box and what is in it?" Gabriel said, "O Friend of God, in it is the secret of God which God does not reveal to anyone except to him whom He loves." I said, "Open its door for me." He said, "I am a slave who follows the divine command. Ask thy Lord until He grants permission to open it." I therefore asked for the permission of God. A voice came from the Divine Throne saying, "O Gabriel open its door," and he opened it. In it I saw spiritual poverty (*faqr*) and a cloak (*muraqqa'*). I said, "What is this *faqr* and *muraqqa'*?" The voice from heaven said, "O Muhammad, there are two things which I have chosen for thee and thy people from the moment I created the two of you. These two things I do not give to anyone save those whom I love, and I have created nothing dearer than these." Then the Holy Prophet said, "God—Exalted be His Name—selected *faqr* and the *muraqqa'* for me, and these two are the dearest things to him." The Prophet directed his attention toward God and when he

returned from the nocturnal ascent (*miraj*) he made ʿAli wear the
cloak with the permission of God and by His command. ʿAli wore it
and sewed patches on it until he said, "I have sewn so many
patches on this cloak that I am embarrassed before the sewer." ʿAli
made his son Hasan to wear it after him and then Husayn and
then the descendants of Husayn one after another until the Mahdi.
The cloak rests with him now.[22]

With only slight modifications, the same *hadith* was told as the
origin of the cloaks worn by Sufi mystics.[23] However, early Sufism
did not understand ascension in a gnostic manner. From Hasan
Basri (d. 772) onward, Sufis interpreted the *miʿraj* of Muhammad
as a metaphor[24]—comparable to the motifs of sexual union, alcoholic intoxication and the like—for the discussion of the introspective type of mystical union that early Sufism favored.[25]

An early and isolated instance of Sufi gnosis may perhaps be
indicated by the legend of Abu Yazid (Bayezid) of Bistam (d. 874),
who first introduced the term *fana,* "annihilation," to describe the
moment of mystical union. The term refers to the subjective loss of
the human ego and permits Sufis to refer summarily to experiences
of both introspective union and nothingness. Abu Yazid was also the
first Sufi to boast a *miʿraj,* or "ascension" into heaven. Michael Sells
has noted several parallels between merkabah mysticism and the
miʿraj of Abu Yazid.[26] Unfortunately, the earliest extant version of
his *miʿraj* is a legendary saying that was preserved by Abu Nasr al-
Sarraj:

> As soon as I reached [God's] unity [he says], I became a bird whose
> body was of oneness and whose wings were of everlastingness, and
> I went on flying in the atmosphere of relativity for ten years until
> I entered into an atmosphere a hundred million times as large;
> and I went on flying until I reached the expanse of eternity and in
> it I saw the tree of oneness. Then [says Sarraj], he described the
> soil [in which it grew] its root and branch, its shoots and fruits, and
> then he said: Then I looked, and I knew that all this was deceit.[27]

In this account, Abu Yazid was said to have "reached [God's]
unity,"—that is, experienced mystical union—before he envisioned
his soul's flight. He was said further to have also had a second experience of mystical union, "the expanse of eternity," before his ecstatic state continued with a vision of "the tree of oneness." Shifts
from union to vision, to union again, and once again to vision, are
otherwise unknown to me in the historical and psychological

records. They are exaggerations that have crept into Abu Yazid's legend. They do suggest, however, a later misunderstanding of an original practice of both visions and unions.

The legendary precedent of Abu Yazid helped make the *mi'raj* of Muhammad become an object of Sufi emulation,[28] but only centuries later, when gnosis entered Sufism.

The Isma'ili

Ja'far al-Sadiq (d. 765), a fifth-generation descendant of 'Ali, articulated the doctrine of the imamate. At all times, there is in the world a divinely appointed and guided leader, immune to sin and error, whose religious teachings are authoritative. Implied by this doctrine is the imam's unsurpassed access to divine revelation, as is consistent with Ja'far's reputation as a teacher of esoteric mysticism.[29] We are ignorant, however, of the content of his practices.[30]

Among the Shiite sects that claim the imamate for their leaders are the Isma'ili. They recognize seven 'Alid imams, culminating in Isma'il b. Jafar, as the rightful successors of Muhammad. They originated as political partisans of Isma'il's heirs, possibly as early as the late eighth century. When the line of imams recognized by the Ithna 'Ashari (Twelver) Shiites became extinct in 874, the Isma'ili became the focus of the Shiite hope for the overthrow of the 'Abbasid caliphate.[31] After several decades of clandestine political organization and missionary activity, a revolt was begun by 'Abd Allah al-Mahdi in 902. In 910 he founded an Isma'ili caliphate that was called Fatimid after Fatima, daughter of Muhammad. The Fatimids completed their conquest of Egypt in 973 and ruled until the dynasty fell to Salah al-Din in 1171. Although Isma'ilism was the official religion of the Fatimid caliphs of North Africa and Egypt, it was otherwise denounced as a heresy and persecuted by both Sunnis and Ithna 'Ashari Shiites. It was consequently organized as an esoteric tradition that reserved its advanced teachings under vows of secrecy to an elite.[32]

The public devotions of the Fatamid Isma'ili differed very little from Ithna 'Ashari Shiism and Sunnism. However, a contrast of the *zahir,* "exoteric," with the *batin,* "esoteric," was fundamental to Fatimid thought. In principle, all Isma'ili doctrines are *batin*. None are to be told outside the community. Actual secrecy is restricted, however, to books and traditions whose proper understanding requires special education and training.[33] Isma'ili *haqa'iq,* "philosophy" or "doctrine," has its basis in *ta'wil,* an esoteric or allegorizing method of Quranic exegesis that relies extensively on alphabetology and numerology.[34] The inner meaning of the Quran, so revealed, proves to be gnostic.

Documents from the early tenth century refer to a system of divine hypostases involving the demiurge *qadar* and the further hypostases *kuni, al-jadd, al-khayal,* and *al-istiftah.*[35] A treatise by Abu 'Isa al-Murshid, a Fatamid jurist of the late tenth century, seems to preserve an early Isma'ili creation myth:

> He existed when there was no space, no eternity, no time, no things occupying space and no minute of time. When he conceived a will and a wish (*irada* and *mashi'a*), He created a light and produced out of this light a creature (*khalq*). This light remained for some length of its eternity not knowing whether it was a creator or a created thing. Then God breathed into it a spirit and directed at it a voice: "Be!" (*kun*), thus it came into being with God's permission. All things were made by God through creating them (*mubda'atan*) from the letters *kaf* and *nun* [making the word *kun*]. There is bringing-into-being, one who brings-into-being, and a thing which is brought-into-being. Then there is Allah. Then through the *waw* and the *ya'*, which became a name for what is above it, calling it therefore *kuni.*[36]

In this narrative, the first hypostasis, *kuni,* was a creature of light. His animation by language pertained to both speech and thought. Interestingly, the narrative bears comparison with the cosmic Adam of Mandaeism.

The pre-Fatamid creation myth continued with an account of the emanation of a second hypostasis, *qadar,* from the first:

> Then the command (*amr*) of the Creator of all things went to *kuni:* "Create for yourself out of your own light a creature to act for you as a vizier and helper and to carry out our command". Thus it created a creature out of its light and gave it a name, calling it *qadar.* Through *kuni* God brought to being (*kawwana*) all things, and through *qadar* He determined (*qaddara*) them.[37]

In Hellenistic Gnosticism, the first hypostasis and the demiurge had been opposing principles. In merkabah mysticism and Isma'ilism, they were regarded as a single entity. Although the texts use masculine pronouns for both, *kuni* and *qadar* were female and male, respectively.[38] Early Fatimid sources treated *kuni* and *qadar,* respectively, as Intellect and Soul.[39] *Kuni* was the collective group of archetypal ideas as God thinks of them, and *qadar* their implementation in the actual structuring of the world.

Later in the text, the first two hypostases were made the basis of a system of seven:

> *Kuni* consists of four letters, *qadar* of three, which makes seven letters. This indicates that when he (*kuni*) had created *qadar,* he created out of the light which is between itself and *qadar* seven Cherubim (*karubiyya*), giving them esoteric names the meaning of which can only be understood by the Friends of God (peace be upon them) and the sincere believers who follow them. These names are: ʿ*azama* (might), ʿ*izza* (glory), *huda* (right guidance), *baha*ʾ (splendour), *ra*ʾ*fa* (mercy), *amr* (command), *mu*ʾ*tamar* (counsel).[40]

The reference to cherubim tends to indicate the influence of merkabah mysticism. The Arabic term *karubiyyun* does not occur in the Quran. A Hebrew loanword, it was borrowed either directly from Jews or else from Christians. The text identified the seven cherubim with the seven skies.[41] After creating the seven cherubim, *kuni* created a series of twelve "Spiritual Beings" that functioned as intermediaries between *kuni* and the prophets and imams.[42] The mechanism was apparently astrological: "The division of the sphere into twelve signs is an indication of the twelve Spiritual Beings."[43]

The physical world was created after the creation of the seven cherubim and twelve spiritual beings.[44] Despite the correspondence of the two worlds, early Ismaʿili gnosis adhered to a fundamental rejection of the material world:

> All that has been created in the upper world has something corresponding to it in the lower world. This is so in order that those with insight may understand that the entirety of subtle beings and spirits belongs to the limit of the First and returns to it; whereas the bodies and all coarse substances belong to the limit of the Follower. Thus that which is coarse is destined to perish, but what is subtle is permanent and is either rewarded or punished.[45]

A trace of the Gnostic myth of the fall of Sophia may be seen in the Ismaʿili account of the origin of the cosmos through a rebellion of the female demiurge against God:

> Know—may God impart you the knowledge of good—that when the First was created as a spirit, he saw no other beings besides

himself. Thus he conceived a proud thought that there is nobody
but himself. Upon this, six dignitaries immediately emanated
from him through God's power, in order to teach him that there is
an omnipotent being above him from Whom he derives his power
and upon Whose will all his actions depend. Three of the dignitaries were above and three beneath him. When the First saw that
this happened neither through his own power nor according to his
own will, he was convinced that there was someone above him and
acknowledged his Creator; it was then that he said: "There is no
god but God"—i.e. "I am not a god."[46]

In this narrative, *kuni*'s sin is the occasion of the world's creation, but God's act of creation has a redemptive function to restore
her faith in Him. The myth mentions dualism only in order to correct the doctrine in favor of monotheism.

Kuni and the six dignitaries may be seen as a monotheistic
reworking of the Hellenistic Gnostic conception of the archons of
the seven heavens. Since *kuni* corresponded to the sun while *qadar*
corresponded to the moon,[47] the entire series may have been astronomical.

Pre-Fatimid Isma'ilism extended theosophical analyses to the
Arabic alphabet, the Quran, and universal history, as well as to
cosmology.[48] The theosophy relied primarily on groups of two,
seven, and twelve. Seven letters composed the name of God (*Bism'l-
lah*), corresponding to the seven verses of the first sura, and the
seven *natiqs*, or "prophets," whose activities each commenced an epoch in world history. The seven letters also generated the seven
heavens, seven earths, seven seas, seven days of the week, and so
forth. By different manipulations, the systems of seven letters and
their consequences were made to generate systems of twelve in the
alphabet, Quran, and cosmos. Other analyses concerned the number two: Muhammad and 'Ali, noon and night, sun and moon, female and male.[49] *Kuni* and *qadar*, the seven hypostatic cherubim,
and the twelve spiritual beings were presumably thought to manifest repeatedly as complete groups throughout creation.

Allegorical exegeses of the Quran, dealing extensively with its
images of wind, water, lightning, and so forth,[50] were cited as further proofs of Isma'ili eschatology. Muhammad was counted as the
sixth *natiq*, and Isma'ilism anticipated the arrival of a seventh, a
messianic *Qa'im* or *Mahdi*, who would inaugurate the seventh and
final epoch of world history. Each previous *natiq* had brought a *zahir* message, and he had been followed by a fundament (*asas*) or silent one (*samit*), who revealed the *batin* of the prophet's message.

Each fundament had been followed by a line of seven imams, the last of whom became the next *natiq*. The seventh imam of the current cycle was Muhammad b. Ismaʿil, who had lived in the eighth century. He was claimed not to have died, but to have gone into occlusion, from which he would reappear in the near future as the seventh *natiq*, the *Qaʾim* or *Mahdi*. He would commence the seventh era by revealing all previously *batin* doctrines and abrogating the *zahir* law. He was then to rule the world, end its physical existence, and preside over the last judgment.[51] Until his arrival, devotion was to be directed to his representative, the leader of the Ismaʿili.

The practical implications of the Ismaʿili doctrine of the imamate are disclosed in an early Fatimid legend[52] about the fourth imam, Muhammad al-Baqir (d. 735?):

> Jabir b. Zayd al-Jufi relates from Imam al-Baqir:—"I went to Our Lord, and, on entering, saw in his hand a rosary made of (dried) olives, while he himself was saying: "Glory be to God, for everything from whence I have taken the "veil," a "door" was opened to me. And over everything at the door of which I was knocking, a "veil" appeared. Glory be to the One who helps and guides those who search after Him, and directs those who speed in the search for His light." Said I to myself: "Verily, thou art the Great One." And the Imam lifted his face towards me, and said: "Verily, great is the One Who has been appointed by the Great One, and all-knowing is the One who has been appointed by the All-knowing, by His blessing emanating from Him to me. I am a slave of God, and it was Divinely revealed to me to bid you not to worship any deity except for God the Great". I said to myself: "This is a *veil*,—why does he conceal himself?" The Imam turned his face to me, and I saw bright light shining and radiating from it,—so much that my eyes could not stand it, and I began to faint. And the Imam uttered:—"This is one of the miracles that some Saints can work." After this he said: "Should I show thee more, Jabir?" And I replied: "No, this is enough for me." And he said: "I will announce to thee, Jabir, the glad tidings: God has purified thee so that His shadow might descend upon thee, by the manifestation of His holy "gate" to thee, the holy Salsal. O Jabir, Salman is one of us, a member of the family of the Prophet. His *zahir*, i.e. as he appears to the eye of an ordinary mortal, is as the outside of a door (which is shut); but his nature (*batin*) is derived from the light of the expression "*ar-Rahman ar-Rahim*" (i.e. from the formula of the *basmala* in the Coran). When thy vision is screened from thy (lower) self, thy (better) self shall become visible in the shining of his light. Thou hast seen as much as thou couldst stand. . . . If thou couldst bear from

Him as much as thou bearest from us, we shall become for thee
what we are from Him. . . . Then hasten to discover the true relation between us and thyself. Then what thou canst not comprehend shall dawn upon thee, if God please."[53]

It is not simply that the angelic hypostasis Salman al-Farsi,
whose mystic name was Salsal, was the *batin* of the living imam.
The living imam functioned as a gnostic redeemer who mediated
the experience of gnosis to his follower. The imam's prayer explained
that the door that opens toward God is simultaneously a veil of God.
The paradox pertained to Salman. The hypostasis was not to be confused with God, and yet was the means of knowing him. When the
imam insisted on his own humanity ("slave of God"), Jabir b. Zayd
concluded that the imam was himself a veil that concealed the light
of God. The imam then asserted that the light that Jabir beheld, by
means of his visionary perception, was both the angel Salman and
Jabir's own "(better) self." Importantly, a macroanthropic angel
must logically be the *batin* not only of the imam, but of all people—
indeed, of all creation. A visionary experience of the angel was non-
allegorical yet intrapsychic. The statement, "Thou hast seen as
much as thou couldst stand," asserted the further gnostic doctrine
of the relativity of visionary experience to the visionary. The imam's
teaching concluded with the suggestion that Jabir dispense with
the imam's intermediacy, so that Jabir would "bear from Him [Sal-
man] as much as thou bearest from us." A full understanding of esoteric truth would then be possible.

Identification of the macroanthropic angel as a gnostic's own
higher self may also be detected in a portion of a pre-Fatimid initiation rite. The candidate was to ask, "Will the name that thou art
going to give me remain mine?" His shaykh would then answer, "If
thou art worshiped." The candidate would query, "How can one
speak like this?" The shaykh would explain, "Thy name is thy owner,
and thou art its slave."[54] What was to be worshiped was the angelic
name, but it was no other than the *batin* of the candidate himself.

Fatimid legend credited the fifth imam, Jafar al-Sadiq, with
the teaching: "Strive to reach the sky gradually (by a ladder), and
you will find what you want." When asked to identify the ladder, he
spoke of "progress in learning, by which one advances higher and
higher in it, and approaches it by his increasing knowledge and
understanding."[55] The Highest Proof, or angelic *batin* of the imam,
was "the top of the spiritual ladder, and its final goal."[56] Although

these formulations are consistent with metaphoric understandings to ascension, they may also be understood imaginally. Fatimid legend had ʿAli teach, "God . . . has given us the Greatest Name, by uttering which we may, if we wish, ascend the Heaven, make the sun, moon, and stars to obey us. But with all this we eat and drink, walk in the market place, and do what we will, by the command of God, our Lord."[57]

Although some Ismaʿili described the macroanthropic hypostasis as Salman, another tradition had ʿAli state: "Muhammad and myself are One Light, from the Light of God. God has ordered this Light to split into two halves, and said to one half: 'Be Muhammad,' and to the other:—'Be ʿAli.' This is why the Prophet said: "Ali is from me, and I am from ʿAli. Nobody can act on my behalf except ʿAli'. "[58]

The hypostatic basis of the the doctrine of the imamate was also expressed in the regard for ʿAli as "the ultimate limit of all limits."[59] He was the "Great [letter] ʿayn . . . the First Reason, the Supreme Creative Substance, which makes itself manifested (to the human perception) in the most perfect guise, while, at the same time, it is deeply hidden at the bottom of every creation."[60] ʿAli was the intermediary of salvific vision and gnosis. Legend had him assert, "A slave of God will not become perfect in his faith until he recognises myself in my (real) Luminous Substance. . . . He, the faithful, can only by this become one seeing what he wants to know."[61] The Ismaʿili conception of ʿAli as the perfect man[62] possibly derived from the early gnostic *ghulat*. It was a general conception among Shiites[63] and an instance of the doctrine, tracing to Hellenistic Gnosticism, that salvation consists of a spiritual transformation, through the mediation of the redeemer, into perfect conformance with the anthropos.

The ecstatic practices of the Ismaʿili, which are attested for the late twelfth century, at the end of the Fatimid rule, involved experiences of communion:

> Prayer (*salat*) is of two kinds. One is the ordinary prescribed prayer. . . . The other form of prayers is spiritual; it is based on high training of the soul and consciousness, and belongs to the sphere of the "worship by knowledge", *al-ʿibadatuʾl-cilmiyya*. It is differently described by terms such as "attachment" (*ittisal*) to God, or "approachment" (*taqarrub*) to Him, or "union" (*ittihad*) with Him, or connection with the higher world (*al-iritibat biʾl-malaʾiʾl-aʿla*).[64]

The term *ittisal* was a technical term among Muslim Neo-Aristotelians and Sufis for the experience of "conjunction" with the intellect. The term *ittihad* denoted introspective union among the Sufis;[65] but because the Isma'ili understood union to proceed not with God, but with a demiurgic hypostasis, they may have used *ittihad* as a synonym for *ittisal* in reference to experiences of communion.

The Isma'ili technique for attaining *ittisal* differed from the practices of Sufi mystics: "It has nothing to do with any fixed formula, or prescribed genuflexions or prostrations, or any special movements of the body. It can only be performed in spirit, by the force of continuous meditation, or by the power of concentration (*bi-quwwati'l-irtibad wa shiddati'l-muhafaza*)."[66]

The Isma'ili did not engage in *dhikr*,[67] the self-hypnotic repetition of a "fixed formula" that is favored by Sufis. Neither did they use "special movements," as, for example, the self-hypnotic whirling of the Mevlevi order of Sufis.

The Isma'ili practice of "continuous meditation" was described more fully in a later passage:

> The human soul (*nafs*) can be given the possibility of admittance to the realm of ideas (*ad-dar as-siwariyya*). . . . With the help of its imagination the soul is able to form a (general) idea (*sura*) of this world, which it abstracts from its materiality. Such abstraction is composed of substances of angels (*dhawatu'l-mala'ika*),—as elemental forces,—and of ideas (*siwar*). The soul continues to increase its knowledge, and its psychical faculties never cease inquiring until it goes to receive the order of God (*amr*), by which it becomes ready to possess the blessing of reason and love (*uns*)- . . . . the final spiritual union (*al-ittisal al-kulli*).[68]

The experience called *ittisal* entailed access to the world of ideas. The ideas were understood in their technical sense in the Platonic tradition, as abstract concepts of universal categories, that might be derived by intellectual abstraction from material phenomena. For example, seeing a great many trees might give rise to the abstract concept, tree. The abstract concept was considered to be a force responsible for structuring material things. The idea "tree" was what caused amorphous matter to assume the form and functions of a tree. As was generally held by philosophers of the era, formative, structuring ideas of this sort were the true nature of angels.

Rational thinking on the topic of angels, so defined, was the "continuous meditation" of the Isma'ili.[69] The meditations eventually precipitated an ecstasy that was characterized by the reception of the Divine *amr*, "order, command, will." The revelations were rational in character and were experienced as a "blessing of reason and love":

> *Wahy*, or Divine inspiration, is what the mind (*nafs*) of the Prophet receives through his intellect (*ʿaql*), in the way of revelation, from the Will (*amr*) of the Creator. It does not come into conflict with the (intellectual) powers of the reasoning soul (*an-nafs an-natiqa*), i.e. human mind, or common sense. . . . *Wahy* repeatedly descends upon the bearer, independently of his own will.[70]

Ittisal, communion, was not an end in itself, but the condition of gnosis. Through repeated experiences of inspiration, an Ismaʿili would gradually acquire otherwise inaccessible spiritual knowledge:

> Those who purify their minds, and obey God, may gradually attain the state when the lights of the Realities are kindled in them by the angels, higher knowledge becomes accessible to them (*yuha ilay-hi wa yulqa ʿalay-hi*), and they receive the highest equality and the greatest happiness (*al-qistuʾl-aʿam waʾl-hazzuʾl-ajzal*). Obstructing veils then become torn before their spiritual vision, and they begin to know many things which are normally hidden from mankind.[71]

Ismaʿili Neoplatonism

The Fatimid dynasty came to power as an expression of Ismaʿili messianism. The leader, ʿAbd Allah, adopted the title al-Mahdi, and designated his son and successor as al-Qaʾim. As the dynasty wore on, however, history failed to culminate and Ismaʿili doctrines were obliged to change. Among the innovations was an embrace of the newly translated legacy of Hellenism. Different Fatamid *daʾis* met the challenge by developing Neoplatonic and Neo-Aristotelian versions of Ismaʿili gnosis.

The Ismaʿili exploitation of Neoplatonism was begun by Muhammad ibn Ahmad al-Nasafi (d. 942) and consolidated by Abu Yaʿqub al-Sijistani (martyred after 971). The *Enneads* of Plotinus, which had been translated into Arabic in the middle of the ninth century under the title *The Theology of Aristotle*,[72] provided Neoplatonic terms and concepts that the Ismaʿili writers employed.

From Plotinus onward, Neoplatonism had recognized a hierarchy of the One, the Intellect, the World-Soul, and the many individual souls that compose it.[73] Al-Nasafi took over these teachings and co-ordinated the Quranic doctrine of creation with the Neoplatonic doctrine of hierarchic emanation by redefining the One. Where Neoplatonism's One is the true nature of being—for the many are illusions—al-Nasafi named God the innovator of both "the thing" (*al-shay*) and "non-thing-ness" (*al-lashay*).[74] This insistence on a strictly negative theology was at least partly indebted to a gnostic distinction between God and the demiurge. In Isma'ili Neoplatonism, God was wholly transcendent, beyond both being and nonbeing; and it was the "First Originated Being," *al-'aql*, the *nous* or Intellect, that al-Nasafi called the "causes of causes."[75]

Although it is conventional to interpret Isma'ili references to God rather than to the Neoplatonic One as a mere shift in nomenclature, the mystical implications are substantive. The early Neoplatonists, followed by most Sufi mystics, favored introspective unitive experiences that accommodated doctrinal affirmations of the mystic's successful achievement of ultimate or absolute reality. The Isma'ili instead favored communion (*ittisal*), which tends to accommodate a wholly negative theology concerning a transcendent God, together with an affirmative theology concerning the presence of a divine hypostasis. Once a tradition acquires a negative theology, however, mystics' concerns with the doctrine may induce the contents of their trances to shift from introspective unions to ecstatic nothingness.[76] Two doctrinal options are then possible. The experiences of theological negativity may be equated or, as in the Neoplatonism of Iamblichus and his Isma'ili successors, they are given hierarchic rank, with absolute indescribability being contrasted with experienced nothingness.

An explicit concern with the latter option was expressed in al-Nasafi's positive conception of *al-lashay*, "non-thing-ness," as something that was itself transcended by God.

Al-Nasafi also introduced a distinct cosmogonic phase between God and the demiurgic Intellect. God directly created "the Word of God" (*Kalimat Allah*) or "existenciation" (*al-Ibda*). This "existenciation" was part of the first hypostasis, the Intellect (*al-'Aql*); but it was the portion that facilitated or directly caused the emanation of the remainder. In its turn, Intellect generated the rest of the Neoplatonic hierarchy.[77] These formulations, which were intended to have esoteric implications for Isma'ili gnostics, reduced the Neoplatonic One to a mere aspect of the Intellect. The ultimate ground of being, the Thinker of the ideas that comprise the Intellect was granted the status of the consciousness (i.e., of nothingness), whose existence individual ideas presuppose.[78]

Al-Nasafi's innovation was endorsed by al-Sijistani, whose formulations received official Fatimid sanction during the reign of the fourth caliph, al-Mu'izz (953–975).[79] Al-Sijistani was responsible for reconceptualizing the idea of Soul. For fourteen centuries, the Platonic tradition had contrasted the One, the archetypal ideas (understood collectively as the Intellect), and their individual activities or implementation (the Soul). Al-Nasafi's hierarchy added a transcendent God; but compensated by following Neo-Aristotelianism in treating the One and its ideas as a single hypostatic phenomenon. Al-Sijistani introduced a distinctly fourth term.

Neoplatonism had traditionally been an acosmist philosophy. Matter was considered an illusion, a mental impression that was produced in the soul. Because matter required no further account, the doctrine of hypostatic emanation meant, in turn, that all was in and of the One. Uncritical adoptions of Neoplatonic acosmism in Islam resulted in the so-called pantheism or monism of Ibn Masarra,[80] Ibn al-'Arabi,[81] and other Sufis.

The Isma'ili Neoplatonists instead adhered to the traditional Muslim view of the material cosmos as a work of divine creation. Al-Nasafi had worked out the distinction between God and the creation. It remained for al-Sijistani to explore how the emanations of intellect and soul might issue in the reality, and not merely the illusion, of materiality. The logical problems were extensive.

Because the Isma'ilis understood Intellect in a Neo-Aristotelian rather than a Neoplatonic manner, they did not think it an undifferentiated transcendent entity that housed and so included static archetypal ideas. Intellect was understood to consist of both the ideas and their active implementation in the world. The traditional Platonic view of soul, as motive or active implementations of ideas, then ceased to be meaningful. On the other hand, because Neoplatonism regarded matter as an illusion produced by soul, Neoplatonism had not had to distinguish between soul and material form. Soul had been treated as an emanation from the Intellect that accounted for the ideas' motions. Like soul, the motions might be either collective or individual.

Al-Sijistani was unable to develop a solution to the problem by equating Neoplatonism's soul with Aristotle's view of forms as entities that are invariably manifest in matter. Souls and forms could not be the same things. Corpses retained form when souls went either to paradise or hell. Forms ranked below soul, together with matter, as the components of a hypostasis that al-Sijistani termed nature.[82]

What then was soul? In gnosticism and the rival theologies of its intellectual milieu, the concept of "soul" may best be compared with our modern concept of consciousness. It was purely spiritual—which is to say, wholly intellectual or abstract. Like Intellect, Soul might be said to consist of an immaterial or spiritual substance that was located within a body; but this substance was equivalent to consciousness. It was purely intelligible. It was a spiritual entity that could be thought, but it had no form, shape, or extension that could be imagined. Notions of the soul's form, shape, or appearance regularly pertained not to the soul, but only to the bodies in which it was found.

In Gnosticism, the soul in its descent into the world put on a series of appearances and so acquired a psychic body. Each accommodated the archon of a heaven through which the soul passed.[83] In Neoplatonism, the descent of the soul caused it to acquire a "clothing" or "garment" of light in each of the seven heavens.[84] Celestial light was regarded as a physical substance, the ether. It was sometimes conceived as a fifth element, but most frequently as an ideal blend of the four elements. St. Paul took the position that the soul, which is to say, consciousness, is removed at death from the physical body and placed in a spiritual body.[85] Most Christians believed, however, that the soul is transferred at the resurrection from a fallible and mortal body to a perfect, immortal, and yet completely physical body.[86]

No one prior to al-Sijistani seems to have entertained a three-tiered hierarchy. Because form was something that an idea assumed when it was extended in space and embodied in substance, there was neither need nor room to conceive of a class of phenomena that were intermediate between ideas and their embodied forms. Al-Sijistani's innovation cannot be explained as a logical consequence of the effort to reconcile Neoplatonism with Muslim views of the soul. Neoplatonism had several times been adapted to monotheistic creationism in Christianity, Judaism, and Islam, without paralleling al-Sijistani's achievement. What was at stake, I suggest, was the esoteric status of visionary experiences. By distinguishing not ideas and souls, but ideas, souls, and the forms in nature, al-Sijistani attributed a status to souls that was consistent with the traditional gnostic view of the imaginal character of visions.

The souls that might be beheld during visions were not contingent on bodies, as forms are. Neither were they reducible to allegorical expressions of ideas that were purely intelligible. Souls were discrete entities in their own right. Visions were subjective, but they were also veridical events that participated in the integrity and autonomy of the soul.

Umm al-kitab

Another important development in early Islamic gnosis is attested in a Shiite work entitled *Umm al-kitab, "The Mother* (or *Archetype) of the Book."* Different authorities date it anywhere from the eighth to the twelfth centuries. The text is extant in a Persian translation that was preserved among the Isma'ilis of the mountains along the Upper Oxus, but the original was probably written in Arabic by a member of a *ghulat* sect.[87]

In several respects, *Umm al-kitab* is a typical work of Shiite gnosis. The demiurge, whom the *Umm al-kitab* called Salman, was a being of pure light, a gnostic anthropos, and the hypostatic Intellect of the creation.[88] *Umm al-kitab* also adhered to the traditional gnostic emphasis on a septad, resulting in a doctrine of seven Intelligences, formed of light—that is, of the demiurge Salman.[89]

The seven intelligences were treated as hypostases, manifestations of divine transcendence in the angelic form of light. Salman was pure light; the seven were each a different color.[90] Each intelligence was the source of an entire series of creations. The seven intelligences were the seven "limbs of God" that determined seven components of the human body, the seven planets, the seven prophets of the seven eras of world history: the eras of Adam, Nuh, Ibrahim, Musa, 'Isa, Muhammad, and Qa'im, prior to the world's reintegration within the infinity of God. The seven prophets were simultaneously the three letters and four diacritical points that form the Arabic word *shakhs,* "person."[91]

Umm al-kitab also discussed a system of twelve lights, termed the "World of the Mothers," that was responsible for the twelve zodiacal signs and twelve regions of the human body (from Aries to Pisces as follows: head, neck, hands, chest, abdomen, navel, genitals, thighs, knees, feet).[92] Taken together, the seven intelligences and the twelve mothers corresponded to the nineteen letters of the Arabic alphabet.[93]

The crucial innovations of *Umm al-kitab* are ascribed by Pio Filippani-Ronconi to the influences of the yogic practices and ideology of the Vajrayana system of Buddhist tantra.[94] Because parallels are only to be expected in the views of mystics who make sequential uses of mystical visions and unions and adhere to philosophies of metaphysical idealism, Islamicists have been reluctant to accept Filippani-Ronconi's argument. However, the evidence of tantra is persuasive.

From Hellenistic Egypt to early Islam, gnostics had envisioned ascensions to heaven that were considered actual—real encounters with real beings whose real powers were manifest in the sky. Experiences of communion and extrovertive union added complexity to the interpretation of visions. The seven heavens were considered objective and external from a human perspective, but subjective and internal from the standpoint of union with the anthropos or first hypostasis.

With *Umm al-kitab* we meet, for the first time in the history of Western mysticism, the now familiar doctrine that ascension through the regions of the cosmos is accomplished internally within the individual mystic, in a manner that is not allegorical but actual.

From its Stoic invention until its medieval reformulation, the traditional understanding of the macrocosm-microcosm relationship involved a doctrine of correspondence or sympathy. The four elements that were understood to constitute the macrocosm were also held to compose the human body. A physical force that acted on the elements in the world was held to have a consistent action in the body. Through the associations of the four elements and humors, external physical forces were thought to have internal psychological consequences. Except that modern analyses of the chemical elements and psychoactive neurohormones are much more complicated, empirical science maintains these theories to this today. It is only the errors of the ancient theories (e.g., that the red light of the planet Mars affects the redness of rusty iron, roses, and blood, and the sanguine humor) that have obscured the scientific character of macrocosm-microcosm correspondence.

A very different and thoroughly mystical approach is presented in *Umm al-kitab*, for it asserts not the correspondence but the identity of the macrocosm and the microcosm. In the Shiite text, the seven heavens were reduced to a series of locations within the human body. It was not simply that the seven intelligences determined the manifestations of both seven planets and seven components of the human body (Moon—marrow, Mercury—bones, Venus—fat,

Sun—veins, Mars—blood, Jupiter—flesh, Saturn—skin).[95] Fatimid Ismaʿilism similarly associated its seven hypostases with seven ages in the evolution of the embryo and in the prophetic history of the world.[96] *Umm al-kitab* presented the temporal correspondence as a complete physical identity. The ascension described in *Umm al-kitab,* which was identified with the *miʿraj* of Muhammad through the seven heavens, proceeded along "the subtle vein connecting heart with brain and brain with the heavens."[97]

The idea of an internalized ascension was previously unknown in the West, but it was traditional in tantra. To attribute its presence in *Umm al-kitab* to an independent innovation is unreasonable, for the notion of an axial vein of nerves, termed *nada,* is a central and distinctive motif of the kundalini yoga of Hindu tantra. Another distinctly tantric element was the establishment of a definite mythic itinerary. Gnosis had traditionally accommodated visions of highly variable contents by attributing their variation to gnostics' differing degrees of spiritual perfection. Tantra instead seeks visions of highly specific traditional contents. *Umm al-kitab* adhered to the tantrist convention in describing the goal of its gnosis as the reunion of the gnostic with his celestial archetype, Adam.[98] Adam was not treated as a macroanthropos, but was instead located in "his own seat in the anterior lobe of the brain," a position that was simultaneously the peak of Sri Lanka.[99] There is no precedent in Islam for such a conception. Adam's location on the peak of Sri Lanka may readily be recognized, however, as a reflection of Siva's location at the summit of Mount Meru—that is, the crown of the head—in kundalini yoga.

In contrast with Filippani-Ronconi's general argument for the influence of tantra, his specific claims regarding the Buddhist Vajrayana school are inconclusive. The seven intelligences of *Umm al-kitab* are each a different color of light, as is consistent with the tantric Vajrasattva.[100] Color-coding of the seven *cakras* is also a commonplace, however, of Hindu tantra. The *Umm al-kitab* presents a primordial pentad that consists of Muhammad, ʿAli, his wife Fatima (daughter of Muhammad), and their sons Hasan and Husayn. Filippani-Ronconi asserted that the pentad originated as a Islamicization of the five Buddhas of the Vajrayana school.[101] However, Bengali tantra worships five Devatas,[102] and Shaivite tantra knows the divine pentad Siva, Visnu, the Goddess, Sun, and Ganesa—like the Muslim pentad, four males and a female.[103]

In the present context, *Umm al-kitab* may be treated as an early instance of a general milieu. Islamic syncretisms of gnosis and tantra presumably happened repeatedly over the centuries. Muslim trade, colonization, and missionary activity in India were all underway well in advance of the Muslim conquests of northern India in 1193 and Bengal, beginning ten years later.[104] The missionary work was begun by Sufis in the late tenth or early eleventh century. Several legendary missionaries are known by name. Interestingly, Nuru'd-Din, known as Nur Satagar, was an Isma'ili of the Nizari sect who was sent to India during the reign of Siddha Raj (1094–1143).[105] The influences were reciprocal. Persian words occur in the songs of Gorakh, whom Hindus remember as the first to popularize yoga along the Muslim borderlands, perhaps in the eleventh and early twelfth centuries.[106] Scholars generally hold that the Sufi meditative technique of *dhikr,* "remembering," was inspired by the tantrist use of mantras, perhaps as early as the twelfth century.[107] Sufism in northern India and Bengal had a unified and strongly Arabic-Persian character through the fifteenth century.[108] Sufism in Bengal later went its own way, becoming a thoroughgoing synthesis of Sufism and Hindu tantra.[109]

Theosophical Sufism

The Fatimids were capable of severely punishing leading government functionaries who failed to maintain the secrecy of Isma'ili esoterica.[110] Individuals with less claim to Fatimid indulgence were presumably all the more circumspect. Outside Isma'ili territories, Isma'ili doctrines were heretical and subject to persecution. Under the circumstances, we need not be troubled that the historical sequels to Shiite gnosis outside the Isma'ili community cannot be linked directly to Isma'ilism. Prudence demanded secrecy, as in the following tradition related that a Sufi might see God in a living Shiite imam:

> The Imam Ja'far Sadiq replied one day to a man who asked him whether it was true that on the day of the Resurrection God would be visible to all: "Yes," said the Imam. "He is visible even before that day; he has been visible since the day when he asked, 'Am I not your Lord?' The True Believers have seen him even in this world. Dost thou not see him?" And the man replied: "O my Lord, I see *thee.* Permit that by thy authority I go and announce it to the others." But the Imam said: "No, say nothing to anyone, for the people are stupid and ignorant, they will not understand; they will disavow you and hurl the anathema at you."[111]

For the Isma'ili, the doctrine of the imamate had political consequences. For the Sufis, it was mystical alone.

Because the distinctive influence of al-Nasafi and al-Sijistani is
discernible in theosophical Sufism, we may safely assume that
Isma'ili gnosis contributed to its development. The internalization
of a mythic itinerary, consistent with tantra, may also be noted.

Sufism seems to have begun in the seventh and eighth centuries as a practice of asceticism. It was not originally a mysticism. It
acquired a unitive mysticism to add to its original ascesis, either in
the ninth century or perhaps late in the eighth. The unions were
then of an introspective type that entailed a sense of identity with
God. Mansur al-Hallaj was executed in 922 for claiming that he was
God, and Sufism remained disreputable until the 1090s when the
venerated philosopher Abu Hamid al-Ghazzali (d. 1111) mounted an
eloquent defense on its behalf. In the interval, Isma'ilis had founded
the Fatimid dynasty, embraced Neoplatonism, and proselytized extensively both within the empire and without.

In the early Fatimid period, Sufism had little to do with gnosis.
Al-Hujwiri (d. 1070), for example, eagerly sought visions of God as
long as vision was a metaphor for experiences of abstract conceptual
understanding. He denounced actual visionary experiences, however, as "utter anthropomorphism and manifest error."[112]

In his defense of Sufism at the height of Fatimid power and influence a few decades later, al-Ghazzali accepted the combination of
union and vision that gnostics practiced. He taught that after the
soul experiences its identity with God, it may proceed to still higher
states. "The form of the spiritual world (*malakut*) begins to reveal
itself to him and the souls of angels and prophets begin to appear
in comely forms, and that which is willed by his Divine Majesty
begins to show forth."[113] This privileging of visions over unitive
experiences, which was to become a Sufi commonplace, was unprecedented in the history of Islamic gnosis. It may have had antecedents, however, not only in tantra, but also in the merkabah mystics'
practice of postinitiatory magic.

The foundation of "theosophical Sufism," as the gnostic schools
of Sufism are known, are conventionally associated with Shihab al-
Din al-Suhrawardi al-Maqtul (1153–1191), Ruzbihan of Shiraz
(1128–1209), and Muhyi al-Din Ibn al-'Arabi (1165–1240). Many
works of theosophical Sufism were composed in a new style of
esotericism. Isma'ili writings had been kept secretly, but apart
from omissions reserved for oral instruction, the secret texts are
plainly stated. With theosophical Sufism, however, Muslim gnostics

adopted a blend of allegory and cipher that amounted to a secretive language.[114] Similar practices may be found in the literature of Western alchemy[115] and Muslim alchemy definitely blended with gnosis around 960, when the Ikhwan al-Safa, "Brethren of Purity," attempted to reunite the non-Fatimid Isma'ilis on a common doctrinal basis.[116] In their encyclopedia, the Ikhwan al-Safa drew on pseudonymous alchemical writings, attributed to Jabir ibn Hayyan, that were probably produced by an associated circle of alchemists.[117] Theosophical Sufis expressed gnostic ideas in an alchemical style of secrecy, in writings that are not themselves alchemical.

Suhrawardi Maqtul

Henry Corbin, who more than anyone was responsible for clarifying the gnostic character of Isma'ilism and theosophical Sufism, drew attention to a profoundly significant innovation of theosophical Sufism: the concept of the world of imagination. Corbin attributed the innovation to Ibn al-'Arabi;[118] subsequent research has assigned precedence to Suhrawardi.[119]

The Sufis' point of departure, we may assume, was the traditional gnostic problem of accounting for the phenomena beheld in visions. Were they fantasies or realities? Subjective or objective? Internal or external? Worthy of faith or not? The older response, that the phenomena were internal to the anthropos or demiurge with whom the gnostic had union, ceased to be adequate when Sufis combined gnosis with the practice of trance. Not only had the very concept of internality to be reconsidered, but the doctrine had to be applicable to both lucid hypnagogia and trance.

Sufi gnostics solved the problem, I suggest, by developing al-Sijistani's concept of souls. Suhrawardi's doctrine *hikmat al-ishraq,* "wisdom of illumination," was explicitly concerned to justify belief in visionary experiences. Drawing on Neoplatonic light imagery, Suhrawardi designated God as the "light of lights." Although he insisted on an ontological distinction between God and all else, he treated existent things as irradiations of divine light of differing intensities. In this context, vision consisted of a soul's illumination by the light that an object constitutes. Sight perception was consequently a mere variant of visionary experience.[120]

In its basic structure, Suhrawardi's system was a simplified and apolitical form of Islamic gnosis. The angel Gabriel was simultaneously the prophet Muhammad, archetype of humanity, and source of human souls, the Holy Spirit of traditional Islam, the Intellect of the philosophers, and the sage or elder who functioned as a gnostic's teacher and guide during visionary experiences.[121] Tantric influences may occasionally be detected in Suhrawardi's gnosis. He described gnostic ascension as an internal itinerary through three major zones: the "Occident" of the material world, with its ten cosmic regions; the "middle Orient" whose heavens constitute the five inner senses of human beings (sensation, fantasy, apprehension, imagination, and memory); and the intellectual or angelic realm of the "Orient of lights."[122]

In his *Treatise of the Birds,* Suhrawardi had birds, signifying gnostics' souls, set out on a journey across nine mountains. The journey was so arduous, however, that they rested on the seventh mountain. It was a place of beautiful gardens: "Then we went to the eighth mountain. It was so high its top reached the sky. As we approached we could hear the song of birds, and so melodious they were that we slowed our flight and descended. We saw all sorts of good things: we saw forms so delightful that one could not take one's eye from them."[123] The delightful forms on the summit of the mystic Mt. Qaf[124] may be understood in a Platonic sense. The seventh mountain was the garden of paradise. The eighth was a world of forms.

Remarkably, in Suhrawardi's tale, the birds never journey onward to the ninth mountain. Their further journey is vertical. They ascend to a city atop the eighth mountain, and it is there that they enter the palace of the king: "We saw a pavilion and courtyard so vast we could not comprehend it visually. . . . Then we came to a chamber and, as we set foot inside, the resplendence of the king could be seen from afar. In that brilliance our eyes were dazzled, our heads spun and we lost consciousness."[125]

The experience began with a phase of extrovertive union in which the unification was "so vast we could not comprehend it visually," for it filled the entire cosmos. The unitive experience next became introspective—"we set foot inside"—and acquired a distinctly theistic character, which was termed "the resplendence of the king." Finally, the experience moved beyond union into a loss of consciousness, an experience, as it were, of nothingness.

Suhrawardi described the *mi'raj* of Muhammad in similarly "psycho-cosmic"[126] terms. It was an ascension through the cosmos and all further states of being into the divine presence, yet it was simultaneously a journey within the microcosm through the soul and intellect to the divine self.[127]

To this basic structure, Suhrawardi added an extensive angelology that blended Neoplatonic conceptions with Zoroastrian
terminology.[128] Suhrawardi's angelology may also be understood,
however, as a presentation of theosophy in visual imagery. Suhrawardi justified his belief in his visionary experiences by reference to an innovative theory of forms:

> He [the Sufi] observes forms of exquisite freshness and subtlety
> through direct communication with the celestial powers. This is
> the intermediate stage in the stages of the People of Love. In a
> state between wakefulness and sleep one hears horrible voices and
> strange cries, and in the unconscious state of the *sakina* one sees
> great lights. . . . Such events happen to masters, not to those who
> shut their eyes in solitude and let their imagination take flight.[129]

This passage contrasted ecstatic deaths during hypnagogic
states and "great lights" envisioned in trance states with ordinary
flights of fancy. Suhrawardi was uninterested in daydreams. He
was instead concerned to account for ecstasies. He sometimes attributed their forms to an "intermediate stage" between sense perception and intellectual reasoning, but his major innovation was to
transform the epistemology into an ontology.[130] Where al-Sijistani
had addressed the question of the *truthfulness* of the soul's visions,
Suhrawardi insisted on the objective *reality* of the forms disclosed.
What gnostics beheld in visions was, for Suhrawardi, an objectively
existing realm, "the world of the unseen," "the other world,"[131] "the
world of suspended images," or "world of pure figures."[132]

Suhrawardi's otherworld was not an invisible aspect of the
world we know, as are the otherworlds of shamanism, Celtic religion, and Arthurian romance. He did not attribute the forms of
physical phenomena to indwelling metaphysical beings that might
be beheld during visionary experiences. Neither was his otherworld
limited to Platonic ideas that were intelligible but not envisionable.
Suhrawardi's otherworld was also not a spatial extension of this
world. It was not an upper world, high in the sky, as is heaven in
Judaism, Christianity, Mandaeism, and Islam. Suhrawardi's otherworld was a different dimension or order of existence, whose mystery defied logical description and explanation. It was spatially
both within a person's earthbound body and a distinct region of the
cosmos. It was not simply upper, or nether, or invisible. It was distinctly other.

Unlike the forms beheld by the senses, conceptualized by rational faculty, and irrationally combined from memory in daydreams,

the forms of the otherworld were disclosed to the imaginative faculty. Suhrawardi prescribed training in self-hypnosis as the means for the other world's perception.

> When the inner eye is opened, the outer eye should be sealed to everything, the lips shut to everything; and the five external senses should cease to be used and the internal senses employed in their place such that when the patient wants to hold something, he should hold it with his inner hand, when he wants to see something, he should see it with his inner eye, when he wants to hear something, he should hear it with his inner ear, when he wants to smell something, he should smell it with his inner nose, and his sense of taste should come from the soul's palate. Once this is accomplished, he can regard the secret of the heavens continually and be informed at every moment from the world of the unseen.[133]

Ibn al-ʿArabi

Ibn al-ʿArabi, the towering genius of medieval Sufism, is called *Muhyi al-Din*, "the Revivifier of Religion," and *al-Shaykh al-Akbar*, "the Greatest Master." He possessed an encyclopedic familiarity with the mystical and philosophic literatures of Islam, and he seems also to have met and exchanged ideas with as many Sufi masters as he was able. His intellectual voracity may have taken him still farther afield. Many of his teachings were deeply influenced by the Ismaʿili and related Shiites such as the Qarmathians and Ikhwan al-Safa ("Brethren of Purity").[134] His thought shares several of the basic perspectives of the early kabbalah; and an Arabic version of a Persian translation of a Sanskrit work on tantric Yoga was attributed to him.[135]

Visionary experiences formed a basic part of his mystical practice. Blending the Neo-Aristotelian allegorism of Ibn Sina and Ibn Tufail[136] with the traditional gnostic view that visions are intrapsychic but nonsymbolic, Ibn al-ʿArabi arrived at the paradox that visions are both symbolic and nonsymbolic simultaneously. Consider the following example:

> Although this mystic "station" (i.e., *manzilat tanzihi'l tawhid*) consists in the intuition of the Absolute unity and transcendence of God, the knowledge revealed in the act of illumination (i.e., in the heart of the Sufi) is "given" in the form of something tangible. It is the shape of a "house" supported on five columns upon which a roof

spreads. The house is surrounded by doorless walls, which make
access to it impossible. Outside the house, however, there is a column adjoining the outside wall. The illuminated mystics touch
and kiss this column as Muslims touch and kiss the Black Stone.
The column is not seen and touched in this mystic station alone,
but in *all* mystic stations. It acts as an interpreter of the knowledge revealed to the mystic in such "stations." It has "an eloquent
tongue." The mystics have no means of entering into some of these
manazil, so they just receive their knowledge (concerning them)
from that column outside, and they take what they are told for
granted, for the Sufis have evidence of its infallibility in all that it
tells them in the world of revelation (*kashf*).[137]

Since the otherworld was beheld through the activity of the
imagination, Ibn al-ʿArabi referred to it as ʿ*alam al-mithal,* the
"world of imagination." He understood imagination to depend on
images acquired by the senses and retained in memory, and he recognized the imaginative character of all speculative thinking.[138] He
accepted Suhrawardi's theory of perception as the illumination of
the soul by the objects of its experience,[139] which enabled him to val-
idate the veridicality of visions. Light was the inherent nature of
the macrocosm;[140] and "the light of . . . luminous Wisdom extends
over the plane of the Imagination."[141]

Ibn al-ʿArabi concretized the realm of imagination more fully
than Suhrawardi had. For Suhrawardi, the assumption of a physical substratum by "pure figures" accounted for the existence of demons and devils in the physical world.[142] For Ibn al-ʿArabi, there
were only the two realms of intelligibles and sensibles.[143] Imaginables were a type of sensible. Unlike intelligibles, which are abstractions that "enjoy no real existence, existing only insofar as they
determine [existent beings],"[144] the world of imagination resembled
the material world in having existence.

Ibn al-ʿArabi conceived of the world of imagination as a phantasmagorical dimension of reality, an otherworld of unlimited variety, where the impossible was real and true. "Many rational
impossibilities, i.e. things which sound reason declares to be absurd
exist there."[145] The world of imagination was limited only by its
experience.

Ibn al-ʿArabi adhered to the traditional gnostic doctrine of the
relativity of visions to their visionaries. "You will never take (such
knowledge) except to the extent of your disposition."[146] "You will see
your form in Him. Whoever imagines that he sees the Reality Himself has no gnosis; he has gnosis who knows that it is his own es-

sential self that he sees."[147] To explain the circumstance, Ibn al-'Arabi opted, not entirely logically, for the Neoplatonic doctrine that revelation is ultimately only of one's true self—that is, the One underlying the perceptible many:

> Whenever a gnostic receives a spiritual intuition in which he looks on a form that brings him new spiritual knowledge and new spiritual graces [he should know] that the form he contemplates is none other than his own essential self, for it is only from the tree of his own self that he will garner the fruits of his knowledge. In the same way his image in a polished surface is naught but he, although the place or plane in which he sees his image effects certain changes in the image in accordance with the intrinsic reality of that plane.[148]

Visionary reflections of oneself as the world of imagination were a means of gnostic transformation. "The reality of imagination is transmutation . . . in every state and manifestation . . . in every form."[149] Because he regarded universal ideas as divine hypostases, Ibn al-'Arabi maintained that every "reality which comprises a species or set of truths" "has a [divine] name peculiar to itself" that "is the lord of its reality."[150] Gnosis of the divine names accomplished the gnostic's transformation from state to state:

> God *makes him journey* through His Names, *in order to cause him to see His Signs* (17:1) within him. Thus (the servant) comes to know that He is what is designated by every divine Name—whether or not that Name is one of those described as "beautiful." It is through those Names that God appears in His servants, and it is through Them that the servant takes on the different "colorings" of his states: for They are Names in God, but "colorings" (of the soul) in us. . . .
>
> Thus when God makes the saint (*al-wali*) travel through His most beautiful Names to the other Names and (ultimately) all the divine Names, he comes to know the transformations of his states and the states of the whole world. And (he knows) that that transformation is what brings those very Names to be in *us*.[151]

Transformation through gnosis of the divine names could also be achieved through theosophical analyses of sensory experiences. Ibn al-'Arabi cited a tradition of Muhammad: "Whatever man sees in his worldly life is like a dream for the sleeper—a fancy requiring an interpretation."[152]

Like Suhrawardi, Ibn al-ʿArabi adhered to a depoliticized version of the doctrine of the imamate. Ibn al-ʿArabi conceived of "the First Intellect" as "the Real Adam," whose spirit is to the universe as the soul is to the body. The macroanthropos was simultaneously "the Spirit of Muhammad," whose historical miniature was "the Perfect Man." All people, male and female, might aspire to be transformed into a "Perfect Man," but the actual achievement was attained by few. Most people were imperfect replications of the First Intellect. All prophets were perfect, but only Muhammad had been both perfect and complete.[153] Perfection was also possible for a Sufi saint, who amounted to a depoliticized variant of an Ismaʿili *natiq*.[154] Ibn al-ʿArabi regarded himself as "the Seal of the Saints," an eschatological figure equivalent to al-Mahdi.[155]

According to a saying attributed to Muhammad, there were ninety-nine names of God in the Quran. For theosophical Sufism, each was a hypostasis.[156] Suhrawardi maintained, however, that angelic intelligences were as many as the stars,[157] and Ibn al-ʿArabi insisted that the hypostases of an omnipotent God were necessarily infinite in number.[158] The ninety-nine Quranic names were the "mothers" or "finite roots" of an infinite number of names, corresponding to the infinite number of things that were possible to exist.[159]

The correspondence of the macrocosm and microcosm necessitated the location of the divine names within the human body. "God . . . is, in His Identity, the limbs themselves that are the servant himself. . . . For each limb or organ there is a particular kind of spiritual knowledge."[160]

In keeping with the infinitude of the divine names, gnostic transformation proceeded not through a specific number of stages, but through an open series:

> [The gnostic] affirms His Reality in every formal transformation, worshiping Him in His infinite forms, since there is no limit to the forms in which He manifests Himself. The same is the case with the gnosis of God, there being no limit for the gnostic in this respect. Always the gnostic is seeking more knowledge of Him, saying, *O Lord, increase me in knowledge.* The possibilities are without end on both sides, that of the Absolute and that of relative being.[161]

A coherent theosophical system, entailing a manageable number of variables, was precluded. The experiences of life were to be treated individually, and no pretension of completion was to be allowed. Ibn al-ʿArabi had definite ideas, however, about the initial hypostases with which creation commenced, for these were recapitulated in reverse order in the final stages of a gnostic's return. The following account is from his *Journey to the Lord of Power:*

> And if you do not stop with all of this, He reveals to you the world of formation and adornment and beauty, what is proper for the intellect to dwell upon from among the holy forms, the vital breathings from beauty of form and harmony, and the overflow of languor and tenderness and mercy in all things characterized by them. And from this level comes the sustenance of poets.[162]

This presentation of the world of forms was a rearward looking toward the world, an observation of the forms within sensible things. It was to be contrasted with a forward-looking toward God through the "reflections" of the world of imagination. Ibn al-ʿArabi commented: "All that you witnessed before is from the world of the left hand, not from the world of the right hand. And this is the place of the heart. If He manifests this world to you, you will know the reflections, and the endlessness of endlessnesses, and the eternity of eternities, and the order of existences and how being is infused into them."[163]

A few pages later, immediately before the Sufi quest culminates in mystical union, Ibn al-ʿArabi reverted to Quranic idioms that the Ismaʿili and Sufis shared:

> And if you do not stop with this, He reveals to you the Pen, the First intellect, the master and teacher of everything. You examine its tracing and know the message it bears and witness its inversion, and its reception and particularization of the comprehensive [knowledge] from the angel *al-Nuni.*
>
> And if you do not stop with this, He reveals the Mover of the Pen, the right hand of the Truth.
>
> And if you do not stop with this, you are eradicated, then withdrawn, then effaced, then crushed, then obliterated.
>
> When the effects of eradication and what follows are terminated, you are affirmed, then made present, then made to remain, then gathered together, then assigned.[164]

The Pen was one of the Quranic terms by which the Ismaʿili, the Aristotelian philosophy of Ibn Sina, and theosophical Sufism referred to the First Intellect.[165] For Ibn al-ʿArabi, it was "the first of the created. . . . There was no created thing before it."[166]

From contemplation of the first created being, a gnostic was to progress to contemplation of its mover. The mover was beyond the creation, but it was not beyond contemplation. From Ismaʿili Neo-platonism Ibn al-ʿArabi accepted the basic ideas that only negative terms may be applied to God, that God creates the Intellect, but emanations proceed thereafter, producing the universal soul and nature.[167] He followed the Quran, however, in asserting the unity of God; and he affirmed God as *al-Haqq*, the Real. In keeping with Sufi views on *fana* during mystical union, he further maintained the "unity of all Being" (*wahdat al-qujud*). The insoluble paradox that the creation cannot differ from God and yet does so,[168] provided Ibn al-ʿArabi with a philosophic foundation for his mysticism. Meditation on the concept was succeeded by the Sufi's annihilation, or loss of the sense of human ego.

A Sufi's capacity to contemplate God affirmatively, before being forced into negative formulations, was resolved by Ibn al-ʿArabi by reference to one of the two views of nonexistence that had been developed by the Kalam philosophers of Islam. In contrast with the view that nonexistence refers to nothing whatever, some authorities maintained that God had entertained ideas, prior to creation, as a model that He later implemented through the act of creation. Because God renews the creation at every instant, these antemundane ideas may also be regarded as presently supermundane. In both events, they transcend creation. They lack the spatial extension and form that the ideas of the First Intellect involve. The transcendent ideas are "nonexistent" in contrast with the "existence" of the creation. They are uncreated, eternal, and divine. They are nevertheless "something," the substance out of which God made the world.[169] Muslim Neo-Aristotelian philosophers termed the "nonexistent" the "first *hayula* (hylé)," in contrast with the "second *hayla*" (or first *maddah*, "matter") underlying the four elements.[170]

Ibn al-ʿArabi conceived of the divine names in a consistent and derivative fashion.[171] The transcendent names of God were intermediate between God and the first intellect, which was their implementation in the sensible creation. Neither existent, as is the creation, nor nonexistent, as God, the transcendent names of God comprised a "third entity" between God and the creation. Called the "Reality of Realities," the third entity was an inert, feminine, intelligible substance: "Prime Matter," the "root (*asl*) of the universe," and "mother (*umm*) of all existents."[172]

Ibn al-ʿArabi explained the act of creation as a transformation of the uncreate but static names of the third entity, through the introduction of divine potency or vitality, into the active or dynamic processes of the First Intellect. Having been an uncreate object of God's thought, God's names acquired the potency of God's subjectivity, shifted from feminine passivity to masculine activity, and so become the First Intellect, or Adam.

For Ibn al-ʿArabi, the cosmos was a mirror in which God beheld Himself:

> The Reality wanted to see the essences of His Most Beautiful Names or, to put it another way, to see His own Essence, in an all-inclusive object encompassing the whole [divine] Command, which, qualified by existence, would reveal to Him His own mystery. For the seeing of a thing, itself by itself, is not the same as its seeing itself in another, as it were in a mirror.[173]

The substance of the mirror replicated the third entity at a lower level of being. "The Reality gave existence to the whole Cosmos [at first] as an undifferentiated thing without anything of the spirit in it, so that it was like an unpolished mirror."[174] God, "qualified by existence," thus became the first hypostasis: the divine names whose extension in space permitted them to exist as intelligible patterns or forms.

From the First Intellect, Soul and Nature emanated. They replicated the previous sequence at a still lower level of being. Through soul's union with the undifferentiated hylic matter underlying the four elements, matter became "Universal Nature . . . the Breath of the Merciful in which are unfolded the forms of the higher and lower Cosmos."[175]

Because creation occurred through the repeated conjunctions of the masculine and feminine within God, creation was an inalienably compound phenomenon:

> The first compound things which God created was the bodies of spirits—the guardian angels—in the Glory of God. Of them are the First Intelligence and the Universal Soul. These two categories comprise the bodies created out of light. There is not a single angel who is created apart from them. Of course, the Soul is inferior to the Spirit. All the angels who are created after these two come under the sway of Nature.[176]

The cosmos was a series of mirror reflections of God, making ignorance of God impossible. "The Prophet said, 'Who [truly] knows himself knows his Lord,' linking together knowledge of God and knowledge of the self."[177] "Know that the Reality, as is confirmed by Tradition, in His Self-manifestation, transmutes Himself in the forms; know also that when the Heart embraces the Reality, it embraces none other than He, since it is as if the Reality fills the Heart."[178]

Importantly, there were aspects of himself that God did not know until he created a mirror in which to see himself. For example, God was not God in the absence of humanity: "The Essence, as being beyond all . . . relationships, is not a divinity. . . . It is we who make Him a divinity by being that through which He knows Himself as Divine. Thus, He is not known [as "God"] until we are known."[179]

Ibn al-ʿArabi regarded human sexuality as an instance of God's self-discovery. Sufis generally considered sexuality an obstacle to spirituality that was either to be avoided through celibacy or accommodated through its containment within marriage. Ibn al-ʿArabi instead venerated sexuality as mystical behavior. Human sexuality reflects, participates in, and contributes to the cosmic sexuality, which is God's self-knowledge.[180] "The relation of woman with man is that of Nature with the Soul. Woman is the medium through which children appear just as Nature is the medium through which bodies appear. They are made and they appear only through this medium. There can be no Soul without Nature and no Nature without Soul."[181]

In making love to a woman, Ibn al-ʿArabi considered himself to be making love to the reflection of God that the woman was. Not only did he entertain the theosophical doctrine as a general belief, but he sought to achieve mystical consciousness of his experiential involvement with God while he performed the sexual act: "When a man loves a woman, he seeks union with her, that is to say the most complete union possible in love, and there is in the elemental sphere no greater union than that between the sexes. . . . His annihilation in her was total at the moment of consummation . . . since it is none other than He Whom he sees in her."[182]

The same ideology underlies a theosophical experience that Ibn al-ʿArabi had in Mecca, when a young girl named Nizam became apparent to his imagination as a manifestation of a feminine hypostasis[183]—presumably the third entity, which alone is virginal:

> Now this *shaikh* had a daughter, a lissome young girl who captivated the gaze of all those who saw her, whose mere presence was the ornament of our gatherings and startled all those who contem-

plated it to the point of stupefaction. Her name was Nizam [Harmonia] and her surname "Eye of the Sun and of Beauty" ['ayn al-Shams wa'l-Baha']. Learned and pious, with an experience of spiritual and mystic life, she personified the venerable antiquity of the entire Holy Land and the candid youth of the great city faithful to the Prophet. The magic of her glance, the grace of her conversation were such an enchantment that when, on occasion, she was prolix, her words flowed from the source; when she spoke concisely, she was a marvel of eloquence; when she expounded an argument, she was clear and transparent. . . . If not for the paltry souls who are ever ready for scandal and predisposed to malice, I should comment here on the beauties of her body as well as her soul, which was a garden of generosity. . . .

At the time when I frequented her, I observed with care the noble endowments that graced her person and those additional charms conferred by the society of her aunt and father. And I took her as model for the inspiration of the poems contained in the present book, which are love poems, composed in suave, elegant phrases, although I was unable to express so much as a part of the emotion which my soul experienced and which the company of this young girl awakened in my heart, or of the generous love I felt, or of the memory which her unwavering friendship left in my memory, or of the grace of her mind or the modesty of her bearing, since she is the object of my Quest and my hope, the Virgin Most Pure [al-Adhra' al-batul]. Nevertheless, I succeeded in putting into verse some of the thoughts connected with my yearning, as precious gifts and objects which I here offer. I let my enamored soul speak clearly, I tried to express the profound attachment I felt, the profound concern that tormented me in those days now past, the regret that still moves me at the memory of that noble society and that young girl.

Whatever name I may mention in this work, it is to her that I am alluding. Whatever the house whose elegy I sing, it is of her house that I am thinking. But that is not all. In the verses I have composed for the present book, I never cease to allude to the divine inspirations [waridat ilahiya], the spiritual visitations [tanazzulat ruhaniya], the correspondences [of our world] with the world of the angelic Intelligences; in this I conformed to my usual manner of thinking in symbols; this because the things of the invisible world attract me more than those of actual life, and because this young girl knew perfectly what I was alluding to [that is, the esoteric sense of my verses].[184]

In their sexuality, Ibn al-'Arabi's doctrines, practices, and ecstasies more closely resemble Bengali tantra and Jewish kabbalah than they do any earlier form of Sufism. Although most tantrists are reputed to "learn to immobilize mind, breath, and the seminal fluid" in order to experience nothingness while copulating,[185] Shakti tantrists in Bengal not only conceptualize themselves and their partners as manifestations of the gods, but they may seek to envision the copulation of the gods' subtle bodies at the moment of their own orgasms.[186]

Najm ad-Din al-Kubra

The possibility of conducting theosophy, not by analysis of the physical world, but by exploration of the world of imagination, had great appeal to the Sufis. "Without formally denying the reality of the physical world, the Muslim spiritualists—in a milieu of political uncertainty, socio-economic imbalance and general external deterioration—sought refuge in a Realm that was more satisfying and certainly more liquid and amenable to imaginative powers."[187] Some visions displayed the distinctive character of active imagination.

Consider, for example, the teachings of Najm ad-Din al-Kubra (1145–1221), who founded the Central Asiatic Kubrawiyya school of Sufism. He maintained that a Sufi's pursuit of perfection required a process of purification by means of visions in which the Sufi is immersed by angels in the seven wells of the seven levels of existence:[188] "It may happen that you visualize yourself as lying at the bottom of a well and the well seemingly in lively downward movement. In reality it is you who are moving upward."[189]

The inner states that a Sufi experienced were translated into visions of deserts, even "cities, countries, houses, which come down from above toward you and later disappear below you, as though you were seeing a dike on the shore crumble and disappear into the sea."[190] The itinerary conformed with an otherworldly geography. An experience of ecstatic death, for example, took form as a vision of the well of the birth of souls. Its sight caused such terror that the Sufi would think that he was about to die. Then a green light would begin to shine from the mouth of the well, and unforgettable marvels would appear.[191]

Moving on, the Sufi might acquire a "Heavenly Witness," an angelic guide through the world of lights:

> When the circle of the face has become pure . . . it effuses lights as
> a spring pours forth its water, so that the mystic has a sensory per-

ception (i.e., through the suprasensory senses) that these lights are gushing forth to irradiate his face. This outpouring takes place between the two eyes and between the eyebrows. Finally it spreads to cover the whole face. At that moment, before you, before your face, there is another Face also of light, irradiating lights; while behind its diaphanous veil a *sun* becomes visible, seemingly animated by a movement to and fro. In reality this Face is your own face and this sun is the sun of the Spirit . . . that goes to and fro in your body. Next, the whole of your person is immersed in purity, and suddenly you are gazing at a person of light . . . who is also irradiating lights. The mystic has the sensory perception of this irradiation of lights proceeding from the whole of his person. Often the veil falls and the total reality of the person is revealed, and then with the whole of your body you perceive the whole. The opening of the inner sight . . . begins in the eyes, then in the face, then in the chest, then in the entire body. This person of light . . . before you is called in Sufi terminology the suprasensory *Guide*. . . . It is also called the suprasensory *personal Master*. . . , or again the suprasensory spiritual *Scales*.[192]

Al-Kubra also described a vision of God. Because God was invisible, the vision took form as a black light.

I saw myself . . . present in a world of light. Mountains and deserts were iridescent with lights of all colors: red, yellow, white, blue. I was experiencing a consuming nostalgia for them; I was as though stricken with madness and snatched out of myself by the violence of the intimate emotion and feeling of the presence. Suddenly I saw that the *black light* was invading the entire universe. Heaven and earth and everything that was there had wholly become black light and, behold, I was totally absorbed in this light, losing consciousness. Then I came back to myself.[193]

Al-Kubra's loss of consciousness probably signified an experience of nothingness. The reported transformation of a visionary experience into nothingness would have been consistent with tantrist techniques for the management of trance.

Al-Kubra claimed that his visionary practice was "the method of alchemy."[194] Through its access to the world of light, it liberated a person's spiritual element from the darkness of the body and transformed the Sufi into a person of light. The development of a body of light required an itinerary through the world of light and constituted the salvific achievement of the "resurrection body."[195]

Chapter 10

The Passage of Gnosis to the Latin West

Gnosticism was present in western Europe at the start of the Italian Renaissance of the late fifteenth century, and has since been a major component of Western esotericism.[1] Since Gnosticism was practiced in western Europe as late as the Albigensian crusade in the thirteenth century, scholars have generally assumed that the gnostic component of Western esotericism had Christian Gnostic antecedents. Henry Corbin noted a number of parallels, however, that instead suggested diffusions from Islam. Islamic theosophers applied esoteric hermeneutics to the Quran in manners that closely resembled the approach to biblical exegesis that was taken by Jacob Boehme, J. G. Gichtel, Valentin Weigel, Swedenborg, and their disciples.[2] Again, the Sufi doctrine of the creative and magical power of the imagination compares closely with the positions taken by Renaissance and Romantic philosophers.[3] Three centuries intervened, however, between the founders of theosophical Sufism and the Renaissance developments of their teachings.

Troubadour Love Songs

The passage of gnosis from Islam to the Latin West was accomplished, so far as I can judge, in at least two waves. The first transmission inspired the love songs of the troubadours in the late eleventh century. Not only is the European word *troubadour* derived from the Arabic verb *taraba,* among whose meanings is "to sing,"[4] but both the genre[5] and the religious ideology underlying medieval European love songs trace to Muslim gnosis. Love poetry had already been an important genre in pre-Islamic Arabic culture, and Sufi poets frequently used images of sexual union to allegorize mystical union.[6] Theosophers provided metaphysical coherence for the literary convention by addressing their poems either to a feminine hypostasis, such as Fatima or wisdom, or to the personification of a hypostasis in a woman or girl. These developments within Sufism influenced the composition of love songs, and the Arabic poetic conventions reached western Europe in the aftermath of the first crusade in the early twelfth century.

Medieval contacts between Islam and Roman Catholicism were not mediated by translators and books alone.[7] At courts and in households in southern Italy, al-Andalus, and Aquitaine, there were interpersonal contacts in every stratum of society from slaves to nobility. Guillaume, the seventh count of Poitiers and the ninth duke of Aquitaine, was either the first troubadour or the earliest whose work has survived.[8] He lived from 1071 to 1127, ruled or misruled perhaps a third of France, was twice excommunicated, and by his example and patronage inaugurated the Western tradition of love songs. Here is an example of his verse:

My companions, I am going to make a *vers* that is refined,
and it will have more foolishness than sense,
and it will all be mixed with love and joy and youth.

Whoever does not understand it, take him for a peasant,
whoever does not learn it deep in his heart.
It is hard for a man to part from love that he finds to his desire.

I have two good and noble horses for my saddle,
they are good, adroit in combat, full of spirit,
but I cannot keep them both, one can't stand the other.

If I could tame them as I wish,
I would not want to put my equipment anywhere else,
for I'd be better mounted then than any man alive.

One of them was the fastest of the mountain horses,
but for a long time now it has been so fierce and shy,
so touchy, so wild, it fights off the currycomb.

The other was nurtured down there around Confolens,
and you never saw a prettier one, I know.
I won't get rid of that one, not for gold or silver.

I gave it to its master as a grazing colt;
but I reserved the right
that for every year he had it, I got it for more than a hundred.

You knights, counsel me in this predicament,
no choice ever caused me more embarrassment:
I can't decide which one to keep, Na Agnes or Na Arsen.

Of Gimel I have the castle and the fief,
and with Niol I show myself proud to everyone,
for both are sworn to me and bound by oath.[9]

The song begins with a comparison of two horses,[10] but the disclosure of the horses' names in the second last verse tends to suggest that two women have been under discussion all along. Agnes and her sister Ermessen appear as Guillaume's physical lovers in another of his songs.[11] Other poems suggest that in the present instance Agnes and Arsen may be treated as a real woman and an idealized, imaginary lover.[12] Since Guillaume devoted another song to the explicitly transcendental joy that his imaginary lover gave him,[13] the reference to joy in the first stanza may be associated with his imaginary love, Arsen. His possession of her for over a century then proceeds without paradox, since it occurs in his imagination. The comparison in the final verse contrasts Guillaume's physical property—castle and fief—with the property of his imagination. It is his imagination, its lady, and especially his poetic art by which he "show[ed] myself proud to everyone."

Guillaume's treatment of his imaginary love, not as the archetype of his real love, but as an alternative and rival to her, accorded her a status that was consistent with the reification of imagination in Islamic gnosis. Indeed, it is possible to adopt a theosophical approach to the poem that treats horses, women, and properties as differing pairs of manifestations of two hypostases. *Fondatz,* foolishness, and *sen,* sense, the twin themes of Guillaume's verse, may be no other than imagination and the world of sense perception.

Although the celebration of imagination in Western literature has continued to the present day, the theosophical impulse in troubadour verse was very short-lived. The genre was adapted almost immediately to a Christian Platonism and so remained for centuries. Sufism gave Europe a genre of mystical poetry, but its Sufi esoterica were replaced by Catholic assumptions. Official contacts and good relations between Guillaume's court at Poitier and the cathedral school of Chartres[14] commenced decades prior to the revival of Christian Platonism in the early twelfth century,[15] and the contacts continued for decades. At least part of the Platonic revival may have been intended to baptize the esoteric dimension of troubadour poetry.

The basic problem was theosophy. The transcendent monotheisms of Islam and Judaism permitted theosophy to become dominant trends in Sufism and the kabbalah, but the Christian doctrine of the incarnation was unable to accommodate a theosophical approach to mysticism. The uniqueness of Christ could not readily be reconciled with a theosophy that comprehended the whole of creation as a series of hypostases. For Christ to be the *only* begotten son of God, his hypostatic union had to be unique. Hypostases could not be universal phenomena, as they are in Ismaiʿilism, Sufism, and the kabbalah.

From the twelfth century onward, Christianity responded to the problem of theosophy by recourse to its Platonic heritage, which was a blend of Middle Platonism with Neoplatonism and some Neo-Aristotelianism. The theological move was less doctrinal than methodological. No differently than theosophy, Christian Platonism distinguished material phenomena and their archetypes, traced the archetypes to God, and so envisioned a universe that manifested God. Platonism used the doctrine as a means to proceed in contemplation from sensible phenomena to pure intelligibles and finally to their source in God. Mystical unions were cultivated, but visionary experiences generally were not. When visions did occur, Christian Platonists interpreted them allegorically, where gnostics accepted them at face value. For gnostic theosophers, unitive experiences were no more than preludes to the theosophical analysis of the worlds of vision and sense experience. This step, the step from mystical union to theosophical analysis, Christian mystics traditionally refrained from taking. Christian Platonism was content with a path of ascension and an ascetic withdrawal from the world. Platonism shunned what theosophy enjoined, a path of subsequent descent and a renewed engagement with God in the world.

The Platonic revival began in the early twelfth century at the cathedral school of Chartres. The principal doctrinal innovation was Bernard of Chartres' distinction between ideas and forms. In his view, ideas were present to the mind of God prior to creation and remain with God eternally. The eternal ideas assumed temporal form (*formae nativae*), however, when they came to subsist in matter upon the divine work of the creation. Bernard's brother and student, Thierry of Chartres, reintroduced the Platonic idea of a world-soul when he added that the form of God included all other forms.[16] What Bernard had called ideas and forms, Thierry distinguished as forms and their images.[17]

Both formulations addressed two orders of transcendent phenomena. The transcendent ideas of Plato, which Middle Platonism had attributed to the *logos,* were considered preexistent in a simple, undifferentiated, collective manner, in the person of God. A second set of ideas existed as individual entities within the world. They differed from the forms of Aristotle's discussion in being transcendent rather than immanent in matter. Because the forms had spatial extensions consistent with the material phenomena whose universal forms they were, the forms were not exclusively intelligible. They were imaginable and could be termed images.

It has not previously been recognized that the distinction between idea and form, which touched off the Platonic revival in medieval Catholicism, was not original with Bernard, but was instead an unacknowledged translation of the concept of soul that the Isma'ili philosopher al-Sijistani had introduced a century and a half earlier. The basic difference between the Isma'ili and Catholic formulations pertained to the status of the first set of ideas. For the Isma'ilis, Intellect was the first created existent, an angelic entity; for Christians, it was the second person of a triune God.

Although the Platonic revival was inspired by Islam, it drew on the writings of Platonists within the church before turning to classical and Hellenistic texts that were available in Arabic translations. Hence, for example, the interest, commencing in the second third of the twelfth century,[18] in the fifth-century writings of the Syriac monk whose pseudonym was Dionysius the Areopagite. Known in the middle ages as St. Denis, he was the patron saint of France.

The unprecedented interest in the writings of Johannes Scotus Eriugena,[19] a ninth-century author who had translated pseudo-Dionysius into Latin, tends to imply an unstated concern to address a crisis within the church. Eriugena's teachings had been condemned by the councils of Vercelli in 1050 and Rome in 1059. They were again to be condemned by a papal Bull of Honorius III in 1225.[20] Eriugena's pantheism,[21] and perhaps also his inclusion of all creation within man,[22] cannot be reconciled with Catholicism. What extraordinary circumstances led to his temporary rehabilitation during the twelfth century? Was it simply the Platonizing fashion of the age? Or did the threat of gnosis make Eriugena seem acceptable?

Eriugena had successfully pushed Platonism about as far as it could go without turning into a theosophy. Everything in Eriugena's cosmos was a manifestation of God, but it was a product of creation rather than emanation. Its consideration led to contemplation of the God beyond being, rather than to a theosophical and theurgic approach to the world of sense experience.

Another notable aspect of the Platonic revival was the introduction of a female figure whom the troubadours might identify as the unnamed beloved of their verses. Both the Western idea of nature[23] and nature's continuing personification as a woman were innovations of the Platonic revival of the twelfth century. Several classical writers had personified nature as a woman, but the tradition had lapsed under Christianity until it was revived by Bernard Silvestris and Alan de Lille.[24] Both writers were important contributors to the Platonic revival of the twelfth century. Silvestris's *Cosmographia* was responsible, among its other contributions, for reviving the doctrine that man is a microcosm, in sympathy or correspondence with the macrocosm, because he contains the four elements within himself.[25]

Anticlaudianus, which Alan de Lille wrote in the 1180s, was probably indebted to the *Phaedrus* of Plato for the motif of heavenly ascension that formed the central event of its poetic narrative. Alan indicated an awareness of gnostic ascensions in his prologue:

> In this work the sweetness of the literal sense will soothe the ears of boys, the moral instruction will inspire the mind on the road to perfection, the sharper subtlety of the allegory will whet the advanced intellect. Let those be denied access to this work who pursue only sense-images and do not reach out for the truth that comes from reason . . . lest the esoteric be impaired if its grandeur is revealed to the unworthy.[26]

Alan advocated an allegorizing interpretation of visionary ascensions and expressly opposed the literalism favored by gnostics.

A third author responsible for bringing the goddess Natura to prominence was Jean de Meun, who wrote a continuation for the *Roman de la Rose* of Guillaume de Lorris around 1277. Jean explicitly condemned visions such as those favored by gnostics on the grounds that they were products of auto-suggestions:

> Some will with great devotion meditate,
> And too much meditation makes appear
> Before them things of which they have but thought;
> But they believe they see them openly.[27]

Once the unnamed beloved of troubadour poetry acquired a name and her theological status had been clarified, the motif of the feminine made her way from ribald love songs to highly formal courtly poetry. We find her throughout the literature of the Middle

Ages and the Renaissance. As in Arabic, the literary convention had much wider distribution than its mystical interpretation. It had immediate popular appeal for romantic, erotic, and esthetic reasons. In Western Christianity, it also attracted a learned understanding. For Platonic philosophy, all women are instances of the archetypal idea "woman." Any woman might consequently be lauded as a manifestation of her type.

Because love poetry accommodated several orders of interpretation, it remained available to facilitate repeated encounters between gnosis and Platonism in the history of Christian mysticism. Consider, for example, the case of Dante (1265–1321). Dante's early work, *La Vita Nuova*,[28] belonged to the European tradition of love poetry; and Dante seems actually to have envisioned Beatrice in much the same ecstatic manner[29] that Ibn al-ʿArabi had beheld the girl Nizam.[30] However, the mysticism of the *Divine Comedy*[31] was an elegant critical response to gnosis. Dante's poetic journey through hell, purgatory, and heaven drew heavily on Ibn al-ʿArabi's account of the *miʿraj* tradition, while explicitly condemning Muhammad, Averroes, and Islam.[32] Dante rejected the imaginal hermeneutic of gnosticism in favor of the allegorizing hermeneutic of biblical and patristic tradition. St. Bernard of Clairvaux had taught, for example, that ministering angels undertook "the construction of certain spiritual images in order to bring the purest intuitions of divine wisdom before the eyes of the soul" in the form of "visions and dreams . . . parables and figures of speech . . . [and] the very beauty of the angels."[33] Dante paired allegorical visions with experiences of ecstatic nothingness[34] in a variant of the pseudo-Dionysian tradition, which similarly concerned two different types of spiritual experience: a communion with "Jesus who is transcendent mind, utterly divine mind," and the nothingness of "the divine unity beyond being."[35] In substituting allegorical visions for communion experiences, Dante remained an impeccably Catholic mystic. His exploitation of the legend of Muhammad's ascension stole Muslim thunder while countering the doctrinal threat of Islam.

Again, in their love poems, some of Dante's circle of poets, the *fedeli d'amore,* conceived of the Madonna Intelligenza in a manner that combined the feminine hypostasis of theosophical Sufism with the Intellect of Neoplatonism.[36] Rather than the preexistent undifferentiated intelligible substance of Sufism, the archetypal feminine of these Christian mystics possessed an intelligence that arrived her rather near the personification of Wisdom in the biblical book of Proverbs. The result compared with the Intellect of Ismaʿili

Neoplatonism, which was similarly intermediate between God and the forms. Because the creator was regarded as beyond being, Wisdom was treated as the primal condition and fountainhead of being. She was consequently the Madonna. God began his work of creation by thinking of her, and God used her in creating all else that exists. She was the mother of all subsequent creation—and consequently of Christ's incarnation within it. Mary, mother of Jesus, was an instance of the Madonna; Christ's incarnation within her womb was his entrance into being as such.

The debt to Ibn al-ʿArabi's doctrine of God's self-creation was fundamental, even as the contrast between the feminine hypostases was acute. Madonna Intelligenza was not hylic being, intelligible substance in a condition of chaos that lacked all differentiation. She was the primal condition of being, but she was the very intelligence that nature reflects.

The Art of Ramon Lull

St. Francis of Assisi (c. 1182-1226) fancied himself a "troubadour of God" and traveled to Egypt in an unsuccessful attempt to convert the Sultan Malik el-Kamil to Christianity. The influence of Sufism on the founder of the Friars Minor has sometimes been suggested.[37] Francis's extant writings[38] attest amply to his asceticism but bear no evidence of mysticism. The extensive legends that portray Francis's love of nature possibly indicate a practice of extrovertive mysticism,[39] but the extraordinary importance assigned to the legend of his seraphic vision[40] suggests that ecstasies were a rare occurrence for him. Although the first Sufis had been ascetics centuries earlier, Francis's contemporaries were mystics, and Catholic monasticism remains the likeliest source of Francis's ascesis.

Francis's reputation as a "troubadour of God" nevertheless influenced Ramon Lull (1232–c. 1316), a Majorcan nobleman who ended his days as a Franciscan Spiritual. Lull was born only three years after the reconquest of Majorca by James I of Aragon, and a substantial portion of the island's population remained Muslim during Lull's life. After years as a courtier, Lull underwent a religious conversion, probably in 1263, and according to his autobiography, he was attempting to compose courtly love poetry at the time:

> Ramon, while still a young man and seneschal to the king of Majorca, was very given to composing worthless songs and poems and

to doing other licentious things. One night he was sitting beside his bed, about to compose and write in his vulgar tongue a song to a lady whom he loved with a foolish love; and as he began to write this song, he looked to his right and saw our Lord Jesus Christ on the cross, as if suspended in midair. This sight filled him with fear; and, leaving what he was doing, he retired to bed and went to sleep.

Upon arising the next day, he returned to his usual vanities without giving the vision a further thought. It was not until almost a week later, however, in the same place as before, and at almost exactly the same hour, when he was again preparing to work on and finish the aforementioned song, that our Lord appeared to him on the cross, just as before. He was even more frightened than the first time, and retired to bed and fell asleep as he had done before.

Again on the next day, paying no attention to the vision he had seen, he continued his licentious ways. Indeed, soon afterwards he was again trying to finish the song he had begun when our Saviour appeared to him, always in the same form, a third and then a fourth time, with several days in between.

On the fourth occasion—or, as is more commonly believed, the fifth—when this vision appeared to him, he was absolutely terrified and retired to bed and spent the entire night trying to understand what these so often repeated visions were meant to signify.... His conscience told him that they could only mean that he should abandon the world at once and from then on dedicate himself totally to the service of our Lord Jesus Christ.[41]

Lull understood visionary experiences in a Catholic rather than a gnostic manner, as revelations whose significance was allegorical. He used the trope of heavenly ascension, for example, in reference to ecstatic experience; theosophy was signified by the return to earth: "The heart of the Lover soared to the heights of the Beloved [God], so that he might not be prevented from loving him in the abyss of this world. And when he reached his Beloved he contemplated him with sweetness and delight. But the Beloved led him down again to this world so that he might contemplate him in tribulations and griefs."[42]

Probably because Lull's Christian asceticism bordered on the world-rejection of Gnosticism, he felt obliged to insist that "the world [is] to be loved ... but as a piece of work, for the sake of its Maker."[43] Lull's mystical theosophy was otherwise profoundly shaped by gnostic orientations.

Lull did not explain how it was that he had five visions, attended by the onset of ecstatic death, on five successive occasions while preparing to compose love poetry. It is clear, however, that he knew a practice of visualization: "With his imagination the Lover formed and pictured the Countenance of his Beloved in bodily form, and with his understanding he beautified it in spiritual things."[44]

Lull was equally reticent regarding his experiences of mystical union. His reference to a climactic loss of affect suggests, however, that he experienced ecstatic nothingness: "Love went apart with the Lover and they were very joyful in the Beloved, and the Beloved revealed himself to them. The Lover wept, and afterwards was in rapture, and at this Love swooned. But the Beloved brought life to his Lover by reminding him of his virtues."[45]

Upon his turn to religion, Lull dedicated his life to the conversion of Muslims. He began by learning Arabic. He also informed himself about Judaism and Islam by engaging rabbis and Muslims in learned conversations. The earliest of his writings emerged from a period of nine years of study on Majorca (c. 1265–1275). The texts presented rudimentary forms of his Art, which Lull intended as a form of Christian mysticism that would secure the conversions of Muslims and Jews—presumably through competition with theosophical Sufism and the kabbalah.[46]

Lull claimed to have learned his Art by revelation: "Ramon went up a certain mountain not far from his home, in order to contemplate God in greater tranquility. When he had been there scarcely a full week, it happened that one day while he was gazing intently heavenward the Lord suddenly illuminated his mind, giving him the form and method for writing . . . the *Ars generalis*."[47]

Although Lull's purpose was not ecumenical but evangelical, his thinking was deeply shaped by his contacts with Muslims and Jews. Lull's debts to Ibn al-ʿArabi were so extensive as to amount occasionally to plagiarism.[48] The parallels to the kabbalah are only slightly less striking. The first system of Christian theosophy to succeed in becoming a living tradition, Lull's Art may fairly be considered the matrix of Western esotericism.

Lull's theosophy found expression, among other manners, in the content of his meditations and ecstasies. Lull claimed to worship "the Countenance of God . . . in all creatures."[49] An instance of empathetic communion with God may be noted in the following self-report:

> One day the Lover was at prayer and he perceived that his eyes did not weep. And so that he might weep, he urged his thoughts to

think about wealth, women, sons, meats, and vanity. And his understanding found that each of the things mentioned above has more men as servants than has his Beloved. And at this his eyes were wet with tears and his soul was in sorrow and pain.[50]

Lull's meditations led him to consider "wealth, women, sons, meats, and vanity" not from his own perspective, nor from any human perspective, but rather from the perspective of God. Lull wept in pity for God, that God had fewer servants than vanity had.

Lull's Art—that is to say, his method or technique—was a formalization of the system or theory of his theosophy. He began with the premise that God was an infinite, eternal, unknowable being.[51] God could be known only through his attributes or "Dignities," a term that Lull derived by translating Ibn al-ʿArabi's term *hadrah*.[52] These attributes were God himself.

They asked the Lover, "In what does your Beloved's glory consist?" He answered, "He is Glory itself." They asked him, "In what does his power consist?" He answered, "He is Power itself." "And in what does his Wisdom consist?" "He is Wisdom itself." "And why is he to be loved?" "Because he is Love itself."[53]

As in the kabbalah, the divine attributes were the principles according to which God had created the world.[54] All things in creation could be analyzed in terms of the attributes that they manifested: "The Lover . . . said, 'Even when my Beloved is no longer in my thoughts, he is never absent from the eyes of my body, for everything that I see shows me my Beloved'. "[55]

In early presentations of the Art, beginning with *Ars Compendiosa (Ars Maior)* of 1273–1275, the Dignities were sixteen in number: Goodness, Greatness, Eternity, Power, Wisdom, Will, Strength, Truth, Glory, Perfection, Justice, Generosity, Mercy, Humility, Ownership, and Patience.[56] The names all occur as Dignities of God in Ibn al-ʿArabi;[57] they also designate most of the ten sefirot of the kabbalah.

Lull's system of sixteen Dignities was indebted to the account of the four elements in the *Periphyseon* of Eriugena, but Lull transformed Eriugena's Neoplatonism into a theosophy. Eriugena had defended the unknowability of God by insisting that the elements could not be traced to their qualities. Because fire differed from heat, earth from cold, air from dryness, and water from humidity, both the elements and the qualities had to have been created *ex nihilo* by a God whose essence was in no manner disclosed by the material creation. In Lull's system, however, mystical union with God was not the ultimate object of an analysis of matter. Rather, "the intellect moves [both] up and down the ladder of being."[58] Lull's theosophy proceeded from the evidence of the senses to an analysis of God's attributes in order to gain confidence in the system of analysis by demonstrating its agreement with theology. Once the principles of analysis were secure, the system was reapplied to the sensible world as a mode of would-be scientific analysis.

The implication that the four elements, or aspects of them, could be discovered in God may have been sufficiently close to the material pantheism of David of Dinant, a twelfth-century heretic, that Lull felt obliged to scrap his initial approach and to develop another that was firmly based on a transcendent trinitarianism.[59] He may have desired to augment his system by adding a rank higher than the divine attributes. Whatever his motivation, Lull brought the persons of the godhead into consideration and redesigned his theosophical system to reflect the number three. Beginning with the *Ars Inventiva Veritatis* of 1289–1290, the divine attributes were restricted to a set of nine: Goodness, Greatness, Eternity, Power, Wisdom, Will, Strength, Truth, and Glory.[60] Lull was influenced by pseudo-Dionysius' celestial hierarchy of three ranks, each of three heavenly powers, which had been incorporated within Eriugena's system but were differently organized by Lull. As well, Lull transformed the Seraphim, Cherubim, Thrones, Dominations, Virtues, Powers, Principalities, Archangels, and Angels from personal beings into divine attributes, which agreed the more closely with theosophical Sufism and the kabbalah.

In the trinitarian version of Lull's Art, the nine divine Dignities were absolute principles or essential attributes. For notational purposes, Lull designated them by the letters BCDEFGHIK. Lull also assigned the same letters to a series of nine relative predicates, or principles of relation, which he subdivided into three triads: difference, equivalence, and opposition; beginning, middle, and end; superiority, equality, and inferiority. There were also twenty-seven correlative principles. Each of the nine divine attributes was understood to be dynamic—as the sefirot are in kabbalah—and they were consequently regarded as triune. Each contained within itself a triad of agent, patient, and action.[61] For example, Goodness does goodly in accomplishing good. Parallel reflections of the trinity were to be found in the four elements, which each existed in three manners. For example, fire entailed the burner, the burned, and burning.[62]

Lull's Art proceeded, in the main, by assigning absolutes, relatives, or correlatives to sensible or intelligible phenomena, juxtaposing two or more of them, and deriving a metaphysical inference from the conjunction. To facilitate the calculations of juxtaposition, Lull used what he described as alphabets and figures. Letters served as notations designating the various terms of the computations. Charts, diagrams, and mechanical aids, such as charts containing rotating wheels, facilitated the calculations. Like the alphanumeric abjad of Sufism and gematria of the kabbalah, Lull's process of alpha-figural computation was entirely mechanical, but interpretations of its results were profoundly subjective.

The procedure of Lull's Art was presumably borrowed from the kabbalah. *Sefer Yesirah,* "The Book of Creation,"[63] which Scholem dated between the third and sixth centuries,[64] identified the ten sefirot with letters of the Hebrew alphabet and suggested that God created the world by combining two letters at once, in all possible bilittoral combinations.[65] Mystics were to replicate God's procedure as a means of meditation. Commentaries on *Sefer Yesirah* by R. Eleazar of Worms (c. 1165–c.1230), leader of the German Hasidism of his generation, and Abraham Abulafia (c. 1240–after 1292), a seminal figure in the early history of the kabbalah, recommended that mystics first vocalize the two letter combinations, next visualize them in a rotating wheel, and finally conceptualize them, in order to induce experiences of communion.[66] Because the texts are equivocal, it is entirely possible that the rotating visualizations were performed by Jews with the aid of charts in the form of rotating wheels; the innovation may otherwise be assigned to Lull.

Frances A. Yates attempted to account for the gnostic elements in Lull's Art with the observation that Eriugena's *Periphyseon* had been popular among the Albigensians, whose descendants among the aristocrats of southern France maintained contacts with the court of Majorca. Although Pope Honorius III ordered the destruction of all copies of the *Periphyseon* in 1225, Lull based part of his Art on the condemned teachings. Perhaps Lull sought to win the conversion of Albigensians, as also Muslims and Jews.[67]

Most of Lull's discussions of his Art applied it to the world of sense perception; but Lull also applied it to imaginable things:

> There are specific principles and rules in the imaginative faculty for the purpose of imagining imaginable things. . . .
>
> The imaginative faculty extracts species from the things senses with the individual senses; and this it does with its

correlatives. . . . With goodness it makes these species good, and with greatness it magnifies them, as when it imagines a great mountain of gold. With minority it lessens them, as when it imagines an indivisible point. The imaginative faculty has instinct . . . [and] an appetite to imagine the imaginable.[68]

Lull was presumably indebted to conversations with Sufis for the idea of imaginables, but he developed the doctrine in an original way. Not only did imagination disclose the divine attributes, but the very process of imagining was subject to analysis in the hypostatic terms of Lull's Art.

Nicholas of Cusa

In 1376, a papal bull censured Lull's teachings and condemned twenty of his books, partly because he had appealed to reason rather than to faith, and otherwise because the Dignities constituted a plurality of gods. In 1390, the faculty of theology of the University of Paris prohibited the teaching of Lull. Although the man and his works were acquitted by a papal court in 1416, the damage to Lull's reputation had been done. Writers who drew on Lull's teachings often concealed their debts to him.[69]

Nicholas of Cusa (1401–1464) was a case in point. Although Cusa's surviving library contains more of the works of Lull than of any other writer, Cusa did not cite Lull in his writings. Cusa was not a mere follower of Lull, however, but was instead a highly original thinker who freely reworked what he borrowed.[70] Cusa retreated, for example, from the pantheism of Lull's theosophy. At the same time, Cusa, more than anyone before him, developed a Catholic account of the imaginable.

In *De Visione Dei,* "On the Vision of God" (1453), Cusa presented a discussion of mystical visions and unions. He began by likening the experience of a vision to the sight of an "omnivoyant" that he termed "the icon of God." Regardless of where onlookers stood, the eyes in the picture seem to gaze directly at them. His theological conclusion proceeded directly from the assumption of divine omniscience:

There is nothing which seemeth proper to the gaze of the icon of God which doth not more really exist in the veritable gaze of God Himself. . . . If the countenance portrayed in a picture can seem to look upon each and all at one and the same time, this faculty (since it is the perfection of seeing) must no less really pertain unto the reality than it doth apparently unto the icon or appearance.[71]

Cusa here made no claim that imagination disclosed an objectively existing world of imagination. He was content to treat imagination at face value as fantasy. At the same time, he affirmed that the apparent manifestation of revelation, during an experience of imagination, was indeed a true occurrence of revelation. When fantasy shifted from ordinary daydreaming to lucid hypnagogia, grace was truly present.

Cusa discussed introspective unitive experience, with its loss of subject-object distinctions, as an experience of the angelic at the threshold of the experience of the divine:

> I begin, Lord, to behold Thee in the door of the coincidence of opposites, which the angel guardeth that is set over the entrance into Paradise. For Thou art there where speech, sight, hearing, taste, touch, reason, knowledge, and understanding are the same, and where seeing is one with being seen, and hearing with being heard, and tasting with being tasted, and touching with being touched, and speaking with hearing, and creating with speaking.[72]

Following such moments of unified cognition, Cusa went on to experience an absence of cognitive content. For Cusa, the climactic moments of nothingness disclosed God directly. God was beheld in "a kind of mental trance" in which "the intellect . . . understandeth by not understanding."[73]

Cusa's retreat from Lull's theosophy to a more traditional Christian Neoplatonism brought him to a mystical theology that was consistent with Dante's *Divine Comedy*. Visionary experience was a meeting ground for human imagining and divine revelation. The grace was real, but imagining selected the subject matters to which grace made reply.

Lullian Alchemy and the Ether

Lull's reputation as an alchemist was posthumous. Lull died in 1315. The *Testamentum*, the earliest alchemical work attributed to him, bears the date of 1332 and was likely written about that period. Lull's Art came to the attention of alchemists because it followed the *Periphyseon* of Eriugena in attempting a theoretic analysis of the four elements.[74] The initial development of the pseudo-Lullian corpus seems to have proceeded by mistake. The *Testamentum* did not claim to have been written by Lull and was not initially attributed to him. It mentioned Roger Bacon's theory of the fifth essence and asserted that the ether is composed of a perfect balance of the four elements. However, it also cited two works by Lull and used Lullian figures and alphabets as mnemonics for the alchemical opus. These debts to Lull's Art apparently gave rise to the misimpression that Lull had composed the tract. A second phase in the development of the pseudo-Lullian alchemical corpus began later in the same century with the production of pseudonymous works that claimed to have been written by Lull. Among them were texts that plagiarized John of Rupescissa's discussion in 1351–52 of the fifth essence; the same texts made use of Lull's figures. By the 1370s, there were biographical legends that portrayed Lull as an alchemist. Before 1400 the two alchemies of the fifth essence that had been attributed to Lull were combined in *Liber de secretis naturae seu de quinta essentia,* which set the standard for later additions to the pseudo-Lullian alchemical corpus.

Once Lullism had influenced the practice of alchemy, alchemy came to the attention of Lullists, and alchemists began to develop interests in Lullism beyond its application to alchemy alone. The synthesis began in the fourteenth and fifteen centuries when Lull's works on medicine were read and discussed in medical circles of Catalonia and southern France.[75] The process presumably continued for a very long time. In the late fifteenth century, Pier Leoni, physician to Lorenzo de' Medici, was familiar with Lull's writings and pseudo-Lullian alchemy.[76] A similar blend proceeded in Paris in the early sixteenth century, where Renaissance circles were initially interested in Lull's Art, but soon acquired a further interest in pseudo-Lullian alchemy.[77] The alchemical works attributed to Lull were printed continuously during the sixteenth and seventeenth centuries.[78]

Lull's art came to the attention of alchemists in the fourteenth century at the precise time that the motif of the quintessence was introduced. Aristotle's concept of the ether or quintessence had received its first Scholastic endorsement at the hands of John Duns Scotus and William of Occam in the late thirteenth and early fourteenth centuries,[79] but it initially entered alchemy only as a secret designation for alcoholic distillations. Late medieval alchemists, including the authors and followers of the pseudo-Lullian corpus, did not conflate Lull's concept of imaginable things with Aristotle's concept of ether. The synthesis was not accomplished until the Renaissance, when Marsilio Ficino (1433–1499) reverted to the pagan sources of Neoplatonism and revived their practices of magic. Among Ficino's contributions was a revival of Aristotle's original concept of the ether, together with its pagan Neoplatonic modifications.

In Aristotle's presentation, the faculty of sensation provided a link between the material body and the intellect or mind. Sensation included both sense perception and what we today describe as extrasensory perception. Sensation also encompassed the faculty of imagination, which proceeded by dividing and recombining sense impressions. Indeed, imagination might be said to be the very character of sensation, for imagination was responsible for transforming messages from the material body into forms that were coherent to the intellect. Imagination was susceptible to the influence of the stars because the senses were composed of ether, the substance of starlight. In its pagan Neoplatonic development, the ethereal composition of the senses was developed with considerable astrological detail into a concept of a "subtle body" that functioned as a vehicle for the soul and was able to accomplish magic by acting on the ether in general.[80]

Ficino understood the imagination not in the sense intended by Aristotle and the Neoplatonists, but in the gnostic tradition derived from Sufism by way of Lull and Cusa. Imagination was not simply a faculty of bodily and extrasensory percepts. It also encompassed fantasying, visualizing, and much else. Ficino also took for granted that he was addressing the ether or quintessence as it was understood by alchemists. He was not. For medieval alchemists, quintessence had been a literary trope, a metaphor for the discussion of alcohol. In reverting to the classical source of the motif, Ficino turned the metaphor back into metaphysics.

Paracelsus

The tradition of spiritual alchemy that has come down to us originated at the height of the Renaissance when Ficino's concept of ethereal bodies was blended with the alchemy of the quintessence. The synthesis, which provided the means for the Europeanization of Sufism's world of imagination, was effected by Philippus Aureolus Theophrastus Bombastus von Hohenheim (1493–1541), who styled himself Paracelsus.

Paracelsus was both a surgeon and an alchemist. He has traditionally been honored as "the father of modern pharmacology." As was possible only for a brief time in the sixteenth century, he stood at the intersection of two currents of Renaissance thought: the occult tradition that passed from Ficino to Bruno, and the protoscientific tradition that passed from Cusa to Bacon. Paracelsus invented not only spiritual alchemy but medical chemistry. Gnostic trends have been recognized in his thought from the sixteenth century onward.[81]

Paracelsus resolved the discrepancy between the quintessence of the alchemists and the Neoplatonic concept of ethereal starlight not by harmonizing them, as Ficino had attempted to do, but by embracing both concepts separately. Alchemists had come to speak of quintessences in the plural, in designation of extracts produced, among other manners, through a use of alcohol. This usage was directly ancestral to modern perfumers' references to essences. The concept of a quintessence as the most pure, concentrated, and essential extract of a substance was also extended from its initial contexts of distilled alcoholic beverages and floral perfumes to chemical substances in general. "The seed is the vital sap, the *quinta essentia* of the herb."[82] In a second sense of the term, a quintessence was not a chemical extract but a postulated theoretic entity that an extract contained. In this latter sense, Paracelsus wrote that "there is another essence and nature which is called Quintessence, or, as the philosophers say, the Elemental Accident, or again, as ancient physics term it, the Specific Form."[83]

Paracelsus understood quintessences in precisely the sense that Western alchemists since Alan de Lille had discussed forms. Both terms denoted the traditional alchemical adaptation of the Stoic concept of a *spermatikos logos:*

> The quinta essentia is a *materia* which is extracted bodily from all things, and from all things in which there is life, separated from all impurity and all that is mortal, made subtle and purified from all, separated from all elements. Now it is to be understood that the *quinta essentia* alone is the natural power, goodness and medicine, which is shut up in things without a harbourage and extraneous incorporation; further it may be the colours, the life and the property of the thing, and is a spirit like the spirit of life, with this difference that the *spiritus vitae* of the thing is permanent and the *spiritus vitae* of man is mortal.[84]

Paracelsus denied that the quintessence was a fifth element.[85] He did not consider it to be an element but an arcanum or mystery.

"An arcanum . . . is incorporeal, immortal, of perpetual life, intelligible above all Nature and of knowledge more than human."[86] "Every Mystery is simple and a single element."[87] Another synonym for quintessence was spirit. "The life of each object is a spiritual, an invisible and incomprehensible being, and a spirit and a spiritual thing."[88]

Although Paracelsus is famous for his triadic formulas—mercury, sulphur, and salt;[89] water, oil, and salt[90] —his distinctions among matter, soul, and spirit perpetuated the concept underlying the medieval distinction between matter and form.[91] Paracelsus perpetuated the traditional designation of earth, water, air, and fire as "matter," and he followed Ficino in referring to "ether" as the substance of both starlight and souls. In Paracelsus's usage, "the sidereal, subtle body" was a synonym for "the ethereal body."[92] Both matter and ether were substances; and both were to be contrasted with the quintessence, arcanum, or spirit, which for Paracelsus were intelligible forms or structures. He did not follow Isma'ilism, Sufism, the kabbalah, and medieval Christian Platonism in equating form with imaginables.

In Paracelsus's view, the primary condition of ether was chaos. The introduction of a form, such as that of a soul, required the action of spirit:

> A figure painted into a picture, when it is there, has been certainly made of *something*. But we are not thus constituted in the aether out of something—like a picture. . . . If the figure be blotted out with a sponge, it leaves nothing behind it, and it returns to its former shape. So, assuredly, all creatures will be reduced [at death] to their primeval state, that is, to nothingness.[93]

In this passage, Paracelsus took implicit exception to a reading of Cusa's *Image of God* that would make a person's soul analogous to a painting. When a painting is erased, the figure ceases to exist, and the paint reverts to a condition of chaos. Similarly, when a person dies, the ether composing the soul reverts to chaos, but the person's immortal portion, the quintessence, spirit, or arcanum that had been responsible for the forms of both the body and the soul, enters into the nothingness of God. "Nothing has been created out of the Great Mystery which will not inhabit a form beyond the aether."[94]

Paracelsus held that "the created universe consisted of four elements."[95] "The four elements exist together in all things."[96] Elements were themselves not material but ethereal. "Fire which burns is not the element of fire, as we see it; but its soul, invisible to us, is the element and the life of fire."[97] Paracelsus's doctrine of the elements enabled him to develop an alchemical theory of the otherworld. Not only were the elements the souls of physical matter, but just "as there are four elements, so there are four worlds, and in each exists a peculiar race, each with its own necessities."[98] Nymphs or undines inhabited water, sylphs or sylvestres the air, pygmies or gnomes the earth, and salamanders or vulcans fire.[99] Necromancy—that is, the conjuring of "these sidereal spirits"—could accomplish a variety of ends.[100] Paracelsus maintained, however, that necromancers "compel, binde, afflict and Torment the Spirits . . . with punishments and Martyrdomes . . . but not without the curse of God."[101] Paracelsus limited his use of magic to exorcism and astrologically sensitive talismans that protected against evil spirits. Magic that was licit for a Christian made "no use of Ceremonies, Consecrations, Conjurations, Blessings or Curses; but of faith alone whereof Christ speaks . . . to compel, loose, and binde all Spirits."[102]

Paracelsus followed Ficino in associating magic with the imagination. Paracelsus wrote of "intention or imagination" as a single faculty. It accomplishes sensation.[103] As intention, it initiates motor action.[104] In further proofs of its power, he cited a variety of psychosomatic phenomena.[105] Imagination was stellar. "Whatever be the impression, influence, constellation, star—such is the imagination."[106] "The inner stars of man are, in their properties, kind, and nature, by their course and position, like his outer stars, and different only in form and in material. For as regards their nature, it is the same in the ether and in the microcosm."[107] The stars were able to influence humanity in a positive manner:

> The stars in him have a different disposition, a different mind, a different orientation than the lower elements; and . . . these elements in turn have a different wisdom and a different disposition than the stars in man. For instance: the elemental, material body wants to live in luxury and lewdness; the stars, the ethereal body, the inner counterpart of the upper sphere, want to study, learn, pursue arts, and so forth. As a result there arises an antinomy in man himself. The visible, material body wants one thing, and the invisible, ethereal body wants another thing, they do not want the same thing.[108]

Divination was accomplished through the imagination. "The spirit of the star which exists in every man . . . knows many things:

future, present, and past, all arts and sciences."[109] There were four "uncertain arts" that divined by means of the four elements: geomancy, pyromancy, hydromancy, and ventinina.[110] Both magic and divination depended on the superiority of human will to the ether at its disposal:

> The imagination . . . draws the star to itself and rules it, so that from the imagination the operation itself may be found in the star. . . . The imagination of the artist in uncertain arts is the chief art and head of all. But in addition to this, imagination is strengthened and perfected by faith, so that it becomes reality. . . . It is . . . imagination by which one thinks in proportion as he fixes his mind on God, or on Nature, or on the Devil. . . . Imagination in the uncertain arts compels the stars to do the pleasure of him who imagines, believes, and operates. But because man does not always imagine or believe perfectly, therefore these arts are called uncertain, though they are certain and can give true results.[111]

Paracelsus reconciled his belief in the devil with a keen sense of human responsibility. "Cast away all evil thoughts and cogitations, and all Phantasies of the Devil, that such Imaginations may not have any place with you; for . . . many have been overwhelmed and besieged by the devil . . . [through] their own wicked and evil thoughts and Imagination."[112] Paracelsus similarly reconciled his belief in astrological determinism with the Catholic doctrine of free will. The stars influenced the ethereal body, but not the human spirit. "Thoughts are free and are subject to no rule. On them rests the freedom of man, and they tower above the light of nature."[113]

Paracelsus asserted that the difference between phantasy and imagination was the participation of perfect spirit in the latter: "Phantasy is not imagination, but the frontier of folly. . . . He who is born in imagination finds out the latent forces of Nature, which the body with its mere phantasy cannot find. . . . Imagination exists in the perfect spirit, while phantasy exists in the body without the perfect spirit."[114]

By perfect spirit, Paracelsus intended a correct knowledge of the arcana or forms: "The first step . . . in these sciences is to beget the spirit from the star by means of imagination, so that it may be present in its perfection. After that perfection is present even in uncertain arts. But where that spirit is not, there neither judgment nor perfect science will be present."[115]

A correct knowledge of forms was a precondition for the reception of divine grace:

> It is not of ourselves that we have wisdom and the arts, but through a mediator. He is the invisible spirit which gives us art in the same way as the fields give us fruit. . . . Thus God's spirit bestows His gifts in accordance with His orders: to one, the invention of the alphabet, to another, of the forge, to a third, of the lyre, and so to each the invention of something that is needed on earth. . . . Everything we invent has its origin in the spirit.[116]

Paracelsus similarly discussed two kinds of visions that occur in dreams, "natural and supernatural." Natural dreams are products of the imagination; supernatural dreams "are nothing else but Angels and Good Spirits."[117] The advice that Paracelsus offered for remembering forgotten dreams was strikingly like Jung's instructions for active imagination: "This night a wonderful dreame appeared to me . . . but it is fallen out of my memory. . . . To whom any such thing hath happened, he ought not to go forth out of his chamber, nor speak with any man, but to remain alone and fast, until he call to remembrance that which he had forgotten."[118]

Paracelsus's account of imagination permits no doubt that a practice of visionary experiences informed his discussions of the ether, with its elements, worlds, and races of living creatures. His writings also display a unitive tendency. "The mysteries of the Great and the Little World are distinguished only by the form in which they manifest themselves; for they are only *one* thing, *one* being."[119] Some of the unitive language expressed the astrological doctrine of sympathy or correspondence. "The outer and the inner are *one* thing, *one* constellation, *one* influence, *one* concordance, *one* duration."[120] Other phrasings suggest an acquaintance with unitive experience. "Heaven is man, and man is heaven, and all men together are the one heaven, and heaven is nothing but one man."[121]

Paracelsus maintained that grace enabled people to know God in his essence. "Man . . . is illumined by the Holy Ghost that he may know God in His essence."[122] Since Paracelsus adhered to a negative theology, the grace that enabled people to know God in his essence can only have been an experience of ecstatic nothingness.

Paracelsus endorsed Cusa's concept of the *coincidentia oppositorum*, the conjunction of the unknowable infinity of God with the finite human body.[123] He attributed longevity to the conjunction:

> Within the testa and over and above that quintessence, there is enclosed something out of which a certain conjunction, both of the corporal and of that which is beyond the body, outside of that quin-

tum, produces the body into long life. Concerning this understand that it is absolutely nothing and invisible.[124]

Paracelsus quarreled in detail with a number of alchemical recipes that pseudo-Lullian literature attributed to Ramon Lull.[125] He also compared Lull with Avicenna, exhibited familiarity with Lull's medical theories,[126] and engaged in controversy with a practitioner of Lull's Art.[127] His debts to the Lullist tradition were probably more than he acknowledged.[128] It is my assumption that the practice of mystical visions and unions, which I have traced from Islamic gnosis to Ramon Lull and his legacy within Roman Catholicism, entered Western alchemy in the company of Lull's Art, as a component of pseudo-Lullian alchemy. If so, it would be legitimate to speak of a pseudo-Lullian alchemical gnosis that Paracelsus transformed into spiritual alchemy by adding his several innovative doctrines.

Lullism was almost certainly the unnamed target of Paracelsus's explicit rejection of theosophy:

> The Great Mystery, by penetrating, reduced every single thing to its own special essence. With wonderful skill it divided and separated everything, so that each substance was assigned to its due form. In truth, that magic which had such an entrance was a special miracle. If it were divinely brought about by Deity, we shall in vain strive to compass it in our philosophy. God has not disclosed Himself to us by means of this.[129]

The Great Mystery was not God. "Not one simple single body but many bodies were included in the Great Mystery. . . . But in how many forms and species the elements produced all things cannot be fully told."[130] Neither was the Great Mystery consistent with Nature. Its action, to bring all things into being by imposing forms on chaos, "certainly was very wonderful, marked by intensest penetration, and most rapid separation, the like whereof Nature can never again give or express."[131] Paracelsus wrote that "the prime matter of the world was the Fiat."[132] This account of the word *fiat,* "Let there be!," as the fountainhead of all creation, rendered into Latin the Isma'ili and theosophical Sufi view that the creation began with the Arabic word *kun,* "Be!" It was an express creationism.

Paracelsus also adhered to a limited emanationism. He wrote:

> The natural objects, they are His, the herb He has created, but its inherent virtue He has not created; for each virtue is uncreated,

> that is, God is without beginning and not created, and thus all vir-
> tues and forces were in God before heaven and earth and before all
> things had been created, at the time when God was a Spirit and
> hovered over the water. . . . Nobody should say that the virtue of
> things, their power, be natural, but it is supernatural and without
> beginning. . . . Herbs are created just as trees and stars; for they
> were not with God in the beginning of the Godhead, that is before
> heaven and earth were created.[133]

Paracelsus did not use the Platonic term "ideas." His views required greater subtlety. Paracelsus followed Cusa in regarding God
as infinite and unknowable; and he followed Catholicism in maintaining a doctrine of *creatio ex nihilo*.[134] However, he was also prepared to insist that whatever virtues, forces, or powers existed in
the world necessarily also existed in God, and did so in God before
God created heaven and earth. The claim was not theosophical. The
infinite creator of all possible worlds did not become knowable by
means of the virtues embodied within one finite realm of creation.

Paracelsus's debts to gnostic cosmology pertained, for the most
part, to his hierarchy of being. God created out of nothing; but what
God created, the primordial water of Genesis 1:2 or *fiat* of Genesis
1:3, inaugurated a typically gnostic process of cosmogonic emanationism:

> There are three different kinds of matrix: the first is the water on
> which the spirit of God was borne, and this was the maternal
> womb in which heaven and earth were created. Then heaven and
> earth each in turn became a matrix, in which Adam, the first man,
> was formed by the hand of God. Then woman was created out of
> man; she became the maternal womb of all men, and will remain
> so to the end of the world. Now, what did that first matrix contain
> within itself? Being the kingdom of God, it encompassed the spirit
> of God.[135]

The Great Mystery was the first matrix. She was not the Spirit,
but she was a spiritual entity in which the spirit of God generated
the macroanthropos, Adam. Adhering to the kabbalistic doctrine of
the division of the macroanthropos into man and woman,[136] Paracelsus held that Adam initially contained both heaven and earth
within himself. When woman was taken from his body, Adam was
then reduced to man, the heaven or ether, while "woman is like the
earth and all the elements."[137] The third matrix was the womb of a
human woman.

Paracelsus elsewhere described the elements as matrices. "All created things in the universe, then, were born of four mothers, that is to say, of four elements."[138] Again, his discussions of Nature, whom he personified as a woman, accorded her a status equivalent to the macroanthropos. Unlike Eve, Nature encompassed the ether. "Nature emits a light, and by its radiance she can be known."[139] The expression emphasized the orderly character that Paracelsus attributed to the ether, as also to matter:

> Know that our world and everything we see in its compass and everything we can touch constitute only one half of the cosmos. The world we do not see is equal to ours in weight and measure, in nature and properties. From this it follows that there exists another half of man in which this invisible world operates. If we know of the two worlds, we realize that both halves are needed to constitute the whole man; for they are like two men united in one body.[140]

In attributing objective reality to the ethereal world, Paracelsus broke with the Catholic tradition of allegorizing the images in visionary experiences. He reverted to a gnostic hermeneutic. Sufi inspiration may be assumed. Although Paracelsus derived his concept of ether from Ficino's renaissance of Neoplatonism, he regarded the ether not as a sheath for the soul but as an entire world. Paracelsus was a Christian cabalist, and the Sufi concept of the world of imagination had long since entered the kabbalah. It may even have reached Paracelsus by way of Renaissance Lullism. When Pico della Mirandola introduced the cabala to the Catholic world, he explained that one type of cabala was an *ars combinandi,* done with revolving alphabets, that resembled "that which is called amongst us the *ars Raymundi.*"[141] Ludovico Lazzarelli, another pioneer of the Christian cabala, also wrote on pseudo-Lullian alchemy.[142] *De auditu cabbalistico,* a pseudo-Lullian work that drew on the Sufism of ibn al-ʿArabi, was published at Venice in 1518 and 1533. The pseudonymous text, which presented Lull's Art under the name of the cabala, had been written by Pietro Mainardi (1456–1529), a Venetian physician and scholar who depended on Pico for his knowledge of cabala.[143] It is not impossible that Paracelsus had access to the book.

The Sufi concept of a phantasmagorical world of imagination provided Paracelsus with no more than a point of departure. The Muslim rejection of the idea of natural law, the insistence that the regularities of nature were merely habits or customs that Allah might abrogate at any time,[144] precluded the systematization of Sufi theosophy no less than it inhibited the Islamic pursuit of science. Whether applied to imaginables or sensibles, the postulation of system was a blasphemy that ran contrary to divine omnipotence.

In the Christian West, the doctrine of the incarnation prompted a different theological move. The hypostases of gnosticism could not be reconciled with the uniqueness of the hypostatic union in the person of Jesus.[145] The intelligence immanent in the sensible world could not be divine, but had instead to be a created intelligence that reflected the divine mind of Christ while differing from it. To solve the problem, a Platonic world-soul, Nature, the Madonna Intelligenza, and a number of other entities were suggested to intervene between God and matter. Nature was the formulation that the Chartres Platonists favored, and the order and lawfulness that they attributed to Nature were extended by Lull to theosophy.

Paracelsus went further still. When he rejected theosophy and interpolated the world of imagination, he conceived of the ethereal world as a rational domain of nature. This expansion of the scope of natural orderliness served simultaneously to renew the currency of animistic conceptions of pagan origin that had persisted in Celtic and Teutonic folklore. The success of Paracelsus's theological move, which so profoundly distanced spiritual alchemy from Islam, had its classic expression, among other manners, in the celebrity subsequently achieved by Ortolanus's mistranslation of *The Emerald Table* of Hermes Trismegisthus: "That which is above is as that which is below, and that which is below is as that which is above."[146]

Nature was not to be confused, however, with supernature. "Those who seek in the light of nature speak from knowledge of nature; but those who seek in the light of man speak from knowledge of super-nature."[147] The light of nature produced wisdom that was perishable and potentially flawed: "There are two kinds of wisdom in this world—one eternal and one perishable. . . . The one that comes from the light of the Holy Ghost is of only one kind—it is the just and flawless wisdom. But the one that originates in the light of nature is of two kinds: good and evil."[148]

Paracelsus's reference to a light of man, that was distinct from the ether or light of nature, pertained to the spirit of the macroanthropos, which was common to all human beings:

> There are more things . . . than those which are comprehended and recognized in the light of nature, things which are above and superior to it. But these cannot be understood . . . [except] in the

light of man which is above the light of nature. There they may be understood. . . . This is the light by which man hears, learns and penetrates supernatural things. Those who search in the light of nature, talk of nature. Those who search in the light of man, talk of more than nature. For man is more than nature. He is nature. He is also a spirit. He is also an angel. He has the qualities of all these three. When he walks in nature, he serves nature. When he walks in the spirit, he serves the spirit. When he walks in the angel, he serves the angel. The first is given the body, the others are given the soul and are its treasure.[149]

Paracelsus was not consistent in avoiding conventional theological terminology. Although he ordinarily used "soul" to mean the astral, ethereal, or sidereal body, he referred to the immortal soul of Christian belief when he instead asserted that "it is just and correct to call the soul a spirit, and to call the spirit God's angel in man."[150] As Paracelsus defined "spirit," the immortal soul of conventional theology was properly termed a spirit. "After the separation of matter from spirit, it returns to the Lord."[151] The human spirit had, however, two distinct types of function. In addition to its function as immortal soul, it had the function of angel. "It is given to man only as a teacher, to enlighten him in things eternal."[152]

Know that nothing could pass from us to God were there not an angel in us, who takes our inner message to Heaven. Nor would anything of God come to us without such an agent, who is swifter than all our thoughts. . . . Before a thought occurs to us, it has been with God and then returned to us. What God wills, He brings about through the spirit in us, which is charged with performing His work in us. . . . It is incumbent upon the [immortal] soul to serve as man's angel, and upon man to make use of his angel; for the angel is nothing other than the immortal part of man.[153]

Not only did Paracelsus establish the basic metaphysical distinctions of spiritual alchemy, but he developed the concept of the alchemical marriage. He may have been indebted to Leo Hebraeus (Jehudah Abarbanel, 1437–1509) for his knowledge of the traditional kabbalistic division of the macroanthropos into Adam and Eve, whose mystical union is the archetype of sexual coitus.[154] In both the kabbalah and the Sufism of Ibn al-ʿArabi, marital sex was regarded as a theurgical rite that united male and female hypostases. In the kabbalah, marital sex was further held to bring divine spirit into the material world. Soul was most fully joined with matter in the conception of a child, but a union of spirit and matter might also be achieved by meditating during the sex act. Spirit was considered active and masculine; matter was regarded passive and feminine. Their union was to be achieved during the sex act, through discursive meditations on the divine purpose of the sex act, which induced an ecstatic experience of the divine presence in the midst of the physical reality of copulation.[155]

Paracelsus preserved the kabbalistic idiom but gave it an original interpretation by having the marriage of Adam and Eve refer not to spirit and matter, but to ether and matter:

> Just as man originates in the Great World, and is inseparably bound to it, so has woman been created from man, and cannot separate from him. For if Lady Eve had been formed otherwise than from the body of man, desire would never have been born from both of them. But because they are of one flesh and one blood, it follows that they cannot let go of each other.[156]

Paracelsus's concept of the alchemical marriage also influenced his theory of the elements. He broke with long-standing tradition when he rejected the idea that the elements were each a compound of two qualities (hot, cold, moist, or dry). He did not accept the view of Rupescissan and pseudo-Lullist alchemy that the quintessence consisted of a perfect balance of the qualities—that is, the particular blend specific to gold. In his view, quintessences were spiritual entities that transcended the four qualities. Conversely, he recognized that all elements vary in temperature and may be hot or cold. He consequently maintained that there were only two qualities: "heat and dryness, are one thing, and in like manner, cold and humidity."[157]

Metallic alchemy had traditionally referred to several dyads or dyadic motifs: mercury and sulphur, silver and gold, the Moon and the Sun, death and life and so forth. Paracelsus augmented the series through his theory of the elements, and validated the application of the entire group of tropes to the ether-matter distinction of his spiritual alchemy. In this manner, the kabbalistic marriage of Adam and Eve became the alchemical marriage of the Sun and the Moon.

The Vegetable Stone

Once Paracelsus developed the concept of the otherworld that has come down to us, the remains of other traditions fed into Renaissance occultism. Not only kabbalah, Sufism, and relics of classical antiquity, but bits of shamanism, druidism, and witchcraft found their way into spiritual alchemy. It was, as it were, the parapsychology of its day: an effort to present mysticism in would-be scientific garb. Spiritual alchemy was never systematized in a manner that became normative. There was instead a proliferation of systems that had greater or smaller appeal for differing periods of time.

One major development of spiritual alchemy after Paracelsus was expressed succinctly in the "Prolegomena" to Elias Ashmole's *Theatrum Chemicum Brittanicum* (1652), where Ashmole broached the topic of psychoactive drugs:

> To come to the Vegitable, Magicall, and Angelicall Stones; the which have in them no part of the Minerall Stone . . . they are marvelously Subtile, and each of them differing in Operation and Nature. . . .
>
> For, by the Vegitable may be perfectly known the Nature of Man, Beasts, Foules, Fishes, together with all kinds of Trees, Plants, Flowers, &c. and how to produce and make them Grow, Flourish & beare Fruit; how to encrease them in Colour and Smell, and when and where we please, and all this not onely at an instant, Experimenti gratis, but Daily, Monethly, Yearly, at any Time, at any Season; yea, in the depth of Winter. And therefore not unlike, but the Walnut-Tree which anciently grew in Glastenbury Church-yard, and never put forth Leaves before S. Barnabies Day, yet then was fully loaded with them, as also the Hawthorne there, so greatly fam'd for shooting forth Leaves and Flowers at Christmas, together with the Oake in New-Forrest in Hampshire that bore greene Leaves at the same Season; may be some Experiments made of the Vegitable Stone.
>
> Besides the Masculine part of it which is wrought up to a Solar Quality, and through its exceeding Heat will burne up and destroy any Creature, Plant, &c. That which is Lunar & Feminine (if immediately applyed) will mitigate it with its extreme Cold: and in like manner the Lunar Quality benums and congeals any Animall, &c. unlesse it be presently helped and resolved by that of the Sun; For though the both are made out of one Natural Substance: yet in working they have contrary Qualities: nevertheless there is such a naturall Assistance between them, that what the one cannot doe, the other both can, and will perform.
>
> Nor are their inward Vertues more then their outward Beauties; for the Solar part is of so resplendent, transparent Lustre, that the Eye of Man is scarce able to indure it; and if the Lunar

part be expos'd abroad in a dark Night, Birds will repair to (and circulate about) it, as a Fly round a Candle, and submit themselves to the Captivity of the Hand. . . .

By the Magicall or Prospective Stone it is possible to discover any Person in what part of the World soever, although never so secretly concealed or hid; in Chambers, Closets, or Cavernes of the Earth; for there it makes a strict Inquisition. In a Word, it fairely presents to your view even the whole World, wherein to behold, heare, or see your Desire. Nay more. It enables Man to understand the Language of the Creatures, as the Chirping of Birds, Lowing of Beasts, &c. To Convey a Spirit into an Image, which by observing the Influence of Heavenly Bodies, shall become a true Oracle: And yet this as E. A. assures you, is not any wayes Necromanticall, or Devilish; but easy, wonderous easy, Naturall and Honest.

Lastly, as touching the Angelicall Stone, it is so subtill, saith the aforesaid Author, that it can neither be seene, felt, or weighed; but Tasted only. The voyce of Man (which bears some proportion to these subtill properties,) comes short in comparison; Nay the Air it selfe is not so penetrable, and yet (Oh mysterious wonder!) A Stone, that will lode in the Fire to Eternity without being prejudiced. It hath a Divine Power, Celestiall, and Invisible, above the rest; and endowes the possessor with Divine Gifts. It affords the Apparition of Angells, and gives a power of conversing with them, by Dreams and Revelations: nor dare any Evill Spirit approach the Place where it lodgeth. Because it is a Quintessence wherein there is no corruptible thing; and where the Elements are not corrupt, no Devill can stay or abide.

S. Dunston calls it the Food of Angels, and by others it is tearmed The Heavenly Viaticum; The Tree of Life. . . . There is a Gift of Prophesie hid in the Red-Stone.[158]

Ashmole explicitly asserted that the magical and angelical stones were psychoactive. The magical stone "presents to your view even the whole World," while the angelical stone "affords the Apparition of Angells." The references contrasted extrovertive mysticism with visions of ethereal beings. The ethereal experience was induced by "the Food of Angels," "Tree of Life," or "the Red-Stone."[159]

In medieval alchemy, the motif of a stone that was mineral, animal, and vegetable had signified the corrosive vapors of the metallic opus.[160] With the introduction of spiritual alchemy, the motif of the one thing that is composed of all things was reinterpreted in perspective of the experience of mystical union. The triple stone was identified as the "Quintessence.... The invisible Godhead.... Prime cause of being, and the Primer Essence," a manifest "Trinity equally knit in One."[161] Ashmole avoided pantheism, but only the macrocosm can answer to his paradoxical description of a stone that is a vegetable that provides knowledge of "Man, Beasts, Foules, Fishes, together with all kinds of Trees, Plants, Flowers, &c."

John Dee's *Monas Hieroglyphica* (1564) had asserted that "this whole magisterial work depends upon the Sun and the Moon."[162] The lunar and solar qualities of Ashmole's vegetable stone may be interpreted as two hypostases that unite in the alchemical marriage. The association of the hypostases with psychoactive drugs was a secret that Ashmole concealed in this passage. The material plane, "the whole World," was sublunar; ether was the substance of starlight, inclusive of the Copernican sun. The alchemist Thomas Vaughan (c. 1622–1665) expressed the same relations with the remark that Adam "heard indeed sometimes of a Tree of Life in Eden, but the vegetables of this world—for aught he knew—might be so many Trees of Death."[163] The tree of immortal souls was ethereal; the vegetable of ecstatic death belonged to this world.

Ashmole's literary trope, that solar and lunar qualities both belong to the vegetable stone, implied that both the magical and angelical stones were vegetable substances. Vaughan made passing mention of the same: "Certainly if it once be granted—as some stick not to affirm—that the Tree of Knowledge was a vegetable and Eden a garden it may be very well inferred that the Tree of Life— being described after the same manner, as the schoolmen express it—was a vegetable also."[164] The precise botanical identities of the plants are not as important, however, as their abilities to induce the appropriate varieties of ecstatic experience. A metaphysics of the material plane, that was derived from experiences such as extrovertive mysticism and ecstatic death, was paired with a metaphysics of the ethereal plane, that was derived from visionary experiences and mystical nothingness. Any plants and, for that manner, any other means by which to induce the two categories of experience merited classification as lunar and solar. Spiritual alchemy was designed as a general theory of mysticism that was able to accommodate a pairing of lucid hypnagogia with self-hypnotic trance, psilocybin mushrooms with amanita muscaria mushrooms, or any equivalent ecstatic techniques. The sun and the moon were theosophical concepts. The union of the two hypostases constituted the alchemical marriage.

Notes

Chapter 1

1. For a classic and still valuable example of the genre, see Theodore Flournoy, *From India to the Planet Mars: A Study of a Case of Somnambulism with Glossolalia* (1900; rpt. New Hyde Park, N.Y.: University Books, 1963).

2. Thomas Merton, *Thomas Merton on Saint Bernard* (Kalamazoo, Mich.: Cistercian Publications, 1980); idem, "The Inner Experience: Infused Contemplation (V)," ed. Patrick Hart, *Cistercian Studies* 19 (1984), 62–78.

3. Dan Merkur, "Unitive Experiences and the State of Trance," in *Mystical Union and Monotheistic Religion: An Ecumenical Dialogue,* ed. Moshe Idel and Bernard McGinn (New York: Macmillan, 1989), 131.

4. Evelyn Underhill, *Mysticism: A Study in the Nature and Development of Man's Spiritual Consciousness* (London [1911], 1930), 72.

5. Friedrich Heiler, *Prayer: A Study in the History and Psychology of Religion* [1920], trans. Samuel McComb with J. Edgar Park (London: Oxford University Press, 1932); Johannes Lindblom, *Prophecy in Ancient Israel* (Philadelphia: Fortress, 1962).

6. Traugott Konstantin Oesterreich, *Possession: Demoniacal and Other among Primitive Races in Antiquity, the Middle Ages, and Modern Times* (1930; rpt. Secaucus, N.J.: University Books, 1966).

7. S. M. Shirokogoroff, *Psychomental Complex of the Tungus* (London: Kegan Paul, Trench, Trubner, 1935); Mircea Eliade, *Shamanism: Archaic Techniques of Ecstasy* (New York: Bollingen Foundation/Pantheon Books, 1964).

8. St. Augustine of Hippo, *The Literal Meaning of Genesis,* trans. John Hammond Taylor (New York and Ramsey, N.J.: Newman, 1982), II, 178–324.

9. William A. Christian, Jr., *Apparitions in Late Medieval and Renaissance Spain* (Princeton: Princeton University Press, 1981), 133–35.

10. Catherine of Genoa, *Purgation and Purgatory. The Spiritual Dialogue,* trans. Serge Hughes (New York: Paulist, 1979), 118.

11. Ernst Arbman, *Ecstasy or Religious Trance: In the Experience of the Ecstatics and from the Scientific Point of View,* 3 vols., ed. Åke Hultkrantz (Stockholm: Svenska Bokforlaget, 1963–68–70), II, 253–54.

12. Arbman, *Ecstasy,* I, 106–7.

13. Ibid., 239, 242, 245.

14. William J. Samarin, *Tongues of Men and Angels: The Religious Language of Pentecostalism* (New York: Macmillan, 1972), 30. The comments in brackets are by Samarin.

15. See Arbman, *Ecstasy,* I, 237.

16. Cited in ibid., II, 343.

17. Ibid., I, 16–17.

18. B. H. Streeter and A. J. Appasamy, *The Sadhu: A Study in Mysticism and Practical Religion* (1921; rpt. London: Macmillan, 1922), 5–7, 54–55.

19. Arbman, *Ecstasy,* I, 349–50, II, 10, 237; Lindblom, *Prophecy,* 15; Sudhir Kakar, *Shamans, Mystics and Doctors: A Psychological Inquiry into India and Its Healing Traditions* (New York: Knopf, 1982), 80.

20. Arbman, *Ecstacy,* II, 10.

21. Ibid., 10.

22. Ibid., 12–16.

23. Ibid., 17–24.

24. Ibid., 10.

25. Ibid., I, 119.

26. Edward Conze, "Buddhist Philosophy and its European Parallels," in *Thirty Years of Buddhist Studies: Selected Essays* (Columbia: University of South Carolina Press, 1968), 213.

27. *Oxford English Dictionary.*

28. St. Teresa of Jesus, *Complete Works,* 3 vols., trans. E. Allison Peers (London: Sheed and Ward, 1946).

29. St. Bernard of Clairvaux, *On the Song of Songs IV,* trans. Irene M. Edmonds (Kalamazoo, Mich.: Cistercian Publications, 1980), Sermon 74:5, pp. 89–90: "Although he has come to me, I have never been conscious of the moment of his coming. I perceived his presence, remembered afterwards

that he had been with me; sometimes I had a presentiment that he would come, but I was never conscious of his coming or his going."

30. Eliade, *Shamanism.*

31. Robert M. Gimello, "Mysticism and Meditation," in *Mysticism and Philosophical Analysis,* ed. Steven T. Katz (London: Sheldon, 1978), 170–99.

32. Dan Merkur, "The Induction of Mystical Union: Two Hasidic Teachings," *Studia Mystica* 14/4 (1991), 70–76.

33. Erika Fromm, "The Nature of Hypnosis and Other Altered States of Consciousness: An Ego Psychological Theory," in *Hypnosis: Developments in Research and New Perspectives,* 2nd ed., ed. Erika Fromm and Ronald E. Shor (New York: Aldine, 1979), 89.

34. Dan Merkur, *Becoming Half Hidden: Shamanism and Initiation Among the Inuit* (Stockholm: Almqvist and Wiksell, 1985), 42–44.

35. Ronald E. Shor, "Three Dimensions of Hypnotic Depth," *International Journal of Clinical and Experimental Hypnosis* 10 (1962):23–38; rpt. in *Altered States of Consciousness,* 2nd ed., ed. Charles T. Tart (Garden City, N.Y.: Doubleday, 1972), 257–67.

36. Ronald E. Shor, "Hypnosis and the Concept of the Generalized Reality Orientation," *American Journal of Psychotherapy* 13 (1959): 582–602; rpt. in *Altered States of Consciousness,* ed. Tart, 239–56.

37. Dan Merkur, "The Nature of the Hypnotic State: A Psychoanalytic Approach," *International Review of Psycho-Analysis* 11/3 (1984), 345–54.

38. Martin T. Orne, "The Nature of Hypnosis: Artifact and Essence," *Journal of Abnormal and Social Psychology* 58 (1959), 277–99.

39. Paul Schilder and Otto Kauders, *The Nature of Hypnosis* (1956; rpt. New York: International Universities Press, 1973), 76–77, 96.

40. Robert Charles Zaehner, *Mysticism Sacred and Profane: An Inquiry into some Varieties of Preternatural Experience* (1957; rpt. London: Oxford University Press, 1961); idem, *Concordant Discord: The Interdependence of Faiths* (Oxford: Clarendon Press, 1970); idem, *Zen, Drugs and Mysticism* (1972; rpt. New York: Random House, 1974).

41. Ninian Smart, "Interpretation and Mystical Experience," *Religious Studies* 1 (1965), 75–87.

42. H. P. Owen, "Christian Mysticism: A Study in Walter Hilton's *The Ladder of Perfection,*" *Religious Studies* 7 (1971), 31–42.

43. Nelson Pike, "Comments," in *Art, Mind and Religion,* ed. W. H. Capitan and D. D. Merill (Pennsylvania, 1965), 147–48; Bruce Garside,

"Language and the Interpretation of Mystical Experience," *International Journal for the Philosophy of Religion* 3 (1972), 101–2; Philip C. Almond, *Mystical Experience and Religious Doctrine: An Investigation of the Study of Mysticism in World Religions* (Berlin: Mouton, 1982), 162, 173–74.

44. Steven T. Katz, "Language, Epistemology, and Mysticism," in *Mysticism and Philosophical Analysis*, ed. Steven T. Katz (London: Sheldon, 1978), 22–74; idem, "Models, Modeling and Mystical Training," *Religion* 12 (1982), 247–75; idem, "The 'Conservative' Character of Mystical Experience," in *Mysticism and Religious Traditions*, ed. Steven T. Katz (Oxford: Oxford University Press, 1983), 3–60.

45. Arbman, *Ecstasy*, I, xv, 478.

46. William James, *The Varieties of Religious Experience: A Study in Human Nature* (1902; New York: New American Library, 1958), 326.

47. Ibid., 387–88.

48. Mircea Eliade, *Yoga: Immortality and Freedom* (1958; rpt. Princeton: Bollingen Foundation/Princeton University Press, 1969), 47; idem, *Patanjali and Yoga*, trans. Charles Lam Markmann (1969; rpt. New York: Schocken, 1975), 61.

49. Arthur J. Deikman, "Experimental Meditation," *Journal of Nervous and Mental Disease* 136 (1963), 329–73; rpt. in *Altered States of Consciousness*, ed. Tart, 203–23.

50. Merkur, "Unitive Experiences."

51. Rudolf Otto, *Mysticism East and West: A Comparative Analysis of the Nature of Mysticism*, trans. Bertha L. Bracey and Richenda C. Payne (New York, 1932; rpt. New York: Macmillan, 1970), 60–88.

52. Mechthild of Magdeburg, *The Revelations of Mechthild of Magdeburg (1219–1297), or, The Flowing Light of the Godhead*, trans. Lucy Menzies (London: Longmans, Green, 1953), 9.

53. W. T. Stace, *Mysticism and Philosophy* (Philadelphia and New York: Lippincott, 1960), 60, 62–81.

54. Angela of Foligno, *The Book of Divine Consolation*, trans. Mary G. Steegmann (New York: Cooper Square, 1966), 172.

55. Abraham Joshua Heschel, The Prophets (New York: Harper and Row, 1962), II, 99–104. Compare Dan Merkur, "The Prophecies of Jeremiah," *The American Imago* 42/1 (1985), 1–37.

56. Gershom G. Scholem, "*Devekut*, or Communion with God," in *The Messianic Idea in Judaism: And Other Essays on Jewish Spirituality* (New York: Schocken, 1971).

57. Angela of Foligno, *Book*, 172.

58. Henry Corbin, *Creative Imagination in the Sufism of Ibn 'Arabi,* trans. Ralph Manheim (1958; rpt. Princeton: Princeton University Press, 1969).

59. See James, *Varieties of Religious Experience,* 67–71.

60. Rodney Stark, "A Taxonomy of Religious Experience," *Journal for the Scientific Study of Religion* 5 (1965), 99.

61. Lindblom, Prophecy, 302.

62. Teresa, *Complete Works,* II, 334–5.

63. Hadewijch, *The Complete Works,* trans. Columba Hart (New York: Paulist, 1980), 296.

64. Merkur, "The Prophecies of Jeremiah."

65. Cavendish Moxon, "Mystical Ecstasy and Hysterical Dream-States," *Journal of Abnormal Psychology* 15 (1920), 329–34; Theodore Schroeder, "Prenatal Psychisms and Mystical Pantheism," *International Journal of Psycho-Analysis* 3 (1922), 445–66; Alfred Carver, "Primary Identification and Mysticism," *British Journal of Medical Psychology* 4 (1924), 102–14; Franz Alexander, "Buddhistic Training As an Artificial Catatonia (The Biological Meaning of Psychic Occurrences)," *Psychoanalytic Review* 18 (1931), 129–45.

66. Sigmund Freud, "Civilization and Its Discontents" (1930), *The Standard Edition of the Complete Psychological Works of Sigmund Freud,* ed. James Strachey, with Anna Freud, Alix Strachey, and Alan Tyson, vol. 21, 64–145 (London: Hogarth, 1966).

67. Richard Sterba, "Remarks on Mystic States," *American Imago* 25 (1968), 81.

68. Dan Merkur, "The Capacity for Religiosity: A Psychoanalytic Theory" [unpublished manuscript].

69. Merkur, "Unitive Experiences," 237, n. 119.

70. Nathaniel Ross, "Affect as Cognition: With Observations on the Meanings of Mystical States," *International Review of Psycho-Analysis* 2 (1975), 89.

71. Julia Kristeva, *In the Beginning Was Love: Psychoanalysis and Faith,* trans. Arthur Goldhammer (New York: Columbia University Press, 1987), 24.

72. Martin Buber, *Between Man and Man* (New York: Macmillan, 1965), 24.

73. Alexandra David-Neel, *With Mystics and Magicians in Tibet* (1931; rpt. London: Penguin, 1936), 237–38; see Eliade, *Yoga,* 208–9, 225.

74. Hildegard of Bingen, *Scivias*, trans. Columba Hart and Jane Bishop (New York: Paulist, 1990).

75. *The Life and Revelations of Saint Gertrude: Virgin and Abbess of the Order of St. Benedict* (1862; rpt. Westminster, Md.: Christian Classics, 1983), 95.

76. Stace, *Mysticism*, 85–6.

77. As argued, for example, by Ninian Smart, "The Purification of Consciousness and the Negative Path," in *Mysticism and Philosophical Analysis,* ed. Steven T. Katz (London: Sheldon, 1978), 117–130; Robert K. C. Forman, ed., *The Problem of Pure Consciousness: Mysticism and Philosophy* (New York and Oxford: Oxford University Press, 1990).

78. As termed by Agehananda Bharati, *The Light at the Center: Context and Pretext of Modern Mysticism* (Santa Barbara: Ross-Erikson, 1976).

79. Robert R. Holt, *Freud Reappraised: A Fresh Look at Psychoanalytic Theory* (New York: Guilford, 1989), 202.

80. Sigmund Freud, *The Interpretation of Dreams* [1900], rpt. in *The Standard Edition of the Complete Psychological Works of Sigmund Freud,* ed. James Strachey, with Anna Freud, Alix Strachey, and Alan Tyson (London: Hogarth, 1966), Vols. 4–5.

81. Edward Conze, *Buddhist Meditation* (1956; rpt. New York: Harper and Row, 1969), 113, 116, 117–8.

82. Eliade, *Yoga,* 174.

83. Paul Federn, "Some Variations in Ego-Feeling," *International Journal of Psycho-Analysis* 7 (1926), 437.

84. Arthur J. Deikman, *The Observing Self: Mysticism and Psychotherapy* (Boston: Beacon, 1982), 94.

85. Merkur, "The Nature of the Hypnotic State."

86. Sigmund Freud, *New Introductory Lectures on Psycho-Analysis,* in *Standard Edition,* XXII, 66; Heinz Hartmann, Ernst Kris, and Rudolph M. Loewenstein, *Papers on Psychoanalytic Psychology* (New York: International Universities Press, 1964), 159–60.

87. St. John of the Cross, *Collected Works,* trans. Kieran Kavanaugh and Otilio Rodriguez (Washington: Institute of Carmelite Studies, 1973).

88. Jan van Ruysbroek, *The Spiritual Espousals,* trans. Eric Colledge (1953; rpt. Westminster, Md.: Christian Classics, 1983).

89. Rudolf Otto, *The Idea of the Holy: An inquiry into the non-rational factor in the idea of the divine and its relation to the rational,* 2nd ed. (London: Oxford University Press, 1950).

90. Daniel C. Matt, *"Ayin:* The Concept of Nothingness in Jewish Mysticism," in *The Problem of Pure Consciousness: Mysticism and Philosophy,* ed. Robert K. C. Forman (New York: Oxford University Press, 1990), 139–45.

91. See Steven T. Katz, "Language, Epistemology, and Mysticism," 59.

92. Charles T. Tart, "Transpersonal Potentialities of Deep Hypnosis," *Journal of Transpersonal Psychology* 2 (1970), 37; idem, "Measuring the Depth of an Altered State of Consciousness, with Particular Reference to Self-Report Scales of Hypnotic Depth," in *Hypnosis: Developments in Research and New Perspectives,* 2nd ed., ed. Erika Fromm and Ronald E. Shor (New York: Aldine, 1979), 595–96; Spencer Sherman, "Brief Report: Very Deep Hypnosis," *Journal of Transpersonal Psychology* 4 (1972), 89.

93. J. N. Sherwood, M. J. Stolaroff, and W. W. Harman, "The Psychedelic Experience—A New Concept in Psychotherapy," *Journal of Psychedelic Drugs* 3/1 (1962), 77–78.

94. Joseph Havens, "A Working Paper: Memo on the Religious Implications of the Consciousness-Changing Drugs (LSD, Mescalin, Psilocybin)," *Journal for the Scientific Study of Religion* 3 (1964), 219–22.

95. Robert Masters and Jean Houston, *"The Varieties of Psychedelic Experience"* (1966; rpt. London: Turnstone, 1973), 154.

96. Pinchas Noy, "A Revision of the Psychoanalytic Theory of the Primary Process," *International Journal of Psycho-Analysis* 50 (1969), 155–78.

97. Bernard S. Aaronson and Humphry Osmond, ed., *Psychedelics: The Uses and Implications of Hallucinogenic Drugs* (1968; rpt. Garden City, N.Y.: Doubleday/Anchor, 1970); John Blofeld, "A High Yogic Experience Achieved with Mescaline," *Psychedelic Review* 7 (1966), 27–32; William Braden, *The Private Sea: LSD and the Search for God* (Chicago: Quadrangle, 1967); W. B. Caldwell, *LSD Psychotherapy: An Exploration of Psychedelic and Psycholytic Therapy* (1968; rpt. New York: Grove, 1969); Walter Houston Clark, *Chemical Ecstasy: Psychedelic Drugs and Religion* (New York: Sheed and Ward, 1969); Walter Houston Clark, H. Newton, Maloney, James Daane, and Alan R. Tippett, *Religious Experience: Its Nature and Function in the Human Psyche* (Springfield, Ill.: Charles C. Thomas, 1973); David R. Crownfield, "Religion in the Cartography of the Unconscious: A Discussion of Stanislav Grof's *Realms of the Human Unconscious,"* *Journal of the American Academy of Religion* 44/2 (1976), 309–15; Richard C. DeBold and Russell Leaf, ed., *LSD, Man and Society* (Middletown, Conn.: Wesleyan University Press, 1968); Stanislav Grof, *Realms of the Human Unconscious: Observations from LSD Research* (New York: Viking, 1975); Willis W. Harman, "The Use of the Consciousness-Expanding Drugs," *Main Currents in Modern Thought* 20 (1963), 5–14; S. I. Hayakawa, ed., *Etc.: A Review of General Semantics* 22/4 (1965); Aldous Huxley, *The Doors of*

Perception [1954] and *Heaven and Hell* [1956] (rpt. London: Granada, 1977); Stanley Krippner and Richard Davidson, "Religious Implications of Paranormal Events Occurring During Chemically-Induced 'Psychedelic' Experience," *Pastoral Psychology* 21 (1970), 206/27–34; Timothy Leary, "The Religious Experience: Its Production and Interpretation," *Psychedelic Review* 1/3 (1964), 324–46; Timothy Leary and Walter Houston Clark, "Religious Implications of Consciousness Expanding Drugs," *Religious Education* 58/2 (1963), 251–66; Ralph Metzner, ed., *The Ecstatic Adventure* (New York: Macmillan, 1968); Albert S. Moraczewski, "Mescaline, Madness and Mysticism," *Thought* 42 (1967), 358–82; Herbert A. Otto, ed., *Explorations in Human Potentialities* (Springfield, Ill.: Charles C. Thomas, 1966); Walter N. Pahnke, "Drugs and Mysticism," *International Journal of Parapsychology* 8/1 (1966), 295–315; idem, "The Contribution of the Psychology of Religion to the Therapeutic Use of the Psychedelic Substances," in *The Use of LSD in Psychotherapy and Alcoholism*, ed. Harold A. Abramson (Indianapolis: Bobbs-Merrill, 1967); idem, "The Psychedelic Mystical Experience in the Human Encounter with Death," *Harvard Theological Review* 62 (1969), 1–21; Walter N. Pahnke and William A. Richards, "Implications of LSD and Experimental Mysticism," *Journal of Religion and Health* 5/3 (1966), 175–208; D. H. Salman and Raymond H. Prince, ed., *Do Psychedelics Have Religious Implications?* (R. M. Bucke Society for the study of religious experiences, Proceedings, 3rd Annual Conference) (Montreal, 1968); Huston Smith, "Do Drugs Have Religious Import?" *Journal of Philosophy* 61/18 (1964), 517–31; idem, "Psychedelic Theophanies and the Religious Life," *Journal of Psychedelic Drugs* 3/1 (1970), 87–91; idem, *Forgotten Truth: The Primordial Tradition* (1976; rpt. New York: Harper and Row, 1977); Peter G. Stafford and Bonnie H. Golightly, *LSD: The Problem-Solving Psychedelic* (New York: Award, 1967); Anthony F. C. Wallace, "Cultural Determinants of Response to Hallucinatory Experiences," *Archives of General Psychiatry* 1 (1959), 58–69; Alan W. Watts, *The Joyous Cosmology: Adventures in the Chemistry of Consciousness* (1962; rpt. New York: Vintage/Random House, 1965); W. David Watts, Jr., *The Psychedelic Experience: A Sociological Study* (Beverly Hills: Sage, 1971).

98. Zaehner, *Mysticism Sacred and Profane;* idem, *Zen, Drugs and Mysticism;* Paul S. Kurtz, "Similarities and Differences Between Religious Mysticism and Drug-Induced Experiences," *Journal of Humanistic Psychology* 3/2 (1963), 146–54; Alvin R. Gilbert, "Pseudo-Mind Expansion Through Psychedelics and Brain-Wave-Programming Versus True Mind-Expansion Through Life Conditioning to the Absolute," *Psychologia* 14 (1971), 187–92; Charles W. Swain, "Drug Experience and 'Mystical' Experience: Reflections on the Problem of Comparison," *Journal of Drug Issues* 7/3 (1977), 247–52. Proponents of mystical traditions that demand a withdrawal from the perceptible world have occasionally taken alarm at the world-validating character of extrovertive mysticism. Having experienced extrovertive mysticism only through psychedelic use, they have argued that psychedelic experiences are not only not religious, but harmful to religion.

Their positions reflect sectarian prejudices that can have no place in scientific discussions. See Koji Sato, "D. T. Suzuki, Zen and LSD 25," *Psychologia* 10 (1967), 129–32; Meher Baba, "L.S.D. and the Highroads," *Journal of Psychedelic Drugs* 1/2 (1967–68), 38–44.

99. Abraham H. Maslow, "Lessons from the Peak-Experiences," *Journal of Humanistic Psychology* 2 (1962), 9–18. See also idem, *Religions, Values, and Peak Experiences* (1964; rpt. Harmondsworth: Penguin, 1976); idem, *Toward a Psychology of Being* (1968; rpt. New York: Van Nostrand, n.d.); idem, *The Farther Reaches of Human Nature* (1971; rpt. Harmondsworth: Penguin, 1978).

100. J. Trevor, *My Quest for God* (London, 1897), 268; as abridged in James, *Varieties of Religious Experience,* 305.

101. Masters and Houston, *Varieties of Psychedelic Experience,* 149–50.

102. W. H. Bexton, W. Heron, and T. H. Scott, "Effects of Decreased Variation in the Sensory Environment," *Canadian Journal of Psychology* 8 (1954), 70–76; Woodburn Heron, B. D. Doane, and T. H. Scott, "Visual Disturbances after Prolonged Perceptual Isolation," *Canadian Journal of Psychology* 10 (1956), 13–18; Philip Solomon et al., ed., *Sensory Deprivation: A Symposium Held at Harvard Medical School* (Cambridge: Harvard University Press, 1961); Louis Jolyon West, ed., *Hallucinations* (New York: Grune and Stratton, 1962); Marvin Zuckerman, "Hallucinations, Reported Sensations, and Images," in *Sensory Deprivation: Fifteen Years of Research,* ed. John P. Zubek (New York: Appleton-Century-Crofts, 1969).

103. John Lilly, "Mental effects of reduction of ordinary levels of physical stimuli on intact, healthy persons," *Psychiatric Research Reports* 5 (1956), 1–9; John C. Lilly and Jay T. Shurley, "Experiments in Solitude, in Maximum Achievable Physical Isolation with Water Suspension, of Intact Healthy Persons," in *Psychophysiological Aspects of Space Flight,* ed. Bernard E. Flaherty (New York: Columbia University Press, 1961), 238–47.

104. Merkur, *Becoming Half Hidden.*

105. Knud Rasmussen, *The Netsilik Eskimos: Social Life and Spiritual Culture,* Report of the Fifth Thule Expedition 1921–1924, 8/1–2 (Copenhagen, 1931; rpt. New York: AMS, 1976), 336–37.

106. See Rasmussen, *Netsilik Eskimos,* 338.

107. Ibid., 228–29.

108. Dan Merkur, "The Visionary Practices of Jewish Apocalyptists," *The Psychoanalytic Study of Society* 14, ed. L. Bryce Boyer and Simon A. Grolnick (Hillsdale, N.J.: Analytic Press, 1989), 119–48.

109. Moshe Idel, *The Mystical Experience in Abraham Abulafia,* trans. Jonathan Chipman (Albany: State University of New York Press, 1988), 40.

110. Joseph Weiss, *Studies in Eastern European Jewish Mysticism,* ed. David Goldstein (Oxford: Oxford University Press, 1985), 95–125.

111. Idel, *Experience,* 40.

112. Conze, *Meditation,* 62–109; David J. Kalupahana, *The Principles of Buddhist Psychology* (Albany: State University of New York Press, 1987), 73–75.

113. Daniel Goleman, "The Buddha on Meditation and States of Consciousness. Part I: The Teachings," *Journal of Transpersonal Psychology* 4 (1972), 1–44; idem, "A Taxonomy of Meditation-Specific Altered States," *Journal of Altered States of Consciousness* 4/2 (1978–79), 203–13; Michael C. Washburn, "Observations Relevant to a Unified Theory of Meditation," *Journal of Transpersonal Psychology* 10/1 (1978), 45–65; Michael A. West, "Traditional and psychological perspectives on meditation," in *The Psychology of Meditation,* ed. Michael A. West (Oxford: Clarendon Press, 1987), 16–18.

114. Roger Walsh, "Initial Meditative Experiences: Part I," *Journal of Transpersonal Psychology* 9 (1977), 151.

115. Jack Kornfield, "Intensive Insight Meditation: A Phenomenological Study," *Journal of Transpersonal Psychology* 11 (1979), 46–50.

116. David Winston, "Introduction," in Philo of Alexandria, *The Contemplative Life, The Giants, and Selections* (New York: Paulist, 1981), 24–35.

117. Jean Daniélou, *A History of Early Christian Doctrine Before the Council of Nicaea, Volume Two: Gospel Message and Hellenistic Culture,* trans. John Austin Baker (London: Darton, Longman and Todd; Philadelphia: Westminster, 1973).

118. Philip Merlan, *Monopsychism Mysticism Metaconsciousness: problems of the soul in the neoaristotelian and neoplatonic tradition* (The Hague: M. Nijhoff, 1963); Pierre Hadot, "Neoplatonist Spirituality, I. Plotinus and Porphyry," in *Classical Mediterranean Spirituality,* ed. A. Hilary Armstrong (New York: Crossroad, 1986), 230–49.

119. Andre Louth, *The Origins of the Christian Mystical Tradition: From Plato to Denys* (Oxford: Clarendon Press, 1981).

120. Pseudo-Dionysius, *The Complete Works,* trans. Colm Luibheid (New York: Paulist, 1987), 145.

121. Geo Widengren, "Researches in Syrian Mysticism: Mystical Experiences and Spiritual Exercises," *Numen* 8/3 (1961), 161–98.

122. Majid Fakhry, "Three Varieties of Mysticism in Islam," *International Journal for the Philosophy of Religion* 2/4 (1971), 193–207; David R.

Blumenthal, "Maimonides' Intellectualist Mysticism and the Superiority of the Prophecy of Moses," *Studies in Medieval Culture*, 10 (1977), 51–68; rpt. *Approaches to Judaism in Medieval Times,* ed. David R. Blumenthal (Chico, Calif.: Scholars, 1984).

123. Gershom G. Scholem, "The Concept of Kavvanah in the Early Kabbalah" [1934], in *Studies in Jewish Thought: An Anthology of German Jewish Scholarship,* ed. Alfred Jospe (Detroit: Wayne State University Press, 1981), 162–80.

124. Henry Corbin, *Avicenna and the Visionary Recital,* trans. Willard R. Trask (1954; rpt. Irving, Tex.: Spring, 1980).

125. Merkur, *Becoming Half Hidden,* 52–54.

126. Patricia Garfield, *Creative Dreaming* (1974; rpt. New York: Ballantine, 1976); Stephen LaBarge, *Lucid Dreaming* (Los Angeles: Jeremy P. Tarcher, 1985); Jayne Gackenbach and Jane Bosveld, *Control Your Dreams: How Lucid Dreaming Can Help You Uncover Your Hidden Desires, Confront Your Hidden Fears, and Explore the Frontiers of Human Consciousness* (New York: Harper and Row, 1989); Keith Harary and Pamela Weintraub, *Lucid Dreams in 30 Days: The Creative Sleep Program* (New York: St. Martin's, 1989).

127. Gershom G. Scholem, *Jewish Gnosticism, Merkabah Mysticism, and Talmudic Tradition,* 2nd ed. (New York: Jewish Theological Seminary of America, 1965), 15.

128. Corbin, *Avicenna and the Visionary Recital,* 156–57; idem, *The Man of Light in Iranian Sufism,* trans. Nancy Pearson (1971; rpt. Boulder, Colo.: Shambhala, 1978), 79.

129. Mircea Eliade, *Rites and Symbols of Initiation: The Mysteries of Birth and Rebirth* (Originally entitled: "Birth and Rebirth"), trans. Willard R. Trask (1958; rpt. New York: Harper and and and and and and Row, 1975).

130. Merkur, *Becoming Half Hidden,* 181–98.

131. Grof, *Realms of the Human Unconscious,* 104–37.

132. Marghanita Laski, *Ecstasy: A Study of some Secular and Religious Experiences* (1962; rpt. New York: Greenwood, 1968), 160–70; Michael Paffard, *Inglorious Wordsworths: A Study of some transcendental experiences in childhood and adolescence* (London: Hodder and Stoughton, 1973).

133. B. M. Sjoberg, Jr. and L. E. Hollister, "The Effects of Psychotomimetic Drugs on Primary Suggestibility," *Psychopharmacologia* 8 (1965), 251–62; Lionel P. Solursh and J. M. Rae, "LSD, Suggestion and Hypnosis," *International Journal of Neuropsychiatry* 2 (1966), 60–64; David Whitman

van Nuys, "Drug Use and Hypnotic Susceptibility," *International Journal of Clinical and Experimental Hypnosis* 20/1 (1972), 31–37.

134. N. Chwelos, D. B. Blewett, C. M. Smith, and A. Hoffer, "Use of d-Lysergic Acid Diethylamide in the Treatment of Alcoholism," *Quarterly Journal for Studies on Alcohol* 20 (1959), 586–87; Robert E. L. Masters and Jean Houston, "Toward an Individual Psychedelic Psychotherapy," in *Psychedelics,* ed. Aaronson and Osmond, 341.

Chapter 2

1. Carl Gustav Jung, "Commentary on 'The Secret of the Golden Flower,'" *Alchemical Studies,* trans. R. F. C. Hull (Collected Works, Vol. 13; Princeton: Princeton University Press, 1967), 16–17.

2. For a list of references, see R. F. C. Hull, "Bibliographical Notes on Active Imagination in the Works of C. G. Jung," *Spring 1971,* 115–20.

3. Carl Gustav Jung, *The Visions Seminars: From the Complete Notes of Mary Foote,* 2 vols. (Zurich: Spring, 1976).

4. Carl Gustav Jung, *Analytical Psychology: Its Theory and Practice. The Tavistock Lectures* (New York: Pantheon/Random House, 1968); rpt. in *The Symbolic Life: Miscellaneous Writings,* 2nd ed; trans. R. F. C. Hull (Collected Works, vol. 18; Princeton: Princeton University Press, 1980).

5. Carl Gustav Jung, *The Process of Individuation: Notes on Lectures at the ETH, Zurich,* trans. and ed. Barbara Hannah (privately issued).

6. Carl Gustav Jung, *"Exercitia Spiritualia* of St. Ignatius of Loyola: Notes on Lectures (1939)," *Spring 1977,* 183–200; *Spring* 1978, 28–36.

7. Barbara Hannah, "Some Remarks on Active Imagination," *Spring 1953,* 38–58.

8. Michael Fordham, "Active Imagination and Imaginative Activity," *Journal of Analytical Psychology* 1 (1955–56), 207–8.

9. Carl Gustav Jung, "The Transcendent Function," in *The Structure and Dynamics of the Psyche,* trans. R. F. C. Hull (Collected Works of C. G. Jung, vol. 8; Bollingen Series 20; New York: Pantheon, 1960).

10. Carl Gustav Jung, *Memories, Dreams, Reflections,* 2nd ed.; ed. Aniela Jaffe; trans. Richard and Clara Winston (1973; rpt. New York: Vintage/Random House, 1989).

11. Hannah, "Remarks," 43.

12. Ibid., 47.

13. Elie G. Humbert, "Active Imagination: Theory and Practice," *Spring 1971,* 112.

14. Marie-Louise von Franz, "Introduction," in Barbara Hannah, *Encounters with the Soul: Active Imagination as Developed by C. G. Jung* (Boston: Sigo, 1981), 1–2.

15. Aniela Jaffe, *Was C. G. Jung A Mystic? And Other Essays* (Einsiedeln, Switzerland: Daimon Verlag, 1989).

16. Colin Wilson, *C. G. Jung: Lord of the Underworld* (Wellingborough, U.K.: Aquarian, 1984).

17. James Webb, *The Occult Establishment* (La Salle, Ill.: Open Court, 1976), 382–407.

18. Henri F. Ellenberger, *The Discovery of the Unconscious: The History and Evolution of Dynamic Psychiatry* (New York: Basic, 1970), 657.

19. Faivre, "Esotericism," 163.

20. Jung, *Memories, Dreams, Reflections,* 171–72.

21. Ibid., 173.

22. Ibid., 174–75.

23. Ibid., 178.

24. Ibid., 179.

25. Ibid., 179–80.

26. Ibid., 176.

27. Ibid.

28. Ibid., 177.

29. Ibid., 182–83.

30. Ibid., 188.

31. Jung, "Transcendent Function," 68.

32. Ibid., 78.

33. Ibid.

34. Ibid., 82.

35. Ibid., 83.

36. Carl Gustav Jung, *Two Essays on Analytical Psychology,* 2nd ed., trans. R. F. C. Hull (Collected Works, vol. 7; Princeton: Princeton University Press, 1966), 201.

37. Ibid., 202.

38. Ibid.

39. Carl Gustav Jung, *The Symbolic Life,* 171.

40. Ibid., 171–72.

41. Ibid., 172.

42. Marie-Louise von Franz, *Alchemical Active Imagination* (Dallas: Spring, 1979).

43. Hannah, *Encounters with the Soul.*

44. Marie-Louise von Franz, "On Active Imagination," in *Methods of Treatment in Analytical Psychology,* ed. Ian F. Baker (Fellbach: Verlag Adolf Bonz, 1980), 90.

45. Robert A. Johnson, *Inner Work: Using Dreams and Active Imagination for Personal Growth* (San Francisco: Harper and Row, 1986), 160, 188–95.

46. Andreas Mavromatis, *Hypnagogia: The Unique State of Consciousness between Wakefulness and Sleep* (London and New York: Routledge, 1987), 64.

47. Fordham, 207–8; idem, "Active Imagination—Deintegration or Disintegration?" *Journal of Analytical Psychology* 12 (1967), 51.

48. Robert Desoille, *The Directed Daydream: A Series of Three Lectures Given at the Sorbonne (January 1965),* trans. F. Haronian (New York: Psychosynthesis Research Foundation, 1966).

49. J. H. van den Berg, "An Existential Explanation of the Guided Daydream in Psychotherapy," *Review of Existential Psychology and Psychiatry* 2 (1962), 12.

50. Ibid., 14–15.

51. Jung, *"Exercitia Spiritualia,"* 32.

52. Desoille, "Daydreams," 26.

53. Max Hammer, "The Directed Daydream Technique," *Psychotherapy* 4 (1967), 174.

54. Freud, *Interpretation of Dreams,* 619.

55. Ibid., 175.

56. Gaston Bachelard, *On Poetic Imagination and Reverie: Selections,* trans. Colette Gaudin (Dallas: Spring, 1987).

57. Hanscarl Leuner, "Guided Affective Imagery (GAI): A Method of Intensive Psychotherapy," *American Journal of Psychotherapy* 23/1 (1969),

4–22; idem, "The Role of Imagery in Psychotherapy," in *New Dimensions in Psychiatry: A World View,* ed. Silvano Arieti and Gerard Chrzanowski (New York: Wiley, 1975), 169–99; idem, "Guided Affective Imagery: An Account of Its Development," *Journal of Mental Imagery* 1/1 (1977), 73–92; idem, "Basic Principles and Therapeutic Efficacy of Guided Affective Imagery (GAI)," trans. Augusta Arthur, in *The Power of Human Imagination: New Methods in Psychotherapy,* ed. Jerome L. Singer and Kenneth S. Pope (New York: Plenum, 1978), 125–66.

58. Leuner, "Guided Affective Imagery," 5.

59. Joseph Reyher, "Spontaneous Visual Imagery: Implications for Psychoanalysis, Psychopathology, and Psychotherapy," *Journal of Mental Imagery* 1/2 (1977), 253–74; idem, "Emergent Uncovering Psychotherapy: The Use of Imagoic and Linguistic Vehicles in Objectifying Psychodynamic Processes," in *The Power of Human Imagination: New Methods in Psychotherapy,* ed. Jerome L. Singer and Kenneth S. Pope (New York: Plenum, 1978), 51–93.

60. Roberto Assagioli, *Psychosynthesis: A Manual of Principles and Techniques* (1965; rpt. Harmondsworth: Penguin, 1976); Martha Crampton, "The Use of Mental Imagery in Psychosynthesis," *Journal of Humanistic Psychology* 9/2 (1969), 139–53; R. Gerard, *Symbolic Visualization: A Method of Psychosynthesis* (Greenville, Del.: Psychosynthesis Research Foundation, 1968).

61. For surveys, see Mary M. Watkins, *Waking Dreams* (1976; rpt. New York: Harper and Row, 1977); Jerome L. Singer and Kenneth S. Pope, "The Use of Imagery and Fantasy Techniques in Psychotherapy," in *The Power of Human Imagination: New Methods in Psychotherapy,* ed. Jerome L. Singer and Kenneth S. Pope (New York: Plenum, 1978), 3–34.

62. For example, see Shakti Gawain, *Creative Visualization* (San Rafael, Calif.: New World Library, 1978); Ursula Markham, *The Elements of Visualisation* (Longmead, U.K.: Element, 1989).

63. Edwin C. Steinbrecher, *The Inner Guide Meditation: A Spiritual Technology for the 21st Century* (York Beach, Maine: Samuel Weiser, 1988), 31.

64. Ibid., 31–32.

65. Ibid., 32–33.

66. Ibid., 35.

67. Henry Corbin, "*Mundus Imaginalis* or the Imaginary and the Imaginal," *Spring 1972,* 8–9.

68. Gilles Quispel, "Gnosis and Psychology," in *The Rediscovery of Gnosticism, Volume One: The School of Valentinus,* ed. Bentley Layton (Leiden: Brill, 1980), 20–21.

69. For a reprint, see Robert A. Segal, ed., *The Gnostic Jung: Selected and Introduced* (Princeton: Princeton University Press, 1992), 179–93.

70. Charles William King, *The Gnostics and Their Remains: Ancient and Modern*, 2nd ed. (1887; Savage: Wizards Bookshelf, 1973).

71. Richard Smith, "The Modern Relevance of Gnosticism," in James Robinson, ed., *The Nag Hammadi Library in English*, 3rd ed. (San Francisco: Harper and Row, 1988), 537–38.

72. Jung, *Memories, Dreams, Reflections*, 200–201.

73. Segal, *Gnostic Jung*, 18–35.

74. Carl G. Jung, "Gnostic Symbols of the Self," in *Aion: Researches into the Phenomenology of the Self*, 2nd ed., trans. R. F. C. Hull (Collected Works, vol. 9, pt. 2; Princeton: Princeton University Press, 1968); rpt. Segal, *Gnostic Jung*, 73.

75. Watkins, *Dreams*, 32–37, erred in citing Theodore Flournoy and Pierre Janet as Jung's precedents. The older psychiatrists used heterosuggestions to alter the contents of their patients' hysterical dreams. They worked with trance states, and they sought not to provoke but to prevent the manifestations of autonomous materials.

76. E. Caslant, *Method of Development of the Supernormal Faculties* (Paris: Meyer, 1927).

77. Dolores Ashcroft-Nowicki, *Highways of the Mind: The Art and History of Pathworking* (Wellingborough, U.K.: Aquarian, 1987), 30–34.

78. Ibid., 201.

79. Jung, *Memories, Dreams, Reflections*, 205; Segal, *Gnostic Jung*, 6.

80. Herbert Silberer, *Hidden Symbolism of Alchemy and the Occult Arts* [first English title: *Problems of Mysticism and Its Symbolism*, 1917], trans. Smith Ely Jelliffe (1914; rpt. New York: Dover, 1971). Further psychological approaches were advanced by Ethan Allen Hitchcock, *Remarks upon Alchemy and the Alchemists* (Boston: Crosby, Nichols, 1857), and Israel Regardie, *The Philosopher's Stone: A Modern Comparative Approach to Alchemy from the Psychological and Magical Points of View*, 2nd ed. [1st ed., London: Rider, 1938] (Saint Paul, Minn.: Llewellyn, 1978). For a survey, see Luther H. Martin, Jr., "A History of the Psychological Interpretation of Alchemy," *Ambix* 22 (1975), 10–20.

81. Jung, *Memories, Dreams, Reflections*, 204.

82. Silberer, *Symbolism*, 240.

83. Ibid., 240–41.

84. Ibid., 255.

85. Ibid., 257.

86. Ibid., 263.

87. Ibid., 225.

88. Herbert Silberer, "Report on a Method of Eliciting and Observing Certain Symbolic Hallucination-Phenomena" (1909), in *Organization and Pathology of Thought: Selected Sources,* ed. David Rapaport (New York: Columbia University Press, 1951), 195–207.

89. Ibid., 196.

90. Silberer, *Hidden Symbolism,* 235.

91. Jung, *Memories, Dreams, Reflections,* 204.

92. Webb, *Establishment,* 388–91.

93. Jung, *Alchemical Studies,* 16.

94. Jung, *Memories, Dreams, Reflections,* 205.

95. Jung, *Psychology and Alchemy,* 346.

96. Carl Gustav Jung, *Psychology and Alchemy,* 2nd ed. (Collected Works, vol. 12; Princeton: Princeton University Press, 1968), 430; idem, *Alchemical Studies,* 205; idem, *Mysterium Coniunctionis: An Inquiry into the Separation and Synthesis of Psychic Opposites in Alchemy,* 2nd ed. (Collected Works, vol. 14; Princeton: Princeton University Press, 1970), 37–41, 90, 262, 437.

97. Jung, *Memories, Dreams, Reflections,* 98–99.

98. Ibid., 106–7.

99. Webb, *Establishment,* 62, 350–52, 359.

100. Ibid., 368–69, 358.

101. Jung, *Memories, Dreams, Reflections,* 212–13.

102. Silberer, *Hidden Symbolism,* 378–79.

103. Ibid., 409.

104. Ibid., 395–96.

105. Ibid., 272–73.

106. Ibid., 279–80; see Stanislav Grof and Christina Grof, ed., *Spiritual Emergency: When Personal Transformation Becomes a Crisis* (Los Angeles: Jeremy P. Tarcher, 1989); Christina Grof and Stanislav Grof, *The Stormy Search for the Self: A Guide to Personal Growth through Transformational Crisis* (Los Angeles: Jeremy P. Tarcher, 1990).

Chapter 3

1. Karl von Reichenbach, *The Odic Force: Letters on Od and Magnetism,* trans. F. D. O'Byrne (London: Hutchinson, 1926; rpt. New Hyde Park, N.Y.: University Books, 1968), 14–16, 93, 30–34.

2. Christopher McIntosh, *The Rosy Cross Unveiled: The History, Mythology, and Ritual of an Occult Order* (Wellingborough, U.K.: Aquarian, 1980), 82, 89, 90.

3. Ibid., 112.

4. Frederick Hockley, *The Rosicrucian Seer: Magical Writings of Frederick Hockley,* ed. John Hamill (Wellingborough, U.K.: Aquarian, 1986).

5. Maurice P. Crosland, *Historical Studies in the Language of Chemistry* (1962; rpt. New York: Dover, 1978).

6. *A Suggestive Inquiry into the Hermetic Mystery, with a Dissertation on the more celebrated Alchemical Philosophers, being an attempt towards the Recovery of the Ancient Experiment of Nature* (London: Trelawney Saunders, 1850). Atwood, 80, referred explicitly to the "New Imponderable" or "*Od*-ic Force."

7. Carl Gustav Jung, *The Practice of Psychotherapy: Essays on the Psychology of the Transference and Other Subjects,* 2nd ed., trans. R. F. C. Hull (Collected Works, vol. 16; Princeton: Princeton University Press, 1966), 297.

8. Eliphas Levi, *Transcendental Magic: Its Doctrine and Ritual,* trans. A. E. Waite, 2nd ed. (London, 1923), 343–44.

9. Arthur Edward Waite, *Azoth; or, The Star in the East* (London: Theosophical Publishing Society, 1893).

10. Atwood, 292–95, 303–4; Waite, *Azoth,* 190–93; Silberer, *Hidden Symbolism,* 294, 296–97, 299, 303–7; Regardie, 121–125; Jung, *Mysterium Coniunctionis,* 349; idem, *The Practice of Psychotherapy,* 260; Mircea Eliade, *The Forge and the Crucible,* trans. Stephen Corrin (London: Rider, 1962; rpt. New York: Harper and Row, 1971), 150–51, 156–57; Titus Burckhardt, *Alchemy: Science of the Cosmos, Science of the Soul,* trans. William Stoddart (1967; rpt. Baltimore: Penguin 1971), 186; Johannes Fabricius, *Alchemy: The Medieval Alchemists and their Royal Art,* 2nd ed. (Wellingborough, U.K.: Aquarian, 1989), 182–203.

11. Atwood, 161, 386–87, 442; Hitchcock, 129, 157–58, 160, 226; Waite, *Azoth,* 168, 204; Silberer, *Hidden Symbols,* 243–45, 279, 336–43, 353, 360–2; Regardie, 135–36; Jung, *Mysterium Coniunctionis,* 171, 380–81, 540; idem, *Practice of Psychotherapy,* 252; Eliade, *Forge and the Crucible,* 166; Burckhardt, *Alchemy,* 106; Fabricius, *Alchemy,* 61, 96, 198.

12. Atwood, 271.

13. Ibid., 289.

14. Ibid., 290.

15. Ibid., 292.

16. Ibid.

17. Ibid., 303.

18. Ibid., 304.

19. Ibid., 322.

20. Ibid., 322.

21. Ibid., 361.

22. Ibid., 386.

23. Ibid., 80–81.

24. Ibid., 354.

25. Ibid., 289.

26. Ibid., 386–87.

27. R. A. Gilbert, *A. E. Waite: Magician of Many Parts* (Wellingborough, U.K.: Crucible, 1987), 76, 110, 116, 120–21, 123, 130, 143.

28. Contra Gilbert, 97, 124, 151.

29. Waite, *Azoth.*

30. Gilbert, *Waite,* 94.

31. Arthur Edward Waite, *Lives of the Alchemystical Philosophers* (London: G. Redway, 1988); rpt. titled: *Alchemists Through the Ages* (Blauvelt, N.Y.: Rudolf Steiner, 1970); idem, *The Secret Tradition in Alchemy: Its Development and Records* (London: Kegan Paul, Trench, Trubner, and New York: Knopf, 1926). Reviewing the latter in *Nature,* 118 (Dec. 18, 1926), 870, Holmyard wrote: "Mr. Waite has, in short, finally and irretrievably demolished the fantastic thesis set up by Mrs. Atwood and others, and has proved beyond refutation that early and medieval alchemy was almost entirely concerned with physics or physic."

32. Waite, *Lives of the Alchemystical Philosophers,* 36.

33. Waite, *Azoth,* 167.

34. Ibid., 180.

35. Ibid., 186–87.

36. Ibid., 154.

37. Ibid., 167.

38. Ibid., 190.

39. Ibid., 168.

40. Ibid., 190.

41. Ibid., 168.

42. Ibid., 197.

43. Ibid., 195.

44. Ibid., 168.

45. Ibid., 202.

46. Ibid., 168.

47. Ibid., 204.

48. Francis King, ed., *The Secret Rituals of the O.T.O.* (New York: Samuel Weiser, 1973), 26–28; Webb, *Establishment*, 59–69.

49. Schelling was indebted to Jacob Boehme, an early seventeenth-century Rosicrucian theosopher. See Robert F. Brown, *The Later Philosophy of Schelling: The Influence of Boehme on the Works of 1809–1815* (Lewisburg: Bucknell University Press, and London: Associated University Presses, 1977).

50. An exception to this rule was Friedrich Nietzsche's discussion of dreamlike "Apollonian consciousness" and "Dionysiac rapture," which involves "the vision of mystical Oneness" (*The Birth of Tragedy* [1887], in *The Birth of Tragedy* and *The Genealogy of Morals,* trans. Francis Golffing [Garden City, N.Y.: Doubleday, 1956], 19, 22–23, 59, 97).

51. Friedrich Willhelm Joseph von Schelling, *The Ages of the World,* trans. Frederick de Wolfe Bolman, Jr. (New York: Columbia University

52. Rudolf Steiner, "On the History of Christian Rosenkreutz," in *A Christian Rosenkreutz Anthology,* ed. Paul M. Allen (Blauvelt, N.Y.: Rudolf Steiner, 1968), 439–40.

53. Rudolf Steiner, *Rosicrucianism and Modern Initiation: Mystery Centres of the Middle Ages (six lectures given in Dornach, 4th–13th January, 1924),* 3rd ed., trans. Mary Adams (London: Rudolf Steiner, 1982), 29–34.

54. Rudolf Steiner, *Secrets of the Threshold: Eight Lectures given from August 24–31, 1913* (Hudson, N.Y.: Anthroposophic; London: Rudolf Steiner, 1987), 23.

55. Ibid., 24–25.

56. Ibid., 19–20.

57. Ibid., 102.

58. Ibid., 103.

59. Ibid., 99.

60. Ibid., 41.

61. Ibid., 41, 43.

62. Ibid., 99, 103–4, 107–8.

63. Ibid., 129–30.

64. Ibid., 139–40.

65. Jung, *Psychology and Religion*, 5.

66. Jung, *Mysterium Coniunctionis*, 300–301.

67. Jung, *Psychology and Alchemy*, 34.

68. Ibid., 245.

69. Ibid., 250.

70. Carl Gustav Jung, *Aion: Researches into the Phenomenology of the Self*, 2nd ed.; trans. R. F. C. Hull (Collected Works, vol. 9, pt. 2; Princeton: Princeton University Press, 1968), 22.

71. Jung, *Mysterium Coniunctionis*, 350.

72. Jung, *Aion*, 8.

73. Ibid., 10.

74. Jung, *Practice of Psychotherapy*, 260.

75. Jung, *Mysterium Coniunctionis*, 106–7.

76. Jung, *Aion*, 13.

77. Ibid., 11.

78. Jung, *Mysterium Coniunctionis*, 89, 176.

79. Jung introduced this wrinkle into the opus in order to compensate for his conformance with Freud's distinction between the secondary-process thought of consciousness and the primary process of the unconscious: "For purely psychological reasons I have, in other of my writings, tried to equate the masculine consciousness with the concept of Logos and the feminine with that of Eros" (Jung, *Mysterium Coniunctionis*, 179).

80. Ibid., 239–46.

81. Ibid., 240.

82. Ibid., 92, 355–57.

83. Ibid., 357.

84. Ibid., 358.

85. Jung, *Practice of Psychotherapy,* 260.

86. Jung, *Mysterium Coniunctionis,* 366, 380–81, 539–40; idem, *Practice of Psychotherapy,* 252.

87. Jung, *Mysterium Coniunctionis,* 110, 540.

88. Jung, *Aion,* 22.

89. By contrast, Israel Regardie, 138, an occultist deeply initiated in the Hermetic Order of the Golden Dawn, acknowledged his inability to explicate the bulk of alchemical symbolism, despite his dependence on the writings of Atwood and Jung.

90. Jung, *Alchemical Studies,* 189.

91. Jung, *Mysterium Coniunctionis,* 250.

92. Segal, *Gnostic Jung,* 33–35.

93. Ibid., 105.

94. Silberer, *Hidden Symbolism,* 261.

95. Fabricius, 37, 40, 43, 49–52, 57–58, 70–71, 73, 75, 215, 218–20.

96. Jung, *Two Essays on Analytical Psychology,* 219.

97. Eliade, *Forge and the Crucible,* 224.

98. Ibid., 149–50.

99. Ibid., 149.

100. Ibid., 150.

101. Ibid., 153.

102. Ibid., 151.

103. Ibid., 165.

104. Ibid., 162.

105. Ibid., 161.

106. Corbin, *Creative Imagination,* 243–44; idem, *Cyclical Time and Ismaili Gnosis,* trans. Ralph Manheim and James W. Morris (London:

Kegan Paul International/Islamic Publications, 1983), 109–10; idem, *Man of Light*, 135; idem, "Le Livre du Glorieux de Jabir Ibn Hayyan (Alchimie et Archetypes)," *Eranos-Jahrbuch* 18 (1950), 47–114.

107. René Guenon, *The Multiple States of Being* [1932], trans. Joscelyn Godwin (New York: Larson, 1984); idem, *The Lord of the World* (Moorcote, U.K.: Coombe Springs, 1983).

108. Andre VandenBroeck, *Al-Kemi: Hermetic, Occult, Political, and Private Aspects of R. A. Schwaller de Lubicz* (Great Barrington, Mass.: Inner Traditions/Lindisfarne, 1987).

109. For a contemporary presentation, see Franz Bardon, *Initiation Into Hermetics: A Course of Instruction of Magic Theory and Practise* [1956], trans. A. Radspieler (Wuppertal, Germany: Dieter Ruggeberg, 1976).

110. Henry Corbin, *Spiritual Body and Celestial Earth: From Mazdean Iran to Shi'ite Iran,* trans. Nancy Pearson (1960; rpt. Princeton: Princeton University Press, 1977), 99.

111. Henry Corbin, *Creative Imagination in the Sufism of Ibn 'Arabi,* trans. Ralph Manheim (Princeton: Princeton University Press, 1969), 243–44.

112. Ellic Howe, ed., *The Alchemist of the Golden Dawn: The Letters of the Revd W. A. Ayton to F. L. Gardner and Others 1886–1905* (Wellingborough, U.K.: Aquarian, 1985), 50–51.

113. Francis King, ed., *Astral Projection, Ritual Magic, and Alchemy: Golden Dawn Material by S. L. MacGregor Mathers and Others* (Rochester, Vt.: Destiny, 1987), 177; Regardie, *The Philosopher's Stone.*

114. Frances A. Yates, *Giordano Bruno and the Hermetic Tradition* (London: Routledge and Kegan Paul, 1964), 97–104.

115. E. M. Butler, *Ritual Magic* (Cambridge: University Press, 1949; rpt. New York: Noonday, 1959), 29–44; Peter Schäfer, *Gershom Scholem Reconsidered: The Aim and Purpose of Early Jewish Mysticism,* The Twelfth Sacks Lecture delivered on 29th May 1985 (Oxford, U.K.: Oxford Centre for Postgraduate Hebrew Studies, 1986).

116. Arthur Edward Waite, trans., *The Alchemical Writings of Edward Kelly* (1893; rpt. London: Robinson and Watkins, 1973); Meric Casaubon, ed., *A True and Faithful Relation of What Passed for many Years Between Dr. John Dee . . . and Some Spirits . . .* (London: D. Maxwell and T. Garthwait, 1659; rpt. Glasgow: Antonine, 1974). The association can also be found in act 3, scene 1 of Shakespeare's *First Part of King Henry IV.* For Hotspur, alchemy and spirit conjuring are distinct; for Glendower, they are a single practice. Neither Worcester nor Mortimer is able to follow the conversation of the two initiates.

117. Lynn Thorndike, *A History of Magic and Experimental Science: During the First Thirteen Centuries of Our Era* (New York and London: Columbia University Press, 1923), vol. II, 313.

118. Lynn Thorndike, *A History of Magic and Experimental Science, Volumes III and IV: Fourteenth and Fifteenth Centuries* (New York and London: Columbia University Press, 1934), vol. III, 41.

119. *The Works of Geber: Englished by Richard Russell, 1678, a New Edition,* introd. E. J. Holmyard (London: J. M. Dent; New York: Dutton, 1928), 39.

120. Thorndike, vol. III, 357–60; Robert P. Multhauf, *The Origins of Chemistry* (London: Oldbourne, 1966), 211–12.

121. Thorndike, *History,* vol. III, 178.

122. E. J. Holmyard, "The Emerald Table," *Nature* 112 (1923), 526.

123. Tenney L. Davis, "The Emerald Table of Hermes Trismegistus: Three Latin Versions Which Were Current Among Later Alchemists," *Journal of Chemical Education* 3 (1926), 874–75.

124. Robert Steele and Dorothea Waley Singer, "The Emerald Table," *Proceedings of the Royal Society of Medicine* 21 (1928), 486, 492.

125. Davis, "Table," 869.

126. Thorndike, *History,* vol. III, 615.

127. Ibid., vol. IV, 37–43; Multhauf, *Origins,* 180 n. 6, 212.

128. Daniel P. Walker, *Spiritual and Demonic Magic: From Ficino to Campanella* (London: Warburg Institute, University of London, 1958; rpt. Notre Dame: University of Notre Dame Press, 1975), 8.

129. Daniel P. Walker, *Spiritual and Demonic Magic;* idem, *The Ancient Theology: Studies in Christian Platonism from the Fifteenth to the Eighteenth Century* (London: Gerald Duckworth, 1972); Yates, *Giordano Bruno and the Hermetic Tradition;* idem, *The Occult Philosophy in the Elizabethan Age* (London: Routledge and Kegan Paul, 1979); idem, *Lull and Bruno* (London: Routledge and Kegan Paul, 1982).

130. John Read, *Through Alchemy to Chemistry: A Procession of Ideas and Personalities* (London: G. Bell, 1957), 24–25.

131. F. Sherwood Taylor, *The Alchemists* (1952; rpt. St. Albans, U.K.: Paladin/Granada, 1976), 174.

Chapter 4

1. Eliade, *The Forge and the Crucible,* 152.

2. Earle Radcliffe Caley, "The Leyden Papyrus X: An English Translation with Brief Notes," *Journal of Chemical Education* 3 (1926), 1149–66.

3. Arthur John Hopkins, "Bronzing Methods in the Alchemistic Leyden Papyri," *The Chemical News* 85 (1902), 49–52; idem, "Earliest Alchemy," *The Scientific Monthly* 6 (1918), 530–37 idem, "A Modern Theory of Alchemy," *Isis* 7 (1925), 58–76; idem, "Transmutation by Color: A Study of Earliest Alchemy," *Studien zür Geschichte der Chemie: Festgabe Edmund O. v. Lippman,* ed. Julius Ruska (Berlin: Julius Springer, 1927); idem, *Alchemy, Child of Greek Philosophy* (New York: Columbia University Press, 1934); idem, "A defence of Egyptian alchemy," *Isis* 28 (1938), 424–31; idem, "A study of the Kerotakis Process as given by Zosimus and later alchemical writers," *Isis* 29 (1938), 326–54.

4. F. Sherwood Taylor, "A Survey of Greek Alchemy," *Journal of Hellenic Studies* 50 (1930), 109–39; idem, "The Origins of Greek Alchemy," *Ambix* 1 *(1937),* 30–47; idem, *The Alchemists.* On Maria, see Raphael Patai, "Maria the Jewess—Founding Mother of Alchemy," *Ambix* 29 (1982), 177–97.

5. One must also beware errors in existing scholarship. Seyyed Hossein Nasr, *Science and Civilization in Islam* (1968; rpt. New York: New American Library, 1970), 248, n. 1, acknowledged that his own discussions of spiritual alchemy in the history of Islam were informed by Titus Burckhardt's view of spiritual alchemy. Unfortunately, Burckhardt's *Alchemy* is among the more theologically innovative—and historically anachronistic—accounts of alchemy presently available.

6. Taylor, *The Alchemists,* 56–57.

7. H. J. Sheppard, "Gnosticism and Alchemy," *Ambix* 6 (1957), 88.

8. Ibid., 47–50; see Hopkins, *Alchemy,* 108–9, 114–15.

9. Taylor, *The Alchemists,* 44.

10. Ibid., 50.

11. Ibid., 49.

12. Ibid., 99.

13. Hopkins, *Alchemy,* 85, identifies *ios* with the philosopher's stone—i.e., the salt.

14. VandenBroeck, *Al-Kemi,* asserts that R. A. Schwaller de Lubicz claimed to have done the alchemical work that was written up under the name of Fulcanelli; but the claim is preposterous. Fulcanelli's Aristotelian chemistry cannot be reconciled with Schwaller de Lubicz's ethereal thaumaturgy.

15. Fulcanelli: Master Alchemist, *Le Mystère des Cathédrales: Esoteric interpretation of the Hermetic Symbols of the Great Work,* trans. Mary

Sworder (Paris: Jean Schemit, 1926; trans. London: Neville Spearman, 1971).

16. Francis King and Isabel Sutherland, *The Rebirth of Magic* (London: Corgi, 1982), 74–78.

17. Fulcanelli, *Mystère,* 65.

18. Ibid., 65–66.

19. Ibid., 80, 85.

20. Ibid., 46.

21. Ibid., 74.

22. Ibid., 81.

23. Ibid., 160.

24. Ibid., 160–61.

25. Ibid., 161.

26. Taylor, *Alchemists,* 47.

27. Fulcanelli, *Mystère,* 98.

28. Taylor, *Alchemists,* 49.

29. Fulcanelli, *Mystère,* 86.

30. Ibid., 89.

31. Ibid., 74.

32. Ibid., 84.

33. Ibid., 56, 77.

34. Ibid., 84.

35. Ibid.

36. Ibid., 78–79.

37. Ibid., 90–91, 102, 108.

38. George Howard Bruce, *High School Chemistry,* 2nd ed. (New York: World Book Company, 1938), 252–61.

39. Taylor, *Alchemists,* 49–50.

40. Fulcanelli, *Mystère,* 109.

41. Taylor, *Alchemists,* 50.

42. Fulcanelli, *Mystère,* 129.

43. Ibid., 110, 111, 114.

44. Ibid., 97–98.

45. Ibid., 50.

46. Ibid., 74–75, 82–83.

47. Ibid., 94.

48. Ibid.

49. Taylor, *Alchemists,* 49.

50. Paracelsus, as cited by Fulcanelli, *Mystère,* 86.

51. R. P. Festugière, *La Révélation d'Hermes Trismégiste, Vol. I. L'Astrologie et les sciences occultes,* 2nd ed. (1950; rpt. Paris: Société d'Edition "les Belles Lettres," 1983), 239.

52. Taylor, "Origins of Greek Alchemy," 8.

53. Carl Gustav Jung, "The Visions of Zosimos," in *Alchemical Studies,* 66.

54. See John J. Collins, "Introduction: Towards the Morphology of a Genre," in *Apocalypse: The Morpholog of a Genre,* ed. John J. Collins (Semeia 14; Missoula, Mont.: Scholars, 1979), 9.

55. On the literary technique of dispersion, see: Crosland, *Historical Studies,* 37.

56. F. Sherwood Taylor, "The Visions of Zosimos: Translation and Prefatory Note," *Ambix* 1, 88; rpt. *The Alchemists* (William Heinnemann, 1952; rpt. Frogmore, U.K.: Paladin/Granada, 1976), 57.

57. Ibid., 88–89.

58. Ibid., 89.

59. Corbin, *Avicenna and the Visionary Recital,* 150; Dov Baer of Lubowitch, *Tract on Ecstasy* (London: Vallentine, Mitchell, 1963), 191–92.

60. Taylor, "Visions of Zosimos," 89.

61. Jung, "Visions of Zosimos," 70.

62. Hermetism is known to have been indebted to Judaism; see: Birger A. Pearson, "Jewish Elements in *Corpus Hermeticum* I (*Poimandres*)," in *Gnosticism, Judaism, and Egyptian Christianity* (Minneapolis, Minn.: Fortress, 1990), 136–47.

63. Bachelard, *On Poetic Imagination and Reverie,* 53.

64. Jung, *Psychology and Alchemy,* 245–50.

65. See Hopkins, *Alchemy,* 112–15.

66. Taylor, "Visions of Zosimos," 89.

67. Ibid., 89–90.

68. Jack Lindsay, *The Origins of Alchemy in Graeco-Roman Egypt* (London: Frederick Muller, 1979), 346–47.

69. Jung, "Visions of Zosimos," 71.

70. Ibid., 73.

71. Walter Scott, *Hermetica: The Ancient Greek and Latin Writings Which Contain Religious or Philosophic Teachings Ascribed to Hermes Trismegistus. Vol. 1: Introduction, Texts and Translations* (1924; rpt. Boulder: Hermes House, n.d.), 151.

72. Ibid., 143.

73. Taylor, "Visions of Zosimos," 90.

74. Scott, *Hermetica,* 185.

75. Taylor, "Visions of Zosimos," 90.

76. Taylor, "Survey of Greek Alchemy," 124.

77. Taylor, "Visions of Zosimos," 91.

78. Festugière, *Révélation,* I, 242–51.

79. "Isis to Her Son Horus" (Paris mss. 2327, 1478 CE; Paris mss. 2250, 17th century), Marcellin Berthelot, *Collection des anciens alchimistes grecs,* 3 vols. (1888; rpt. Osnabruck: Otto Zeller, 1967), vol. II, 28–31, vol. III, 31–33.

80. H. E. Stapleton, G. L. Lewis, and F. Sherwood Taylor, "The Sayings of Hermes Quoted in the *MA' AL-WARAQI* of Ibn Umail," *Ambix* 3 (1949), 71. The Arabic language compilation was probably assembled around the tenth century.

81. Moshe Idel, "The Origin of Alchemy According to Zosimos and a Hebrew Parallel," *Revue des Études juives* 145 (1986), 117–24.

82. Plutarch, *De Iside et Osiride,* 32.

83. Earle Radcliffe Caley, "The Stockholm Papyrus: An English Translation with Brief Notes," *Journal of Chemical Education* 4/8 (1927), 981.

84. Festugière, *Révélation,* I, 225.

85. Georg Dieter Betz, ed., *The Greek Magical Papyri in Translation: Including the Demotic Spells* (Chicago: University of Chicago Press, 1986), 140–41; see 119–20.

86. As cited in C. Anne Wilson, *Philosophers, Iosis and Water of Life* (Leeds, U.K.: Leeds Philosophical and Literary Society, 1984), 5.

87. Taylor, "Origins of Greek Alchemy," 37–38.

88. Taylor, *The Alchemists*, 33; citing Berthelot, *Collection des anciens alchimistes grecs,* texte grec, 191.

89. Ridicule of Greco-Egyptian magic may also be found in Zosimos of Panopolis, *On the Letter Omega,* ed. and trans. Howard M. Jackson (Missoula: University of Montana/Scholars Press, 1978).

90. Zosimos, "Sur la Mésure du Jaunissement" (St.-Marc, Venice mss., 11th century; Paris mss. 2327, 1478 CE; Paris mss. 2329, 16–17th centuries; Paris mss. 2249, 16th century), Berthelot, vol. II, 182, vol. III, 180.

91. The works of Islamic alchemy available in English translation are concerned exclusively with chemical processes, as though there were no other alchemy in Islam. The same conclusion has been reached by Islamicists who command the Arabic and Persian literatures; see E. Wiedemann, "al-Kimiya, alchemy," *The Encyclopedia of Islam,* 2nd ed. (Leiden: Brill; London, Luzac, 1960), II, pt. 2, 1010–17. As evidence of spiritual alchemy, Burckhardt and Nasr incorrectly cite an allegorical passage from Abu 'L-Qasim Muhammad ibn Ahmad al- 'Iraqi, *Kitab al-'Ilm Al-Muktasab Fi Zira'at Adh-Dhahab: Book of Knowledge Acquired Concerning the Cultivation of Gold,* ed. and trans. E. J. Holmyard (Paris: Paul Geuthner, 1923). The subtext of the passage concerns sulphuric acid, not mysticism.

92. Hopkins, *Alchemy, Child of Greek Philosophy.*

93. Lee Stavenhagen, ed and trans., *A Testament of Alchemy: Being the Revelations of Morienus to Khalid ibn Yazid* (Hanover: Brandeis University Press-University Press of New England, 1974); Arthur Edward Waite, trans., *The Turba Philosophorum* (1896; rpt. New York: Samuel Weiser, 1976).

94. Sheppard, 101.

95. H. J. Sheppard, "Gnosticism and Alchemy"; idem, "Egg Symbolism in Alchemy," *Ambix* 6 (1958), 3/140–48; idem, "The Redemption Theme and Hellenistic Alchemy," *Ambix* 7 (1959), 1/42–46; idem, "The Origin of the Gnostic-Alchemical Relationship," *Scientia* 97 (1962), 146–49; idem, "The Ouroboros and the Unity of Matter in Alchemy: A Study in Origins," *Ambix* 10 (1962), 2/83–96; idem, "Serpent Symbolism in Alchemy," *Scientia* 101 (1966), 203–7.

96. Jung, *Psychology and Alchemy,* 430.

97. John Dillon, *The Middle Platonists: A Study of Platonism 80 BC to AD 220* (London: Gerald Duckworth, 1977), 106–10.

98. F. H. Sandbach, *The Stoics* (London: Chatto and Windus, 1975), 72.

99. Ibid., 73, 75.

100. Ibid., 75.

101. Sheppard, "Gnosticism and Alchemy," 90–91.

102. Scott, 115–17. See Arthur Darby Nock and André-Jean Marie Festugière, ed. and trans., *Corpus Hermeticum* (Paris: Société d'Edition "Les Belles Lettres," 1945), I, 6–8.

103. Alan of Lille, *Anticlaudianus, or, The Good and Perfect Man,* trans. James J. Sheridan (Toronto: Pontifical Institute of Medieval Studies, 1973), 63.

104. Ibid.

105. Ibid., 64.

106. Ibid.

107. Ibid.

108. Ibid.

109. Ibid., 64–65.

110. David Knowles, *The Evolution of Medieval Thought* (New York: Random House, 1962), 113–14.

111. Segal, *Gnostic Jung,* 31–32.

Chapter 5

1. Hans Jonas, *The Gnostic Religion: The message of the alien God and the beginnings of Christianity,* 2nd ed. (Boston: Beacon, 1963).

2. Ugo Bianchi, ed., *The Origins of Gnosticism: Colloquium of Messina, 13–18 April 1966* (Leiden: Brill, 1970), xxvi.

3. Jonas, *Religion,* 33; Kurt Rudolph, *Gnosis: The Nature and History of Gnosticism* (San Francisco: Harper and Row, 1983), 57–67; Robert M. Grant, "Gnostic Spirituality," in *Christian Spirituality: Origins to the Twelfth Century,* ed. Bernard McGinn and John Meyendorff, with Jean Leclercq (New York: Crossroad, 1987), 44.

4. Jonas, *Gnostic Religion,* 93–94.

5. See, for example, George W. MacRae "The Jewish Background of the Gnostic Sophia Myth," *Novum Testamentum* 12 (1970), 86–101; Birger Albert Pearson, "Jewish Haggadic Traditions in *The Testimony of Truth* from Nag Hammadi (CG IX, 3)," in *Ex Orbe Religionum: Studia Geo Widengren,* ed. C. J. Bleeker, S. G. F. Brandon, and M. Simon (Leiden: Brill,

1972), 457–70; idem, "Jewish Elements in Gnosticism and the Development of Gnostic Self-Definition," in *Jewish and Christian Self-Definition, Volume One: The Shaping of Christianity in the Second and Third Centuries,* ed. E. P. Sanders (Philadelphia: Fortress, 1980), 151–60, 240–45; Edwin M. Yamauchi, "The Descent of Ishtar, the Fall of Sophia, and the Jewish Roots of Gnosticism," *Tyndale Bulletin* 29 (1978), 143–75; Ithamar Gruenwald, "Halakhic Material in Codex Gnosticus V, 4: *The Second Apocalypse of James?*" in *From Apocalypticism to Gnosticism: Studies in Apocalypticism, Merkavah Mysticism and Gnosticism* (Frankfurt am Main: Verlag Peter Lang, 1988), 279–94; idem, "Jewish Sources for the Gnostic Texts from Nag Hammadi?" in *Proceedings of the Sixth World Congress of Jewish Studies* (Jerusalem: World Union of Jewish Studies, 1977); rpt. *From Apocalypticism to Gnosticism,* 207–20; Gedaliahu A. G. Stroumsa, *Another Seed: Studies in Gnostic Mythology* (Leiden: Brill, 1984).

6. William R. Schoedel, "'Topological' Theology and Some Monistic Tendencies in Gnosticism," *Ex Orbe Religionum: Studia Geo Widengren,* ed. Bleeker, Brandon, and Simon; idem, "Gnostic Monism and the Gospel of Truth," in *The Rediscovery of Gnosticism, Volume One: The School of Valentinus,* ed. Bentley Layton (Leiden: Brill, 1980), 379–90.

7. Arthur Darby Nock, "Gnosticism," *Harvard Theological Review* 57 (1964), 4/255–79.

8. Similarly, Ninian Smart, "Interpretation and Mystical Experience," rightly criticized the bias in R. C. Zaehner's *Mysticism Sacred and Profane,* which treated Hindu Yoga and Buddhist meditation together as a single type of "panenhenic" mysticism, differing from the "theistic" mysticism of Catholicism.

9. Bernard McGinn, *The Foundations of Mysticism (Vol. I of The Presence of God: A History of Western Christian Mysticism;* New York: Crossroad, 1991), 71–73.

10. Ibid., 75, 77.

11. Ibid., 72.

12. Morton Smith, "The History of the Term Gnostikos," in *The Rediscovery of Gnosticism, Volume Two: Sethian Gnosticism,* ed. Bentley Layton (Leiden: Brill, 1981).

13. Kurt Rudolph, " 'Gnosis' and 'Gnosticism'—The Problem of Their Definition and Their Relation to the Writings of the New Testament," in *The New Testament and Gnosis: Essays in Honour of Robert McL. Wilson,* ed. A. H. B. Logan and A. J. M. Wedderburn (Edinburgh: Clark, 1983), 27–28.

14. Jean Daniélou, *A History of Early Christian Doctrine Before the Council of Nicaea, Volume Two: Gospel Message and Hellenistic Culture,*

trans. and ed. John Austin Baker (London: Darton, Longman and Todd; Philadelphia: Westminster, 1973), 449, 469, 477.

15. Margaret Smith, *The Way of the Mystics: The Early Christian Mystics and the Rise of the Sufis* (Original title: *Studies in Early Mysticism in the Near and Middle East;* 1931; rpt. London: Sheldon, 1976), 171; A. J. Arberry, *Sufism: An Account of the Mystics of Islam* (1950; rpt. London: George Allen and Unwin, 1969), 52.

16. Gershom G. Scholem, *Origins of the Kabbalah,* ed. R. J. Zwi Werblowsky, trans. Allan Arkush (Princeton: Jewish Publication Society-Princeton University Press, 1987), 21, n. 24.

17. Jung, *Aion,* 202–7; rpt. Segal, *Gnostic Jung,* 73–78.

18. Jung, *Psychology and Religion,* 287–88; rpt. Segal, *Gnostic Jung,* 123.

19. Jung, *Aion,* 223; rpt. Segal, *Gnostic Jung,* 103.

20. Gershom G. Scholem, *Jewish Gnosticism, Merkabah Mysticism, and Talmudic Tradition,* 2nd ed. (New York: Jewish Theological Seminary of America, 1965), 1.

21. Gershom G. Scholem, *Major Trends in Jewish Mysticism,* 3rd ed. (New York: Schocken, 1954), 49.

22. Steven Runciman, *The Medieval Manichee: A Study of the Christian Dualist Heresy* (Cambridge: Cambridge University Press, 1947); Rudolph, 374–76.

23. Ioan Petru Couliano, *The Tree of Gnosis: Gnostic Mythology from Early Christianity to Modern Nihilism,* trans. H. S. Wiesner and Ioan P. Couliano (New York: HarperCollins, 1992).

24. Rudolph, *Gnosis,* 343–66.

Chapter 6

1. E. C. Krupp, "Astronomers, Pyramids, and Priests," in *In Search of Ancient Astronomies,* ed. E. C. Krupp (Garden City, N.Y.: Doubleday, 1977), 225.

2. James Henry Breasted, *The Dawn of Conscience* (1933; rpt. New York: Scribner's, 1968), 73–74.

3. B. L. van der Waerden, "History of the Zodiac," *Archiv für Orientforschung* 16 (1953), 216–17, 220, 224.

4. Ibid., 223.

5. D. R. Dicks, *The Geographical Fragments of Hipparchus* (London: University of London Press, 1960), 17.

6. Rupert Gleadow, *The Origin of the Zodiac* (New York: Atheneum, 1969), 19, 31, 75.

7. Dillon, *Middle Platonists*, 106–10.

8. S. James Tester, *A History of Western Astrology* (New York: Ballantine, 1987), 19, 52, 49–50, 46.

9. David Ulansey, *The Origins of the Mithraic Mysteries: Cosmology and Salvation in the Ancient World* (New York: Oxford University Press, 1989).

10. Tester, *History of Western Astrology*, 18–19.

11. For other debts of Gnosticism to Egyptian religion, see C. J. Bleeker, "The Egyptian Background of Gnosticism," in *The Origins of Gnosticism: Colloquium of Messina, 13–18 April 1966*, ed. Ugo Bianchi (Leiden: Brill, 1967), 229–37.

12. Simone Petrement, *A Separate God: The Christian Origins of Gnosticism*, trans. Carol Harrison (New York: HarperCollins, 1990), 21, 59–72.

13. Irenaeus, *Adversus haereses*, I, 24; ed. A. Stieren, 2 vols. (Leipzig 1848–1853), I, 247; as translated in Robert Haardt, *Gnosis: Character and Testimony*, trans. J. F. Hendry (Leiden: Brill, 1971), 44.

14. *1 Apoc. Jas.* 26; Robinson, 262.

15. *1 Apoc. Jas.* 26; Robinson, 263.

16. *Testim. Truth* 55; Robinson, 455–56.

17. *Paraph. Shem* 46; Robinson, 360.

18. *Zost.* 6; Robinson, 405.

19. *Gos. Eg.* 41, 58, Ibid., 209, 214–15.

20. *Ap. John* 10–11; Robinson, 110–11; Compare the conception of the material world as chaos, darkness, and Hades in *Ap. John* 30–31; Robinson, 122.

21. *Gos. Eg.* 58; Robinson, 215.

22. The Mandaeans continue to identify hell with the seven planetary spheres; see Kurt Rudolph, "Mandean Sources," in *Gnosis: A Selection of Gnostic Texts, II: Coptic and Mandean Sources*, ed. Werner Foerster, trans. R. McL. Wilson (Oxford: Clarendon Press, 1974), 133 n.

23. Ugo Bianchi, "Mithraism and Gnosticism," in *Mithraic Studies*, ed. John R. Hinnells (Manchester: Manchester University Press, 1975), vol. II, 463–65.

24. The Gnostic position had some Greek antecedents but was basically original; see Jaap Mansfeld, "Bad World and Demiurge: A 'Gnostic' Motif from Parmenides and Empedocles to Lucretius and Philo," in *Studies in Gnosticism and Hellenistic Religions,* ed. R. van den Broek and M. J. Vermaseren (Leiden: Brill, 1981), 261–314.

25. Jonas, *Gnostic Religion,* 42–43.

26. Rudolph, *Gnosis,* 92–93.

27. Deirdre J. Good, *Reconstructing the Tradition of Sophia in Gnostic Literature* (Atlanta: Scholars Press, 1987), 72–73.

28. *Tri. Trac.* 76; Robinson, 73.

29. *Ap. John* 9–10; *1 Apoc. Jas* 35; *Treat. Seth* 50–51; Robinson, 110, 266, 363; Compare. *Eugnostos* 85; *Soph. Jes. Chr.* 107; Robinson, 236.

30. Michael Allen Williams, *The Immovable Race: A Gnostic Designation and the Theme of Stability in Late Antiquity* (Leiden: Brill, 1985), 62–63, 175.

31. *Steles Seth* 121; Robinson, 398.

32. Hippolytus, ref. v, 8,9–21; as cited by Robert Haardt, *Gnosis: Character and Testimony,* trans. J. F. Hendry (Leiden: Brill, 1971), 89–91.

33. St. Clement of Alexandria, *Stromateis,* 2.36.2–4; as cited by Bentley Layton, trans., in *The Gnostic Scriptures* (Garden City, N.Y.: Doubleday, 1987), 235.

34. *Steles Seth* 118; Robinson, 397.

35. Jonas, *Gnostic Religion;* Compare Rudolph, *Gnosis.*

36. Edward Conze, "Prajna and Sophia," in *Thirty Years of Buddhist Studies: Selected Essays* (Columbia: University of South Carolina Press, 1968), 207–9; idem, "Buddhism and Gnosis," in *The Origins of Gnosticism: Colloquium of Messina, 13–18 April 1966,* ed. Ugo Bianchi (Leiden: Brill, 1970), 651–67.

37. David Dawson, *Allegorical Readers and Cultural Revision in Ancient Alexandria* (Berkeley: University of California Press, 1992), 151, 149.

38. Elaine H. Pagels, "Visions, Appearances, and Apostolic Authority: Gnostic and Orthodox Traditions," in *Gnosis: Festschrift für Hans Jonas,* ed. Ugo Bianchi, Martin Krause, James M. Robinson, and Geo Widengren (Gottingen: Vandenhoeck and Ruprecht, 1978), 427.

39. Dan Merkur, "Adaptive Symbolism and the Theory of Myth: The Symbolic Understanding of Myths in Inuit Religion," in *Psychoanalytic Study of Society,* ed. L. Bryce Boyer and Simon Grolnick, 13 (1988), 81.

40. Jonas, *Gnostic Religion,* 45.

41. *Tri. Tract.* 79–80; Robinson, 74.

42. *Tri. Tract.* 83; Robinson, 76.

43. Martin Persson Nilsson, "The High God and the Mediator," *Harvard Theological Review* 56 (1963), 101–20; Alan F. Segal, "Ruler of This World: Attitudes about Mediator Figures and the Importance of Sociology for Self-Definition," in *Jewish and Christian Self-Definition, Volume Two: Aspects of Judaism in the Graeco-Roman Period,* ed. E. P. Saunders, with A.I. Baumgarten and A. Mendelson (Philadelphia: Fortress, 1981), 245–68, 403–13.

44. *Tri. Tract.* 80; *Ap. John* 13–14; *Trim. Prot.* 43–44; Robinson, 75, 112, 518.

45. Ithamar Gruenwald, *Apocalyptic and Merkavah Mysticism* (Leiden: Brill, 1980), 112–18; idem, "Merkavah Mysticism and Gnosticism," *Studies in Jewish Mysticism,* ed. Joseph Dan and Frank Talmage (Cambridge, Mass.: Association for Jewish Studies, 1982), 43–44.

46. *Orig. World* 102–4; Robinson, 174–76. The same tale is mentioned briefly in *Hyp. Arch.* 95; Robinson, 168.

47. Jonas, *Gnostic Religion,* 80–86; George W. MacRae, "Sleep and Awakening in Gnostic Texts," in *The Origins of Gnosticism: Colloquium of Messina, 13–18 April 1966,* ed. Ugo Bianchi (Leiden: Brill, 1967), 496–507.

48. Jonas, *Gnostic Religion,* 42–43.

49. Charles H. Talbert, "The Myth of a Descending-Ascending Redeemer in Mediterranean Antiquity," *New Testament Studies* 22 (1975–76), 418–40.

50. The term "Sethian Gnosticism" refers to a group of texts that concern or mention Seth. The term does not imply a distinct sect; see Frederik Wisse, "Stalking Those Elusive Sethians," *The Rediscovery of Gnosticism, Volume Two: Sethian Gnosticism,* ed. Bentley Layton (Leiden: Brill, 1981), 563–87.

51. Birger A. Pearson, "The Figure of Seth in Gnostic Literature," *The Rediscovery of Gnosticism, Volume Two: Sethian Gnosticism,* ed. Bentley Layton (Leiden: Brill, 1981), 491–500.

52. Rudolph, *Gnosis,* 131–32.

53. Ugo Bianchi, "Docetism: A Peculiar Theory about the Ambivalence of the Presence of the Divine," *Selected Essays on Gnosticism, Dualism and Mysteriosophy* (Leiden: Brill, 1978). However, it is a gross overstatement to suggest that "the entire problem of gnosticism amounts to defining a

specific mode of presence for heavenly beings in this world. . . . It is the problem of docetism" (p. 265).

54. See Geo Widengren, *The Ascension of the Apostle and the Heavenly Book* (Uppsala Universitets Arsskrift 1950:7; Uppsala: A. B. Lundequist; Leipzig: Otto Harrassowitz, 1950), 40–47.

55. Alexander Böhlig, "Jacob as an Angel in Gnosticism and Manicheism," *Nag Hammadi and Gnosis,* ed. R. McL. Wilson (Leiden: Brill, 1978), 122–30.

56. Jonathan Z. Smith, *Map is Not Territory: Studies in the History of Religions* (Leiden: Brill, 1978), 24–66.

57. Rudolph, *Gnosis,* 157–65.

58. Hans Jonas, "Myth and Mysticism: A Study of Objectification and Interiorization in Religious Thought," *Journal of Religion* 49 (1969), 316–17.

59. Ibid., 318.

60. Ibid., 324.

61. Ibid., 318.

62. Jonas, "Delimitation of the Gnostic Phenomenon," 107.

63. Rudolph, *Gnosis,* 171; compare Jonas, *Gnostic Religion,* 165–69.

64. Rudolph, *Gnosis,* 214–15.

65. Ibid., 208–9, 214.

66. *Gos. Thom.* 43–44, saying 62; Robinson, 133.

67. Rudolph, *Gnosis,* 225.

68. R. McL. Wilson, "Gnosis and the Mysteries," *Studies in Gnosticism and Hellenistic Religions,* ed. R. van den Broek and M. J. Vermaseren (Leiden: Brill, 1981), 455–56.

69. Jonathan Z. Smith, *Drudgery Divine: On the Comparison of Early Christianities and the Religions of Late Antiquity* (Chicago: University of Chicago Press, 1990).

70. Walter Burkert, *Ancient Mystery Cults* (Cambridge: Harvard University Press, 1987), 11.

71. Ibid., 3–4, 8, 10.

72. Hutton Webster, *Primitive Secret Societies: A Study in Early Politics and Religion,* 2nd ed. (1932; rpt. New York: Octagon, 1968).

73. Dan Merkur, "Prophetic Initiation in Israel and Judah," in *The Psychoanalytic Study of Society, Volume 12: Essays in honor of George De-*

vereux, ed. L. Bryce Boyer and Simon A. Grolnick (Hillsdale, N.J.: Analytic Press, 1988), 37–67; idem, "Prophecies of Jeremiah," 7.

74. Wilson, "Gnosis and the Mysteries," 454.

75. Pagels, "Visions," 427.

76. Ibid., 427–28.

77. H. Ch. Puech, "Gnostic Gospels and Related Documents," in *New Testament Apocrypha, Volume One: Gospels and Related Writings,* ed. W. Schneemelcher, trans. R. McL. Wilson (London: Lutterworth, 1963), 246.

78. Pagels, "Visions," 420.

79. Henry Corbin, *Cyclical Time and Ismaili Gnosis,* trans. Ralph Manheim and James W. Morris (London: Kegan Paul International-Islamic Publications, 1983), 59.

80. Edgar Hennecke, *New Testament Apocrypha, Volume Two: Writings Relating to the Apostles; Apocalypses and Related Subjects,* ed. Wilhelm Schneemelcher and R. McL. Wilson (Philadelphia: Westminster Press, 1964), 302–4.

81. Ibid., 225.

82. Ibid., 232–4.

83. Corbin, 62.

84. Ibid., 61.

85. Acts of John 100; Hennecke, 233–4.

86. David J. Halperin, *The Merkabah in Rabbinic Literature* (New Haven, CT: American Oriental Society, 1980); idem, *Faces of the Chariot;* Ira Chernus, *Mysticism in Rabbinic Judaism: Studies in the History of Midrash* (Berlin and New York: Walter de Gruyter, 1982).

87. In folkloristics, legends are conventionally defined as tales that (1) are believed true by their culture of origin, (2) have human protagonists, and (3) are set in times and places that are purported to be historical; see: William R. Bascom, "The Forms of Folklore: Prose Narratives," *Journal of American Folk-Lore* 78 (1965) 3–20. Belief-legends are a subset of legends that meet three additional criteria: (4) they are narrated in the third person, (5) their antagonists are numina, and (6) their actions concern human encounters with numina. Memorates, or autobiographical accounts of personal religious experiences, become belief-legends when they are retold in the third person; see Lauri Honko, *Geisterglaube in Ingermanland,* FF Communications, 185 (Helsinki: Academia Scientiarum Fennica, 1962); idem, Memorates and the Study of Folk Beliefs," *Journal of the Folklore Institute* 1 (1964), 5–19. Because people trust personal testimony more than

hearsay, personal religious experiences tend to be retold in the first person when there is a risk of the tales' reception as fictions; see Linda Degh and Andrew Vazsonyi, "The Memorate and the Proto-Memorate," *Journal of American Folk-Lore* 87 (1974), 225–39. For the tales to be retold in the third person, belief in the tales must ordinarily be shared by the story-tellers and their audiences. Honko's term "belief-legend" refers to the tales' value as evidence of living religious beliefs. Belief-legends exemplify religious experiences of their types. The tales contribute traditional themes and motifs to the contents of peoples' religious experiences, unconsciously when not also consciously. The tales also provide paradigms for the interpretations of religious experiences. People draw on their familiarity with belief-legends in efforts to comprehend their own religious experiences. Again, the tales frequently have pedagogical use as classic illustrations of religious experiences. Belief-legends are concerned less with historical truth than with the experiential truths of living religiosity. When the tales are retold, changes may be introduced in order to keep the tales current, modern, or up to date. Matters no longer understood tend to be omitted, while new matters are introduced in order that the tales retain their relevance. Geographical references may be revised to reflect the locations of retelling. Other types of change are less typical of tales in general, and more specific to belief-legends. Very frequently there is schematizing simplification through the omission of biographically accurate but idiosyncratic details. The omissions delete materials that are irrelevant to the tales' functions as exemplars of their types of religious experience. With time, the biographical legend of a particular individual will come to be retold as the paradigmatic tale of an everyman. Another type of change involves the tales' expansion through the introduction of new materials. The additional motifs are frequently of mythic rather than legendary character.

88. Frederik Wisse, in Robinson, 104.

89. *Ap. John* 2; Robinson, 105.

90. *Treat. Seth* 56; Robinson, 365.

91. Wesley W. Isenberg, in Robinson, 139, 141.

92. *Gos. Phil.* 57–58; Robinson, 144–45.

93. *Ap. Jas.* 15; Robinson, 36–37.

94. *Gos. Thom.* 32–33, saying 3; Robinson, 126.

95. *Paraph. Shem* 41; Robinson, 358.

96. Dan Merkur, "The Visionary Practices of Jewish Apocalyptists," *The Psychoanalytic Study of Society* 14, ed. L. Bryce Boyer and Simon A. Grolnick (Hillsdale, N.J.: Analytic Press, 1989), 119–48.

97. *Ap. John* 1–2; Robinson, 105.

98. *Treat. Res.* 45–46; *Tri. Tract.* 118; *Apoc. Paul* 18–19; *Auth. Teach.* 32, 34; *Paraph. Shem* 1; Robinson, 55, 94, 257–58, 309, 310, 341.

99. *Steles Seth* 125; Robinson, 401.

100. Karen L. King, in Robinson, 524.

101. *Gos. Mary* 14; Robinson, 525–26.

102. *Gos. Thom.* 51, saying 112; Robinson, 138.

103. *Auth. Teach.* 23; Robinson, 306.

104. Maddalena Scopello, in Robinson, 192.

105. *Exeg. Soul* 131; Robinson, 194.

106. Rudolph, *Gnosis,* 257.

107. *Zost.* 1; Robinson, 403.

108. *Paraph. Shem* 1; Robinson, 341. Compare *Paraph. Shem.* 41, 45–46; Robinson, 358, 360.

109. *Treat. Res.* 45–46; Robinson, 54–55.

110. *Exeg. Soul* 134; Robinson, 196.

111. *Gos. Phil.* 73; Robinson, 153.

112. *Eugnostos* 71; Robinson, 223–24.

113. *Treat. Res.* 48–49; Robinson, 56.

114. *Gos. Phil.* 63; Robinson, 148.

115. *Ap. Jas.* 6; Robinson, 32.

116. *Ap. Jas.* 12; Robinson, 35.

117. Harold W. Attridge and George W. MacRae, in Robinson, 38.

118. *Gos. Truth* 29; Robinson, 45.

119. Jonas, *Gnostic Religion,* 68–73; MacRae, 96–507.

120. Elaine Pagels, *The Gnostic Gospels* (New York: Random House, 1979), 125.

121. *Gos. Phil.* 56; Robinson, 144.

122. Stanislav Grof and Christina Grof, *Beyond Death: The gates of consciousness* (London: Thames and Hudson, 1980), 24–28.

123. Dan Merkur, *Becoming Half Hidden: Shamanism and Initiation Among the Inuit* (Stockholm: Almqvist and Wiksell International, 1985), 181–98.

124. *Gos. Thom.* 32, 51, sayings 1, 111; *Gos. Phil.* 52, 77; Robinson, 126, 138, 141, 155.

125. *Gos. Thom.* 36, saying 18; Robinson, 128.

126. *Gos. Thom.* 43, saying 60; Robinson, 133; compare *Gos. Thom.* 45, saying 70; Robinson, 134.

127. *Dial. Sav.* 122–23; Robinson, 247.

128. Pagels, *Gospels,* 135.

129. *Zost.* 1–2; Robinson, 403–4.

130. *Zost.* 3–6; Robinson, 404–5.

131. *Zost.* 6–7; Robinson, 405.

132. *Zost.* 53; Robinson, 417.

133. Gilles Quispel, "The Birth of the Child: Some Gnostic and Jewish Aspects," trans. Ruth Horine, *Eranos Jahrbuch* 40—1971 (Ascona: Eranos Foundation, 1973), 285–309.

134. *Gos. Phil.* 64; Robinson, 148.

135. *Exeg. Soul* 131; Robinson, 194.

136. Francois-M.-M. Sagnard, *Le Gnose Valentinienne et le Témoignage de Saint Irénée* (Paris: Librairie Philosophique J. Vrin, 1947), 243–44.

137. *Gos. Phil.* 61; Robinson, 146–47.

138. Mandaeism concretized the Stoic concept and accorded the transformative power to the mythic sperm of Adam; see E. S. Drower, *The Secret Adam: A Study of Nasoraean Gnosis* (Oxford: Clarendon Press, 1960), 76–77.

139. *Gos. Thom.* 50, saying 108; Robinson, 137.

140. *Great Pow.* 36; Robinson, 312.

141. *Gos. Thom.* 33, saying 7; Robinson, 127.

142. See Scholem, *Jewish Gnosticism,* 71–72.

143. Gos. Phil. 67; Robinson, 150.

144. Harold W. Attridge and Elaine Pagels, in Robinson, 58.

145. *Tri. Tract.* 97; Robinson, 83.

146. *Tri. Tract.* 60–61; Robinson, 65.

147. *Treat. Res.* 48–49; Robinson, 56.

148. *Gos. Phil.* 76; Robinson, 155.

149. George W. MacRae and William R. Murdock, in Robinson, 257.

150. *Apoc. Paul* 23–24; Robinson, 259.

151. *Gos. Eg.* 58–59; Robinson, 211.

152. John D. Turner, in Robinson, 513.

153. *Trim. Prot.* 48–50; Robinson, 521.

154. Roy Kotansky, "Incantations and Prayers for Salvation on Inscribed Greek Amulets," in *Magika Hiera: Ancient Greek Magic and Religion,* ed. Christopher A. Faraone and Dirk Obbink (New York and Oxford: Oxford University Press, 1991), 107–37.

155. Jacques E. Menard, "Normative Self-Definition in Gnosticism," in *Jewish and Christian Self-Definition, Volume One: The Shaping of Christianity in the Second and Third Centuries,* ed. E. P. Sanders (Philadelphia: Fortress, 1980), 149.

156. *Gos. Truth* 21–22; Robinson, 42.

157. *Gos. Mary* 16–17; Robinson, 526.

158. Michael A. Williams, "Stability as a Soteriological Theme in Gnosticism," in *The Rediscovery of Gnosticism, Volume Two: Sethian Gnosticism,* ed. Bentley Layton (Leiden: Brill, 1981), 819–29; idem, *The Immovable Race,* 46–47, 78–85.

159. Antoinette Clark Wire, in Robinson, 490.

160. *Allogenes* 58–59; Robinson, 496–97.

161. Jonas, *Gnostic Religion,* 104–5.

162. Allogenes 59–60; Robinson, 497.

163. Hadot, 242.

164. Louth, 81, 95.

165. *Allogenes* 60–64; Robinson, 497–98.

166. *Eugnostos* 74; Robinson, 226–27.

167. *Soph. Jes. Chr.* 98; Robinson, 226–27.

168. *Tri. Tract.* 66–67; Robinson, 67–68.

169. *Gos. Thom.* 27, saying 22; Robinson, 129.

170. *Gos. Thom.* 32–33, saying 3; Robinson, 126.

171. *Gos. Thom.* 36, saying 17; Robinson, 128.

172. *Tri. Tract.* 73; Robinson, 71.

173. *Marsanes* 27; Robinson, 467.

174. *Gos. Phil.* 68; Robinson, 150.

175. *Auth. Teach.* 34; Robinson, 310.

176. Rudolph, *Gnosis,* 245. Jorunn Jacobsen Buckley, "'The Holy Spirit is a Double Name': Holy Spirit, Mary, and Sophia in the *Gospel of Philip,*" in *Images of the Feminine in Gnosticism,* ed. Karen L. King (Philadelphia: Fortress, 1988), 225, suggested that "the possibility of a 'carnal' ritual does not seem precluded." Equally tenable, however, is the hypothesis of an ascetic rite consistent with the spiritual marriage in second-century Christianity; see Richard A. Horsley, "Spiritual Marriage with Sophia," *Vigiliae Christianae* 33 (1979), 30–54.

177. *Gos. Phil.* 67; Robinson, 150.

178. Irenaeus, *Adv. haer.* 121, 3; as cited by Rudolph, *Gnosis,* 245.

179. Rudolph, *Gnosis,* 142, 154, 196.

180. Ibid., 245–46.

181. *Zost.* 129; Robinson 429.

Chapter 7

1. David J. Halperin, *The Faces of the Chariot: Early Jewish Responses to Ezekiel's Vision* (Tübingen: J. C. Mohr [Paul Siebeck], 1988), ably criticized most previous criteria for dating the *hekhalot* literature. However, his demonstration of the relation, on the one hand, between two synagogue midrashim, *The Visions of Ezekiel* and the tale of Moses' ascension, and on the other, the *hekhalot* literature, leads me to a different conclusion than he reached. A methodological point is at issue. Halperin, 451, claimed that it is not particularly important whether the *hekhalot* texts reflect fantasies or hallucinations. I disagree. For the purpose of dating, it is very significant that the synagogue midrashim contain folkloristic portraits of visionary experiences that are sometimes accurate even in very little known points of detail. Halperin, 387–407, claimed that the synagogue midrashim inspired the origin of the *hekhalot* literature; but because the midrashim bear witness, at one or more removes, to a living knowledge of visionary practices, we must instead conclude that merkabah mysticism was already in progress when the relevant portions of the midrashim originated in third-century Caesarea (Halperin, 309–10). Halperin, 11–37, argued that Palestinian tannaim first became alarmed about the discussion of the merkabah in the late second century. Is this when merkabah mysticism originated, or when it first came to rabbinical attention? Confirmation of these dates is available through the impact of merkabah mysticism on "tan-

naitic and early amoraic liturgy;" see Lawrence A. Hoffman, "Censoring In and Censoring Out: A Function of Liturgical Language," in *Ancient Synagogues: The State of Research,* ed. Joseph Gutmann (Chico, Calif.: Scholars Press, 1981), 19–37.

2. Gershom G. Scholem, *Major Trends,* 40–74; idem, *Jewish Gnosticism;* idem, *Kabbalah* (New York: Quadrangle-New York Times Book Company, 1974), 8–41, 373–76.

3. Peter Schäfer, *Gershom Scholem Reconsidered: The Aim and Purpose of Early Jewish Mysticism,* the twelfth Sacks Lecture delivered on 29th May 1985 (Oxford, U.K.: Oxford Centre for Postgraduate Hebrew Studies, 1986), 3.

4. Compare Ithamar Gruenwald, "Prophecy, Jewish Apocalyptic Literature and the Problem of Uncanonical Books," *Aufsteig und Niedergang der römischen Welt,* 2 Reihe, 19/1 (Berlin: Walter de Gruyter, 1979); rpt. in *From Apocalypticism to Gnosticism: Studies in Apocalypticism, Merkavah Mysticism and Gnosticism* (Frankfurt am Main: Peter Lang, 1988), 24–26.

5. David Flusser, "Scholem's recent book on Merkabah Literature," *Journal of Jewish Studies* 11 (1960), 65.

6. Scholem, *Major Trends,* 54–55, 65–66.

7. The common origin of Gnosticism and merkabah mysticism in Jewish apocalypticism has since been phrased, somewhat more subtly, by Philip S. Alexander, "Comparing Merkavah Mysticism and Gnosticism: An Essay in Method," *Journal of Jewish Studies* 35 (1984), 1–18.

8. Ithamar Gruenwald, "Knowledge and Vision: Towards a Clarification of two 'gnostic' concepts in the light of their alleged origins," *Israel Oriental Studies* 3 (1973), 63–107; idem, "Jewish Merkavah Mysticism and Gnosticism," in *Studies in Jewish Mysticism,* ed. Joseph Dan and Frank Talmage (Cambridge, Mass.: Association for Jewish Studies, 1982), 41–55.

9. David J. Halperin, "A New Edition of the Hekhalot Literature," *Journal of the American Oriental Society* 104 (1984), 3/543–52; Schäfer, *Gershom Scholem Reconsidered.*

10. Scholem, *Kabbalah,* 15.

11. Joseph Dan, "The Seventy Names of Metatron," in *World Congress of Jewish Studies, Jerusalem, August 16–21, 1981: Division C. Talmud and Midrash, Philosophy and Mysticism, Hebrew and Yiddish Literature* (Jerusalem: World Union of Jewish Studies, 1982), 23.

12. Ira Chernus, "Individual and Community in the Redaction of the Hekhalot Literature," *Hebrew Union College Annual* 52 (1981), 252–74.

13. David J. Halperin, *The Merkabah in Rabbinic Literature* (New Haven, Conn.: American Oriental Society, 1980); idem, *Faces of the Chariot;*

Ira Chernus, *Mysticism in Rabbinic Judaism: Studies in the History of Midrash* (Berlin and New York: Walter de Gruyter, 1982).

14. Moshe Idel, *Kabbalah: New Perspectives* (New Haven: Yale University Press, 1988), 77–78.

15. Ibid., 78.

16. MS New York, JTS 1786, fol. 26a; as cited in Idel, 79, 313 n. 32.

17. Halperin, *Faces of the Chariots,* 355.

18. Louis Jacobs, *Jewish Mystical Testimonies* (New York: Schocken, 1977), 27–28.

19. Ibid., 28.

20. Ibid., 28–29.

21. Gruenwald, followed by Idel, suggested that the passage reflects a practice of water divination, remarked in the Greek magical papyri, that made use of a vessel filled with water, atop which oil was often placed; see Ithamar Gruenwald, "Re'uyot Yehezqel (The Visions of Ezekiel)," in *Temirin: Texts and Studies in Kabbala and Hasidism,* ed. Israel Weinstock (Jerusalem: Mossad Harav Kook, 1972), I, 112–4; idem, "Ha-'Ispeqlariyah we-ha-Tekhiniqah shel ha-Hazon ha-Nebu'i we-ha-'Apoqalipti (Mirrors and the Technique of Prophetic and Apocalyptic Vision), *Beth Mikra* 40 (1970), 95–97; Moshe Idel, "Le-Gilgulleha shel Tekhiniqah Qedumah shel Hazon Nebu'i Bime ha-Benayim (On the Medieval Development of an Ancient Technique for Prophetic Vision), *Sinai* 86 (1979–80), 1–2/1–7. As I understand the practices, however, they did not use water as a mirror surface. In some cases, divination was based on interpretations of the shapes assumed by drops of oil on the surface of the water. In other cases, a glint of light on the surface of a sheet of water or oil was used as a focus for inducing self-hypnosis, resulting in a variant of scrying (crystal-gazing); see Yoram Bilu, "Pondering 'The Princes of the Oil': New Light on an Old Phenomenon," *Journal of Anthropological Research* 37 (1981), 3/269–78; Herbert Silberer, "The Origin and the Meaning of the Symbols of Freemasonry," part IV, *Psyche and Eros* 2 (1921), 308. In no event was a mirror reflection involved.

22. Halperin, *Faces of the Chariot,* 233.

23. *Ma'aseh Merkabah* 6; Naomi Janowitz, *The Poetics of Ascent: Theories of Language in a Rabbinic Ascent Text* (Albany: State University of New York Press, 1989), 37.

24. *Hekhalot Rabbati* 22:3; David R. Blumenthal, *Understanding Jewish Mysticism: A Source Reader. The Merkabah Tradition and the Zoharic Tradition* (New York: Ktav Publishing House, 1978), 73. The interpretation of the verse was suggested by Morton Smith, "Observations on Hekhalot Rabbati," in Alexander Altmann, ed., *Biblical and Other Studies* (Cambridge: Harvard University Press, 1963), 156.

25. *Hekhalot Rabbati* 16:4–5; Blumenthal, 60–61.

26. *Hekhalot Rabbati* 20:1–3; Blumenthal, 69–70.

27. Lawrence H. Schiffman, "The Recall of Rabbi Nehuniah ben Ha-Qanah from Ecstasy in the *Hekhalot Rabbati*," *Association for Jewish Studies Review* 1 (1976), 269–81.

28. *Ma'aseh Merkabah* 21–23; Janowitz, 51–52.

29. *Hekhalot Rabbati* 19:6; Blumenthal, 67–68.

30. *Hekhalot Rabbati* 20:4; Blumenthal, 70–71.

31. Mavromatis, 62, 64.

32. As cited in Scholem, *Major Trends,* 52.

33. Scholem, *Major Trends,* 52.

34. Ms. Munich 22 f. 162b, "an elaboration of the explanations" in *Hekhalot Zutarti* and *Hekhalot Rabbati* 26:1–2; as cited in Scholem, *Major Trends,* 53, 361, n. 47.

35. Scholem, *Jewish Gnosticism,* 15.

36. Merkur, *Becoming Half Hidden,* 181–96.

37. Shor, "Hypnosis and the Concept of the Generalized Reality Orientation."

38. Carl Gustav Jung, *Psychology and Religion: West and East,* 2nd ed., trans. R. F. C. Hull (Collected Works, vol. 11; Princeton: Princeton University Press, 1969), 26.

39. Halperin, *Faces of the Chariot,* 206.

40. Ibid., 200–201.

41. Ibid., 157–93.

42. Ibid., 93–96, 220.

43. Merkur, "Visionary Practices of Jewish Apocalyptists," 121–22.

44. Hoffman, "Censoring In and Censoring Out."

45. *Ma'aseh Merkabah* 16; Janowitz, 50.

46. *Ma'aseh Merkabah* 27; Janowitz, 56.

47. *Ma'aseh Merkabah* 17; Janowitz, 51.

48. *Ma'aseh Merkabah* 4; Janowitz, 33.

49. Ibid., 34.

50. *Ma'aseh Merkabah* 5; Janowitz, 35–36.

51. *Hekhalot Rabbati* 24:1–5; Blumenthal, 78–79.

52. For a psychoanalysis of the motif, see David J. Halperin, "A Sexual Image in Hekhalot Rabbati and Its Implications," in *Proceedings of the First International Conference on the History of Jewish Mysticism: Early Jewish Mysticism,* ed. Joseph Dan (*Jerusalem Studies in Jewish Thought,* vol. VI, 1–2; Jerusalem: Magnes Press, 1987), 117–32.

53. *Ma'aseh Merkabah* 9; Janowitz, 41.

54. Scholem, *Major Trends,* 79.

55. *3 Enoch* 9:1–5; Philip S. Alexander, "3 (Hebrew Apocalypse of) Enoch (Fifth-Sixth Century A.D.): A New Translation," in James H. Charlesworth, ed., *The Old Testament Pseudepigrapha: Volume 1: Apocalyptic Literature and Testaments* (Garden City, N.Y.: Doubleday, 1983), 263.

56. Drower, *Secret Adam,* 19.

57. Alexander Altmann, "The Gnostic Background of the Rabbinic Adam Legends," *Jewish Quarterly Review* 35 (1944–45), 371–91; Susan Niditch, "The Cosmic Adam: Man as Mediator in Rabbinic Literature," *Journal of Jewish Studies* 35/2 (1983), 137–46.

58. *3 Enoch* 11:1, 3; Alexander, 264.

59. Saul Lieberman, in Gruenwald, *Apocalyptic and Merkavah Mysticism,* 235–41.

60. For a theory of myth and the manner of its interpretation, see Merkur, "Adaptive Symbolism and the Theory of Myth."

61. In a version of the legend of Muhammad's ascension that was heavenly influenced by merkabah mysticism, R. Ishmael appears as the angel Isma'il and aids the ascending Muhammad, much as Metatron aids the visionary in *III Enoch.* See David J. Halperin, "Hekhalot and Mi'raj: Observations on the Heavenly Journey in Judaism and Islam," paper delivered to the University of Chicago conference, "Other Realms: Death, Ecstasy and Otherworldly Journeys in Recent Scholarship," May 16–17, 1991. Unpublished.

62. Peter Schäfer, *Geniza-Fragmente zur Hekhalot-Literatur* (Tübingen: J. C. B. Mohr, 1984), 105; translated by Elliot R. Wolfson, "*Yeridah la-Merkavah:* Typology of Ecstasy and Enthronement in Ancient Jewish Mysticism," in *Typologies of Mysticism,* ed. R. Herrera (New York: Peter Lang, 1993) [forthcoming].

63. Wolfson, "*Yeridah la-Merkavah.*"

64. Ibid.

65. Rachel Elior, "The Concept of God in Hekhalot Literature, in *Binah, Volume 2: Studies in Jewish Thought,* ed. Joseph Dan (New York: Praeger, 1989), 99.

66. Gruenwald, *Apocalyptic and Merkavah Mysticism,* 159–60.

67. Martin Samuel Cohen, *The Shiʿur Qomah: Texts and Recensions* (Tübingen: J. C. B. Mohr [Paul Siebeck], 1985), 17.

68. Scholem, *Major Trends,* 65.

69. Joseph Dan, "The Concept of Knowledge in the *Shiʿur Qomah,*" *Studies in Jewish Religious and Intellectual History: Presented to Alexander Altmann on the Occasion of His Seventieth Birthday,* ed. Siegfried Stein and Raphael Loewe (London: Institute of Jewish Studies; University: University of Alabama Press, 1979), 68–69.

70. Martin Samuel Cohen, *The Shiʿur Qomah: Liturgy and Theurgy in Pre-Kabbalistic Jewish Mysticism* (Lanham, Md.: University Press of America, 1983), 221.

71. Scholem, *Major Trends,* 79.

72. Plotinus is the earliest Western mystic who left unequivocal extant record of introspective unitive experiences (A. Hilary Armstrong, personal communication, 1987); and the spread of Neoplatonism in Christianity, Judaism, and Islam saw to the dissemination of the practice in the West.

73. Geo Widengren, *Ascension of the Apostle;* idem, *Muhammad, the Apostle of God, and His Ascension* (Uppsala Universitets Arsskrift 1955:1; Uppsala: A.-B. Lundequistska Bokhandeln; Wiesbaden: Otto Harrassowitz, 1955); idem, "Baptism and Enthronement in Some Jewish-Christian Gnostic Documents," in *The Saviour God,* ed. S. G. F. Brandon (Manchester: Manchester University Press, 1963), 205–17; idem, "Royal Ideology and the Testaments of the Twelve Patriarchs," in *Promise and Fulfilment,* ed. F. F. Bruce (Edinburgh: Clark, 1963), 202–12.

74. Also found at Qumran was ascension imagery related to the later *hekhalot* literature; see: Carol Newsom, *Songs of the Sabbath Sacrifice: A Critical Edition* (Atlanta: Scholars Press, 1985).

75. Halperin, *Faces of the Chariot,* 436.

76. Randolf Alnaes, "Therapeutic Application of the Change in Consciousness Produced by Psycholytica (LSD, Psilocybin, Etc.): The Psychedelic Experience in the Treatment of Neurosis," *Acta Psychiatrica Scandinavica,* Supplementum 180 (1964), 397–409; Stanislav Grof, *Realms of the Human Unconscious: Observations from LSD Research* (New York: Dutton, 1976), 138–49.

77. Merkur, *Becoming Half Hidden,* 195–98.

78. As cited in Gruenwald, *Apocalyptic and Merkavah Mysticism,* 145.

79. *3 Enoch* 13:1; Alexander, 265–66.

80. *3 Enoch* 13:2; Alexander, 266. A slightly longer list of creative letters occurs in *3 Enoch* 41:1–3; Alexander, 292.

81. *Ma'aseh Merkabah* 27; Janowitz, 56.

82. *Ma'aseh Merkabah* 28; Janowitz, 57.

83. *Ma'aseh Merkabah* 33; Janowitz, 64.

84. Elior, "Concept," 100.

85. Scholem, *Kabbalah*, 19.

86. A. Leo Oppenheim, "The Interpretation of Dreams in the Ancient Near East: With a Translation of an Assyrian Dream-Book," *Transactions of the American Philosophical Society* 46 (1956), 3/198.

87. Philip S. Alexander, "The Historical Setting of the Hebrew Book of Enoch," *Journal of Jewish Studies* 28 (1977), 179.

88. Gruenwald, *Apocalyptic and Merkavah Mysticism*, 144.

89. Ibid., 167–68.

90. Ibid., 102–3.

91. Ibid., 108.

92. *Ma'aseh Merkabah* 33; Janowitz, 64.

93. Scholem, *Jewish Gnosticism*, 32–33; Rudolph, *Gnosis*, 173–74; Robinson, *Nag Hammadi Library*, 211, 216, 259, 521 (*Gos. Eg., Apoc. Paul, Trim. Prot.*).

94. *Ma'aseh Merkabah* 13; Janowitz, 43.

95. *Ma'aseh Merkabah* 14; Janowitz, 47.

96. Scholem, *Jewish Gnosticism*, 12; see Gruenwald, *Apocalyptic and Merkavah Mysticism*, 143, 179.

97. Halperin, *Faces of the Chariot*, 372–75; citations, pp. 382, 385.

98. Michael A. Morgan, trans., *Sepher Ha-Razim: The Book of the Mysteries* (Chico, Calif.: Scholars Press, 1983).

99. Gruenwald, *Apocalyptic and Merkavah Mysticism*, 231. For an English translation of the papyri, see Hans Dieter Betz, ed., *The Greek Magical Papyri in Translation: Including the Demotic Spells* (Chicago: University of Chicago Press, 1986).

100. Betz, 74, 99, 127, 137, 138, 139, 147, 158.

101. Ibid., 5, 33, 35, 56–60, 102, 126, 139, 147, 159, 160, 200, 201.

102. Ibid., 55, 101–2, 127, 133, 219, 222.

103. Ibid., 122.

104. Morgan, *Sepher,* 34.

105. Ibid., 38.

106. Ibid., 39.

107. Ibid., 42.

108. Ibid., 69–70.

109. Ibid., 70–72.

110. Ibid., 80.

Chapter 8

1. Richard Bell, "Muhammad's Visions," *Muslim World* 24 (1934), 146.

2. W. Montgomery Watt, *Bell's Introduction to the Qur'an* (Edinburgh: University Press, 1970), 24.

3. Bell, "Muhammad's Visions," 147.

4. Ibid., 153.

5. Ibid., 148.

6. For a survey of early Muslim understandings of prophetic experience, see William A. Graham, *Divine Word and Prophetic Word in Early Islam: A Reconsideration of the Sources, with Special Reference to the Divine Saying or* Hadith Qudsi (The Hague: Mouton, 1977), 9–48.

7. All quotations from the Quran are taken from *The Koran: with a Parallel Arabic Text,* trans. N. J. Dawood (London: Penguin, 1990).

8. Merkur, "Prophecies of Jeremiah."

9. Merkur, "Visionary Experiences of Jewish Apocalyptists."

10. Watt, *Introduction,* 22.

11. Tor Andrae, *Mohammed: The Man and His Faith,* trans. Theophil Menzel (New York: Barnes and Noble, 1935), 49.

12. Muhammad ibn Ishaq, *The Life of Muhammad: A Translation of Ishaq's* Sirat Rasul Allah, trans. A. Guillaume (London: Geoffrey Cumberlege-Oxford University Press, 1955), 255.

13. Andrae, *Mohammed,* 49–50; citing Ibn Sa'd. i, I. p. 131 f. Bukhari, *K. bad' al-wahi.*

14. Theodor Noldeke, *Geschichte des Qorans,* 2nd ed., ed. Friedrich Schwally (Leipzig, 1909), I, 26; David Samuel Margoliouth, *Mohammed*

and the Rise of Islam (New York and London: Putnam's, 1905), 45–46; Duncan Black Macdonald, *The Religious Attitude and Life in Islam* (Chicago, 1909), 33–40; *Koran,* trans. J. M. Rodwell (London: Dent; New York: Dutton, 1909), 21 n. 1; Frank R. Freemon, "A Differential Diagnosis of the Inspirational Spells of Muhammad the Prophet of Islam," *Epilepsia* 17 (1976), 423–27.

15. Arbman, *Ecstasy,* III, 369.

16. *The Qur'an,* trans. Edward Henry Palmer (Oxford: Clarendon, 1880), xx-xxii; A. Sprenger, *Das Leben Muhammads,* I, 207–9; K. Birnbaum, *Psychopathologische Dokumente* (Berlin, 1920), 272–73; Eugen Bleuler, *Lehrbuch der Psychiatrie,* 6th ed. (Berlin, 1937), 273; Arbman, *Ecstasy,* III, 371.

17. Owen Berkeley-Hill, "A Short Study of the Life and Character of Mohammed," *International Journal of Psychoanalysis* 2 (1921), 31–53.

18. Ibn Ishaq, *Life,* 106.

19. Ernest Jones, *On the Nightmare,* 2nd ed. (New York: Liveright, 1951).

20. Ibn Ishaq, *Life,* 121, 130, 135–6.

21. Andrae, *Mohammed,* 98.

22. Richard Bell, "Mohammed's Call," *Muslim World* 24 (1934), 16.

23. Ibid., 43.

24. Ibn Ishaq, *Life,* 136.

25. Watt, *Introduction,* 25–6.

26. Joseph M. Baumgarten, "The Book of Elkesai and Merkabah Mysticism," in *Proceedings of the Eighth World Congress of Jewish Studies, Jerusalem, August 16–21, 1981, Division C: Talmud and Midrash, Philosophy and Mysticism, Hebrew and Yiddish Literature* (Jerusalem: World Union of Jewish Studies, 1982), 13–18.

27. Gedaliahu G. Stroumsa, "Esotericism in Mani's Thought and Background," in *Codex Manichaicus Coloniensis: Atti del Simposio Internazionale (Rende-Amantea 3–7 settembre 1984),* ed. Luigi Cirillo with Amneris Roselli (Mana: Editore Cosenza, 1986), 153–68.

28. Rudolph, *Gnosis,* 327–30, 339.

29. Ibid., 376.

30. Charles Cutler Torrey, "Mysticism in Islam," in *At One With the Invisible: Studies in Mysticism,* ed. E. Hershey Sneath (New York: Macmillan, 1921), 144; John Clark Archer, *Mystical Elements in Mohammed* (New Haven: Yale University Press, 1924), 9.

31. Ibid., 19.

32. Because Muhammad first adopted the doctrine of the mediation of revelation at a mid-point in his career, the Gnostic idea of a hypostasis was presumably unknown to him previously. The Manichean doctrines that are discernible at the beginning of his career (see Andrae, *Mohammed,* 97, 107, 122–23) may be treated as stray elements among the many competing cultural influences in Muhammad's Arabia. Richard Bell, *The Origin of Islam in its Christian Environment* (London: Macmillan, 1926), 154, argued persuasively that the Quran's docetic account of the crucifixion (sura 4.156–58) was probably not intended in a Gnostic fashion. It served instead to reconcile the story of Jesus with Muhammad's standard claim that God invariably rescued God's prophets from catastrophe.

33. Ibn Ishaq, *Life,* 165–66.

34. Ibid., 166.

35. Ibid., 300.

36. Alexander Altmann, *Studies in Religious Philosophy and Mysticism* (Ithaca: Cornell University Press, 1969; rpt. Plainview, N.Y.: Books for Libraries Press, 1975), 42–44, 150–51.

37. Ibn Ishaq, *Life,* 295–96.

38. Ibid., 371.

39. Ibid., 590.

40. Ibid., 648.

41. Watt, *Introduction,* 36.

42. Charles Cutler Torrey, *The Jewish Foundation of Islam* (1933; rpt. New York: Ktav, 1967), 79–81.

43. Torrey, *Foundation,* 66, 68, 110–12; Julian Obermann, "Islamic Origins: A Study in Background and Foundation," in *The Arab Heritage,* ed. Nabih Amin Faris (Princeton: Princeton University Press, 1946), 110–12; S. D. Goitein, "Muhammad's Inspiration by Judaism," *Journal of Jewish Studies* 9 (1958), 153–54; Abraham I. Katsh, *Judaism and the Koran: Biblical and Talmudic Backgrounds of the Koran and Its Commentaries* (New York: A. S. Barnes, 1962).

44. Gordon D. Newby, "Observations about an Early Judaeo-Arabic," *Jewish Quarterly Review* 61 (1971), 220–21.

45. Goitein, *Inspiration,* 155.

46. Bell, "Muhammad's Visions," 149.

47. In some Mandaean texts, the demiurge Ptahil is also called "Gabriel, the messenger" (Rudolph, "Mandean Sources," 136, 182). The influence of Islam on Mandaeism may be assumed.

48. David J. Halperin, "The Ibn Sayyad Traditions and the Legend of Al-Dajjal," *Journal of the American Oriental Society* 96 (1976), 213–14. For a discussion of "Islamic Reflections of Merkabah Traditions," see also Halperin, *Faces of the Chariot,* 467–90.

49. Ibid., 217.

50. Ibid.

51. Ibid., 219.

52. Ibid., 220.

53. Altmann, *Studies,* 41–42.

54. *Hekhalot Rabbati* 22:3; Blumenthal, 73. The comparison was noted by Altmann, *Studies,* 42. An acquaintance with merkabah mysticism may also have influenced legendary addenda to the remark in sura 6.35. Legend ascribed the remark to one of Muhammad's cousins, shortly after Muhammad first began preaching in Mecca. "By God, I will never believe in you until you get a ladder to the sky, and mount up it until you come to it, while I am looking on, and until four angels shall come with you, testifying that you are speaking the truth, and by God, even if you did that I do not think I should believe you" (Ibn Ishaq, *Life,* 135). The four angels may be compared with the angels of the four seasons. Synagogues of the fifth and sixth centuries frequently had mosaic floors that depicted the merkabah as the sun-god Helios in a chariot drawn by four horses, surrounded by anthropomorphic angels of the seasons and the signs of the zodiac; see Lee I. Levine, ed., *Ancient Synagogues Revealed* (Jerusalem: Israel Exploration Society, 1981), 8–9, 15–16, 66–67. Helios was identified as "he on the cherubim" in the Greek magical papyrus XIII.355–8 (see Betz, 170).

55. A. A. Bevan, "Mohammed's Ascension to Heaven," in *Studien zur Semitischen Philologie und Religionsgeschichte: Julius Wellhausen zum Siebzigsten Geburtstag am 17. Mai 1914,* ed. Karl Marti (Giessen: Alfred Topelmann [vormals J. Ricker], 1914), 53.

56. Bell, "Muhammed's Visions," 152.

57. Bevan, "Ascension, 56.

58. Similarly, the motif of the opening of Muhammad's breast earliest occurs in a tale of his childhood, but was later given initiatory significance and added to the account of the *mi'raj;* see Harris Birkeland, "The Legend of the Opening of Muhammed's Breast," *Avhandlinger utgitt av Det Norske Videnskaps-Akademi i Oslo, II. Historisk-Filosofisk Klasse* (Oslo: Jacob Dybwad, 1955), 3.

59. Bevan, "Ascension, 56–7.

60. Ibid., 56; J. R. Porter, "Muhammad's Journey to Heaven," *Numen* 21/1 (1974), 71–73.

61. Halperin, "Hekhalot and Mi'raj."

62. Annemarie Schimmel, *And Muhammad Is His Messenger: The Veneration of the Prophet in Islamic Piety* (Chapel Hill: University of North Carolina Press, 1985), 123–43.

Chapter 9

1. Irenaeus, *Adv. Haer.* I 14, 1; translation in Werner Foerster, *Gnosis: A Selection of Gnostic Texts, I. Patristic Evidence,* trans. R. McL. Wilson (Oxford: Clarendon, 1972), 203.

2. Irenaeus, *Adv. Haer.* I 14, 3; Foerster, 205.

3. Ibid., I 14, 1; Foerster, 203.

4. Ibid., Foerster, 204.

5. Ibid., I, 14, 2; Foerster, 204.

6. Ibid., I 15, 1–18,4; Foerster, 208–16.

7. Kurt Rudolph, "Mandaean Sources," in *Gnosis: A Selection of Gnostic Texts, Vol. 2: Coptic and Mandaean Sources,* ed. Werner Foerster, trans. R. McL. Wilson (Oxford: Clarendon, 1972), 132, 140–41.

8. T. Säve-Söderbergh, *Studies in the Coptic Manichaean Psalm Book* (Uppsala, 1949), as cited by Edwin M. Yamauchi, *Gnostic Ethics and Mandaean Origins* (Cambridge: Harvard University Press, 1970), 5–6.

9. E. S. Drower, *The Secret Adam: A Study of Nasoraean Gnosis* (Oxford: Clarendon, 1960), 17–19; 'Daniel Cohn-Sherbot, 'The Alphabet in Mandaean and Jewish Gnosticism," *Religion* 11 (1981), 227–34.

10. Drower, *Adam,* 19, 25, 38.

11. Steve Wasserstrom, "The Moving Finger Writes: Mughira b. Sa'id's Islamic Gnosis and the Myths of Its Rejection," *History of Religions* 25/1 (1985), 15.

12. Marshall G. S. Hodgson, "How Did the Early Shi'a Become Sectarian?" *Journal of the American Oriental Society* 75 (1955), 1–13.

13. Wasserstrom, "Finger," 3.

14. William F. Tucker, "Rebels and Gnostics: Al-Mugira ibn Sa'id and the Mugiriyya," *Arabica* 22 (1975), 33–47.

15. Matti Moosa, *Extremist Shiites: The Ghulat Sects* (Syracuse: Syracuse University Press, 1988), xvii-xxi.

16. Al-Maqdisi, 5:140; as cited by Wasserstrom, "Finger," 19.

17. William F. Tucker, "Abu Mansur al-'Ijli and the Mansuriyya: a study in medieval terrorism," *Der Islam* 54 (1977), 66–76.

18. Sahrastani, *Kitab al-Milal,* ed. Cureton, 136:3–6; as cited in Widengren, *Muhammad,* 29–30.

19. Mutahhar, *Le livre de la création* V, 130–31; as cited in Widengren, *Muhammad,* 86.

20. Louis Massignon, *Salman Pak and the Spiritual Beginnings of Iranian Islam,* trans. Jamshedji Maneckji Unvala (Bombay: Bombay University Press, 1955), 25.

21. Schimmel, *And Muhammad Is His Messenger,* 159–75. See also Najm ad-Din al-Ghaiti, "The Story of the Night Journey and the Ascension," in *A Reader on Islam: Passages from Standard Arabic Writings Illustrative of the Beliefs and Practices of Muslims,* ed. Arthur Jeffery ('S-Gravenhage: Mouton, 1962), 621–39.

22. Ibn Abi Junhur, *Kitab al-mujli* (Tehran, 1329), 370, as cited in Seyyed Hossein Nasr, *Sufi Essays* (New York: Schocken, 1977), 109–10.

23. Muhammad 'Ali Sabziwari, *Tuhfat al-abbasiyah* (Shiraz, 1326), 93–94, as cited in Nasr, *Sufi Essays,* 110.

24. Altmann, 43; A. E. Affifi, "The Story of the Prophet's Ascent (*Mi'raj*) in Sufi Thought and Literature," *Islamic Quarterly* 2 (1955), 26–27; Louis Massignon, *The Passion of al-Hallaj: Mystic and Martyr of Islam, Vol. 3: The Teaching of al-Hallaj,* trans. Herbert Mason (Princeton: Princeton University Press, 1982), 293–98.

25. Göran Ogén, "Religious Ecstasy in Classical Sufism," in *Religious Ecstasy: Based on Papers read at the Symposium on Religious Ecstasy held at Abo, Finland, on the 26th-29th of August 1981,* ed. Nils G. Holm (Stockholm: Almqvist and Wiksell International, 1982), 226–40.

26. Michael Sells, "3 Enoch (Sefer Hekhalot) and the Mi'raj of Abu Yazid al-Bistami," paper read before the American Academy of Religion, 1989. [Unpublished].

27. Ibid., 95.

28. Nazeer el-Azma, "Some Notes on the Impact of the Story of the Mi'raj on Sufi Literature," *Muslim World* 63/2 (1973), 96–98; Earle H. Waugh, "Religious Aspects of the Mi'raj Legends," in *Etudes Arabes et Islamique I—histoire et civilisation, Vol. 4. Actes du XXIXe Congrès international des Orientalistes,* ed. Claude Caher (Paris: L'Asiatheque, 1975), 236–44; idem, "Following the Beloved: Muhammad as Model in the Sufi Tradition," in *The Biographical Process: Studies in the History and Psychology of Religion,* ed. Frank E. Reynolds and Donald Capps (The Hague: Mouton, 1976), 63–85.

29. John B. Taylor, "Ja'far al-Sadiq, Spiritual Forebear of the Sufis," *Islamic Culture* 40 (1966), 97–113; idem, "Man's Knowledge of God in the Thought of Ja'far al-Sadiq," *Islamic Culture* 40 (1966), 195–206.

30. Wilferd Madelung, "Shiism: An Overview," in *The Encyclopedia of Religion*, ed. Mircea Eliade (New York: Macmillan, 1987), XIII, 243.

31. W. Ivanow, *Studies in Early Persian Ismailism*, 2nd ed. (Bombay: Ismaili Society, 1955), 128.

32. W. Ivanow, *A Creed of the Fatimids* (Bombay: Qayyimah Press, 1936), 1.

33. W. Ivanow, *Ismaili Tradition concerning the Rise of the Fatimids* (London: Humphrey Milford-Oxford University Press, 1942), xxi, 3–4.

34. W. Madelung, "Isma'iliyya," in *Encyclopaedia of Islam*, 2nd ed., ed. E. van Donzel, B. Lewis, and Ch. Pellat (Leiden: Brill, 1978), vol. 4, 202.

35. S. M. Stern, *Studies in Early Isma'ilism* (Jerusalem: Magnes Press; Leiden: Brill, 1983), 4–5.

36. Ibid., 18.

37. Ibid.

38. Madelung, "Isma'iliyya," 203.

39. Paul E. Walker, "Cosmic Hierarchies in Early Isma'ili Thought: The View of Abu Ya'qub al-Sijistani," *Muslim World* 66 (1976), 18–21.

40. Stern, *Studies*, 20.

41. Ibid.

42. Ibid., 21.

43. Ibid., 23.

44. Ibid.

45. Ibid.

46. Ibid., 25.

47. Ibid.

48. Ivanow, *Early Persian Ismailism*, 69.

49. Ibid., 29–59, 67–68, 70.

50. Ibid., 48–50.

51. Madelung, "Isma'iliyya," 203.

52. Ivanow, *Ismaili Tradition*, 117, n 1

53. Ibid., 253–54.

54. Ivanow, *Early Persian Ismailism,* 77.

55. Ivanow, *Ismaili Tradition,* 249.

56. Ibid., 253.

57. Ibid., 271.

58. Ibid., 269.

59. Ibid., 256.

60. Ibid., 257.

61. Ibid., 267.

62. Marshall G. S. Hodgson, *The Order of Assassins: The Struggle of the Early Nizari Isma'ilis Against the Islamic World* ('S-Gravenhage: Mouton, 1955), 10, 19.

63. Uri Rubin, "Pre-existence and light: Aspects of the concept of Nur Muhammad," *Israel Oriental Studies* 5 (1975), 112–16.

64. Ivanow, *Creed of the Fatimids,* 56–57.

65. Blumenthal, "Maimonides' Intellectualist Mysticism."

66. Ivanow, *Creed of the Fatimids,* 57.

67. For a survey of *dhikr,* see Marshall G. S. Hodgson, *The Venture of Islam: Conscience and History in a World Civilization, Volume Two: The Expansion of Islam in the Middle Periods* (Chicago: University of Chicago Press, 1974), 211–13.

68. Ibid., 67.

69. The Isma'ili emphasis on particulars, leading to communion, is to be contrasted with the global approach, leading to introspective union, of a Sufi who "sees in all things the Secret Oneness of God and continually cognizes this Presence with Attraction and Love" (J. G. Bennett, "Sufi Spiritual Techniques," *Systematics* 7 [1969–70], 248).

70. Ivanow, *Creed of the Fatimids,* 33–34.

71. Ibid., 63.

72. Paul E. Walker, "An Isma'ili Answer to the Problem of Worshiping the Unknowable, Neoplatonic God," *American Journal of Arabic Studies* 2 (1974), 11.

73. Hadot, "Neoplatonist Spirituality."

74. Ian Richard Netton, *Allah Transcendent: Studies in the Structure and Semiotics of Islamic Philosophy, Theology and Cosmology* (London: Routledge, 1989), 210–14.

75. Sami N. Makarem, "Isma'ili and Druze Cosmogony in Relation to Plotinus and Aristotle," in *Islamic Theology and Philosophy: Studies in Honor of George F. Hourani,* ed. Michael E. Marmura (Albany: State University of New York Press, 1984), 81.

76. Compare, for example, pseudo-Dionysius the Areopagite.

77. Netton, 211.

78. A similar reworking of Neoplatonism was achieved, possibly independently, by al-Nasafi's contemporary, the Spanish Sufi Muhammad ibn Masarra (883–931). In Ibn Masarra's system, God created the first hypostasis. Termed "primal matter," it was a hylic substance equivalent to the intelligible matter of Neoplatonism's One. Four further hypostases—intellect, soul, nature, and secondary (perceptible) matter—followed. See Miguel Asin Palacios, *The Mystical Philosophy of Ibn Masarra and His Followers,* trans. Elmer H. Douglas and Howard W. Yoder (Leiden: Brill, 1978), 32–33, 42, 50–51, 62–69. Where ibn Masarra's God was ultimate being, al-Nasafi's was beyond both being and nonbeing.

79. Madelung, "Isma'iliyya," 193, 204; Stern, *Studies,* 75.

80. Asin Palacios, *Mystical Philosophy of Ibn Masarra,* 33, 62–69.

81. S. A. Q. Husaini, *The Pantheistic Monism of Ibn al-'Arabi* (Lahore, Pakistan: Sh. Muhammad Ashraf, 1970).

82. Paul E. Walker, "The Ismaili Vocabulary of Creation," *Studia Islamica* 40 (1974), 80–81; Netton, 218–21.

83. R. van den Broek, "The Creation of Adam's Psychic Body in the Apocryphon of John," in *Studies in Gnosticism and Hellenistic Religions: presented to Gilles Quispel on the Occasion of his 65th Birthday,* ed. R. van den Broek and M. J. Vermaseren (Leiden: Brill, 1981), 38–57.

84. Couliano, *Eros and Magic,* 56–57.

85. Colleen McDannell and Bernhard Lang, *Heaven: A History* (New Haven: Yale University Press, 1988; rpt. New York: Vintage Books, 1990), 35–36.

86. Ibid., 52, 61.

87. Ivanow, *Early Persian Ismailism,* 8; Madelung, "Isma'iliyya," 203; Hodgson, *Order of Assassins,* 331; Pio Filippani-Ronconi, "The Soteriological Cosmology of Central-Asiatic Isma'ilism," in *Isma'ili Contributions to Islamic Culture,* ed. Seyyed Hossein Nasr (Tehran: Imperial Iranian Academy of Philosophy, 1977); Farhad Daftary, *The Isma'ilis: their history and doctrines* (Cambridge: Cambridge University Press, 1990), 100.

88. Filippani-Ronconi, "Cosmology," 111–12.

89. Ibid., 113.

90. Ibid., 112.

91. Ibid., 109, 113.

92. Ibid., 113.

93. Ibid., 115.

94. Ibid., 105–6, 111, 114; Daftary, *Isma'ilis,* 100–102.

95. Filippani-Ronconi, "Cosmology," 113.

96. Ivanow, *Ismaili Tradition,* 232, n. 1.

97. Filippani-Ronconi, "Cosmology," 110–11.

98. Ibid., 110.

99. Ibid., 111.

100. Ibid., 112.

101. Ibid., 111.

102. Arthur Avalon and Sriyukta Barada Kanta Majumdar, ed., *Principles of Tantra: The Tantratattva of Sriyukta Siva Candra Vidyarnava Bhattacarya Mahodaya* (1914; rpt. Madras: Ganesh, 1960), 344.

103. Sanjukta Gupta, Dirk Jan Hoens, and Teun Goudriaan, *Hindu Tantrism* (Leiden: Brill, 1979), 24.

104. Jagadish Narayan Sarkar, *Islam in Bengal (Thirteenth to Nineteenth Century)* (Calcutta: Ratna Prakashan, 1972), 2, 20.

105. Enamul Haq, "Sufi Movement in Bengal," *Indo-Iranica* 3/1 (1948) 10–12.

106. Mohan Singh, "Iranian Influence on Medieval Indian Mystics," *Indo-Iranica* 6/4 (1952–53), 37–38.

107. Eliade, *Yoga,* 216–19, 408.

108. Md. Enamul Haq, "Sufi Movement in India," *Indo-Iranica* 3/3 (1949), 11–41.

109. Asim Roy, *The Islamic Syncretistic Tradition in Bengal* (Princeton: Princeton University Press, 1983), 111–206.

110. Madelung, "Shiism: Isma'iliyah," 252.

111. Corbin, *Creative Imagination,* 129.

112. 'Ali b. 'Uthman al-Jullabi al-Hujwiri, *The Kashf al-Mahjub: The Oldest Persian Treatise on Sufiism,* 2nd ed., trans. Reynold A. Nicholson (London: Luzac, 1936), 330–32.

113. Zaehner, 168–69.

114. A. E. Affifi, "Ibn 'Arabi," in *A History of Muslim Philosophy: with Short Accounts of Other Disciplines and the Modern Renaissance in Muslim Lands,* ed. M. M. Sharif (Wiesbaden: Otto Harrassowitz, 1963), I, 405.

115. Crosland.

116. Madelung, "Karmati," 662.

117. Paul Kraus, *Jabir ibn Hayyan: Contribution à L'Histoire des Idées Scientifiques dans l'Islam. Volume 1: Le Corpus des Ecrits Jabiriens* (*Mémoires Présentes à l'Institut d'Egypte* 44; 1943); Seyyed Hossein Nasr, *An Introduction to Islamic Cosmological Doctrines: Conceptions of Nature and Methods Used for Its Study by the Ikhwan al-Safaʾ, al-Biruni, and Ibn Sina* (Cambridge: Belknap Press, Harvard University Press, 1964), 90–91.

118. Henry Corbin, *Creative Imagination in the Sufism of Ibn 'Arabi,* trans. Ralph Manheim (Bollingen Series 91; 1958; rpt. Princeton: Princeton University Press, 1969).

119. Fazlur Rahman, "Dream, Imagination and *'Alam al-Mithal,*" *Islamic Studies* 3 (1964), 167–80.

120. Seyyed Hossein Nasr, "Shihab al-Din Suhrawardi Maqtul," in *A History of Muslim Philosophy: With Short Accounts of Other Disciplines and the Modern Renaissance in Muslim Lands,* ed. M. M. Sharif (Wiesbaden: Otto Harrasowitz, 1963), I, 387; Netton, 258–59.

121. Nasr, "Suhrawardi Maqtul," 390–91; Netton, 264–65.

122. Nasr, "Suhrawardi Maqtul," 381, 393.

123. Shihabuddin Yahya Suhrawardi, *The Mystical and Visionary Treatises of Shihabuddin Yahya Suhrawardi,* trans. W. M. Thackston, Jr. (London: Octagon, 1982), 24.

124. Giselda Webb, "An Exegesis of Suhrawardi's *The Purple Intellect* (*'Aql-i surkh*)," *Islamic Quarterly* 26 (1982), 202, 208.

125. Suhrawardi, 24.

126. Webb, 202.

127. Nasr, "Suhrawardi Maqtul," 394–95.

128. Netton, 263–64, 266–67.

129. Suhrawardi, 92.

130. Rahman, 169.

131. Suhrawardi, 49, 58.

132. Rahman, 169.

133. Suhrawardi, 49.

134. A. E. Affifi, *The Mystical Philosophy of Muhyid Din-Ibnul Arabi* (Cambridge: University Press, 1939), 75, 89, 164, 184–88; Rom Landau, "The Philosophy of Ibn 'Arabi," *Muslim World* 47 (1957), 158; Netton, *Allah Transcendent,* 282–83, 303.

135. R. W. J. Austin, "Introduction," in Ibn al-'Arabi, *The Bezels of Wisdom,* trans. R. W. J. Austin (New York: Paulist, 1980), 23.

136. Corbin, *Avicenna and the Visionary Recital;* Abu Bakr Muhammad bin Tufail, *The Journey of the Soul: The Story of Hai bin Yaqzan,* trans. Riad Kocache (London: Octagon, 1982).

137. Ibn al-'Arabi, *Futuhat,* II, 767, l. 2 from foot; as cited by Affifi, *Mystical Philosophy,* 76.

138. Ibn al-'Arabi, *Futuhat,* I, 289; as cited by Husaini, *Pantheistic Monism,* 149–50.

139. Affifi, *Mystical Philosophy,* 125.

140. Muhyiddin Ibn al-'Arabi, "Ibn al-'Arabi's Shajarat al-Kawn, trans. Arthur Jeffery," *Studia Islamica* 10–11 (1959–60), 74, 76, 124–25, 129.

141. Ibn al-'Arabi, *Bezels of Wisdom,* 120.

142. Rahman, 170.

143. Ibn al-'Arabi, *Bezels of Wisdom,* 55, 76.

144. Ibid., 53.

145. Ibn al-'Arabi, as cited by Rahman, 173.

146. James Winston Morris, "The Spiritual Ascension: Ibn 'Arabi and the Mi'raj," *Journal of the American Oriental Society* 108/1 (1988), 67.

147. Ibn al-'Arabi, *Bezels of Wisdom,* 77.

148. Ibid., 69.

149. William C. Chittick, "Death and the World of Imagination: Ibn al-'Arabi's Eschatology," *Muslim World* 78 (1988), 55.

150. Ibn al-'Arabi, *Futuhat,* I, 99–100, as cited by Husaini, 167.

151. Morris, "Spiritual Ascension," 640–61.

152. Fassu Sulaymani, cited in Ibn al-'Arabi, *Futuhat,* III, 378; as cited by Husaini, 187.

153. Schimmel, *And Muhammad Is His Messenger,* 132–35; Affifi, *Mystical Philosophy,* 71–72; Husaini, 79, 106–7.

154. Affifi, *Mystical Philosophy,* 89.

155. Ibid., 100–101

156. William C. Chittick, *The Sufi Path of Knowledge: Ibn al-'Arabi's Metaphysics of Imagination* (Albany: State University of New York Press, 1989), 8–9.

157. Seyyed Hossein Nasr, *Three Muslim Sages: Avicenna—Suhrawardi—Ibn 'Arabi* (Cambridge: Harvard University Press, 1964), 71.

158. Ibn al-'Arabi, *Bezels of Wisdom,* 150.

159. Chittick, *Sufi Path of Knowledge,* 42.

160. Ibn al-'Arabi, *Bezels of Wisdom,* 130–31.

161. Ibn al-'Arabi, *Bezels of Wisdom,* 149–50.

162. Muhyiddin Ibn 'Arabi, *Journey to the Lord of Power: A Sufi Manual on Retreat,* trans. Rabia Terri Harris (New York: Inner Traditions International, 1981), 43.

163. Ibid.

164. Ibid., 47–48.

165. Wilfred Madelung, "Aspects of Isma'ili Theology: The Prophetic Chain and the God beyond Being," in *Isma'ili Contributions to Islamic Culture,* ed. Seyyed Hossein Nasr (Tehran: Imperial Iranian Academy of Philosophy, 1977), 56–57.

166. Ibn al-'Arabi, *Futuhat,* I, 139; as cited by Husaini, 74.

167. Netton, *Allah Transcendent,* 303.

168. Ibid., 274.

169. H. A. Wolfson, "The Kalam Problem of Nonexistence and Saadia's Second Theory of Creation," *Jewish Quarterly Review* 36 (1946), 380–82.

170. H. A. Wolfson, "Arabic and Hebrew Terms for Matter and Element with Especial Reference to Saadia," *Jewish Quarterly Review* 38 (1947), 48–51. The distinction had entered Sufism in Spain with Muhammad Ibn Masarra (883–931), who considered primal matter to be the substance out of which the intellect was formed. Secondary matter was the basis of the four elements. See: Asin Palacios, *Mystical Philosophy of Ibn Masarra,* 50–51.

171. Asin Palacios, *Mystical Philosophy of Ibn Masarra,* 124.

172. Masataka Takeshita, "An Analysis of Ibn 'Arabi's *Insha al-Dawa'ir* with Particular Reference to the Doctrine of the 'Third Entity'," *Journal of Near Eastern Studies* 41 (1982), 243–45, 248. The term *al-umm* had already been used by Muslim philosophers; see Wolfson, "Arabic and Hebrew Terms," 55, 57.

173. Ibn al-ʿArabi, *Bezels of Wisdom,* 50.

174. Ibid.

175. Ibid., 277.

176. Ibn al-ʿArabi, *Futuhat,* I, 147; as cited by Husaini, 78.

177. Ibn al-ʿArabi, *Bezels of Wisdom,* 74.

178. Ibid., 148.

179. Ibid., 92.

180. Valerie J. Hoffman-Ladd, "Mysticism and Sexuality in Sufi Thought and Life," *Mystics Quarterly* (1992) [forthcoming].

181. Ibn al-ʿArabi, *Futuhat,* III, 90; as cited by Husaini, 90–91.

182. Ibn al-ʿArabi, *Bezels of Wisdom,* 274.

183. Corbin, *Creative Imagination,* 100, 137–39.

184. Ibid., 136–38.

185. Agehananda Bharati, *The Tantric Tradition* (London: Rider, 1965), 293.

186. June McDaniel, *The Madness of the Saints: Ecstatic Religion in Bengal* (Chicago: University of Chicago Press, 1989), 109, 111, 118–19.

187. Rahman, 177.

188. S. Babs Mala, "Self-Realization in the Mystical Thought of al-Kubra: An Interpretation," *Orita* 12/1 (1978), 61.

189. Corbin, *Man of Light,* 77.

190. Ibid.

191. Ibid., 79.

192. Ibid., 85.

193. Ibid., 112.

194. Ibid.

191. Ibid., 121.

Chapter 10

1. Faivre, "Esotericism," 157, 160.

2. Corbin, *Creative Imagination,* 92.

3. Ibid., 179, 182.

4. Ibid., ix.

5. Ibid., 71–90.

6. Michael Sells, "Bewildered Tongue: The Semantics of Mystical Union in Islam," in *Mystical Union and Monotheistic Religion: An Ecumenical Dialogue,* ed. Moshe Idel and Bernard McGinn (New York: Macmillan, 1989), 89–95.

7. Maria Rosa Menocal, *The Arabic Role in Medieval Literary History: A Forgotten Heritage* (Philadelphia: University of Pennsylvania Press, 1987).

8. Frederick Goldin, *Lyrics of the Troubadours and Trouveres: An Anthology and a History* (Garden City, N.Y.: Anchor Press/Doubleday, 1973), 5.

9. Ibid., 21–23.

10. The image possibly alluded to the motif of the horse-drawn chariot of the soul, whose source was the *Phaedrus* of Plato.

11. L. T. Topsfield, *Troubadours and Love* (Cambridge: Cambridge University Press, 1975), 16–17.

12. Ibid., 30–32.

13. Ibid., 37.

14. Ibid., 3, 34.

15. Raymond Klibansky, *The Continuity of the Platonic Tradition During the Middle Ages: Outlines of a Corpus Platonicum Medii Aevi* (London: Warburg Institute, 1937); Marie-Dominique Chenu, "The Platonisms of the Twelfth Century," in his *Nature, Man, and Society in the Twelfth Century: Essays on New Theological Perspectives in the Latin West,* ed. and trans. Jerome Taylor and Lester K. Little (Chicago: University of Chicago Press, 1968), 49–98.

16. David Knowles, *The Evolution of Medieval Thought* (New York: Random House, 1962), 113–14.

17. Stephen Gersh, "Platonism-Neoplatonism-Aristotelianism: A Twelfth-Century Metaphysical System and Its Sources," in *Renaissance and Renewal in the Twelfth Century,* ed. Robert L. Benson and Giles Constable, with Carol D. Lanham (Cambridge: Harvard University Press, 1982; rpt. Toronto: University of Toronto Press, 1991), 518.

18. Chenu, "Platonisms," 80.

19. Nikolaus M. Haring, "John Scottus in Twelfth-Century Angelology," *The Mind of Eriugena: Papers of a Colloquium, Dublin, 14–18 July 1970,* ed. John J. O'Meara and Ludwig Bieler (Dublin: Irish University Press-Royal

Irish Academy, 1973), 158–69; Edouard Jeauneau, "Le renouveau erigenien du XIIᵉ siècle," *Eriugena Redivivus: Zur Wirkungsgeschichte seines Denkens im Mettelalter und im Übergang zur Neuzeit,* ed. Werner Beierwaltes (Heidelberg: Carl Winter-Universitätsverlag, 1987), 26–46.

20. John J. Omeara, "Introduction," in Eriugena, *Periphyseon (The Division of Nature),* trans. I. P. Sheldon-Williams and John J. O'Meara (Montreal: Bellarmin; Washington: Dumbarton Oaks, 1987), 21.

21. Eriugena, *Periphyseon,* 300–304.

22. Ibid., 431.

23. Marie-Dominique Chenu, "Nature and Man—The Renaissance of the Twelfth Century," in his *Nature, Man, and Society in the Twelfth Century,* 1–48.

24. George D. Economou, *The Goddess Natura in Medieval Literature* (Cambridge: Harvard University Press, 1972), 53.

25. Bernardus Silvestris, *The Cosmographia,* trans. Winthrop Wetherbee (New York: Columbia University Press, 1973).

26. Alan of Lille, *Anticlaudianus, or, The Good and Perfect Man,* trans. James J. Sheridan (Toronto: Pontifical Institute of Mediaeval Studies, 1973), 40–41.

27. Guillaume de Lorris and Jean de Meun, *The Romance of the Rose,* trans. Harry W. Robbins (New York: Dutton, 1962), 390.

28. Dante Alighieri, *La Vita Nuova (Poems of Youth),* trans. Barbara Reynolds (Harmondsworth: Penguin, 1969).

29. Stanford Gwilliam, "Divine Light and the *Divine Comedy:* the Shekinah Experience of Dante Alighieri," *Journal of Altered States of Consciousness* 3 (1977–78), 2/181–90.

30. Corbin, *Creative Imagination,* 51–52, 100, 139.

31. Dante Alighieri, *The Divine Comedy,* 3 vols., trans. Mark Musa, 2nd ed. (Harmondsworth: Penguin, 1984–86).

32. Miguel Asin Palacios, *Islam and the Divine Comedy,* ed. and trans. Harold Sutherland (1926; rpt. London: Frank Cass, 1968).

33. St. Bernard of Clairvaux, *On the Song of Songs,* 4 vols., trans. Kilian Walsh and Irene M. Edmonds (Kalamazoo, Mich.: Cistercian Publications, 1971–80), Sermon 2:2, 41:3–5; see 7:7; 31:5; 45:5.

34. For a dated but still valuable study, see Edmund G. Gardner, *Dante and the Mystics: A Study of the Mystical Aspect of the Divina Commedia and Its Relations with some of its Mediaeval Sources* (London: Dent; New York: Dutton, 1913).

35. Pseudo-Dionysius, *The Complete Works,* trans. Colm Luibheid and Paul Rorem (New York: Paulist, 1987), 195, 61.

36. Corbin, *Creative Imagination,* 18; idem, *Cyclical Time,* 76.

37. Idries Shah, *The Sufis* (Garden City, N.Y.: Doubleday, 1964), 228–34.

38. Francis and Clare, *The Complete Works,* trans. Regis J. Armstrong and Ignatius C. Brady (New York: Paulist, 1982).

39. For an inconclusive argument, see Edward A. Armstrong, *Saint Francis: Nature Mystic. The derivation and significance of the nature stories in the Franciscan Legend* (Berkeley: University of California Press, 1973).

40. See Bonaventure, *The Life of St. Francis,* in Bonaventure, *The Soul's Journey Into God. The Tree of Life. The Life of St. Francis,* trans. Ewert Cousins (New York: Paulist, 1978).

41. [Ramon Lull], *Selected Works of Ramon Llull (1232–1316),* 2 vols., ed. and trans. Anthony Bonner (Princeton: Princeton University Press, 1985), I, 13–15.

42. Ramon Lull, *The Book of the Lover and the Beloved,* 2nd ed., trans. E. Allison Peers; ed. Kenneth Leech (1946; rpt. London: Sheldon, 1978), 26.

43. Ibid., 111.

44. Ibid., 99.

45. Ibid., 35.

46. J. N. Hillgarth, *Ramon Lull and Lullism in Fourteenth-Century France* (Oxford: Clarendon, 1971), 1–4, 6–8, 15–18.

47. Lull, *Selected Works,* I, 22.

48. Asin Palacios, *Mystical Philosophy of Ibn Masarra,* 138.

49. Ibid., 99.

50. Lull, *Book of the Lover,* 106.

51. Ibid., 119–21, 156.

52. Asin Palacios, *Mystical Philosophy of Ibn Masarra,* 140.

53. Lull, *Book of the Lover,* 22.

54. Lull, *Selected Works,* I, 60–61.

55. Lull, *Book of the Lover,* 22.

56. Frances A. Yates, *Lull and Bruno: Collected Essays, Volume 1* (London: Routledge and Kegan Paul, 1982), 3–125.

57. Ibid.

58. Ibid., 42.

59. Urszula Szulakowska, "Thirteenth Century Material Pantheism in the Pseudo-Lullian 'S'–Circle of the Powers of the Soul," *Ambix* 35 (1988), 127–28, 133.

60. R. D. F. Pring-Mill, "The Trinitarian World Picture of Ramon Lull," *Romanistisches Jahrbuch* 7 (1955–56), 232; Lull, *Book of the Lover,* 59–60.

61. Pring-Mill, 232–33.

62. Ibid., 251–52.

63. Ithamar Gruenwald, "A Preliminary Critical Edition of *Sefer Yezira,*" *Israel Oriental Studies* 1 (1971), 132–77. For an English translation, which enumerates the paragraphs differently, see David R. Blumenthal, ed., *Understanding Jewish Mysticism: A Source Reader. The Merkabah Tradition and the Zoharic Tradition* (New York: Ktav, 1978), 15–44.

64. Gershom G. Scholem, *On the Kabbalah and Its Symbolism,* trans. Ralph Manheim (New York: Schocken, 1965), 167.

65. Gershom G. Scholem, *Origins of the Kabbalah,* trans. Allen Arkush, ed. R. J. Zwi Werblowsky (Princeton: Jewish Publication Society-Princeton University Press, 1987), 30.

66. Moshe Idel, *Kabbalah: New Perspectives* (New Haven: Yale University Press, 1988), 97–102; idem, *The Mystical Experience in Abraham Abulafia* (Albany: State University of New York Press, 1988), 20–25.

67. Yates, *Lull and Bruno,* 114–15.

68. Lull, *Selected Works,* I, 609.

69. Ibid., 71–3.

70. Hillgarth, 270–74.

71. Nicholas of Cusa, *The Vision of God,* trans. Emma Gurney Salter (New York: Dutton; and London: Dent, 1928; rpt. New York: Frederick Ungar, 1960), 7.

72. Ibid., 46–47.

73. Ibid., 78.

74. Yates, *Lull and Bruno,* 28–29.

75. Michela Pereira, *The Alchemical Corpus Attributed to Raymond Lull* (London: Warburg Institute, University of London, 1989), 2, 4, 6–7, 10–11, 13–15.

76. Hillgarth, 280–81.

77. Pereira, 30.

78. Hillgarth, 293.

79. Ernst Cassirer, *The Individual and the Cosmos in Renaissance Philosophy,* trans. Mario Domandi (1963; rpt. Philadelphia: University of Pennsylvania Press, 1972), 25.

80. Ioan P. Couliano, *Eros and Magic in the Renaissance,* trans. Margaret Cook (Chicago: University of Chicago Press, 1987), 4–5, 27, 43–44.

81. Walter Pagel, *Paracelsus: An Introduction to Philosophical Medicine in the Era of the Renaissance* (Basel and New York: S. Karger, 1958), 315.

82. Paracelsus, *Selected Writings,* ed. Jolande Jacobi, trans. Norbert Guterman, 3rd ed. (Princton: Princeton University Press, 1969), 29.

83. Paracelsus, *The Hermetic and Alchemical Writings of Paracelsus,* ed. Arthur Edward Waite (London: James Elliott, 1894; rpt. Berkeley: Shambhala, 1976), II, 185.

84. As cited by F. Sherwood Taylor, "The Idea of the Quintessence," in *Science Medicine and History: Essays on the Evolution of Scientific Thought and Medical Practice, written in honour of Charles Singer,* ed. E. Ashworth Underwood (London: Oxford University Press, 1953; rpt. New York: Arno, 1975), I, 262.

85. Paracelsus, *Hermetic and Alchemical Writings,* II, 23.

86. Ibid., 37.

87. Ibid., 265.

88. Paracelsus, *Die neun Bucher de natura rerum* (Villach, 1537); as cited by Walter Pagel, "Paracelsus and the Neoplatonic and Gnostic Tradition," *Ambix* 8 (1960), 132, n. 32.

89. Paracelsus, *Selected Writings,* 14.

90. Paracelsus, *Hermetic and Alchemical Writings,* II, 137.

91. Pagel, "Paracelsus and the Neoplatonic and Gnostic Tradition," 127, instead maintained that Paracelsus adhered to the Platonic contrast of matter and *ideas.*

92. Paracelsus, *Selected Writings,* 217–18.

93. Paracelsus, *Hermetic and Alchemical Writings,* II, 259.

94. Ibid., 269.

95. Ibid., 263.

96. Ibid., 10.

97. Ibid., 266.

98. Ibid., 270.

99. Theophrastus von Hohenheim, called Paracelsus, *Four Treatises,* ed. Henry E. Sigerist (Baltimore: Johns Hopkins Press, 1941), 231.

100. Paracelsus, *Hermetic and Alchemical Writings,* II, 303.

101. Paracelsus, *The Archidoxes of Magic,* trans. Robert Turner (London, 1656; rpt. London: Askin Publishers; New York: Samuel Weiser, 1975), 37.

102. Ibid., 82.

103. Paracelsus, *Hermetic and Alchemical Writings,* II, 291.

104. Ibid., 7.

105. Ibid., 120; Paracelsus, *Archidoxes of Magic,* 60–63.

106. Paracelsus, *Hermetic and Alchemical Writings,* II, 308–9; see idem, *Selected Writings,* 32.

107. Paracelsus, *Selected Writings,* 21.

108. Ibid., 41.

109. Paracelsus, *Hermetic and Alchemical Writings, II, 306.*

110. Ibid., 297.

111. Ibid., 307.

112. Paracelsus, *Archidoxes of Magic,* 72.

113. Paracelsus, *Selected Writings,* 45.

114. Ibid., 307.

115. Ibid., 308.

116. Paracelsus, *Selected Writings,* 117.

117. Paracelsus, *Archidoxes of Magic,* 45–47.

118. Ibid., 47.

119. Paracelsus, *Selected Writings,* 19.

120. Ibid., 21.

121. Ibid., 39.

122. Ibid., 44.

123. On Paracelsus's relation to Cusa, see Pagel, *Paracelsus*, 279–84.

124. Paracelsus, *Hermetic and Alchemical Writings*, II, 339.

125. Ibid., 332, 335.

126. Yates, *Lull and Bruno*, 27, 67, 27, n. 54.

127. Paracelsus, *Hermetic and Alchemical Writings*, II, 346.

128. Pagel, *Paracelsus*, 241–47.

129. Ibid., 252.

130. Paracelsus, *Hermetic and Alchemical Writings*, II, 269.

131. Ibid., 252–53.

132. Walter Pagel, "The Prime Matter of Paracelsus," *Ambix* 9 (1961), 118.

133. As cited in Walter Pagel and Marianne Winder, "The Higher Elements and Prime Matter in Renaissance Naturalism and in Paracelsus," *Ambix* 21 (1974), 108.

134. Pagel, "Paracelsus and the Neoplatonic and Gnostic Tradition," 144–45.

135. Paracelsus, *Selected Writings*, 23–24.

136. Pagel and Winder, "Elements," 95.

137. Ibid., 25. See also Walter Pagel and Marianne Winder, "The Eightness of Adam and Related 'Gnostic' Ideas in the Paracelsian Corpus," *Ambix* 16 (1969), 119–39.

138. Paracelsus, *Hermetic and Alchemical Writings*, II, 264.

139. Paracelsus, *Selected Writings*, 43.

140. Ibid., 43.

141. Frances A. Yates, *The Art of Memory* (1966; rpt. Harmondsworth: Penguin, 1969), 189.

142. Pereira, 29.

143. Yates, *Art of Memory*, 189–90; Lull, *Selected Works*, I, 74. For a detailed bibliography, see Hillgarth, 18, n. 86.

144. Nasr, *Science and Civilization in Islam*, 35; Stanley L. Jaki, *The Savior of Science* (Washington, D.C.: Regnery Gateway, 1988), 71.

145. Jaki, 73.

146. Steele and Singer, "The Emerald Table," 492.

147. Paracelsus, *Selected Writings,* 43–44.

148. Ibid., 161.

149. Paracelsus, *Four Treatises,* 223–24.

150. Paracelsus, *Selected Writings,* 199–200.

151. Ibid., 182.

152. Ibid.

153. Ibid., 164.

154. Pagel and Winder, "The Higher Elements," 95.

155. *Sefer Ha-Zohar* II, 89a-89b; as cited in *The Wisdom of the Zohar: An Anthology of Texts,* ed. Isaiah Tishby with Fischel Lachower, trans. David Goldstein (Oxford: Littman Library/Oxford University Press, 1989), III, 1391; Joseph Karo, *Shulkhan Arukh (Orah Hayyim)* 231:1; Elliot K. Ginsburg, *The Sabbath in the Classical Kabbalah* (Albany: State University of New York Press, 1989), 109, 114.

156. Paracelsus, *Selected Writings,* 33.

157. Paracelsus, *Hermetic and Alchemical Writings,* 172.

158. Elias Ashmole, ed., *Theatrum Chemicum Britannicum,* new intro. Allen G. Debus (1652; rpt. New York: Johnson Reprint Corp., 1967), 8–10.

159. Ibid., 11.

160. Ibid., 389–90, 405.

161. Ibid., 306–7.

162. C. H. Josten, "A Translation of John Dee's 'Monas Hieroglyphica' (Antwerp, 1564), With an Introduction and Annotations," *Ambix* 12 (1964), 2–3/165.

163. [Thomas Vaughan], *The Works of Thomas Vaughan: Mystic and Alchemist (Eugenius Philalethes),* ed. Arthur Edward Waite (1919; rpt. New Hyde Park, N.Y.: University Books, 1968), 144.

164. Ibid., 36.

Works Cited

Aaronson, Bernard S., and Humphry Osmond, ed. *Psychedelics: The Uses and Implications of Hallucinogenic Drugs.* 1968. Rpt. Garden City, N.Y.: Doubleday/Anchor, 1970.

Affifi, A. E. "Ibn ʿArabi." In *A History of Muslim Philosophy: with Short Accounts of Other Disciplines and the Modern Renaissance in Muslim Lands.* Ed. M. M. Sharif, I. Wiesbaden: Otto Harrassowitz, 1963.

————. *The Mystical Philosophy of Muhyid Din-Ibnul Arabi.* Cambridge: University Press, 1939.

————. "The Story of the Prophet's Ascent (*Miʿraj*) in Sufi Thought and Literature." *Islamic Quarterly* 2 (1955), 23–27.

Alexander, Franz. "Buddhistic Training As an Artificial Catatonia (The Biological Meaning of Psychic Occurrences)." *Psychoanalytic Review* 18 (1931), 129–45.

Alexander, Philip S. "Comparing Merkavah Mysticism and Gnosticism: An Essay in Method." *Journal of Jewish Studies* 35 (1984), 1–18.

————. "The Historical Setting of the Hebrew Book of Enoch." *Journal of Jewish Studies* 28 (1977), 156–80.

————. "3 (Hebrew Apocalypse of) Enoch (Fifth-Sixth Century A.D.): A New Translation." In *The Old Testament Pseudepigrapha: Volume 1: Apocalyptic Literature and Testaments.* Ed. James H. Charlesworth. Garden City, N.Y.: Doubleday, 1983.

Almond, Philip C. *Mystical Experience and Religious Doctrine: An Investigation of the Study of Mysticism in World Religions.* Berlin: Mouton, 1982.

Alnaes, Randolf. "Therapeutic Application of the Change in Consciousness Produced by Psycholytica (LSD, Psilocybin, Etc.): The Psychedelic Experience in the Treatment of Neurosis." *Acta Psychiatrica Scandinavica,* Supplementum 180 (1964), 397–409.

Altmann, Alexander. "The Gnostic Background of the Rabbinic Adam Legends." *Jewish Quarterly Review* 35 (1944–45), 371–91.

———. *Studies in Religious Philosophy and Mysticism.* Ithaca: Cornell University Press, 1969; rpt. Plainview, N.Y.: Books for Libraries Press, 1975.

Andrae, Tor. *Mohammed: The Man and His Faith.* Trans. Theophil Menzel. New York: Barnes and Noble, 1935.

Angela of Foligno. *The Book of Divine Consolation.* Trans. Mary G. Steegmann. New York: Cooper Square, 1966.

ʿArabi, Muhyiddin Ibn al-. *The Bezels of Wisdom.* Trans. R. W. J. Austin. New York: Paulist, 1980.

———. "Ibn al-ʿArabi's Shajarat al-Kawn." Translated by Arthur Jeffery. *Studia Islamica* 10–11 (1959–60), 43–77, 113–60.

———. *Journey to the Lord of Power: A Sufi Manual on Retreat.* Trans. Rabia Terri Harris. New York: Inner Traditions International, 1981.

Arberry, A. J. *Sufism: An Account of the Mystics of Islam.* 1950; rpt. London: George Allen and Unwin, 1969.

Arbman, Ernst. *Ecstasy or Religious Trance: In the Experience of the Ecstatics and from the Scientific Point of View,* 3 vols. Ed. Åke Hultkrantz. Stockholm: Svenska Bokforlaget, 1963–68–70.

Archer, John Clark. *Mystical Elements in Mohammed.* New Haven: Yale University Press, 1924.

Armstrong, Edward A. *Saint Francis: Nature Mystic. The derivation and significance of the nature stories in the Franciscan Legend.* Berkeley: University of California Press, 1973.

Ashcroft-Nowicki, Dolores. *Highways of the Mind: The Art and History of Pathworking.* Wellingborough, U.K.: Aquarian, 1987.

Ashmole, Elias, ed. *Theatrum Chemicum Britannicum.* New intro. Allen G. Debus. 1652; rpt. New York: Johnson Reprint, 1967.

Asin Palacios, Miguel. *Islam and the Divine Comedy.* Ed. and trans. Harold Sutherland. 1926; rpt. London: Frank Cass, 1968.

———. *The Mystical Philosophy of Ibn Masarra and His Followers* Trans. Elmer H. Douglas and Howard W. Yoder. Leiden: Brill, 1978.

Assagioli, Roberto. *Psychosynthesis: A Manual of Principles and Techniques.* 1965; rpt. Harmondsworth: Penguin, 1976.

Atwood, Mary Anne. *A Suggestive Inquiry into the Hermetic Mystery, with a Dissertation on the more celebrated Alchemical Philosophers, being an attempt towards the Recovery of the Ancient Experiment of Nature.* London: Trelawney Saunders, 1850; rpt. Belfast: William Tait; London: J. M. Watkins, 1918.

Augustine of Hippo, St. *The Literal Meaning of Genesis,* 2 vols. Trans. John Hammond Taylor. New York and Ramsey, NJ: Newman, 1982.

Avalon, Arthur, and Sriyukta Barada Kanta Majumdar, ed. *Principles of Tantra: The Tantratattva of Sriyukta Siva Candra Vidyarnava Bhattacarya Mahodaya.* 1914; rpt. Madras: Ganesh, 1960.

Azma, Nazeer el-. "Some Notes on the Impact of the Story of the Mi'raj on Sufi Literature." *Muslim World* 63/2 (1973), 93–104.

Baba, Meher. "L.S.D. and the Highroads." *Journal of Psychedelic Drugs* 1/2 (1967–68), 38–44.

Bachelard, Gaston. *On Poetic Imagination and Reverie: Selections.* Trans. Colette Gaudin. Dallas: Spring, 1987.

Bardon, Franz. *Initiation Into Hermetics: A Course of Instruction of Magic Theory and Practise.* Trans. A. Radspieler. 1962; rpt. Wuppertal, Germany: Dieter Ruggeberg, 1976.

Bascom, William R. "The Forms of Folklore: Prose Narratives." *Journal of American Folk-Lore* 78 (1965), 3–20.

Baumgarten, Joseph M. "The Book of Elkesai and Merkabah Mysticism." In *Proceedings of the Eighth World Congress of Jewish Studies, Jerusalem, August 16–21, 1981, Division C: Talmud and Midrash, Philosophy and Mysticism, Hebrew and Yiddish Literature,* 13–18. Jerusalem: World Union of Jewish Studies, 1982.

Bell, Richard. "Mohammed's Call." *Muslim World* 24 (1934), 13–19.

——— . "Muhammad's Visions." *Muslim World* 24 (1934), 145–54.

——— . *The Origin of Islam in its Christian Environment.* London: Macmillan, 1926.

Bennett, J. G. "Sufi Spiritual Techniques." *Systematics* 7 (1969–70), 244–60.

Berkeley-Hill, Owen. "A Short Study of the Life and Character of Mohammed." *International Journal of Psychoanalysis* 2 (1921), 31–53.

Bernard of Clairvaux, St. *On the Song of Songs,* 4 vols. Trans. Kilian Walsh or Irene M. Edmonds. Kalamazoo, Mich.: Cistercian Publications, 1971–80.

Berthelot, Marcellin. *Collection des Anciens Alchimistes Grecs,* 3 vols. 1888; rpt. Osnabruck: Otto Zeller, 1967.

Betz, Hans Dieter, ed. *The Greek Magical Papyri in Translation: Including the Demotic Spells.* Chicago: University of Chicago Press, 1986.

Bevan, A. A. "Mohammed's Ascension to Heaven." In *Studien zur Semitischen Philologie und Religionsgeschichte: Julius Wellhausen zum Siebzigsten Geburtstag 17. Mai 1914,* ed. Karl Marti. Giessen: Alfred Töpelmann (vormals J. Ricker), 1914.

Bexton, W. H., W. Heron, and T. H. Scott. "Effects of Decreased Variation in the Sensory Environment." *Canadian Journal of Psychology* 8 (1954), 70–76.

Bharati, Agehananda. *The Light at the Center: Context and Pretext of Modern Mysticism.* Santa Barbara: Ross-Erikson, 1976.

———. *The Tantric Tradition.* London: Rider, 1965.

Bianchi, Ugo. "Docetism: A Peculiar Theory about the Ambivalence of the Presence of the Divine." In *Selected Essays on Gnosticism, Dualism and Mysteriosophy.* Leiden: Brill, 1978.

———. "Mithraism and Gnosticism." In *Mithraic Studies.* Ed. John R. Hinnells. Manchester: Manchester University Press, 1975.

———, ed. *The Origins of Gnosticism: Colloquium of Messina, 13–18 April 1966.* Leiden: Brill, 1970.

Bilu, Yoram. "Pondering 'The Princes of the Oil': New Light on an Old Phenomenon." *Journal of Anthropological Research* 37/3 (1981), 269–278.

Birkeland, Harris. "The Legend of the Opening of Muhammed's Breast." *Avhandlinger utgitt av Det Norske Videnskaps-Akademi i Oslo, II. Historisk-Filosofisk Klasse,* no. 3. Oslo: Jacob Dybwad, 1955.

Bleeker, C. J. "The Egyptian Background of Gnosticism." In *The Origins of Gnosticism: Colloquium of Messina, 13–18 April 1966.* Ed. Ugo Bianchi. 229–37. Leiden: Brill, 1967.

Blofeld, John. "A High Yogic Experience Achieved with Mescaline." *Psychedelic Review* 7 (1966), 27–32.

Blumenthal, David R. "Maimonedes' Intellectualist Mysticism and the Superiority of the Prophecy of Moses." *Studies in Medieval Culture* 10 (1977), 51–68; rpt. in *Approaches to Judaism in Medieval Times.* Ed. David R. Blumenthal. Chico, Calif.: Scholars Press, 1984.

———, ed. *Understanding Jewish Mysticism: A Source Reader. The Merkabah Tradition and the Zoharic Tradition.* New York: Ktav, 1978.

Bohlig, Alexander. "Jacob as an Angel in Gnosticism and Manicheism." In *Nag Hammadi and Gnosis.* Ed. R. McL. Wilson. 122–30. Leiden: E. J. Brill, 1978.

Bonaventure. *The Soul's Journey Into God. The Tree of Life. The Life of St. Francis.* Trans. Ewert Cousins. New York: Paulist, 1978.

Braden, William. *The Private Sea: LSD and the Search for God.* Chicago: Quadrangle, 1967.

Breasted, James Henry. *The Dawn of Conscience.* 1933; rpt. New York: Scribner's, 1968.

Brown, Robert F. *The Later Philosophy of Schelling: The Influence of Boehme on the Works of 1809–1815.* Lewisburg: Bucknell University Press; London: Associated University Presses, 1977.

Bruce, George Howard. *High School Chemistry,* 2nd ed. New York: World Book Company, 1938.

Buber, Martin. *Between Man and Man.* New York: Macmillan, 1965.

Buckley, Jorunn Jacobsen. " 'The Holy Spirit is a Double Name': Holy Spirit, Mary, and Sophia in the *Gospel of Philip.*" In *Images of the Feminine in Gnosticism,* ed. Karen L. King. Philadelphia: Fortress, 1988.

Burckhardt, Titus. *Alchemy: Science of the Cosmos, Science of the Soul.* Trans. William Stoddart. 1967; rpt. Baltimore: Penguin, 1971.

Burkert, Walter. *Ancient Mystery Cults.* Cambridge: Harvard University Press, 1987.

Butler, E. M. *Ritual Magic.* Cambridge: University Press, 1949; rpt. New York: Noonday, 1959.

Caldwell, W. B. *LSD Psychotherapy: An Exploration of Psychedelic and Psycholytic Therapy.* 1968; rpt. New York: Grove, 1969.

Caley, Earle Radcliffe. "The Leyden Papyrus X: An English Translation with Brief Notes." *Journal of Chemical Education* 3 (1926), 1149–66.

———. "The Stockholm Papyrus: An English Translation with Brief Notes." *Journal of Chemical Education* 4/8 (1927), 979–1002.

Carver, Alfred. "Primary Identification and Mysticism." *British Journal of Medical Psychology* 4 (1924), 102–14.

Casaubon, Meric, ed. *A True and Faithful Relation of What Passed for many Years Between Dr. John Dee . . . and Some Spirits . . . .* London: D. Maxwell and T. Garthwait, 1659; rpt. Glasgow: Antonine, 1974.

Caslant, E. *Method of Development of the Supernormal Faculties.* Paris: Meyer, 1927.

Cassirer, Ernst. *The Individual and the Cosmos in Renaissance Philosophy.* Trans. Mario Domandi. 1963; rpt. Philadelphia: University of Pennsylvania Press, 1972.

Catherine of Genoa. *Purgation and Purgatory. The Spiritual Dialogue.* Trans. Serge Hughes. New York: Paulist, 1979.

Chenu, Marie-Dominique. *Nature, Man, and Society in the Twelfth Century: Essays on New Theological Perspectives in the Latin West.* Ed. and trans. Jerome Taylor and Lester K. Little. Chicago: University of Chicago Press, 1968.

Chernus, Ira. "Individual and Community in the Redaction of the Hekhalot Literature." *Hebrew Union College Annual* 52 (1981), 252–74.

———. *Mysticism in Rabbinic Judaism: Studies in the History of Midrash.* Berlin and New York: Walter de Gruyter, 1982.

Chittick, William C. "Death and the World of Imagination: Ibn al-ʿArabi's Eschatology." *Muslim World* 78 (1988), 51–82.

———. *The Sufi Path of Knowledge: Ibn al-ʿArabi's Metaphysics of Imagination.* Albany: State University of New York Press, 1989.

Christian, Jr., William A. *Apparitions in Late Medieval and Renaissance Spain.* Princeton: Princeton University Press, 1981.

Chwelos, N., D. B. Blewett, C. M. Smith, and A. Hoffer. "Use of d-Lysergic Acid Diethylamide in the Treatment of Alcoholism." *Quarterly Journal for Studies on Alcohol* 20 (1959), 577–90.

Clark, Walter Houston. *Chemical Ecstasy: Psychedelic Drugs and Religion.* New York: Sheed and Ward, 1969.

Clark, Walter Houston, H. Newton Maloney, James Daane, and Alan R. Tippett. *Religious Experience: Its Nature and Function in the Human Psyche.* Springfield: Charles C. Thomas, 1973.

Cohen, Martin Samuel. *The Shiʿur Qomah: Liturgy and Theurgy in Pre-Kabbalistic Jewish Mysticism.* Lanham, Md.: University Press of America, 1983.

———. *The Shiʿur Qomah: Texts and Recensions.* Tubingen: J. C. B. Mohr (Paul Siebeck), 1985.

Cohn-Sherbok, Daniel. "The Alphabet in Mandaean and Jewish Gnosticism." *Religion* (1981), 227–234.

Conze, Edward. "Buddhism and Gnosis." In *The Origins of Gnosticism: Colloquium of Messina, 13–18 April 1966,* ed. Ugo Bianchi. Leiden: E. J. Brill, 1970.

———. *Buddhist Meditation.* 1956; rpt. New York: Harper and Row, 1969.

———. "Buddhist Philosophy and its European Parallels." In *Thirty Years of Buddhist Studies: Selected Essays,* 210–28. Columbia: University of South Carolina Press, 1968.

———. "Prajna and Sophia." In *Thirty Years of Buddhist Studies.*

Corbin, Henry. *Avicenna and the Visionary Recital.* Trans. Willard R. Trask. 1954; rpt. Irving, Tex.: Spring, 1980.

——. *Creative Imagination in the Sufism of Ibn ʿArabi.* Trans. Ralph Manheim. 1958; rpt. Princeton: Princeton University Press, 1969.

——. *Cyclical Time and Ismaili Gnosis.* Trans. Ralph Manheim and James W. Morris. London: Kegan Paul International-Islamic Publications, 1983.

——, "Le Livre du Glorieux de Jabir Ibn Hayyan (Alchimie et Archetypes)." *Eranos-Jahrbuch* 18 (1950), 47–114.

——. *The Man of Light in Iranian Sufism.* Trans. Nancy Pearson. 1971; rpt. Boulder, Colo.: Shambhala, 1978.

——. "*Mundus Imaginalis* or the Imaginary and the Imaginal." *Spring 1972*, 1–18.

——. *Spiritual Body and Celestial Earth: From Mazdean Iran to Shi'ite Iran.* Trans. Nancy Pearson. 1960; rpt. Princeton: Bollingen Foundation-Princeton University Press, 1977.

Couliano, Ioan Petru. *Eros and Magic in the Renaissance.* Trans. Margaret Cook. Chicago: University of Chicago Press, 1987.

——. *The Tree of Gnosis: Gnostic Mythology from Early Christianity to Modern Nihilism.* Trans. H. S. Wiesner and Ioan P. Couliano. New York: Harper Collins, 1992.

Crampton, Martha. "The Use of Mental Imagery in Psychosynthesis." *Journal of Humanistic Psychology* 9/2 (1969), 139–53.

Crosland, Maurice P. *Historical Studies in the Language of Chemistry.* 1962; rpt. New York: Dover, 1978.

Crownfield, David R. "Religion in the Cartography of the Unconscious: A Discussion of Stanislav Grof's *Realms of the Human Unconscious.*" *Journal of the American Academy of Religion* 44/2 (1976), 309–15.

Cusa, Nicholas of. *The Vision of God.* Trans. Emma Gurney Salter. New York: Dutton; London: Dent, 1928; rpt. New York: Frederick Ungar, 1960.

Daftary, Farhad. *The Ismaʿilis: their history and doctrines.* Cambridge: Cambridge University Press, 1990.

Dan, Joseph. "The Concept of Knowledge in the *Shiʿur Qomah.*" In *Studies in Jewish Religious and Intellectual History: Presented to Alexander Altmann on the Occasion of His Seventieth Birthday.* Ed. Siegfried Stein and Raphael Loewe. London: Institute of Jewish Studies; University: University of Alabama Press, 1979.

————. "The Seventy Names of Metatron." In *World Congress of Jewish Studies, Jerusalem, August 16–21, 1981: Division C. Talmud and Midrash, Philosophy and Mysticism, Hebrew and Yiddish Literature.* Jerusalem: World Union of Jewish Studies, 1982.

Daniélou, Jean. *A History of Early Christian Doctrine Before the Council of Nicaea, Volume Two: Gospel Message and Hellenistic Culture.* Trans. and ed. John Austin Baker. London: Darton, Longman and Todd; Philadelphia: Westminster, 1973.

Dante Alighieri, *The Divine Comedy,* 3 vols. Trans. Mark Musa. 2nd ed. Harmondsworth: Penguin, 1984–86.

————. *La Vita Nuova (Poems of Youth).* Trans. Barbara Reynolds. Harmondsworth: Penguin, 1969.

David-Neel, Alexandra. *With Mystics and Magicians in Tibet.* 1931; rpt. London: Penguin, 1936.

Davis, Tenney L. "The Emerald Table of Hermes Trismegistus: Three Latin Versions Which Were Current Among Later Alchemists." *Journal of Chemical Education* 3 (1926), 863–75.

Dawson, David. *Allegorical Readers and Cultural Revision In Ancient Alexandria.* Berkeley: University of California Press, 1992.

DeBold, Richard C., and Russell Leaf, ed. *LSD, Man and Society.* Middletown, Conn.: Wesleyan University Press, 1968.

Degh, Linda, and Andrew Vazsonyi. "The Memorate and the Proto-Memorate." *Journal of American Folk-Lore* 87 (1974), 225–39.

Deikman, Arthur J. "Experimental Meditation." *Journal of Nervous and Mental Disease* 136 (1963), 329–73. Rpt. in *Altered States of Consciousness,* 2nd ed., ed. Charles T. Tart, 203–23. Garden City, N.Y.: Doubleday Anchor Books, 1972.

————. *The Observing Self: Mysticism and Psychotherapy.* Boston: Beacon, 1982.

Desoille, Robert. *The Directed Daydream: A Series of Three Lectures Given at the Sorbonne (January 1965).* Trans. Frank Haronian. New York: Psychosynthesis Research Foundation, 1966.

Dicks, D. R. *The Geographical Fragments of Hipparchus.* London: University of London Press, 1960.

Dillon, John. *The Middle Platonists: A Study of Platonism 80 BC to AD 220.* London: Gerald Duckworth, 1977.

Drower, E. S. *The Secret Adam: A Study of Nasoraean Gnosis.* Oxford: Clarendon, 1960.

Economou, George D. *The Goddess Natura in Medieval Literature*. Cambridge: Harvard University Press, 1972.

Eliade, Mircea. *The Forge and the Crucible*. Trans. Stephen Corrin. London: Rider, 1962; rpt. New York: Harper and Row, 1971.

————. *Rites and Symbols of Initiation: The Mysteries of Birth and Rebirth*. Originally entitled: *Birth and Rebirth*. Trans. Willard R. Trask. 1958; rpt. New York: Harper Colophon, 1975.

————. *Patanjali and Yoga*. Trans. Charles Lam Markmann. 1969; rpt. New York: Schocken, 1975.

————. *Shamanism: Archaic Techniques of Ecstasy*. New York: Bollingen Foundation-Pantheon, 1964.

————. *Yoga: Immortality and Freedom*. 1958; rpt. Princeton: Bollingen Foundation-Princeton University Press, 1969.

Ellenberger, Henri F. *The Discovery of the Unconscious: The History and Evolution of Dynamic Psychiatry*. New York: Basic, 1970.

Elior, Rachel. "The Concept of God in Hekhalot Literature." In *Binah, Volume 2: Studies in Jewish Thought*. Ed. Joseph Dan. 97–120. New York: Praeger, 1989.

Eriugena. *Periphyseon (The Division of Nature)*. Trans. I. P. Sheldon-Williams and John J. O'Meara. Montreal: Bellarmin; Washington: Dumbarton Oaks, 1987.

Fabricius, Johannes. *Alchemy: The Medieval Alchemists and their Royal Art*, 2nd ed. Wellingborough, U.K.: Aquarian, 1989.

Faivre, Antoine. "Esotericism." In *The Encyclopedia of Religion*. Ed. Mircea Eliade. New York: Macmillan; London: Collier Macmillan, 1987. Rpt. in *Hidden Truths: Magic, Alchemy, and the Occult*, ed. Lawrence E. Sullivan. New York: Macmillan; London: Collier Macmillan, 1989.

Fakhry, Majid. "Three Varieties of Mysticism in Islam." *International Journal for the Philosophy of Religion* 2/4 (1971), 193–207.

Federn, Paul. "Some Variations in Ego-Feeling." *International Journal of Psycho-Analysis* 7 (1926), 434–44.

Festugière, R. P. *La Révélation d'Hermès Trismégiste, Vol. I. L'Astrologie et les sciences occultes*, 2nd ed. 1950; rpt. Paris: Société d'Edition "Les Belles Lettres," 1983.

Filippani-Ronconi, Pio. "The Soteriological Cosmology of Central-Asiatic Isma'ilism." In *Isma'ili Contributions to Islamic Culture*. Ed. Seyyed Hossein Nasr. Tehran: Imperian Iranian Academy of Philosophy, 1977.

Flournoy, Theodore. *From India to the Planet Mars: A Study of a Case of Somnambulism with Glossolalia.* 1900; rpt. New Hyde Park, N.Y.: University Books, 1963.

Flusser, David. "Scholem's recent book on Merkabah Literature." *Journal of Jewish Studies* 11 (1960), 59–68.

Foerster, Werner. *Gnosis: A Selection of Gnostic Texts,* 2 vols. Trans. R. McL. Wilson. Oxford: Clarendon, 1972.

Fordham, Michael. "Active Imagination and Imaginative Activity." *Journal of Analytical Psychology* 1 (1955–56), 207–8.

———. "Active Imagination—Deintegration or Disintegration?" *Journal of Analytical Psychology* 12 (1967), 51–66.

Forman, Robert K. C., ed. *The Problem of Pure Consciousness: Mysticism and Philosophy.* New York and Oxford: Oxford University Press, 1990.

Francis and Clare. *The Complete Works.* Trans. Regis J. Armstrong and Ignatius C. Brady. New York: Paulist, 1982.

Freemon, Frank R. "A Differential Diagnosis of the Inspirational Spells of Muhammad the Prophet of Islam." *Epilepsia* 17 (1976), 423–27.

Freud, Sigmund. "Civilization and Its Discontents" [1930]. Rpt. in *Standard Edition,* vol. 21, 64–145.

———. *The Interpretation of Dreams* [1900]. Rpt. in *The Standard Edition of the Complete Psychological Works of Sigmund Freud.* Ed. James Strachey, with Anna Freud, Alix Strachey, and Alan Tyson. Vols. 4–5. London: Hogarth, 1966.

———. *New Introductory Lectures on Psycho-Analysis* [1933]. Rpt. in *Standard Edition,* vol. 22.

Fromm, Erika. "The Nature of Hypnosis and Other Altered States of Consciousness: An Ego Psychological Theory." In *Hypnosis: Developments in Research and New Perspectives,* 2nd ed. Ed. Erika Fromm and Ronald E. Shor. New York: Aldine, 1979.

Fulcanelli: Master Alchemist. *Le Mystère des Cathèdrales: Esoteric interpretation of the Hermetic Symbols of the Great Work* [Paris: Jean Schemit, 1926]. Trans. Mary Sworder. London: Neville Spearman, 1971.

Gackenbach, Jayne, and Jane Bosveld. *Control Your Dreams: How Lucid Dreaming Can Help You Uncover Your Hidden Desires, Confront Your Hidden Fears, and Explore the Frontiers of Human Consciousness.* New York: Harper and Row, 1989.

Gardner, Edmund G. *Dante and the Mystics: A Study of the Mystical Aspect of the Divina Commedia and Its Relations with some of its Mediaeval Sources.* London: Dent; New York: E. P. Dutton, 1913.

Garfield, Patricia. *Creative Dreaming.* 1974; rpt. New York: Ballantine, 1976.

Garside, Bruce. "Language and the Interpretation of Mystical Experience." *International Journal for the Philosophy of Religion* 3 (1972), 93–102.

Gawain, Shakti. *Creative Visualization.* San Rafael, Calif.: New World Library, 1978.

Geber. *The Works of Geber: Englished by Richard Russell, 1678, a New Edition.* Introd. E. J. Holmyard. London: Dent; New York: Dutton, 1928.

Gerard, R. *Symbolic Visualization: A Method of Psychosynthesis.* Greenville, Del: Psychosynthesis Research Foundation, 1968.

Gersh, Stephen. "Platonism-Neoplatonism-Aristotelianism: A Twelfth-Century Metaphysical System and Its Sources." In *Renaissance and Renewal in the Twelfth Century.* Ed. Robert L. Benson and Giles Constable, with Carol D. Lanham, 512–34. Cambridge: Harvard University Press, 1982; rpt. Toronto: University of Toronto Press, 1991.

[Gertrude, St.] *The Life and Revelations of Saint Gertrude: Virgin and Abbess of the Order of St. Benedict.* 1862; rpt. Westminster, Md: Christian Classics, 1983.

Ghaiti, Najm ad-Din al-. "The Story of the Night Journey and the Ascension." In *A Reader on Islam: Passages from Standard Arabic Writings Illustrative of the Beliefs and Practices of Muslims.* Ed. Arthur Jeffery. 621–39. 'S-Gravenhage: Mouton, 1962.

Gilbert, Alvin R. "Pseudo-Mind Expansion Through Psychedelics and Brain-Wave-Programming Versus True Mind-Expansion Through Life Conditioning to the Absolute." *Psychologia* 14 (1971), 187–92.

Gilbert, R. A. *A. E. Waite: Magician of Many Parts.* Wellingborough, U.K.: Crucible, 1987.

Gimello, Robert M. "Mysticism and Meditation." In *Mysticism and Philosophical Analysis.* Ed. Steven T. Katz. 170–99. London: Sheldon, 1978.

Ginsburg, Elliot K. *The Sabbath in the Classical Kabbalah.* Albany: State University of New York Press, 1989.

Gleadow, Rupert. *The Origin of the Zodiac.* New York: Atheneum, 1969.

Goitein, S. D. "Muhammad's Inspiration by Judaism." *Journal of Jewish Studies* 9 (1958), 149–62.

Goldin, Frederick. *Lyrics of the Troubadours and Trouveres: An Anthology and a History.* Garden City, N.Y.: Anchor-Doubleday, 1973.

Goleman, Daniel. "The Buddha on Meditation and States of Consciousness. Part I: The Teachings." *Journal of Transpersonal Psychology* 4 (1972), 1–44.

———. "A Taxonomy of Meditation-Specific Altered States." *Journal of Altered States of Consciousness* 4/2 (1978–79), 203–13.

Good, Deirdre J. *Reconstructing the Tradition of Sophia in Gnostic Literature.* Atlanta: Scholars Press, 1987.

Graham, William A. *Divine Word and Prophetic Word in Early Islam: A Reconsideration of the Sources, with Special Reference to the Divine Saying or Hadith Qudsi.* The Hague: Mouton, 1977.

Grant, Robert M. "Gnostic Spirituality." In *Christian Spirituality: Origins to the Twelfth Century.* Ed. Bernard McGinn and John Meyendorff, with Jean Leclercq. New York: Crossroad, 1987.

Grof, Christina, and Stanislav Grof. *The Stormy Search for the Self: A Guide to Personal Growth through Transformational Crisis.* Los Angeles: Jeremy P. Tarcher, 1990.

Grof, Stanislav. *Realms of the Human Unconscious: Observations from LSD Research.* New York: Viking, 1975.

Grof, Stanislav, and Christina Grof. *Beyond Death: The gates of consciousness.* London: Thames and Hudson, 1980.

———, eds. *Spiritual Emergency: When Personal Transformation Becomes a Crisis.* Los Angeles: Jeremy P. Tarcher, 1989.

Gruenwald, Ithamar. *Apocalyptic and Merkavah Mysticism.* Leiden: E. J. Brill, 1980.

———. *From Apocalypticism to Gnosticism: Studies in Apocalypticism, Merkavah Mysticism and Gnosticism.* Frankfurt am Main: Peter Lang, 1988.

———. "Ha-ʾIspeqlariyah we-ha-Tekhiniqah shel ha-Hazon ha-Nebuʾi we-ha-ʾApoqalipti (Mirrors and the Technique of Prophetic and Apocalyptic Vision)." *Beth Mikra* 40 (1970), 95–97.

———. "Halakhic Material in Codex Gnosticus V, 4: *The Second Apocalypse of James?*" In *From Apocalypticism to Gnosticism: Studies in Apocalypticism, Merkavah Mysticism and Gnosticism,* 279–94. Frankfurt am Main: Verlag Peter Lang, 1988.

———. "Jewish Sources for the Gnostic Texts from Nag Hammadi?" In *Proceedings of the Sixth World Congress of Jewish Studies.* Jerusalem:

World Union of Jewish Studies, 1977. Rpt. *From Apocalypticism to Gnosticism: Studies in Apocalypticism, Merkavah Mysticism and Gnosticism,* 207–20. Frankfurt am Main: Verlag Peter Lang, 1988.

———. "Knowledge and Vision: Towards a Clarification of two 'gnostic' concepts in the light of their alleged origins." *Israel Oriental Studies* 3 (1973), 63–107.

———. "Merkavah Mysticism and Gnosticism." In *Studies in Jewish Mysticism.* Ed. Joseph Dan and Frank Talmage. 41–55. Cambridge, Mass.: Association for Jewish Studies, 1982.

———. "A Preliminary Critical Edition of *Sefer Yezira.*" *Israel Oriental Studies* 1 (1971), 132–77.

———. "Re'uyot Yehezqel (The Visions of Ezekiel)." In *Temirin: Texts and Studies in Kabbala and Hasidism,* ed. Israel Weinstock. Vol 1, 101–39. Jerusalem: Mossad Harav Kook, 1972.

Guenon, Rene. *The Lord of the World.* Moorcote, U.K.: Coombe Springs, 1983.

———. *The Multiple States of Being* [1932]. Trans. Joscelyn Godwin. New York: Larson, 1984.

Gupta, Sanjukta, Dirk Jan Hoens, and Teun Goudriaan. *Hindu Tantrism.* Leiden: Brill, 1979.

Gwilliam, Stanford. "Divine Light and the *Divine Comedy:* the Shekinah Experience of Dante Alighieri." *Journal of Altered States of Consciousness* 3/2 (1977–78), 181–90.

Haardt, Robert. *Gnosis: Character and Testimony.* Trans. J. F. Hendry. Leiden: Brill, 1971.

Hadewijch. *The Complete Works.* Trans. Columba Hart. New York: Paulist, 1980.

Hadot, Pierre. "Neoplatonist Spirituality. I. Plotinus and Porphyry." In *Classical Mediterranean Spirituality.* Ed. A. Hilary Armstrong, 230–49. New York: Crossroad, 1986.

Halperin, David J. *The Faces of the Chariot: Early Jewish Responses to Ezekiel's Vision.* Tübingen: J. C. Mohr [Paul Siebeck], 1988.

———. "Hekhalot and Mi'raj: Observations on the Heavenly Journey in Judaism and Islam." Paper delivered at the University of Chicago conference, "Other Realms: Death, Ecstasy, and Otherworldly Journeys in Recent Scholarship," May 16–17, 1991. Unpublished.

———. "The Ibn Sayyad Traditions and the Legend of Al-Dajjal." *Journal of the American Oriental Society* 96 (1976), 213–25.

——— . *The Merkabah in Rabbinic Literature*. New Haven, Conn.: American Oriental Society, 1980.

——— . "A New Edition of the Hekhalot Literature." *Journal of the American Oriental Society* 104 (1984), 3/543–52.

——— . "A Sexual Image in Hekhalot Rabbati and Its Implications." In *Proceedings of the First International Conference on the History of Jewish Mysticism: Early Jewish Mysticism*. Ed. Joseph Dan. *Jerusalem Studies in Jewish Thought* VI/1–2, 117–32. Jerusalem: Magnes Press, 1987.

Hammer, Max. "The Directed Daydream Technique." *Psychotherapy* 4 (1967), 173–81.

Hannah, Barbara. *Encounters with the Soul: Active Imagination as Developed by C. G. Jung*. Boston: Sigo, 1981.

——— . "Some Remarks on Active Imagination." *Spring 1953,* 38–58.

Haq, Md. Enamul. (1948) "Sufi Movement in Bengal." *Indo-Iranica* 3/1, 9–32.

——— . (1949) "Sufi Movement in India." *Indo-Iranica* 3/3, 11–41.

Harary, Keith, and Pamela Weintraub. *Lucid Dreams in 30 Days: The Creative Sleep Program*. New York: St. Martin's, 1989.

Haring, Nikolaus M. "John Scottus in Twelfth-Century Angelology." In *The Mind of Eriugena: Papers of a Colloquium, Dublin, 14–18 July 1970*. Ed. John J. O'Meara and Ludwig Bieler. 158–69. Dublin: Irish University Press-Royal Irish Academy, 1973.

Harman, Willis W. "The Use of the Consciousness-Expanding Drugs." *Main Currents in Modern Thought* 20 (1963), 5–14.

Hartmann, Heinz, Ernst Kris, and Rudolph M. Loewenstein. *Papers on Psychoanalytic Psychology*. New York: International Universities Press, 1964.

Havens, Joseph. "A Working Paper: Memo on the Religious Implications of the Consciousness-Changing Drugs (LSD, Mescalin, Psilocybin)." *Journal for the Scientific Study of Religion* 3 (1964), 216–26.

Hayakawa, S. I., ed. *Etc.: A Review of General Semantics* 22/4 (1965).

Heiler, Friedrich. *Prayer: A Study in the History and Psychology of Religion* [1920]. Trans. Samuel McComb with J. Edgar Park. London: Oxford University Press, 1932.

Hennecke, Edgar. *New Testament Apocrypha, Volume Two: Writings Relating to the Apostles; Apocalypses and Related Subjects,* ed. Wilhelm Schneemelcher and R. McL. Wilson. Philadelphia: Westminster Press, 1964.

Heron, Woodburn, B. D. Doane, and T. H. Scott. "Visual Disturbances after Prolonged Perceptual Isolation." *Canadian Journal of Psychology* 10 (1956), 13–18.

Heschel, Abraham Joshua. *The Prophets,* 2 vols. New York: Harper and Row, 1962.

Hildegard of Bingen. *Scivias.* Trans. Columba Hart and Jane Bishop. New York: Paulist, 1990.

Hillgarth, J. N. *Ramon Lull and Lullism in Fourteenth-Century France.* Oxford: Clarendon, 1971.

Hitchcock, Ethan Allen. *Remarks upon Alchemy and the Alchemists.* Boston: Crosby, Nichols, 1857; rpt. Los Angeles: Philosophical Research Society, 1976.

Hockley, Frederick. *The Rosicrucian Seer: Magical Writings of Frederick Hockley.* Ed. John Hamill. Wellingborough, U.K.: Aquarian, 1986.

Hodgson, Marshall G. S. "How Did the Early Shi'a Become Sectarian?" *Journal of the American Oriental Society* 75 (1955), 1–13.

——— . *The Order of Assassins: The Struggle of the Early Nizari Isma'ilis Against the Islamic World.* 'S-Gravenhage: Mouton, 1955.

——— . *The Venture of Islam: Conscience and History in a World Civilization, Volume Two: The Expansion of Islam in the Middle Periods.* Chicago: University of Chicago Press, 1974.

Hoffman, Lawrence A. "Censoring In and Censoring Out: A Function of Liturgical Language." In *Ancient Synagogues: The State of Research.* Ed. Joseph Gutmann. 19–37. Chico, Calif.: Scholars Press, 1981.

Hoffman-Ladd, Valerie J. "Mysticism and Sexuality in Sufi Thought and Life." *Mystics Quarterly* (1992) [forthcoming].

Holmyard, Erik John. *Alchemy.* Harmondsworth: Penguin, 1957.

——— . "Alchemy and Mysticism." *Nature* 118, no. 2981 (1926), 869–70.

——— . "The Emerald Table." *Nature* 112 (1923), 525–26.

Holt, Robert R. *Freud Reappraised: A Fresh Look at Psychoanalytic Theory.* New York: Guilford, 1989.

Honko, Lauri. *Geisterglaube In Ingermanland.* FF Communications, 185. Helsinki: Academia Scientiarum Fennica, 1962.

——— . "Memorates and the Study of Folk Beliefs." *Journal of the Folklore Institute* 1 (1964), 5–19.

Hopkins, Arthur John. *Alchemy, Child of Greek Philosophy.* New York: Columbia University Press, 1934.

———. "Bronzing Methods in the Alchemistic Leyden Papyri." *The Chemical News* 85 (1902), 49–52.

———. "A defence of Egyptian alchemy." *Isis* 28 (1938), 424–31.

———. "Earliest Alchemy." *The Scientific Monthly* 6 (1918), 530–37.

———. "A Modern Theory of Alchemy." *Isis* 7 (1925), 58–76.

———. "A study of the Kerotakis Process as given by Zosimus and later alchemical writers." *Isis* 29 (1938), 326–54.

———. "Transmutation by Color: A Study of Earliest Alchemy." *Studien zur Geschichte der Chemie: Festgabe Edmund O. v. Lippman*. Ed. Julius Ruska. Berlin: Julius Springer, 1927.

Horsley, Richard A. "Spiritual Marriage with Sophia." *Vigiliae Christianae* 33 (1979), 30–54.

Howe, Ellic, ed. *The Alchemist of the Golden Dawn: The Letters of the Revd W. A. Ayton to F. L. Gardner and Others 1886–1905*. Wellingborough, U.K.: Aquarian, 1985.

Hull, R. F. C. "Bibliographical Notes on Active Imagination in the Works of C. G. Jung." *Spring 1971*, 115–20.

Humbert, Elie G. "Active Imagination: Theory and Practice." *Spring 1971*, 101–14.

Husaini, S. A. Q. *The Pantheistic Monism of Ibn al-'Arabi*. Lahore, Pakistan: Sh. Muhammad Ashraf, 1970.

Huxley, Aldous. *The Doors of Perception* [1954] and *Heaven and Hell* [1956]. Rpt. London: Granada, 1977.

Idel, Moshe. *Kabbalah: New Perspectives*. New Haven: Yale University Press, 1988.

———. "Le-Gilgulleha shel Tekhiniqah Qedumah shel Hazon Nebu'i Bime ha-Benayim (On the Medieval Development of an Ancient Technique for Prophetic Vision)." *Sinai* 86 (1979–80), 1–2/1–7.

———. *The Mystical Experience in Abraham Abulafia*. Trans. Jonathan Chipman. Albany: State University of New York Press, 1988.

———. "The Origin of Alchemy According to Zosimos and a Hebrew Parallel." *Revue des Études juives* 145 (1986), 117–24.

'Iraqi, Abu 'L-Qasim Muhammad ibn Ahmad al-. *Kitab al-'Ilm Al-Muktasab Fi Zira'at Adh-Dhahab: Book of Knowledge Acquired Concerning the Cultivation of Gold*. Ed. and trans. E. J. Holmyard. Paris: Paul Geuthner, 1923.

Ishaq, Muhammad Ibn. *The Life of Muhammad: A Translation of Ishaq's Sirat Rasul Allah.* Trans. A. Guillaume. London: Geoffrey Cumberlege-Oxford University Press, 1955.

Ivanow, W. [Ivanov, Vladimir Alekseevich]. *Ismaili Tradition Concerning the Rise of the Fatimids.* London: Humphrey Milford-Oxford University Press, 1942.

————. *Studies in Early Persian Ismailism,* 2nd ed. Bombay: Ismaili Society, 1955.

Jacobs, Louis. *Jewish Mystical Testimonies.* New York: Schocken, 1977.

Jaffe, Aniela. *Was C. G. Jung A Mystic? And Other Essays.* Einsiedeln, Switzerland: Daimon, 1989.

Jaki, Stanley L. *The Savior of Science.* Washington, DC: Regnery Gateway, 1988.

James, William. *The Varieties of Religious Experience: A Study in Human Nature.* 1902; New York: New American Library, 1958.

Janowitz, Naomi. *The Poetics of Ascent: Theories of Language in a Rabbinic Ascent Text.* Albany: State University of New York Press, 1989.

Jeauneau, Edouard. "Le renouveau erigenien du XIIᵉ siècle." In *Eriugena Redivivus: Zur Wirkungsgeschichte seines Denkens im Mittelalter und im Übergang zur Neuzeit.* Ed. Werner Beierwaltes, 26–46. Heidelberg: Carl Winter-Universitätsverlag, 1987.

John of the Cross, St. *Collected Works.* Trans. Kieran Kavanaugh and Otilio Rodriguez. Washington: Institute of Carmelite Studies, 1973.

Johnson, Robert A. *Inner Work: Using Dreams and Active Imagination for Personal Growth.* San Francisco: Harper and Row, 1986.

Jonas, Hans. *The Gnostic Religion: The message of the alien God and the beginnings of Christianity,* 2nd ed. Boston: Beacon, 1963.

————. "Myth and Mysticism: A Study of Objectification and Interiorization In Religious Thought." *Journal of Religion* 49 (1969), 315–29.

Jones, Ernest. *On the Nightmare,* 2nd ed. New York: Liveright, 1951.

Josten, C. H. "A Translation of John Dee's 'Monas Hieroglyphica' " (Antwerp, 1564), With an Introduction and Annotations.' *Ambix* 12 (1964), 84–221.

Jung, Carl Gustav. *Aion: Researches into the Phenomenology of the Self,* 2nd ed. Trans. R. F. C. Hull. Collected Works, vol. 9, pt. 2. Princeton: Princeton University Press, 1968.

————. *Alchemical Studies.* Trans. R. F. C. Hull. Collected Works, vol. 13. Princeton: Princeton University Press, 1967.

————. *Analytical Psychology: Its Theory and Practice. The Tavistock Lectures.* New York: Pantheon Books-Random House, 1968.

————. *"Exercitia Spiritualia* of St. Ignatius of Loyola: Notes on Lectures (1939)." *Spring 1977,* 183–200; *Spring 1978,* 28–36.

————. *Memories, Dreams, Reflections,* 2nd ed. Ed. Aniela Jaffe. Trans. Richard and Clara Winston. 1973; rpt. New York: Vintage-Random House, 1989.

————. *Mysterium Coniunctionis: An Inquiry into the Separation and Synthesis of Psychic Opposites in Alchemy,* 2nd ed. Trans. R. F. C. Hull. Collected Works, vol. 14. Princeton: Princeton University Press, 1970.

————. *The Practice of Psychotherapy: Essays on the Psychology of the Transference and Other Subjects,* 2nd ed. Trans. R. F. C. Hull. Collected Works, vol. 16. Princeton: Princeton University Press, 1966.

————. *The Process of Individuation: Notes on Lectures at the ETH, Zurich.* Trans. and ed. Barbara Hannah. Privately issued.

————. *Psychology and Alchemy,* 2nd ed. Trans. R. F. C. Hull. Collected Works, vol. 12. Princeton: Princeton University Press, 1968.

————. *Psychology and Religion: West and East,* 2nd ed. Trans. R. F. C. Hull. Collected Works, vol. 11. Princeton: Princeton University Press, 1969.

————. *The Symbolic Life: Miscellaneous Writings,* 2nd ed. Trans. R. F. C. Hull. Collected Works, vol. 18. Princeton: Princeton University Press, 1980.

————. *"The Transcendent Function."* In *The Structure and Dynamics of the Psyche.* Trans. R. F. C. Hull. Collected Works, vol. 8. New York: Pantheon Books, 1960.

————. *Two Essays on Analytical Psychology,* 2nd ed. Trans. R. F. C. Hull. Collected Works, vol. 7. Princeton: Princeton University Press, 1966.

————. *"The Visions of Zosimos."* In *Alchemical Studies,* 57–108.

————. *The Visions Seminars: From the Complete Notes of Mary Foote.* 2 vols. Zurich: Spring Publications, 1976.

Kakar, Sudhir. *Shamans, Mystics and Doctors: A Psychological Inquiry into India and Its Healing Traditions.* New York: Knopf, 1982.

Kalupahana, David J. *The Principles of Buddhist Psychology.* Albany: State University of New York Press, 1987.

Katsh, Abraham I. *Judaism and the Koran: Biblical and Talmudic Backgrounds of the Koran and Its Commentaries.* 1954; rpt. New York: A. S. Barnes and Company, 1962.

Katz, Steven T. "Language, Epistemology, and Mysticism." In *Mysticism and Philosophical Analysis*. Ed. Steven T. Katz. 22–74. London: Sheldon, 1978.

———. "Models, Modeling and Mystical Training." *Religion* 12 (1982), 247–75.

———. "The 'Conservative' Character of Mystical Experience." In *Mysticism and Religious Traditions*. Ed. Steven T. Katz. 3–60. Oxford: Oxford University Press, 1983.

King, Charles William. *The Gnostics and Their Remains: Ancient and Modern*, 2nd ed. 1887; rpt. Savage: Wizards Bookshelf, 1973.

King, Francis, ed. *Astral Projection, Ritual Magic, and Alchemy: Golden Dawn Material by S. L. MacGregor Mathers and Others*. Rochester, Vt.: Destiny, 1987.

———. *The Secret Rituals of the O.T.O.* New York: Samuel Weiser, 1973.

King, Francis, and Isabel Sutherland. *The Rebirth of Magic*. London: Corgi, 1982.

Klibansky, Raymond. *The Continuity of the Platonic Tradition During the Middle Ages: Outlines of a Corpus Platonicum Medii Aevi*. London: Warburg Institute, 1937.

Knowles, David. *The Evolution of Medieval Thought*. New York: Random House, 1962.

Kornfield, Jack. "Intensive Insight Meditation: A Phenomenological Study." *Journal of Transpersonal Psychology* 11 (1979), 41–58.

Kotansky, Roy. "Incantations and Prayers for Salvation on Inscribed Greek Amulets." In *Magika Hiera: Ancient Greek Magic and Religion*. Ed. Christopher A. Faraone and Dirk Obbink. 107–37. New York and Oxford: Oxford University Press, 1991.

Krippner, Stanley, and Richard Davidson. "Religious Implications of Paranormal Events Occurring During Chemically-Induced 'Psychedelic' Experience." *Pastoral Psychology* 21/206 (1970), 27–34.

Kristeva, Julia. *In the Beginning Was Love: Psychoanalysis and Faith*. Trans. Arthur Goldhammer. New York: Columbia University Press, 1987.

Krupp, E. C. "Astronomers, Pyramids, and Priests." In *In Search of Ancient Astronomies*. Ed. E. C. Krupp. Garden City, N.Y.: Doubleday, 1977.

Kurtz, Paul S. "Similarities and Differences Between Religious Mysticism and Drug-Induced Experiences." *Journal of Humanistic Psychology* 3/2 (1963), 146–54.

LaBarge, Stephen. *Lucid Dreaming*. Los Angeles: Jeremy P. Tarcher, 1985.

Landau, Rom. "The Philosophy of Ibn 'Arabi." *Muslim World* 47 (1957), 146–60.

Laski, Marghanita. *Ecstasy: A Study of some Secular and Religious Experiences*. 1962; rpt. New York: Greenwood, 1968.

Layton, Bentley, trans. *The Gnostic Scriptures*. Garden City, N.Y.: Doubleday, 1987.

Leary, Timothy. "The Religious Experience: Its Production and Interpretation." *Psychedelic Review* 1/3 (1964), 324–46.

Leary, Timothy, and Walter Houston Clark. "Religious Implications of Consciousness Expanding Drugs." *Religious Education* 58/2 (1963), 251–56.

Leuner, Hanscarl. "Basic Principles and Therapeutic Efficacy of Guided Affective Imagery (GAI)." Trans. Augusta Arthur. In *The Power of Human Imagination: New Methods in Psychotherapy*, ed. Jerome L. Singer and Kenneth S. Pope, 125–66. New York: Plenum, 1978.

——— . "Guided Affective Imagery (GAI): A Method of Intensive Psychotherapy." *American Journal of Psychotherapy* 23/1 (1969), 4–22.

——— . "Guided Affective Imagery: An Account of Its Development." *Journal of Mental Imagery* 1/1 (1977), 73–92.

——— . "The Role of Imagery in Psychotherapy." In *New Dimensions in Psychiatry: A World View*. Ed. Silvano Arieti and Gerard Chrzanowski. 169–99. New York: Wiley, 1975.

Levi, Eliphas. *Transcendental Magic: Its Doctrine and Ritual*, 2nd ed. Trans. A. E. Waite. London, 1923.

Levine, Lee I., ed. *Ancient Synagogues Revealed*. Jerusalem: Israel Exploration Society, 1981.

Lewis, Bernard. *The Assassins: A Radical Sect in Islam*. New York: Basic Books, 1968.

——— . *The Origins of Isma'ilism: A study of the historical background of the Fatimid Caliphate*. Cambridge: W. Heffer, 1940.

Lille, Alan of. *Anticlaudianus, or, The Good and Perfect Man*. Trans. James J. Sheridan. Toronto: Pontifical Institute of Mediaeval Studies, 1973.

Lilly, John. "Mental effects of reduction of ordinary levels of physical stimuli on intact, healthy persons." *Psychiatric Research Reports* 5 (1956), 1–9.

Lilly, John C., and Jay T. Shurley. "Experiments in Solitude. In Maximum Achievable Physical Isolation with Water Suspension, of Intact

Healthy Persons." In *Psychophysiological Aspects of Space Flight*. Ed. Bernard E. Flaherty. 238–47. New York: Columbia University Press, 1961.

Lindblom, Johannes. *Prophecy in Ancient Israel*. Philadelphia: Fortress, 1962.

Lindsay, Jack. *The Origins of Alchemy in Graeco-Roman Egypt*. London: Frederick Muller, 1979.

Lorris, Guillaume de, and Jean de Meun. *The Romance of the Rose*. Trans. Harry W. Robbins. New York: Dutton, 1962.

Louth, Andrew. *The Origins of the Christian Mystical Tradition: From Plato to Denys*. Oxford: Clarendon Press, 1981.

Lull, Ramon. *The Book of the Lover and the Beloved*, 2nd ed. Trans. E. Allison Peers; ed. Kenneth Leech. 1946; rpt. London: Sheldon Press, 1978.

———. *Selected Works of Ramon Llull (1232–1316)*. 2 vols., ed. and trans. Anthony Bonner. Princeton: Princeton University Press, 1985.

MacDonald, Duncan Black. *The Religious Attitude and Life in Islam*. Chicago, 1909.

MacRae, George W. "The Jewish Background of the Gnostic Sophia Myth." *Novum Testamentum* 12 (1970), 86–101.

———. "Sleep and Awakening in Gnostic Texts." In *The Origins of Gnosticism: Colloquium of Messina, 13–18 April 1966*. Ed. Ugo Bianchi. Leiden: Brill, 1967.

Madelung, Wilferd. "Isma'iliyya." In *Encyclopaedia of Islam*, 2nd ed. Ed. E. van Donzel, B. Lewis, and Ch. Pellat, vol. 4, 198–206. Leiden: Brill, 1978.

———. "Karmati." *In Encyclopaedia of Islam*, 2nd ed. Ed. E. van Donzel, B. Lewis, and Ch. Pellat, vol. 4, 660–65. Leiden: Brill, 1978.

———. "Shiism: Isma'iliyah." In *The Encyclopedia of Religion*. Ed. Mircea Eliade, Vol. 13, 247–60. New York: Macmillan, 1987.

———. "Shiism: An Overview." In *The Encyclopedia of Religion*. Ed. Mircea Eliade, Vol. 13, 242–47. New York: Macmillan, 1987.

Makarem, Sami N. "Isma'ili and Druze Cosmogony in Relation to Plotinus and Aristotle." In *Islamic Theology and Philosophy: Studies in Honor of George F. Hourani*. Ed. Michael E. Marmura, 81–91. Albany: State University of New York Press, 1984.

Mala, S. Babs. "Self-Realization in the Mystical Thought of al-Kubra: An Interpretation." *Orita* 12/1 (1978), 51–65.

Mansfeld, Jaap. "Bad World and Demiurge: A 'Gnostic' Motif from Parmenides and Empedocles to Lucretius and Philo." In *Studies in Gnosticism and Hellenistic Religions.* Ed. R. van den Broek and M. J. Vermaseren. 261–314. Leiden: Brill, 1981.

Margoliouth, David Samuel. *Mohammed and the Rise of Islam.* New York and London: Putnam's, 1905.

Markham, Ursula. *The Elements of Visualisation.* Longmead, U.K.: Element Books, 1989.

Martin, Jr., Luther H. "A History of the Psychological Interpretation of Alchemy." *Ambix* 22 (1975), 10–20.

Maslow, Abraham H. *The Farther Reaches of Human Nature.* 1971; rpt. Harmondsworth: Penguin, 1978.

———. "Lessons from the Peak-Experiences." *Journal of Humanistic Psychology* 2 (1962), 9–18.

———. *Religions, Values, and Peak Experiences.* 1964; rpt. Harmondsworth: Penguin, 1976.

———. *Toward a Psychology of Being.* 1968; rpt. New York: Van Nostrand, n.d.

Massignon, Louis. *The Passion of al-Hallaj: Mystic and Martyr of Islam,* 4 vols. Trans. Herbert Mason. Princeton: Princeton University Press, 1982.

———. *Salman Pak and the Spiritual Beginnings of Iranian Islam.* trans. Jamshedji Maneckji Unvala. Bombay: Bombay University Press, 1955.

Masters, Robert E. L. and Jean Houston. "Toward an Individual Psychedelic Psychotherapy." In *Psychedelics: The Uses and Implications of Hallucinogenic Drugs.* Ed. Bernard S. Aaronson and Humphry Osmond. 1968; rpt. Garden City, N.Y.: Doubleday-Anchor, 1970.

———. *The Varieties of Psychedelic Experience.* 1966; rpt. London: Turnstone, 1973.

Matt, Daniel C. "*Ayin:* The Concept of Nothingness in Jewish Mysticism." In *The Problem of Pure Consciousness: Mysticism and Philosophy.* Ed. Robert K. C. Forman. 121–59. New York: Oxford University Press, 1990.

Mavromatis, Andreas. *Hypnagogia: The Unique State of Consciousness between Wakefulness and Sleep.* London and New York: Routledge, 1987.

McDaniel, June. *The Madness of the Saints: Ecstatic Religion in Bengal.* Chicago: University of Chicago Press, 1989.

McDannell, Colleen, and Bernhard Lang. *Heaven: A History.* New Haven: Yale University Press, 1988; rpt. New York: Vintage Books, 1990.

McGinn, Bernard. *The Foundations of Mysticism. (Vol. I of The Presence of God: A History of Western Christian Mysticism.)* New York: Crossroad, 1991.

McIntosh, Christopher. *The Rosy Cross Unveiled: The History, Mythology, and Ritual of an Occult Order.* Wellingborough, U.K.: Aquarian, 1980.

Mechthild of Magdeburg. *The Revelations of Mechthild of Magdeburg (1219–1297), or, The Flowing Light of the Godhead.* Trans. Lucy Menzies. London: Longmans, Green, 1953.

Menard, Jacques E. "Normative Self-Definition in Gnosticism." In *Jewish and Christian Self-Definition, Volume One: The Shaping of Christianity in the Second and Third Centuries.* Ed. E. P. Sanders, 134–50, 238–40. Philadelphia: Fortress, 1980.

Menocal, Maria Rosa. *The Arabic Role in Medieval Literary History: A Forgotten Heritage.* Philadelphia: University of Pennsylvania Press, 1987.

Merkur, Dan. "Adaptive Symbolism and the Theory of Myth: The Symbolic Understanding of Myths in Inuit Religion." In *Psychoanalytic Study of Society, Volume 13: Essays in honor of Weston LaBarre.* Ed. L. Bryce Boyer and Simon Grolnick. 63–94. Hillsdale, N.J.: Analytic Press, 1988.

———. *Becoming Half Hidden: Shamanism and Initiation Among the Inuit.* Stockholm: Almqvist and Wiksell, 1985.

———. "The Capacity for Religiosity: A Psychoanalytic Theory" [unpublished manuscript].

———. "The Induction of Mystical Union: Two Hasidic Teachings." *Studia Mystica* 14/4 (1991), 70–76.

———. "The Nature of the Hypnotic State: A Psychoanalytic Approach." *International Review of Psycho-Analysis* 11/3 (1984), 345–54.

———. "The Prophecies of Jeremiah." *The American Imago* 42/1 (1985), 1–37.

———. "Prophetic Initiation in Israel and Judah." In *The Psychoanalytic Study of Society, Volume 12: Essays in honor of George Devereux.* Ed. L. Bryce Boyer and Simon A. Grolnick. 37–67. Hillsdale, N.J.: Analytic Press, 1988.

———. "Unitive Experiences and the State of Trance." In *Mystical Union and Montheistic Religion: An Ecumenical Dialogue.* Ed. Moshe Idel and Bernard McGinn. New York: Macmillan, 1989.

——— . "The Visionary Practices of Jewish Apocalyptists." *The Psycho-analytic Study of Society, Volume 14: Essays in honor of Paul Parin.* Ed. L. Bryce Boyer and Simon A. Grolnick. 119–48. Hillsdale, N.J.: Analytic Press, 1989.

Merlan, Philip. *Monopsychism Mysticism Metaconsciousness: problems of the soul in the neoaristotelian and neoplatonic tradition.* The Hague: Nijhoff, 1963.

Merton, Thomas. "The Inner Experience: Infused Contemplation (V)." Ed. Patrick Hart. *Cistercian Studies* 19 (1984), 62–78.

——— . *Thomas Merton on Saint Bernard.* Kalamazoo, Mich.: Cistercian, 1980.

Metzner, Ralph. ed. *The Ecstatic Adventure.* New York: Macmillan, 1968.

Moosa, Matti. *Extremist Shiites: The Ghulat Sects.* Syracuse: Syracuse University Press, 1988.

Moraczewski, Albert S. "Mescaline, Madness and Mysticism." *Thought* 42 (1967), 358–82.

Morgan, Michael A., trans. *Sepher Ha-Razim: The Book of the Mysteries.* Chico, Calif.: Scholars Press, 1983.

Morris, James Winston. "The Spiritual Ascension: Ibn ʿArabi and the Miʿraj." *Journal of the American Oriental Society* 106 (1986), 539–51, 733–56; 107 (1987), 101–19.

Moxon, Cavendish. "Mystical Ecstasy and Hysterical Dream-States." *Journal of Abnormal Psychology* 15 (1920), 329–34.

Multhauf, Robert P. *The Origins of Chemistry.* London: Oldbourne, 1966.

Nasr, Seyyed Hossein. *An Introduction to Islamic Cosmological Doctrines: Conceptions of Nature and Methods Used for Its Study by the Ikhwan al-Safaʾ, al-Biruni, and Ibn Sina.* Cambridge: Belknap Press, Harvard University Press, 1964.

——— . *Science and Civilization in Islam.* 1968; rpt. New York: New American Library, 1970.

——— . "Shihab al-Din Suhrawardi Maqtul." In *A History of Muslim Philosophy: With Short Accounts of Other Disciplines and the Modern Renaissance in Muslim Lands.* Ed. M. M. Sharif. Vol. I, 372–98. Wiesbaden: Otto Harrasowitz, 1963.

——— . *Sufi Essays.* New York: Schocken, 1977.

Netton, Ian Richard. *Allah Transcendent: Studies in the Structure and Semiotics of Islamic Philosophy, Theology and Cosmology.* London: Routledge, 1989.

Newby, Gordon D. "Observations about an Early Judaeo-Arabic." *Jewish Quarterly Review* 61 (1971), 212–21.

Newsom, Carol. *Songs of the Sabbath Sacrifice: A Critical Edition.* Atlanta: Scholars Press, 1985.

Nicholson, Reynold A. "An Early Arabic Version of the *Mi'raj* of Abu Yazid al-Bistami." *Islamica* 2 (1926), 402–15.

————. *The Mystics of Islam.* 1914; rpt. New York: Schocken, 1975.

Niditch, Susan. "The Cosmic Adam: Man as Mediator in Rabbinic Literature." *Journal of Jewish Studies* 35/2 (1983), 137–46.

Nietzsche, Friedrich. *The Birth of Tragedy* [1887]. In *The Birth of Tragedy* and *The Genealogy of Morals.* Trans. Francis Golffing. Garden City, N.Y.: Doubleday Anchor, 1956.

Nilsson, Martin Persson. "The High God and the Mediator." *Harvard Theological Review* 56 (1963), 101–20.

Nock, Arthur Darby. "Gnosticism." *Harvard Theological Review* 57 (1964), 255–79.

Nock, Arthur Darby, and Andre-Jean Marie Festugière, ed. and trans. *Corpus Hermeticum.* Paris: Société d'Edition "Les Belles Lettres," 1945.

Noy, Pinchas. "A Revision of the Psychoanalytic Theory of the Primary Process." *International Journal of Psycho-Analysis* 50 (1969), 155–78.

Obermann, Julian. "Islamic Origins: A Study in Background and Foundation." In *The Arab Heritage.* Ed. Nabih Amin Faris. 58–120. Princeton: Princeton University Press, 1946.

Oesterreich, Traugott Konstantin. *Possession: Demoniacal and Other among Primitive Races in Antiquity, the Middle Ages, and Modern Times.* 1930; rpt. Secaucus, N.J.: University Books, 1966.

Ogén, Göran. "Religious Ecstasy in Classical Sufism." In *Religious Ecstasy: Based on Papers read at the Symposium on Religious Ecstasy held at Abo, Finland, on the 26th–29th of August 1981.* Ed. Nils G. Holm. 226–40. Stockholm: Almqvist and Wiksell International, 1982.

Oppenheim, A. Leo. "The Interpretation of Dreams in the Ancient Near East: With a Translation of an Assyrian Dream-Book." *Transactions of the American Philosophical Society* 46/3 (1956).

Orne, Martin T. "The Nature of Hypnosis: Artifact and Essence." *Journal of Abnormal and Social Psychology* 58 (1959), 277–99.

Otto, Herbert A., ed. *Explorations in Human Potentialities.* Springfield: Charles C. Thomas, 1966.

Otto, Rudolf. *The Idea of the Holy: An inquiry into the non-rational factor in the idea of the divine and its relation to the rational,* 2nd ed. London: Oxford University Press, 1950.

——. *Mysticism East and West: A Comparative Analysis of the Nature of Mysticism.* Trans. Bertha L. Bracey and Richenda C. Payne. New York, 1932; rpt. New York: Macmillan, 1970.

Owen, H. P. "Christian Mysticism: A Study in Walter Hilton's *The Ladder of Perfection.*" *Religious Studies* 7 (1971), 31–42.

Paffard, Michael. *Inglorious Wordsworths: A Study of some transcendental experiences in childhood and adolescence.* London: Hodder and Stoughton, 1973.

Pagel, Walter. *Paracelsus: An Introduction to Philosophical Medicine in the Era of the Renaissance.* Basel and New York: S. Karger, 1958.

——. "Paracelsus and the Neoplatonic and Gnostic Tradition." *Ambix* 8 (1960), 125–66.

——. "The Prime Matter of Paracelsus." *Ambix* 9 (1961), 117–35.

Pagel, Walter, and Marianne Winder. "The Eightness of Adam and Related 'Gnostic 'Ideas in the Paracelsian Corpus." *Ambix* 16 (1969), 119–39.

——. "The Higher Elements and Prime Matter in Renaissance Naturalism and in Paracelsus." *Ambix* 21 (1974), 93–127.

Pagels, Elaine H. *The Gnostic Gospels.* New York: Random House, 1979.

——. "Visions, Appearances, and Apostolic Authority: Gnostic and Orthodox Traditions." In *Gnosis: Festschrift für Hans Jonas.* Ed. Ugo Bianchi, Martin Krause, James M. Robinson, and Geo Widengren. 415–30. Göttingen: Vandenhoeck and Ruprecht, 1978.

Pahnke, Walter N. "The Contribution of the Psychology of Religion to the Therapeutic Use of the Psychedelic Substances." In *The Use of LSD in Psychotherapy and Alcoholism.* Ed. Harold A. Abramson. Indianapolis: Bobbs-Merrill, 1967.

——. "Drugs and Mysticism." *International Journal of Parapsychology* 8/1 (1966), 295–315.

——. "The Psychedelic Mystical Experience in the Human Encounter with Death." *Harvard Theological Review* 62 (1969), 1–21.

Pahnke, Walter N., and William A. Richards. "Implications of LSD and Experimental Mysticism." *Journal of Religion and Health* 5/3 (1966), 175–208.

Paracelsus. *The Archidoxes of Magic.* Trans. Robert Turner. London, 1656; rpt. London: Askin; New York: Samuel Weiser, 1975.

———. *Four Treatises.* Ed. Henry E. Sigerist. Baltimore: Johns Hopkins Press, 1941.

———. *The Hermetic and Alchemical Writings of Paracelsus,* 2 vols. Ed. Arthur Edward Waite. London: James Elliott, 1894; rpt. Berkeley: Shambhala, 1976.

———. *Selected Writings.* Ed. Jolande Jacobi. trans. Norbert Guterman, 3rd ed. Princeton: Princeton University Press, 1969.

Patai, Raphael. "Maria the Jewess—Founding Mother of Alchemy." *Ambix* 29 (1982), 177–97.

Pearson, Birger A. "The Figure of Seth in Gnostic Literature." *The Rediscovery of Gnosticism, Volume Two: Sethian Gnosticism.* Ed. Bentley Layton. 491–500. Leiden: Brill, 1981.

———. "Jewish Elements in *Corpus Hermeticum* I *(Poimandres)*." In *Gnosticism, Judaism, and Egyptian Christianity,* 136–47. Minneapolis, Minn.: Fortress, 1990.

———. "Jewish Elements in Gnosticism and the Development of Gnostic Self-Definition." In *Jewish and Christian Self-Definition, Volume One: The Shaping of Christianity in the Second and Third Centuries.* Ed. E. P. Sanders. 151–60, 240–45. Philadelphia: Fortress, 1980.

———. "Jewish Haggadic Traditions in *The Testimony of Truth* from Nag Hammadi (CG IX, 3)." In *Ex Orbe Religionum: Studia Geo Widengren.* Ed. C. J. Bleeker, S. G. F. Brandon, and M. Simon. 457–70. Leiden: Brill, 1972.

Pereira, Michela. *The Alchemical Corpus Attributed to Raymond Lull.* London: Warburg Institute, University of London, 1989.

Petrement, Simone. *A Separate God: The Christian Origins of Gnosticism.* Trans. Carol Harrison. New York: Harper Collins, 1990.

Pike, Nelson. "Comments." In *Art, Mind and Religion.* Ed. W. H. Capitan and D. D. Merill, 147–48. Pittsburgh, Pennsylvania, University of Pittsburgh Press, 1965.

Porter, J. R. "Muhammad's Journey to Heaven." *Numen* 21/1 (1974), 64–80; rpt. in *The Journey to the Other World.* Ed. Hilda R. Ellis Davidson. Cambridge, U.K.: D. S. Brewer; Totowa, N.J.: Rowman and Littlefield, 1975.

Pring-Mill, R. D. F. "The Trinitarian World Picture of Ramon Lull." *Romanistisches Jahrbuch* 7 (1955–56), 229–56.

Pseudo-Dionysius. *The Complete Works.* Trans. Colm Luibheid and Paul Rorem. New York: Paulist, 1987.

Puech, H. Ch. "Gnostic Gospels and Related Documents." In *New Testament Apocrypha, Volume One: Gospels and Related Writings.* Ed. W. Schneemelcher. trans. R. McL. Wilson. London: Lutterworth, 1963.

Quispel, Gilles. "The Birth of the Child: Some Gnostic and Jewish Aspects." Trans. Ruth Horine. *Eranos Jahrbuch* 40 (1971), 285–309.

———. "Gnosis and Psychology." In *The Rediscovery of Gnosticism, Volume One: The School of Valentinus.* Ed. Bentley Layton. Leiden: Brill, 1980.

[Quran]. *Koran.* Trans. J. M. Rodwell. London: Dent; New York: Dutton, 1909.

———. *The Koran: with a Parallel Arabic Text.* Trans. N. J. Dawood. Harmondsworth: Penguin, 1990.

———. *The Qur'an.* Trans. Edward Henry Palmer. Oxford: Clarendon, 1880.

Rasmussen, Knud. *The Netsilik Eskimos: Social Life and Spiritual Culture.* Report of the Fifth Thule Expedition 1921–1924, 8/1–2. Copenhagen, 1931; rpt. New York: AMS, 1976.

Read, John. *Through Alchemy to Chemistry: A Procession of Ideas and Personalities.* London: G. Bell, 1957.

Regardie, Israel. *The Philosopher's Stone: A Modern Comparative Approach to Alchemy from the Psychological and Magical Points of View.* London: Rider, 1938.

Reichenbach, Karl von. *The Odic Force: Letters on Od and Magnetism.* Trans. F. D. O'Byrne. London: Hutchinson, 1926; rpt. New Hyde Park, N.Y.: University Books, 1968.

Reyher, Joseph. "Emergent Uncovering Psychotherapy: The Use of Imagoic and Linguistic Vehicles in Objectifying Psychodynamic Processes." In *The Power of Human Imagination: New Methods in Psychotherapy.* Ed. Jerome L. Singer and Kenneth S. Pope, 51–93. New York: Plenum, 1978.

———. "Spontaneous Visual Imagery: Implications for Psychoanalysis, Psychopathology, and Psychotherapy." *Journal of Mental Imagery* 1/2 (1977), 253–74.

Robinson, James, ed. *The Nag Hammadi Library in English,* 3rd ed. San Francisco: Harper and Row, 1988.

Ross, Nathaniel. "Affect as Cognition: With Observations on the Meanings of Mystical States." *International Review of Psycho-Analysis* 2 (1975), 79–93.

Roy, Asim. *The Islamic Syncretistic Tradition in Bengal*. Princeton: Princeton University Press, 1983.

Rubin, Uri. "Pre-existence and light: Aspects of the concept of Nur Muhammad." *Israel Oriental Studies* 5 (1975), 62–119.

———. "Prophets and Progenitors in the Early Shiʿa Tradition." *Jerusalem Studies in Arabic and Islam* 1 (1979), 41–65.

Rudolph, Kurt. *Gnosis: The Nature and History of Gnosticism*. San Francisco: Harper and Row, 1983.

———. " 'Gnosis' and 'Gnosticism'—The Problem of Their Definition and Their Relation to the Writings of the New Testament." In *The New Testament and Gnosis: Essays In Honour of Robert McL. Wilson*. Ed. A. H. B. Logan and A. J. M. Wedderburn. 21–37. Edinburgh: Clark, 1983.

———. "Mandaean Sources." In *Gnosis: A Selection of Gnostic Texts, II: Coptic and Mandean Sources*. Ed. Werner Foerster. trans. R. McL. Wilson, 121–319. Oxford: Clarendon, 1974.

Runciman, Steven. *The Medieval Manichee: A Study of the Christian Dualist Heresy*. Cambridge: Cambridge University Press, 1947.

Sagmard, François-M.-M. *Le Gnose Valentinienne et le Témoignage de Saint Irénée*. Paris: Librairie Philosophique J. Vrin, 1947.

Salman, D. H., and Raymond H. Prince, ed. *Do Psychedelics Have Religious Implications?* (R. M. Bucke Society for the Study of Religious Experiences, Proceedings, 3rd Annual Conference). Montreal: R. M. Bucke Memorial Society, 1968.

Samarin, William J. *Tongues of Men and Angels: The Religious Language of Pentecostalism*. New York: Macmillan, 1972.

Sandbach, F. H. *The Stoics*. London: Chatto and Windus, 1975.

Sarkar, Jagadish Narayan. *Islam in Bengal (Thirteenth to Nineteenth Century)*. Calcutta: Ratna Prakashan, 1972.

Sato, Koji. "D. T. Suzuki, Zen and LSD 25." *Psychologia* 10 (1967), 129–32.

Schafer, Peter. *Gershom Scholem Reconsidered: The Aim and Purpose of Early Jewish Mysticism*. The Twelfth Sacks Lecture delivered on 29th May 1985. Oxford, U.K.: Oxford Centre for Postgraduate Hebrew Studies, 1986.

Schelling, Friedrich Willhelm Joseph von. *The Ages of the World*. Trans. Frederick de Wolfe Bolman, Jr. New York: Columbia University Press, 1942.

Schiffman, Lawrence H. "The Recall of Rabbi Nehuniah ben Ha-Qanah from Ecstasy in the *Hekhalot Rabbati.*" *Association for Jewish Studies Review* 1 (1976), 269–81.

Schilder, Paul, and Otto Kauders. *The Nature of Hypnosis.* 1956; rpt. New York: International Universities Press, 1973.

Schimmel, Annemarie. *And Muhammad Is His Messenger: The Veneration of the Prophet in Islamic Piety.* Chapel Hill: University of North Carolina Press, 1985.

————. "Eros—Heavenly and Not So Heavenly—in Sufi Literature and Life." In *Society and the Sexes in Medieval Islam.* Ed. Afaf Lutfi al-Sayyid-Marsot. Malibu, Calif.: Undena, 1979.

Schoedel, William R. "Gnostic Monism and the Gospel of Truth." In *The Rediscovery of Gnosticism, Volume One: The School of Valentinus.* Ed. Bentley Layton. Leiden: Brill, 1980.

————. " 'Topological' Theology and Some Monistic Tendencies in Gnosticism." In *Ex Orbe Religionum: Studia Geo Widengren.* Ed. C. J. Bleeker, S. G. F. Brandon, and M. Simon. Leiden: Brill, 1972.

Scholem, Gershom G. "*Devekut,* or Communion with God." In *The Messianic Idea in Judaism: And Other Essays on Jewish Spirituality.* New York: Schocken, 1971.

————. *Jewish Gnosticism, Merkabah Mysticism, and Talmudic Tradition,* 2nd ed. New York: Jewish Theological Seminary of America, 1965.

————. *Kabbalah.* New York: Quadrangle-New York Times Book Company, 1974.

————. *Major Trends in Jewish Mysticism,* 3rd ed. New York: Schocken, 1954.

————. *On the Kabbalah and Its Symbolism.* Trans. Ralph Manheim. New York: Schocken Books, 1965.

————. *Origins of the Kabbalah.* Trans. Allen Arkush. ed. R. J. Zwi Werblowsky. Princeton: Jewish Publication Society-Princeton University Press, 1987.

Schroeder, Theodore. "Prenatal Psychisms and Mystical Pantheism." *International Journal of Psycho-Analysis* 3 (1922), 445–66.

Scott, Walter. *Hermetica: The Ancient Greek and Latin Writings Which Contain Religious or Philosophic Teachings Ascribed to Hermes Trismegistus, Vol. 1: Introduction, Texts and Translations.* 1924; rpt. Boulder: Hermes House, n.d.

Segal, Alan F. "Ruler of This World: Attitudes about Mediator Figures and the Importance of Sociology for Self-Definition." In *Jewish and Chris-*

tian Self-Definition, Volume Two: Aspects of Judaism in the Graeco-Roman Period. Ed. E. P. Saunders, with A.I. Baumgarten and A. Mendelson, 245–68, 403–13. Philadelphia: Fortress, 1981.

Segal, Robert A.. ed. *The Gnostic Jung: Selected and Introduced.* Princeton: Princeton University Press, 1992.

———. "Jung and Gnosticism." *Religion* 17 (1987), 301–36.

Sells, Michael. "Bewildered Tongue: The Semantics of Mystical Union in Islam." In *Mystical Union and Monotheistic Religion: An Ecumenical Dialogue.* Ed. Moshe Idel and Bernard McGinn. New York: Macmillan, 1989.

Shah, Idries. *The Sufis.* Garden City, N.Y.: Doubleday, 1964.

Sheppard, H. J. "Egg Symbolism in Alchemy." *Ambix* 6 (1958), 140–48.

———. "Gnosticism and Alchemy." *Ambix* 6 (1957), 86–101.

———. "The Origin of the Gnostic-Alchemical Relationship." *Scientia* 97 (1962), 146–49.

———. "The Ouroboros and the Unity of Matter in Alchemy: A Study in Origins." *Ambix* 10 (1962), 83–96.

———. "The Redemption Theme and Hellenistic Alchemy." *Ambix* 7 (1959), 42–46.

———. "Serpent Symbolism in Alchemy." *Scientia* 101 (1966), 203–7.

Sherman, Spencer. "Brief Report: Very Deep Hypnosis." *Journal of Transpersonal Psychology* 4 (1972), 87–91.

Sherwood, J. N., M. J. Stolaroff, and W. W. Harman. "The Psychedelic Experience—A New Concept in Psychotherapy." *Journal of Psychedelic Drugs* 3/1 (1962), 13–19.

Shirokogoroff, S. M. *Psychomental Complex of the Tungus.* London: Kegan Paul, Trench, Trubner, 1935.

Shor, Ronald E. "Hypnosis and the Concept of the Generalized Reality Orientation." *American Journal of Psychotherapy* 13 (1959), 582–602; rpt. in *Altered States of Consciousness,* 2nd ed.. ed. Charles T. Tart, 239–56. Garden City, N.Y.: Doubleday Anchor Books, 1972.

———. "Three Dimensions of Hypnotic Depth." *International Journal of Clinical and Experimental Hypnosis* 10 (1962), 23–38; rpt. in *Altered States of Consciousness.* ed. Tart, 257–67.

Silberer, Herbert. *Hidden Symbolism of Alchemy and the Occult Arts.* First English title: *Problems of Mysticism and Its Symbolism.* Trans. Ely Jelliffe Smith. 1917; rpt. New York: Dover, 1971.

———. "The Origin and the Meaning of the Symbols of Freemasonry."
Psyche and Eros 1 (1920), 17–24, 84–97; 2 (1921), 81–89, 299–309.

———. "Report on a Method of Eliciting and Observing Certain Symbolic
Hallucination-Phenomena." In *Organization and Pathology of
Thought: Selected Sources.* Ed. David Rapaport. New York: Columbia
University Press, 1951.

Silvestris, Bernardus. *The Cosmographia.* Trans. Winthrop Wetherbee.
New York: Columbia University Press, 1973.

Singer, Jerome L., and Kenneth S. Pope. "The Use of Imagery and Fantasy
Techniques in Psychotherapy." In *The Power of Human Imagination:
New Methods in Psychotherapy.* Ed. Jerome L. Singer and Kenneth S.
Pope. 3–34. New York: Plenum, 1978.

Singh, Mohan. "Iranian Influence on Medieval Indian Mystics," *Indo-
Iranica* 6/4 (1952–53), 37–43.

Sjoberg, Jr., B. M., and L. E. Hollister. "The Effects of Psychotomimetic
Drugs on Primary Suggestibility." *Psychopharmacologia* 8 (1965),
251–62.

Smart, Ninian. "Interpretation and Mystical Experience." *Religious Studies* 1 (1965), 75–87.

———. "The Purification of Consciousness and the Negative Path." In *Mysticism and Philosophical Analysis.* Ed. Steven T. Katz. London: Sheldon, 1978.

Smith, Huston. "Do Drugs Have Religious Import?" *Journal of Philosophy*
61/18 (1964), 517–31.

———. *Forgotten Truth: The Primordial Tradition.* 1976; rpt. New York:
Harper Colophon, 1977.

———. "Psychedelic Theophanies and the Religious Life." *Journal of Psychedelic Drugs* 3/1 (1970), 87–91.

Smith, Jonathan Z. *Drudgery Divine: On the Comparison of Early Christianities and the Religions of Late Antiquity.* Chicago: University of
Chicago Press, 1990.

———. *Map is Not Territory: Studies in the History of Religions.* Leiden:
Brill, 1978.

Smith, Margaret. *The Way of the Mystics: The Early Christian Mystics and
the Rise of the Sufis.* Original title: *Studies in Early Mysticism in the
Near and Middle East.* 1931. Rpt. London: Sheldon, 1976.

Smith, Morton. "The History of the Term Gnostikos." In *The Rediscovery of
Gnosticism, Volume Two: Sethian Gnosticism.* Ed. Bentley Layton.
Leiden: Brill, 1981.

————— . "Observations on Hekhalot Rabbati." In *Biblical and Other Studies.* Ed. Alexander Altmann. Cambridge: Harvard University Press, 1963.

Solmsen, Friedrich. *Plato's Theology.* Ithaca: Cornell University Press, 1942.

Solomon, Philip, et alii, ed. *Sensory Deprivation: A Symposium Held at Harvard Medical School.* Cambridge: Harvard University Press, 1961.

Solursh, Lionel P., and J. M. Rae. "LSD, Suggestion and Hypnosis." *International Journal of Neuropsychiatry* 2 (1966), 60–64.

Stace, W. T. *Mysticism and Philosophy.* Philadelphia and New York: Lippincott, 1960.

Stafford, Peter G., and Bonnie H. Golightly. *LSD: The Problem-Solving Psychedelic.* New York: Award, 1967.

Stapleton, H. E., G. L. Lewis, and F. Sherwood Taylor. "The Sayings of Hermes Quoted in the *MA' AL-WARAQI* of Ibn Umail." *Ambix* 3 (1949), 70–90.

Stark, Rodney. "A Taxonomy of Religious Experience." *Journal for the Scientific Study of Religion* 5 (1965), 97–116.

Stavenhagen, Lee, ed. and trans. *A Testament of Alchemy: Being the Revelations of Morienus to Khalid ibn Yazid.* Hanover: Brandeis University Press-University Press of New England, 1974.

Steele, Robert, and Dorothea Waley Singer. "The Emerald Table." *Proceedings of the Royal Society of Medicine* 21 (1928), 485–501.

Steinbrecher, Edwin C. *The Inner Guide Meditation: A Spiritual Technology for the 21st Century.* York Beach, Me.: Samuel Weiser, 1988.

Steiner, Rudolf. "On the History of Christian Rosenkreutz." In *A Christian Rosenkreutz Anthology.* Ed. Paul M. Allen. Blauvelt, N.Y.: Rudolf Steiner Publications, 1968.

————— . *Rosicrucianism and Modern Initiation: Mystery Centres of the Middle Ages (Six lectures given in Dornach, 4th–13th January, 1924),* 3rd ed. Trans. Mary Adams. London: Rudolf Steiner Press, 1982.

————— . *Secrets of the Threshold: Eight Lectures given from August 24–31, 1913.* Hudson, N.Y.: Anthroposophic Press; London: Rudolf Steiner Press, 1987.

Sterba, Richard. "Remarks on Mystic States." *American Imago* 25 (1968), 77–85.

Stern, S. M. *Studies in Early Isma'ilism.* Jerusalem: Magnes Press; Leiden: Brill, 1983.

Streeter, B. H., and A. J. Appasamy. *The Sadhu: A Study in Mysticism and Practical Religion.* 1921; rpt. London: Macmillan, 1922.

Stroumsa, Gedaliahu G. *Another Seed: Studies in Gnostic Mythology.* Leiden: Brill, 1984.

――――. "Esotericism in Mani's Thought and Background." In *Codex Manichaicus Coloniensis: Atti del Simposio Internzaionale (Rende-Amantea 3–7 settembre 1984).* Ed. Luigi Cirillo with Amneris Roselli, 153–68. Mana: Editore Cosenza, 1986.

Suhrawardi, Shihabuddin Yahya. *The Mystical and Visionary Treatises of Shihabuddin Yahya Suhrawardi.* Trans. W. M. Thackston, Jr. London: Octagon, 1982.

Swain, Charles W. "Drug Experience and 'Mystical' Experience: Reflections on the Problem of Comparison," *Journal of Drug Issues* 7/3 (1977), 247–52.

Szulakowska, Urszula. "Thirteenth Century Material Pantheism in the Pseudo-Lullian 'S'-Circle of the Powers of the Soul." *Ambix* 35 (1988), 127–54.

Talbert, Charles H. "The Myth of a Descending-Ascending Redeemer in Mediterranean Antiquity." *New Testament Studies* 22 (1975–76), 418–40.

Tart, Charles T. "Measuring the Depth of an Altered State of Consciousness, with Particular Reference to Self-Report Scales of Hypnotic Depth." In *Hypnosis: Developments in Research and New Perspectives,* 2nd ed. Ed. Erika Fromm and Ronald E. Shor. 567–601. New York: Aldine, 1979.

――――. "Transpersonal Potentialities of Deep Hypnosis." *Journal of Transpersonal Psychology* 2 (1970); rpt. in *The Highest State of Consciousness.* Ed. John White. 344–51. Garden City, N.Y.: Anchor Books-Doubleday, 1972.

Taylor, F. Sherwood. *The Alchemists.* London: William Heinemann, 1952; rpt. St. Albans, U.K.: Paladin-Granada, 1976.

――――. "The Idea of the Quintessence." In *Science Medicine and History: Essays on the Evolution of Scientific Thought and Medical Practice, written in honour of Charles Singer.* Ed. E. Ashworth Underwood. Vol. 1, 247–65. London: Oxford University Press, 1953; rpt. New York: Arno, 1975.

――――. "The Origins of Greek Alchemy," *Ambix* 1 (1937), 30–47.

――――. "A Survey of Greek Alchemy." *Journal of Hellenic Studies* 50 (1930), 109–39.

———. "The Visions of Zosimos: Translation and Prefatory Note." *Ambix* 1, 88–92.

Taylor, John B. "Ja'far al-Sadiq, Spiritual Forebear of the Sufis." *Islamic Culture* 40 (1966), 97–113.

———. "Man's Knowledge of God in the Thought of Ja'far al-Sadiq," *Islamic Culture* 40 (1966), 195–206.

Teresa of Jesus, St. *Complete Works,* 3 vols. Trans. E. Allison Peers. London: Sheed and Ward, 1946.

Tester, S. James. *A History of Western Astrology.* New York: Ballantine, 1987.

Thorndike, Lynn. *A History of Magic and Experimental Science,* 7 vols. New York and London: Columbia University Press, 1923–38.

Tishby, Isaiah, with Fischel Lachower, ed. *The Wisdom of the Zohar: An Anthology of Texts.* Trans. David Goldstein. Oxford: Littman Library/ Oxford University Press, 1989.

Topsfield, L. T. *Troubadours and Love.* Cambridge: Cambridge University Press, 1975.

Torrey, Charles Cutler. *The Jewish Foundation of Islam.* 1933; rpt. New York: Ktav, 1967.

———. "Mysticism in Islam." In *At One With the Invisible: Studies in Mysticism.* Ed. E. Hershey Sneath. 142–79. New York: Macmillan, 1921.

Tucker, William F. "Abu Mansur al-'Ijli and the Mansuriyya: a study in medieval terrorism." *Der Islam* 54 (1977), 66–76.

———. "Rebels and Gnostics: Al-Mugira ibn Sa'cid and the Mugiriyya." *Arabica* 22 (1975), 33–47.

Tufail, Abu Bakr Muhammad bin. (1982), *The Journey of the Soul: The Story of Hai bin Yaqzan.* Trans. Riad Kocache. London: Octagon Press.

Ulansey, David. *The Origins of the Mithraic Mysteries: Cosmology and Salvation in the Ancient World.* New York: Oxford University Press, 1989.

Underhill, Evelyn. *Mysticism: A Study in the Nature and Development of Man's Spiritual Consciousness,* 12th ed. London, 1930; rpt. New York: New American Library, 1955.

van den Berg, J. H. "An Existential Explanation of the Guided Daydream in Psychotherapy." *Review of Existential Psychology and Psychiatry* 2 (1962), 5–35.

VandenBroeck, Andre. *Al-Kemi: Hermetic, Occult, Political, and Private Aspects of R. A. Schwaller de Lubicz.* Great Barrington, Mass.: Inner Traditions-Lindisfarne Press, 1987.

van den Broek, R. "The Creation of Adam's Psychic Body in the Apocryphon of John." In *Studies in Gnosticism and Hellenistic Religions: Presented to Gilles Quispel on the Occasion of his 65th Birthday.* Ed. R. van den Broek and M. J. Vermaseren. 38–57. Leiden: Brill, 1981.

van der Waerden, B. L. "History of the Zodiac." *Archiv für Orientforschung* 16 (1953).

van Nuys, David Whitman. "Drug Use and Hypnotic Susceptibility." *International Journal of Clinical and Experimental Hypnosis* 20/1 (1972), 31–37.

van Ruysbroek, Jan. *The Spiritual Espousals.* Trans. Eric Colledge. 1953; rpt. Westminster, Md.: Christian Classics, 1983.

Vaughan, Thomas. *The Works of Thomas Vaughan: Mystic and Alchemist (Eugenius Philalethes).* Ed. Arthur Edward Waite. 1919; rpt. New Hyde Park, N.Y.: University Books, 1968.

von Franz, Marie-Louise. *Alchemical Active Imagination.* Dallas: Spring, 1979.

———. "On Active Imagination." In *Methods of Treatment in Analytical Psychology.* Ed. Ian F. Baker. 88–99. Fellbach: Adolf Bonz, 1980.

Waite, Arthur Edward. *Azoth; or, The Star in the East.* London: Theosophical Publishing Society, 1893.

———. *Lives of the Alchemystical Philosophers.* London: G. Redway, 1888.

———. *The Secret Tradition in Alchemy: Its Development and Records.* London: Kegal Paul, Trench, Trubner; New York: Knopf, 1926.

———, trans. *The Alchemical Writings of Edward Kelly.* 1893; rpt. London: Robinson and Watkins, 1973.

———, trans. *The Turba Philosophorum.* 1896; rpt. New York: Samuel Weiser, 1976.

Walker, Daniel P. *The Ancient Theology: Studies in Christian Platonism from the Fifteenth to the Eighteenth Century.* London: Gerald Duckworth, 1972.

———. *Spiritual and Demonic Magic: From Ficino to Campanella.* London: Warburg Institute, University of London, 1958; rpt. Notre Dame: University of Notre Dame Press, 1975.

Walker, Paul E. "Cosmic Hierarchies in Early Isma'ili Thought: The View of Abu Ya'qub al-Sijistani." *Muslim World* 66 (1976), 14–28.

———. "An Isma'ili Answer to the Problem of Worshiping the Unknowable, Neoplatonic God." *American Journal of Arabic Studies* 2 (1974), 7–21.

———. "The Ismaili Vocabulary of Creation." *Studia Islamica* 40 (1974), 75–85.

Wallace, Anthony F. C. "Cultural Determinants of Response to Hallucinatory Experiences." *Archives of General Psychiatry* 1 (1959), 58–69.

Walsh, Roger. "Initial Meditative Experiences: Part I." *Journal of Transpersonal Psychology* 9 (1977), 151–92.

Wasserstrom, Steve. "The Moving Finger Writes: Mughira b. Sa'id's Islamic Gnosis and the Myths of Its Rejection." *History of Religions* 25/1 (1985), 1–29.

Washburn, Michael C. "Observations Relevant to a Unified Theory of Meditation." *Journal of Transpersonal Psychology* 10/1 (1978), 45–65.

Watkins, Mary M. *Waking Dreams.* 1976; rpt. New York: Harper Colophon, 1977.

Watt, W. Montgomery. *Bell's Introduction to the Qur'an.* Edinburgh: University Press, 1970.

Watts, Alan W. *The Joyous Cosmology: Adventures in the Chemistry of Consciousness.* 1962; rpt. New York: Vintage-Random House, 1965.

Watts, Jr., W. David. *The Psychedelic Experience: A Sociological Study.* Beverly Hills: Sage, 1971.

Waugh, Earle. "Following the Beloved: Muhammad as Model in the Sufi Tradition." In *The Biographic Process: Studies in the History and Psychology of Religion.* Ed. Frank E. Reynolds and Donald Capps. 63–85. The Hague: Mouton, 1976.

———. "Religious Aspects of the Mi'raj Legends." In *Etudes Arabes et Islamique I—histoire et civilisation, Vol. 4. Actes du XXIXᵉ Congrès international des Orientalistes.* Ed. Claude Caher. 236–44. Paris: L'Asiatheque, 1975.

Webb, Giselda. (1982), An Exegesis of Suhrawardi's *The Purple Intellect* ('Aql-i surkh). *Islamic Quarterly* 26, 194–210.

Webb, James. *The Occult Establishment.* La Salle, Ill.: Open Court, 1976.

Weiss, Joseph. *Studies in Eastern European Jewish Mysticism.* Ed. David Goldstein. Oxford: Oxford University Press, 1985.

West, Louis Jolyon, ed. *Hallucinations.* New York: Grune and Stratton, 1962.

West, Michael A. "Traditional and psychological perspectives on meditation." In *The Psychology of Meditation*. Ed. Michael A. West. Oxford: Clarendon, 1987.

Widengren, Geo. *The Ascension of the Apostle and the Heavenly Book*. Uppsala Universitets Arsskrift 1950:7. Uppsala: A. B. Lundequistska Bokhandeln; Leipzig: Otto Harrassowitz, 1950.

———. "Baptism and Enthronement in Some Jewish-Christian Gnostic Documents." In *The Saviour God*. Ed. S. G. F. Brandon. 205–17. Manchester: Manchester University Press, 1963.

———. *Muhammad, the Apostle of God, and His Ascension*. Uppsala Universitets Arsskrift 1955:1. A.-B. Lundequistska Bokhandeln; Wiesbaden: Otto Harrassowitz, 1955.

———. "Researches in Syrian Mysticism: Mystical Experiences and Spiritual Exercises." *Numen* 8/3 (1961), 161–98.

———. "Royal Ideology and the Testaments of the Twelve Patriarchs." In *Promise and Fulfilment*. Ed. F. F. Bruce, 202–12. Edinburgh: Clark, 1963.

Wiedemann, E. "al-Kimiya, alchemy." In *The Encyclopedia of Islam*, 2nd ed., vol 2, pt. 2, 1010–17. Leiden: Brill; London: Luzac, 1960.

Williams, Michael Allen. *The Immovable Race: A Gnostic Designation and the Theme of Stability in Late Antiquity*. Leiden: Brill, 1985.

——— "Stability as a Soteriological Theme In Gnosticism." In *The Rediscovery of Gnosticism, Volume Two: Sethian Gnosticism*. Ed. Bentley Layton, 819–29. Leiden: E. J. Brill, 1981.

Wilson, C. Anne. *Philosophers, Iosis and Water of Life*. Leeds, U.K.: Leeds Philosophical and Literary Society, 1984.

Wilson, Colin. *C. G. Jung: Lord of the Underworld*. Wellingborough, U.K.: Aquarian, 1984.

Wilson, R. McL. "Gnosis and the Mysteries." In *Studies in Gnosticism and Hellenistic Religions*. Ed. R. van den Broek and M. J. Vermaseren. Leiden: Brill, 1981.

Winston, David. "Introduction." In Philo of Alexandria, *The Contemplative Life, The Giants, and Selections*. New York: Paulist, 1981.

Wisse, Frederik. "Stalking Those Elusive Sethians." *The Rediscovery of Gnosticism, Volume Two: Sethian Gnosticism*. Ed. Bentley Layton. 563–87. Leiden: Brill, 1981.

Wolfson, Elliot R. "*Yeridah la-Merkavah:* Typology of Ecstasy and Enthronement in Ancient Jewish Mysticism." In *Typologies of Mysticism*. Ed. R. Herrera. New York: Peter Lang, 1993 [forthcoming].

Wolfson, H. A. "Arabic and Hebrew Terms for Matter and Element with Especial Reference to Saadia." *Jewish Quarterly Review* 38 (1947), 47–61.

———. "The Kalam Problem of Nonexistence and Saadia's Second Theory of Creation." *Jewish Quarterly Review* 36 (1946), 371–91.

Yamauchi, Edwin M. "The Descent of Ishtar, the Fall of Sophia, and the Jewish Roots of Gnosticism." *Tyndale Bulletin* 29 (1978), 143–75.

———. *Gnostic Ethics and Mandaean Origins.* Cambridge: Harvard University Press, 1970.

Yates, Frances A. *The Art of Memory.* 1966; rpt. Harmondsworth: Penguin, 1969.

———. *Giordano Bruno and the Hermetic Tradition.* London: Routledge and Kegan Paul, 1964; rpt. Chicago: University of Chicago Press, 1967.

———. *Lull and Bruno: Collected Essays, Volume 1.* London: Routledge and Kegan Paul, 1982.

———. *The Occult Philosophy in the Elizabethan Age.* London: Routledge and Kegan Paul, 1979.

Zaehner, Robert Charles. *Concordant Discord: The Interdependence of Faiths.* Oxford: Clarendon Press, 1970.

———. *Hindu and Muslim Mysticism.* 1960; rpt. New York: Schocken, 1969.

———. *Mysticism Sacred and Profane: An Inquiry into some Varieties of Preternatural Experience.* 1957; rpt. London: Oxford University Press, 1961.

———. *Zen, Drugs and Mysticism.* 1972; rpt. New York: Random House, 1974.

Zosimos of Panopolis. *On the Letter Omega.* Ed. and trans. Howard M. Jackson. Missoula: University of Montana-Scholars Press, 1978.

Zuckerman, Marvin. "Hallucinations, Reported Sensations, and Images." In *Sensory Deprivation: Fifteen Years of Research.* Ed. John P. Zubek. New York: Appleton-Century-Crofts, 1969.

Index

Abu Yazid of Bistam, 204–5
Abulafia, Abraham, 32, 35, 249
active imagination, 37, 39–44, 52–44,
70, 89, 258; in alchemy, 53, 66; in
Gnosticism, 53, 123, 135, 146; and
psychotherapy, 123
Acts of John, The, 130–32, 133
Acts of Peter, The, 129–30, 131, 133
Aggadat R. Ishmael, 158
Alan de Lille, 103–6, 242, 254
Albigensians, 114, 237, 249
alchemy, metallic: in Alan de Lille,
103–6; and Gnosticism, 100–1,
142–43; gold-making recipes in,
79–85; Hellenistic, 77–80, 85–103,
106–7; Latin, 103–6, 251–53; Muslim, 78, 222. *See also Emerald Table* of Hermes; ether
alchemy, spiritual: and active imagination, 53, 66; alchemical marriage
in, 58, 60, 62, 68, 72, 263–64, 267;
Atwood on, 55–58, 59, 60, 63, 65,
66, 68, 70, 73; communion in, 57,
58, 59, 62, 63, 64, 65, 68; ecstatic
death in, 56, 57, 60, 63, 65, 67,
70–71, 267; Eliade on, 70–72;
experience of nothingness in, 63,
267; extrovertive union in, 59, 62,
65, 266, 267; intellect (*nous*) in,
56–57, 60, 63, 67–68; introspective
union in, 56, 58, 59, 60, 61, 62, 63,
68, 71; Jung on, 50, 53–4, 56, 65–
70, 101, 106; Paracelsian, 55, 56,
73; psychoactive drug use in, 265–
67; and psychotherapy, 69; and Silberer, 50–1; Sufism as, 235;

transport in, 57–58, 60, 63, 65, 68,
71; vegetable stone in, 264–67;
visions in, 266, 267. *See also
Emerald Table* of Hermes; ether;
Paracelsus; pseudo-Lullian
alchemy
Alexander, Philip S., 176
allegorical vision, 32, 33, 88–89, 107,
132; in Christian Platonism, 240,
242, 243; in Dante, 243; in *Hekhalot Rabbati,* 164–65; in Lull,
245; in Matthew, 164–65; in Muslim Neo-Aristotelianism, 225; of
Muhammad, 192–93; in rabbinic
mysticism, 157
Alnaes, Randolf, 173
alphabetology: in *ghulat* sects, 202; in
Isma'ilism, 206, 208; in Lull's Art,
248–49; in Mandaeism, 201; in
Marcosian Gnosticism, 199–200;
in pseudo-Lullian alchemy, 252; in
Umm al-kitab, 217
Andrae, Tor, 185
androgyne: in Gnosticism, 121; in the
kabbalah, 263; in Paracelsus, 260
Angela of Foligno, 7, 16–17
anthropos, 64–65; in Ibn al-'Arabi, 228;
in Gnosticism, 122, 200; in
Isma'ilism, 210, 211; in the
kabbalah, 260, 263; in Mandaeism,
201, 206; in Paracelsus, 260, 261–
63; in *Umm al-kitab,* 217.
Anthroposophy, 56, 61, 62, 64
apocalypticism, Christian: allegorical,
88–89, 165; heavenly ascension in,
114, 165